AN ACCIDENTAL JEWEL

WISCONSIN'S
TURTLE-FLAMBEAU FLOWAGE

MICHAEL HITTLE

LITTLE CREEK PRESS
AND BOOK DESIGN

Mineral Point, Wisconsin USA

Little Creek Press®
A Division of Kristin Mitchell Design, Inc.
5341 Sunny Ridge Road
Mineral Point, Wisconsin 53565

Book Design and Project Coordination:
Little Creek Press

Fourth Printing
October 2020

For more information or to order books: turflamhist@gmail.com
or visit www.littlecreekpress.com

Library of Congress Control Number: 2017963081

ISBN-10: 1-942586-31-0
ISBN-13: 978-1-942586-31-9

To Marcia

About the Author

Michael Hittle received his B.A. degree from Brown University and his M.A. and Ph.D. degrees from Harvard University. His principal area of interest was the history of Russia. In 1979, Harvard University Press published his study, *The Service City: State and Townsmen in Russia, 1600-1800.*

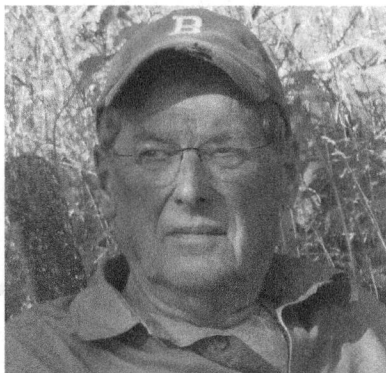

Mr. Hittle joined the faculty of Lawrence University in 1966. His teaching focused on the history of Russia, historiography, and various introductory courses in history, but he also participated regularly in the college's inter-disciplinary Freshman Studies program. Mr. Hittle served as Dean of the Faculty from 1980 to 1988. At the time of his retirement in 2001 Mr. Hittle held the David G. Ormsby Chair in History and Political Economy.

Mr. Hittle grew up in Indianapolis, Indiana, where his love of fishing emerged at an early age. His angling life has ranged from small Hoosier streams to Wisconsin lakes and rivers, from High Arctic waters to Bahamian saltwater flats, and beyond. In 1972 he and his wife, Marcia, purchased property on the Turtle-Flambeau Flowage; and after camping on it for a number of years, they had the shell of a cabin erected on the site. After twenty years of off and on work, he and his family finished the building's interior.

Since retirement, Mr. Hittle has become an increasingly active sportsman/conservationist who is committed to the protection and intelligent use of Wisconsin's natural resources. To that end he has served on the board of the Turtle-Flambeau Flowage and Trude Lake Property Owners' Association and as a member of the editorial board of *Driftwood,* the association's newsletter.

Table of Contents

Part II

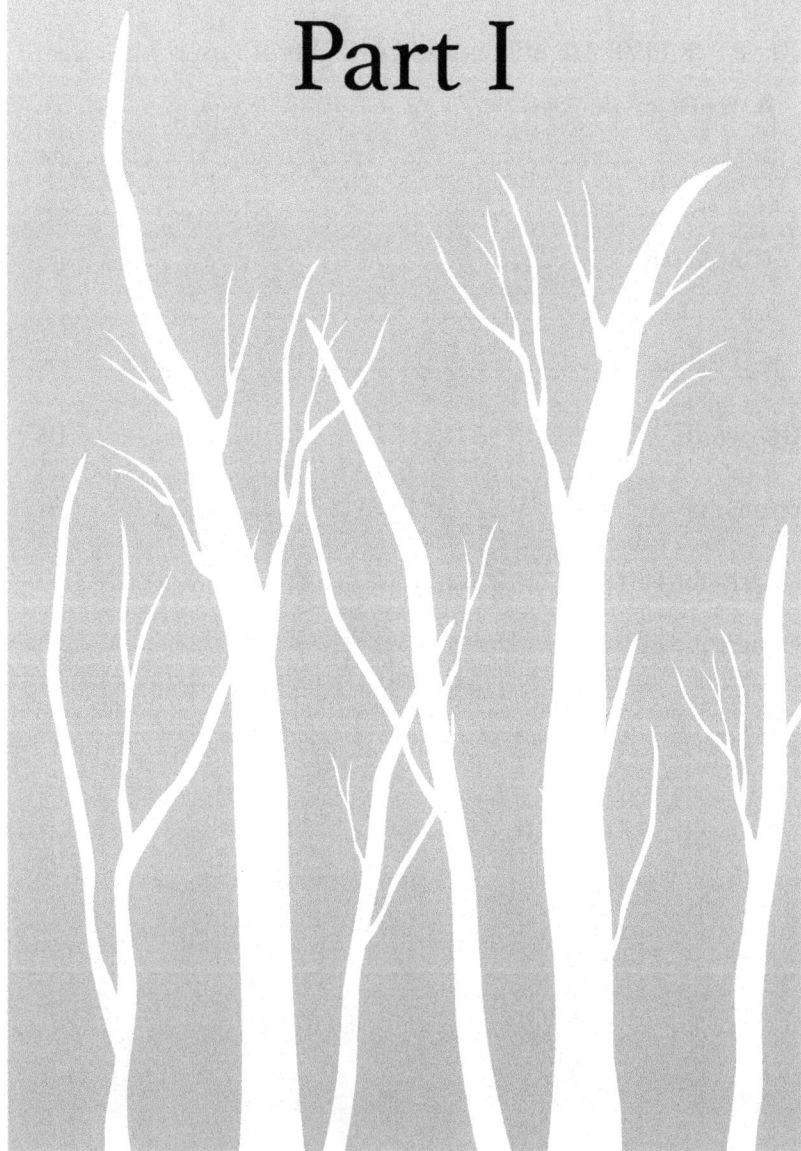

Part I

Preface

My connection with and love for Wisconsin's northwoods began when I was 11 years old and accompanied my parents, Bob and Mary Hittle, on a week-long vacation at Wawona Lodge on Big St. Germain Lake. I think they had in mind a restful week of long walks, swims, boat rides, good food, and relaxation from the demands of workaday life. Little did they know, however, the effect the lake, with its muskies, northerns, and walleyes, would have on their son. I was already an obsessed fisherman back home in Indiana, but the targets of my angling there were mostly panfish and the occasional bass. However, once acquainted with the fishing possibilities of the northwoods— something that was helped along no end by the large fish in coolers outside bait stores—I raised my sights toward the predator species and ratcheted my obsession to a new level. Happily, my folks indulged me, and vacations to the St. Germain and Sayner areas became annual rituals well into my college years. Though we fished numerous area lakes, sometimes skillfully guided by my piscatorial role model, Lionel Rux, we never laid eyes on, or even heard of, the Turtle-Flambeau Flowage.

It would not be until the mid 1960s that the flowage entered my life. In 1966, after 10 years of study on the East Coast, I took a job in the history department at Lawrence University in Appleton. It did not take long for my wife, Marcia, and our sons, Alex and Sam, to find our way back to my old Vilas County stomping grounds; but a few years later, when we started looking around for a cabin to buy, we ran head on into the financial limitations imposed by the salary of a beginning college instructor. And so we started looking for vacant lake frontage and tried to persuade ourselves that a tent was a more than adequate substitute for a cabin. While on the hunt for a suitable piece of property, one March day in 1972 we ate lunch at the Duck Shack in Mercer. Noticing that Marlen Realty had an office adjacent to the restaurant, we stopped in, had a chat with Tom Ponik, and learned about some lots that had just gone on sale on the flowage. The lots were inaccessible that day due to snow cover, but we returned in the spring, drove as far as we could on the logging road that led into the properties, and walked the entire shoreline under development—accompanied every step of the way by a swarm of blackflies. Putting aside a number of worries—when will there be a useable road, or power, or an end to the bugs—we succumbed to the charms of the location, and by the end of the year we owned our own piece of the flowage.

Five years of tent-camping followed during which we experienced the full array of nature's offerings: beautiful sun-drenched days and soggy rain-drenched nights; stringers of fish and trips to town for protein; juicy burgers cooked over coals and mosquitoes diving into scrambled eggs. Always, though, there was the flowage right at our campsite; and the more we came to know it, the more our attachment to it grew. And so it was, also, that the North Fork of the Flambeau River, with its churning coppery waters, aggressive fish, and rugged beauty exerted its own magical draw on the family. In time we came to understand the deep and intimate relationship between these two different bodies of water and to revere them even more.

A major turning point in our flowage experience took place in 1978, when our straight-talking guide to the history and culture of Iron County, Louis Ledvina, cleared a building site, and shortly thereafter we had the shell of a cabin erected. That began a 20-year family project of finishing the interior, literally one board at a time. It was a period when the table saw vied with the woodstove for pride of place in our open-plan cabin, and sawdust rose on the woodstove's thermals and settled everywhere. The work, performed on weekends and odd chunks of summers, did not, however, keep us from our favorite outdoor pursuits. Memories of our camping days prompted us to haul the tent to some island for an overnight, complete with campfire and lumpy ground. Marcia mentally cataloged every tree on our property, and brashly transplanted trees to correct nature's failure to put them in just the right places. Alex, Sam, and I threw baits at whatever we thought might be hungry, sometimes with surprisingly good results, and chased grouse in the autumn with our setters. And so the flowage played a central role in our lives as gardeners, builders, fishers and hunters, and lovers of the natural world. Today, of course, our sons have lives of their own and children to raise. Getting to the flowage is no longer as easy for them as it once was; but still they come when they can and introduce yet another generation to the wonders of the northwoods.

A few years after I retired in 2001, Marcia and I attended an annual meeting of the Turtle-Flambeau Flowage and Trude Lake Property Owners' Association. At the conclusion of his remarks to the group, flowage property manager Roger Jasinski expressed his wish that someone would write a "cultural history" of the flowage. For some time, Marcia and I mulled over the possibility that I might take on such a task. After all, I had more than a passing familiarity with the flowage, and it seemed that my profession as an historian should stand me in good stead when it came to research and writing. Eventually, with Marcia's encouragement, I decided to explore the matter further. After a conversation with Roger helped clarify what he had in mind, I concluded that writing a history of the flowage would be a fitting retirement project and got down to business.

Works of history emerge less from facts than from questions. In this case, it took a while before the proper questions became apparent. This only happened when I examined, with expert counsel from Harry Miller, an extensive collection of materials that the Wisconsin Historical Society had obtained from the estate of E.P. Sherry, a major figure in the paper and power industries. More than anyone else, Sherry had been the driving force behind the creation of the flowage, and the issues he dealt with and the actions he took provided a useful framework for looking at the flowage in terms of the broader issues of Wisconsin history. From then on, the questions came more readily, and in response to those questions the narrative line of the book took shape. Soon a familiar pattern was at work: write and research, research and write, and so on.

A study of this sort—especially one that comes almost to the present day—is of necessity a collaborative effort, and I am deeply grateful to everyone who helped out, whether with a single anecdote or photo or through ongoing consultation over a number of years. That said, I owe a particular debt of gratitude to the following individuals. Maryann Brown, in her role as president of the flowage property owners' association, early on endorsed the project on behalf of the organization; and subsequently she drew from her amazing memory every kind of detail possible, from the ownership history of certain resorts, to colorful local characters, to some key moments in the flowage story with which she had personal involvement. And when she did not know something—which was rare—she knew where to send me. Neil Koshak, with his own vast storehouse of facts and anecdotes, ably and delightfully tutored me on early days of the flowage, as did his childhood pal, the late Art Schmidt Jr. Terry Daulton helped put me in touch with a number of valuable sources of information. Marcia Bjornerud, a colleague from Lawrence University, guided my foray into the geology of the area and vetted the product of that effort.

I received gracious and invaluable help from folks at the Wisconsin Department of Natural Resources. Roger Jasinski and Chris Paulik, the two property managers of the flowage, shared their considerable knowledge of the property, the rules by which it operates, and the improvements that have been made over time. Fisheries biologists Jeff Roth, Lawrence Eslinger, and Zach Lawson provided me with a bag-limit of reports and patiently explained the science that underlay them. And Eleanor Lawry, an archivist at the WDNR in Madison, efficiently tracked down a host of crucial documents pertaining to the construction of the dam, its early operation, and state supervision of it.

The following individuals kindly granted permission to quote selected passages from copyrighted materials or to use photos: Barbara Singer for Eli Singer, author of *The Musky Chronicles* and *The Big Fat Musky Book*; Larry Ramsell for *A Compendium of Musky Angling History*; Bob Leff of Video Art Productions LLC for use of parts of the audio track of the video "The Old Masters of Musky Hunting;" Lisa Marine and Lee Grady for maps and photos from the State Historical Society; Jerry Slivinski of the Mercer Historical Society for photographic images from its collection; Doug Severt for photographic images and a personal memoir; and Paul Rothenberger for photographic images.

I am indebted to the following people who kindly read portions of the manuscript at various stages in its development and made helpful suggestions for its revision: Maryann Brown, Lawrence Eslinger, Marcia Hittle, Carla Kloess, Walter Kloess, Neil Koshak,

Zach Lawson, Jeff Malison, Art Schmidt Jr., Jeff Wilson, Richard Yatzeck, and Carol Zilinger. My principal editor, Tim Solinger, applied a keen eye to the technical aspects of the manuscript and a challenging intellect to its substantive content. Most of all, he kept the reader in mind throughout the process, and the manuscript has been vastly improved by his work. The editor for Little Creek Press brought a fresh set of eyes to the manuscript and sharpened it still further. It is, of course, a time-honored practice for authors to say that in spite of all kinds of assistance from others, they alone remain responsible for their works, including the mistakes that inevitably creep into them. And so, in keeping with that practice, I plead "responsible," though heaven knows I have had time and help enough to get it right.

Introduction

In the early summer of 2012, I was invited to discuss the history of the Turtle-Flambeau Flowage with a group of students from Mercer High School. Standing near the shore at the Sturgeon Bay landing, I pointed out over the water and asked the group what they thought this area had looked like 100 years ago. The students seemed puzzled and remained silent. Perhaps, I thought, they had not expected me to turn the tables and ask them questions about something they had presumably come to learn from me; but after several efforts to rephrase the question and listening to some tentative responses, I realized what the problem was. In these young people's minds, the flowage had always been there; it was as much a part of the Iron County landscape as the cluster of natural lakes around Mercer itself.

And why shouldn't they feel that way? For they were casting their eyes at but one part of a body of water nearly 14,000 acres in size, a sprawling wonder that includes 377 islands (give or take a floating bog island or two), 229 miles of intricate mainland shoreline, and 105 miles of island shoreline. The overwhelming percentage of its combined 334 miles of shoreline is totally wild; some of it is lined with pencil reeds and some of it glistens with exposed ledge rock, while other parts of it are guarded by the stumpy remains of virgin pines, hemlock, spruce, and birch. Almost the entire shoreline is overlooked by northern forests. The flowage's coppery waters, stained by tamarack roots and iron-bearing rock, hide an unpredictable lake bed—one crafted, it would seem, by sentient glaciers that understood the value of structure to fish and fishermen alike and so dispensed, hither and yon, rock piles, sand or gravel flats, steep drop-offs, and bays large and small. Throw in some shallow weed beds here and there and a plentiful supply of downed and drowned timber, and all the ingredients are present for an extraordinarily rich habitat for a host of north country fish species. The flowage is home to walleye and perch for the table; acrobatic smallmouth for the light tackle enthusiast; moody muskies for those who like long odds but big and nasty returns; panfish for the children and the child in us all; and the occasional giant sturgeon, ready to leap from the water to remind humans who, in this neighborhood at least, has the oldest pedigree.

It is little wonder, then, that the Turtle-Flambeau Flowage so often draws comparisons to archetypal Canadian Shield lakes or that it provokes feelings of wilderness and timelessness. Indeed, these attributes played a major role in the decision by the state of Wisconsin to obtain control of the flowage and its surrounding lands and to transform them into a state scenic area. As a result, it should come as no surprise that the Mercer students with whom I spoke, who knew of the flowage but not of its past, should be so enthralled by its "natural" character that they could not imagine that the flowage and its environs were the products of human initiatives.

The facts are these. The flowage is, in historical terms, a recent arrival; indeed, it has yet to mark its first centennial. Moreover, its creation in 1926 by the Chippewa and Flambeau Improvement Company (CFIC), a representative of interested industrial parties in the greater Chippewa watershed, had nothing to do with promoting or conserving the natural world. The dam that held back the waters of the Turtle and Flambeau rivers had the sole purpose of serving as a storage reservoir for waters that could be strategically released to the benefit of downstream users of water power. But over the course of its 90-year existence, the flowage and human interactions with it both evolved to the point where it has taken its place among Wisconsin's most treasured waters—even while it has continued to fulfill its originally intended purpose.

The story of the flowage, like the rivers and lakes from which it was formed, embraces a variety of historical moments, some peaceful, others more turbulent. Its creation, for example, took place amid two important struggles—one constitutional, one economic. The former involved a contest between public and private interests over the use of Wisconsin's considerable water powers; and the latter represented a conflict between a declining logging industry, on the one hand, and a rising electrical power industry, on the other, over the use of Wisconsin's rivers. As it turned out, the future belonged to the power industry, one of whose talented and foresighted leaders, E.P. Sherry, was the driving force behind the construction of the flowage.

Once built, the flowage entered a quiet time during which a fishery blossomed, a resort industry arose, and anglers, hunters, and nature lovers from around the state and nation found their way to its shores and waters. The flowage also attracted the attention of state conservation officials who conducted surveys of the fishery and worked to enhance habitat for valued bird species. Turbulent times resumed, however, in the 1980s when federal courts validated the claims of Wisconsin's Chippewa tribes to their "retained" rights to hunt and fish in areas ceded to the United States in treaties negotiated in 1837, 1842, and 1854. The troubled aftermath of these judicial rulings brought an increased presence of the state of Wisconsin to the northwoods. The continuing threat of violence, and the occasional outbreak of violent activity, prompted a major intervention by state law enforcement personnel in the pursuit of public safety. Less visible, but perhaps equally important over the long run, the Wisconsin Department of Natural Resources set to work with the Chippewa tribes to develop new arrangements for managing area fisheries. The flowage was front and center in the events of these difficult years.

Even as the conflict over the tribes' exercise of their rights continued, the state of Wisconsin, for reasons quite independent of this conflict, decided to purchase from Northern States Power (the dominant shareholder in the CFIC) the flowage itself and adjacent NSP lands. This move was followed by the creation of the Turtle-Flambeau Scenic Waters Area. At that moment, the Wisconsin Department of Natural Resources assumed the principal role in shaping the future of the flowage, a role embodied in the master plan that it developed for the property. A more stable period for the flowage seemed in the making. That said, one more significant event occurred that was to affect these waters: namely, a legal contest between the CFIC and the Federal Energy Regulatory Commission, which was seeking regulatory authority over the flowage dam. In the end, the federal agency won the day and established its authority over the industrial use of the flowage's waters.

The present status of the Turtle-Flambeau Flowage, as a predominantly state-owned resource that also serves private-sector interests, is something of an anomaly: a pragmatic arrangement designed to enable both public and private use of a precious and finite resource. Predictably, this arrangement has become increasingly subject to an ever-growing array of outside pressures—from the state, from industry, from the federal government, from the Chippewa tribes, and from various private interests. As a consequence, the flowage, which like its waters has never stood still, can hardly be considered a "finished" product. But even as we step into its waters in midstream, its story has much to tell about the past, and much to prompt thought about the future.

Clio, the muse of history, can be served in many ways. In the first part of this book, I have mixed narrative and analysis to tell the story of the Turtle-Flambeau Flowage from its beginning to the present day. In so doing, I have sought to place the events and trends that are at the forefront of the story in broader or deeper contexts. For example, a quick look at the geology of the area not only lays out the origins of the physical features that made the flowage possible, but it also underscores just how brief a moment this seemingly timeless body of water has had upon earth's stage. So too have I undertaken to examine relevant economic, social, and political contexts—largely at the state level—that have left their mark on the flowage, and will no doubt continue to do so. In short, I have tried to weave the uniqueness of the Turtle-Flambeau Flowage into the broader fabric of its time.

Clio, whose embrace of the past knows no bounds, can also be served through efforts to capture the very experience of life in a different time and place from our own. Here the historian sets aside the big moments and outsized public personalities and turns to ordinary individuals, whether at work or at play. How did they go about their various pursuits, and how did they perceive them? What was it like to build and run a resort? To catch a musky? To guide a party of anglers? To eat a shore lunch? It is these types of experiences, at once unique to each individual yet held in common by many, piled one upon another, that build an ethos for a moment in time and that can ultimately create both legend and mystique. In the second part of this book, I have sought to share

Michael Hittle

a variety of flowage-related experiences that have meant so much to those who have lived them. I have not, however, tried to impose any order or greater meaning to this material. It is my hope that readers will let the flowage speak directly to them through these individual testimonies.

CHAPTER ONE
The Long, Slow Stretch

A Rocky Start

The peacefulness of the Turtle-Flambeau Flowage today belies the monumental turbulence of its deep past. For the terrain that underlies the flowage and the lands surrounding it originated in three cataclysmic episodes in the geological history of Wisconsin. In the first episode, which occurred around 2,800 million years ago, vast forces—driven by widespread volcanism—shaped and reshaped the crust of the earth and brought forth an embryonic North American continent, known to geologists as the Archean Superior Continent. The bedrock of this continent represented the southernmost extension of the Canadian Shield—a huge area characterized by exposed rock of Precambrian origin—that is, rock more than 545 million years old. The next episode occurred a little over 1,800 million years ago, when a volcanic island chain, along with another smaller continent, collided with the Superior continent. Volcanic action and vast pressures welded the two continents together along a line (the Niagara fault) that runs west from Niagara, Wisconsin, through Woodruff and then crosses State Highway

13 midway between Park Falls and Phillips. These forces raised up the Penokean mountain range, whose character was akin to the Rockies or the Appalachians before a lengthy process of erosion ultimately reduced it to a vast, gently undulating plain. The third episode that affected the area occupied by the flowage was the Midcontinent or Superior Rift, a massive event that took place around 1,100 million years ago. For some 20 million years, violent volcanic activity along a line that parallels contemporary Lake Superior threatened to tear the North American continent in two before it finally subsided. This rifting process, which exerted massive uplifting pressures on adjacent bedrock formations, created the Wisconsin dome that today underlies the state's entire Northern Highland area.

Between the first two episodes, as the oceans washed the Superior continent's southern shallow coastal plain, oxidation of dissolved iron in the ocean led to the depositing of rusty, iron-rich sediments on the sea bed. Known today as banded iron formations for their alternate layers of iron-rich and iron-poor materials, these deposits later formed the basis for an extensive iron mining industry from Minnesota across northern Wisconsin and into upper Michigan.

Today, visible evidence of the billions of years of transformation described above is scarce within the Turtle-Flambeau Scenic Waters Area, thanks in large part to the glacial deposits that cover it. But there are some exposures of Precambrian rock that connect the area with its distant past. A drive along Iron County Trunk FF, for example, takes one past three significant outcrops: Penokean volcanic rock at Lake of the Falls; pillow basalt just west of Third Black Lake; and foliated greenstone schist on the east side of Kimmear Road. Although the properties of the rocks at each site vary, they are all part of a larger sequence of metamorphic rocks of volcanic origin. By way of contrast, a boating trip on the flowage past the outcrops on the islands where campsites R8 and R9 are located or down the North Fork of the Flambeau River from the dam to Pete's Landing will take one past outcrops of a different kind—rocks that belong to a sequence of metamorphic rocks of sedimentary origin. Both sequences date well into the Precambrian Era, so one is looking at rocks possibly dating as far back as 1,800 million years ago.

For some years, the boundary between these two sequences, which runs northeast to southwest on a line that more or less bisects Big Island, was a source of some puzzlement. In the 1950s, geologists working for Kennecott Copper Corporation identified an area, running from Mercer to Park Falls, where electrical signals sent into the earth showed alternating patterns of conductive and non-conductive rocks. Bore holes, however, turned up no explanation. In the 1970s, academic geophysicists once again explored the region with electrical signals and found a location south of the Flambeau River where their signals did not return from the earth. They dubbed this phenomenon the "Flambeau Anomaly." Further exploration revealed the presence of four to six parallel conductive formations that extended in depth to 10 kilometers and that covered an area 15 kilometers wide and 100 kilometers long. Moreover, they found a correspondence between these conductive anomalies and magnetic ones. (Anyone who has ever used a compass on certain parts of Big Island must surely be aware of these magnetic anomalies.) Today geophysicists believe that the Flambeau Anomaly lies along a fault line (called the Flambeau Flowage Fault) that exists at the juncture of the two bedrock sequences—though no surface evidence of a fault has been found. In addition, they attribute the extreme conductivity largely to graphite deposits, though some iron and copper may be present as well, the former possibly accounting for magnetic irregularities.

Whether the geological record is clear or hidden, we are left to wonder at these numerous transformations. Anyone heading out onto the flowage for a little ice fishing on a frosty January morning would be hard-pressed, indeed, to imagine volcanic forces bubbling up from miles below or ocean waters gently lapping upon a continental shelf.

The Ice Age Cometh

If it took billions of years to lay down, transform, and shape the bedrock foundation of the Northern Highland, it took only a miniscule fraction of that time to create its current topography. For that was primarily the work of glaciation, a process which began approximately 1.8 million years ago. In cycles of roughly 100,000 years each, the great ice sheets that descended southward from polar and subpolar regions scoured the landscape, carrying along debris as fine as flour and as large as train cars, depositing some of these materials as they advanced and leaving still others behind as they melted their way northward. The greater part of Wisconsin may have been overrun with ice more than a dozen times, though the exact number cannot be precisely determined as each successive cycle of advance and retreat tended to wipe clean the traces of its predecessor. The last great glacial epoch, called the Wisconsinan or, simply Wisconsin, because its imprint shows most dramatically on this state, began around 90,000 years ago. It made three main advances—and two noteworthy retreats—before completely departing the state around 9,500 years ago.

The most readily interpreted record of Wisconsin glaciation derives from the third, or Valderan, advance. It began 26,000 years ago as the great Labrador Ice Sheet from which it flowed underwent an expansion. After spreading beyond the Lake

Superior Basin, this advance reached its maximum extent around 18,000 years ago and started its main retreat around 15,000 years ago. A lesser resurgence of the ice some 13,000 years ago attained its southernmost extent along a ragged moraine line that runs across Vilas County a few miles north of Manitowish Waters and then crosses Highway 51 to the north of Mercer. This hummocky band, known as the Winegar Moraine, rises to a sufficient elevation to form a continental divide between waters that flow into the Mississippi River Basin and those that flow into the Great Lakes. The area on which the flowage is located, and a good part of the territory that makes up its watershed, lie just to the south of the margin of this last significant glacial advance into the Northern Highland.

Glaciers, thanks to their immense power, can shape topography in many different ways. They can scour and gouge. They can impart direction to physical features of the landscape. They can raise hills, create lakes, or leave huge expanses of level land. In the case of southern Iron County and adjacent Vilas County, glacial activity created a topography populated by innumerable small lakes, often linked by short, irregular streams; vast swamps and marshes; and upland terrain of poor soil quality. Prior to the construction of the flowage, some 200 lakes lay within a 20-mile radius of Mercer, to say nothing of the huge swaths of marshland and swamp that lay largely to the south of the town. Indeed, marshes cover approximately 21 percent of the land in this part of Wisconsin. Overall, the areas of the state that boast the most lakes have few rivals worldwide for the number of lakes per square mile. Only northern Minnesota, parts of Ontario, and one area of Finland are comparable.

Not only did the glaciers bring into being this land of lakes, streams, rivers, marshes, and swamps, but they also left a variety of calling cards that remind us of their powers and whims.

Donut Lake, for example, located on the north side of Big Island in the Turtle-Flambeau Flowage, is a classic kettle lake. It was created when the retreating glacier left a block of ice trapped in a depression. As the ice melted, the sediment that was contained in the ice fell into the cavity, which then filled with water up to the level of the water table. A kettle lake that has gradually lost its water through natural processes can be seen on the south side of County Road FF just to the west of the road that leads to the Bastine Lake area.

The vast swamps and marshlands that lie to the east and south of the Horseshoe Lake portion of the flowage, and the lowlands visible from State Highway 182 going west from Manitowish, are the products of meltwater that flowed from the Winegar Moraine in vast braided rivers. Geologists and geographers regard the presence of such extensive marshes as an indication of an "immature" or "inefficient" post-glacial drainage system. That is, existing rivers and streams, still recovering from the ice age, have yet to reorganize themselves into an efficient drainage network in a relatively flat area.

The up and down terrain of the Springstead Peninsula that divides the flowage into two distinct arms owes its distinct topography to a number of eskers—ridges of sand and gravel made when rivers that flowed beneath glaciers deposited materials that had been embedded in the ice. A geological map of the area shows most of these eskers to be running on a slightly northwest to southeast line. Anglers headed to the Springstead Landing might wish to reflect on the distant origins of the twists and turns that characterize this road: namely, the sinuous curves of an ancient subglacial river.

Glaciers also decorated the landscape in ways great and small with erratics—rocks that differ from indigenous bedrock and that have been carried however far and then dropped in place when the glaciers melted. The granitic Pink Rock, near the river channel in the Turtle part of the flowage, is a classic example of a highly visible erratic, sitting as it does upon exposed local bedrock. Erratics can show up in numbers as well. About six-tenths of a mile to the east of the Pink Rock there is a large, circular rock pile that lurks just beneath the surface of the water. This hazard, it would seem, was deposited by a mischievous glacier to remind boaters of who is really in charge of navigation on the flowage. And any rocky beach will be studded with erratics, whose journeys we can only speculate upon.

Glacial activity also determined the character of the area's parent soils: that is, those that lie below the organically derived surface matter. To the north of the Turtle River, the dominant soil types are sandy and silty loams of a kind also found in the Manitowish River Basin. Where the southwest and southeast arms of the flowage are, the soils are predominantly peaty, as might be expected from the swampy nature of the lands there. On Big Island and on the Springstead Peninsula, rough silty loam and Rodman gravel, a coarse mix of sand and rocks, predominate. These two soil types also run from the Fox Lake area east to near Lake of the Falls. Differing parent soil types give rise to the various kinds of vegetative communities that can be found in the region.

The Flambeau River

The North Fork of the Flambeau River is very much a creature of the glacially formed topography of the Northern Highland. Following contemporary mapping practice and local understanding, I will regard the confluence of the Bear and Manitowish rivers as the starting point of the Flambeau. Each of these rivers has its recognized source in a lake of glacial origin—Flambeau

Lake in the case of the Bear and Boulder Lake in the case of the Manitowish. The Bear passes through an extensive marshland before it hits the Manitowish; and the latter river wends its way in and out of lakes large and small and then traverses a broad marshland before encountering the Bear a little more than five miles south of Mercer. Just a few miles downstream from this junction, the historic Flambeau, after passing over a couple of small rapids (now hidden beneath the waters of the flowage), was joined by the Turtle River and began its dazzling descent toward the Chippewa River. For its part, the historic Turtle River made its way on a course not unlike that of the Manitowish: that is, it rose in South Turtle Lake in Vilas County and flowed through 11 named lakes and several small, unnamed basins before meeting the Flambeau at the site of the present-day flowage dam. In 1820 James Duane Doty, secretary to an exploratory expedition led by Henry Schoolcraft, noted that "the small river formed by the junction of the Turtle and Old Plantation (Manitowish) Rivers, is almost entirely a rapid; and, running over a bed of rocks, is very dangerous. It takes seven days to descend it, and is one hundred and seventy-five miles long." He did not, however, give the river a name.

One might well ask why a river as prominent as the Flambeau begins in midstream, as it were. Why not trace it straight to Boulder Lake? There is a good reason to do so, for that would maximize the length of the river. Or to Turtle Lake? In this case, one could point, as F.L. King did in 1882, to two facts: that the Turtle flowed in such a direct line that it never varied more than five miles to either side of a straight line linking South Turtle Lake with the river's mouth; and that the Turtle is well aligned with the Flambeau's overall southwesterly flow. If consistent direction of flow is a consideration in giving a name to a watershed, then a quick look at the map would suggest that the Flambeau ought to run all the way to the Mississippi, or, to turn things around, that the Chippewa River should have its source in Boulder Lake or South Turtle Lake.

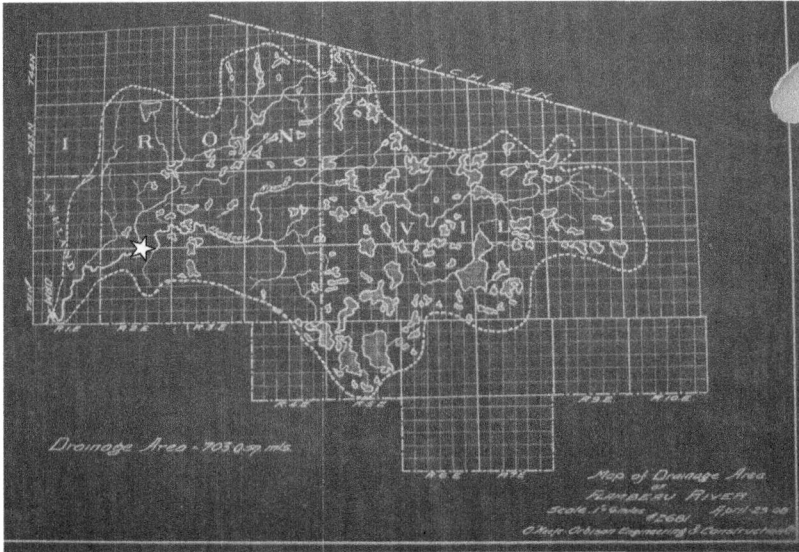

The dam indicated in the lower left corner of this 1908 drawing is likely a proposed site for a major dam. The actual site of the flowage dam is in R.2.E, on the line between T41N and T42N. Wisconsin Historical Society

These speculations might make some sense from a geographer's or cartographer's perspective, but they are irrelevant to the historian. For the latter, the very names of the tributaries that form the upper reach of the North Fork of the Flambeau are telling. Manitowish is an Ojibwa word, the root of which, "manito," means "spirit." According to the Jesuit missionary, Father Baraga, "manitowish" referred to a "small animal" (such as a marten or a weasel). John Tanner, who spent some time as a captive of the Ojibwa, took the word "manito-waise-se" to mean "spirit-beast," because the Ojibwa thought that there were "evil spirits in the waters here." Turtle and Bear could either be translations of Ojibwa words or simply names attached to these rivers by early English-speaking settlers. And Flambeau itself is a straightforward translation into French of the Ojibwa word "wauswagaming," which means "at the lake of the torches." The torches, of course, were those of the Ojibwa fishermen. Somewhere, then, in the comings and goings of people—indigenous, transient, and settling—the names were set. Precisely by whom and when will likely never be known. But these tributaries did their work, unmindful of their labels, draining as best they could this terrain and forming a legendary river.

In 1908, the geologist Leonard Smith calculated the drainage area of the Flambeau River above Park Falls to be 760 square miles. This area ranged north to No Man's Lake, located just south of the Michigan border in extreme northwestern Vilas County; east to Lake Laura and Siphon Springs in the northeastern portion of the Northern Highland American Legion State Forest; and south to Whitefish Lake, which lies just below the Flambeau chain. In his geologic and topographic description of the Flambeau, King noted that both the north and south forks of the Flambeau (the South Fork at that time was known as the Dore Flambeau— the golden Flambeau—perhaps for the color of its water when struck by sunlight) drew their waters from four roughly parallel valleys. These valleys, he proposed, might well be artifacts of a southwesterly trending glacial advance. Whether or not these valleys reflect the movement of a glacier or have their origins in other glacial processes, they funneled sufficient water to set in motion the two branches of the Flambeau.

The drainage basin of the North Fork was not, of course, just any old 760 square miles, as it embraced a sizeable part of this unique, water-rich, post-glacial landscape. Moreover, this drainage area was located in the highest portion of the state, with elevations ranging from 1,560 to 1,650 feet above sea level. It is not surprising, then, that the Flambeau River Basin should attract attention to itself as the geographic understanding of the area began to firm up around the end of the 19th century. In his 1908 evaluation of the water power potential of the Flambeau River, Smith observed: "The Flambeau River has its source in the largest number of lakes and connecting swamps with the greatest aggregate storage capacity of any river in the state." Destiny, it was to turn out, was glacially determined.

From its juncture with the Turtle River, the Flambeau flows in a decidedly southwesterly direction. Its stained waters, which derive their characteristic color both from iron-rich soil and swampland vegetation, rush through a landscape of mixed geological background. They pass outcroppings of staurolite; and they swirl over and around indurate bedrock, as in the case of the Ledge—the challenging rapids a little less than a mile below Holts Landing. The Flambeau's waters also provide a tutorial in the area's glacial history. They pass by sandbars, whose fine grains were likely sorted by the action of meltwater rivers, and race over long chutes of medium-size rubble. They tumble over boulder-studded rapids, some of which may well be the worn down remnants of moraines. And they pass by and over numerous erratics. Bearskull Rock, a well-known landmark to canoeists and anglers on the North Fork, is a glacial erratic.

The Flambeau grows in size and pace as it moves beyond the drop at present-day Park Falls. Its rate of drop from there to its mouth at the Chippewa River is 4.4 feet per mile, almost double its rate of fall from Boulder Lake to Park Falls. The south and north forks of the river finally come together in the southern part of the Flambeau River State Forest. The full stream then wends its way past Ladysmith and on to its final destination—the Chippewa River—in southeastern Rusk County. Their merged waters then descend to the country's great riverine artery, the Mississippi.

Michael Hittle

Sprucing Up

Today, the Flambeau and its tributaries flow through resurgent post-cutover forests, as well as swamps and slow-changing marshlands. But what one sees today along the river's banks is but the latest iteration in a long series of vegetative transformations that have occurred as this region has emerged from the great ice sheets. At the height of the last major glacial advance, around 18,000 years ago, it is likely that only two vegetative communities occupied those parts of Wisconsin not actually covered in ice. On the margin of the ice sheet, a band of permafrost up to 125 miles in width gave rise to tundra-like conditions. Grasses, sedges, and assorted plants that were adapted to permafrost made for an open landscape of the kind that exists today beyond the tree line in Alaska and northern Canada. To the south of the tundra lay a vegetative regime dominated by spruce, sparsely present to the north, denser to the south.

Scientific knowledge of Wisconsin's vegetative history is on firmer footing when it comes to studying events starting around 12,000 years ago. With the ice sheet in full retreat, the vegetation that followed in its wake left traces of pollen—which is strongly resistant to degeneration—in bogs and on lake bottoms. With no further ice advances to obliterate these deposits, they remain available for scientific analysis to the present day. The story told by the pollen, put in simplest terms, describes the advances—in some cases from south to north, in others from east to west—of those trees and plants that were to make up the northern vegetative zone of Wisconsin. This zone, as it existed just prior to the arrival of Europeans on the scene, comprised boreal forests, conifer-hardwood forests, and pine savannas. The process of its formation was shaped by a long-term warming of temperatures, various climatic fluctuations (especially changing moisture patterns), and disturbances brought on by drought and fires.

The forest-building process began with the replacement of tundra vegetation by the arrival of spruce, initially at a level of intensity that formed semi-open woodlands. These woodlands, in turn, gave way to increasingly dense forests, still dominated by spruce. But as the spruce forest moved farther north in the footsteps of the retreating ice, other species moved onto the scene to join remnant spruce. These were ready colonizers, such as paper birch, black ash, aspen, balsam fir, and alder. The next phase in the process began when pine—particularly jack pine—entered Wisconsin from the east in the vicinity of 10,000 years ago and began its spread westward. A thousand years later, a boreal forest dominated by spruce, jack pine, and birch ran from northern Minnesota across northwestern Wisconsin and into the Upper Peninsula of Michigan. To the south of this forest lay a belt of pine-dominated forests that gave way in central Wisconsin to a deciduous forest. Around 8,000 years before the present, two new arrivals—white pine from the east and oak from the south—appeared in the Northern Highlands. They were followed a thousand years later by maple. The white pine ruled mixed northern forests until sometime around 6,000 years ago, only to give way to an increasing presence of oak. The latter trend reached its maximum around 3,500 years ago and was especially prominent in Sawyer and Douglas counties. At the same time that the presence of oak was peaking, hemlock arrived in Wisconsin from the Upper Peninsula, where it had been established for more than two millennia. Hemlock became a staple feature of the mixed pine and hardwood forests of the north. By 3,500 years ago, then, the mix of species that characterized the forests of pre-settlement northern Wisconsin was fully in place, though that is not to say that short- and intermediate-term variations did not take place over time or in different locations. Indeed, contemporary ecological understanding finds natural systems to be dynamic rather than static. The vegetative history of the Northern Highland is a case in point.

The mental images we are likely to entertain of pre-settlement northern forests focus largely on towering conifers—preferably white or red pines—and canopy-enshrouded hardwoods. Yet as early European visitors to the area noted, that was not the case. Of course they encountered impressive stands of timber, but they also took note of scrubby, stunted trees and substantial openings in wooded lands. These conditions extended across the northern part of the state from border to border. The situation was substantially unchanged in 1877 when F.L. King engaged in field research on the geology of the upper Flambeau River. In a brief commentary on vegetation at the end of his analysis of the geology and topography of the area, King identified two distinct regimes of vegetation along the river valley. "In the Upper Lake Region the trees are small, stunted, and scattering; in the Lower Valley they are large, vigorous, and dense," he noted. He attributed the difference to soil quality, which he asserted was sandy in the lakes region and considerably richer downstream. The dividing line between these soil and vegetative areas seems to have been in the vicinity of the junction of the Turtle and the Flambeau rivers.

The first more or less systematic information about the forest cover in the area now occupied by the flowage comes not from scientists, however, but from surveyors. The General Land Office, a part of the Department of the Interior, began its land survey of Wisconsin in 1832. By 1857 some township lines had been laid out in southeastern Iron County, but the full survey of the area took place in 1864 and 1865. The surveyors laid out and marked the 36 sections that make up each township. Because it readily lends itself to measuring acres, the Gunter's chain was used by surveyors. This instrument consisted of 100 interlocked links, each of which was

7.92 inches in length, for a total length of 66 feet for a chain. The Gunter's chain enabled surveyors to measure distances between specific features—such as streams, swamps, or survey markers—in terms of chains and decimal fractions of chains.

As they went about their work, surveyors recorded both their activities and their observations of the land in field notes. For example, at the end of each mile surveyed, they listed, in descending order of frequency, the species of trees present along their recently completed course. They also drew plat maps based on their work, and they often wrote a general description of an entire township. The surveyors paid special attention to those features of the land or vegetation that had some economic potential such as soil and topography suitable for farming, bottom land covered in marsh hay, or timber suitable for logging. It is this information that leads us to a sense of what the forest cover looked like prior to the major logging of the area.

The four townships in which the flowage now lies (T41N R2E, T41N R3E, T42N R2E, and T42N R3E) were surveyed by Deputy Surveyor James McBride, with his assistants, Lewis Wood and Henry Bugela, who served as his chainsmen, and Armsted Henderson, who was his axeman. According to the general descriptions of these townships, McBride and his companions encountered a great deal of swampland where the dominant tree species were tamarack, cedar, and fir. For example, along and approximately a mile to either side of Beaver Creek (today's Big Water), the field notes describe swampy terrain where the soil is third-rate and the trees largely cedar and tamarack—usually listed in that order. The situation was the same for the vast lowland to the south of Horseshoe Lake. On higher ground, different species took prominence. What is now called Big Island, with its sandy, stony soil (also described as third-rate), was home to pine, sugar maple, hemlock, aspen, and birch, as well as cedar, fir, and tamarack in swampy pockets. Indeed, this area and the land lying immediately to the east of it seem to have been the best habitat in the locality for pine, at least in terms of numbers of trees if not their suitability for timber. Interestingly, the field notes make no mention of oak in the Big Island area, where today an oak ridge caps the high ground on the north side of the island. North of the Turtle River, where loamy soils predominate, McBride and his team again found a mixed forest of hemlock, maple, birch, aspen, and pine—though the latter was not quite as well-represented as it was on sandier soils. Someone wishing to retrace McBride's course could do so by walking west along the line separating sections 10 and 11 in the Four Mile Creek area. This line today forms the boundary between state and private property. After traversing 20 chains along this line through land he declared unfit for cultivation, McBride encountered a cedar swamp. At 75 chains, he came across a stream 20 links (13.2 feet) wide—no doubt Four Mile Creek—and then entered a tamarack swamp before hitting the section corner at 80 chains. The timber along this line included hemlock, birch, cedar, and tamarack. The yellow birch stumps—massive remnants that can still be seen in this area, often with new growth arising from or over them—give decaying witness to the surveyor's brief notes. All in all, McBride's notebooks, though limited to his observations along the section lines he was establishing, provide a clear portrait of the kind of mixed conifer-hardwood forest that had slowly come into being since the retreat of the great ice.

Whose Woods Are These?

In all likelihood, the first footprints left on the ground or in the snow along the glacial edge and in the slowly emerging woodlands of northern Wisconsin belonged to herbivores well adapted to tundra and parkland tundra environments. These would include some megafauna of the Pleistocene Epoch, such as mammoths, mastodons, woodland muskox, and giant moose. Also present were woodland caribou and barren-ground caribou, and perhaps moose and elk. It cannot, however, be said with certainty that any or all of these animals foraged across early post-glacial Iron County, let alone the area occupied by the flowage. The archeological record simply does not support such a claim. Yet their presence could be seen as consistent with finds in other Great Lakes states and with knowledge of their distribution elsewhere.

Whatever the precise composition of the animal community may have been along the edge and to the south of the retreating ice sheet, many of the species that comprised it had bleak prospects. As the climate warmed and as the northern forest went through its gradual transformations, the Pleistocene megafauna suffered total extinction for reasons that are not fully understood. And other species, like the woodland and barren-ground caribou, gradually shifted to more northerly climes. As some species dropped out, others moved in—the whitetail deer being an important example of a newcomer that was to leave a lasting imprint on the state. Somewhere between 5,000 and 3,500 BC—roughly the time when forests took on the basic characteristics they retain to the present day—the present cast of animal characters was on the scene as well. This synchrony should come as no surprise, given their mutual dependence.

Our knowledge of the makeup of the northern animal community at the time of European exploration comes from many sources—from the languages and legends of Indians of the region, from writings of explorers and traders, and from studies by archeologists. Taken together, these materials portray a diverse animal community on whose members the Indians were critically dependent. How abundant larger game animals were, however, is less clear. A.W. Schorger, in an essay on Wisconsin wildlife, contends that "extreme northern Wisconsin and the Upper Peninsula of Michigan were extremely poor in game," and he goes on to assert that fish and wild rice made up the staple diet of both Indians and European traders. Perhaps the earliest formal inventory of the mammals of Wisconsin was prepared by Moses Strong, a geologist who drowned tragically while engaged in a survey of the Flambeau River in 1877. Among the larger mammals that Strong studied, he listed black and cinnamon bear (the latter, a color variant of the black bear, was very rare), moose and elk (both of which he claimed were nearing extinction in the state), whitetail deer, panthers (rare in the north), wolverines (also rarely seen in the north), and gray wolves. Other familiar forest dwellers on his list are lynx, bobcats, prairie wolves (coyotes), badgers, red and gray foxes, pine martens, fishers, otters, beavers, mink, weasels, raccoons, porcupines, skunks, squirrels, and numerous species of mice, moles, shrews, and other rodents. Strong's notations that some species were becoming rare to the point of extinction surely reflect the increased impact of Homo sapiens upon the area over the previous 200-plus years. By the same token, it might be said that the presence of so many of these species in the contemporary TFF Scenic Area reflects well on our capacity to be responsible stewards of the land and its creatures when we set our minds to it.

Where game is, there will be hunters, whether four- or two-footed. And so it was that the first human feet to tread upon Wisconsin soil—sometime around 9,500 B.C.—belonged to small groups of highly mobile hunters who anthropologists call Paleo-Indians. These people developed distinctive styles of projectile points, the subsequent discovery of which has made it possible to map their geographic spread and to gain some sense of their way of life. In parts of the western United States, for example, scholars have found clear evidence that Paleo-Indians hunted some of the

Pleistocene megafauna, and from this evidence have surmised that the focused pursuit and killing of these and other large animals uniquely shaped the economic, social, and cultural lives of these early indigenous people. Archeological investigations carried out during the 1970s in the lakes region of Wisconsin turned up a number of Paleo-Indian sites, some of which were located in Price and Oneida counties. Located on rivers or on the outlet streams of lakes, these were small in size and apparently used once and abandoned—features consistent with the notion of Paleo-Indians as small, highly mobile groups in pursuit of game. Studies of these sites indicate that the first human presence in this part of the state occurred around 7,000 B.C.

After the Paleo-Indians, a succession of cultures inhabited the area, which anthropologists have divided into stages—Archaic, Woodland, Oneota, and Historic—going from old to new. Whether these cultures were the products of migrants to the area or adaptations by existing peoples or some combination of the two cannot be said with certainty. What does seem clear, however, is that the northwoods remained home to Indians in a more or less continuing way across thousands of years.

Only two registered archeological sites fall within the bounds of the TFF Scenic Area. One involves a single, unclassified projectile point found at a time of low water. The other, however, has been described as a Late Woodland village, which places it somewhere between 600 A.D. and 1400 A.D. Late Woodland people can be distinguished from some of their early predecessors by, among other things, the use of pottery and the presence of some copper items, such as fishhooks. They also used bows and arrows for hunting and warring. This particular site has not been systematically studied, as it is located on private land. The meager official archeological record for the flowage area should not, however, be taken as an indication that only a handful of Indians were ever present in the area. The lakes, streams, and rivers that now lie beneath the 13,000-plus acres of the flowage constitute precisely the kind of environment to which Indians were drawn from their first arrival on the scene. One can only imagine what artifacts lie beneath the coppery waters of the flowage.

As the archeological record gives way to the historical, our ability to identify the moccasins on the ground advances by several orders of magnitude. This transition occurs in the early 17th century, as a complex tide of trade, cooperation, and conflict among Indian nations, movements of Indian peoples, and French-dominated exploration swept into the western Great Lakes. Though people from many Indian nations—Ottawa, Hurons, Petuns, and Santee Sioux, for example—moved into and through northern Wisconsin during the 17th century, the people of greatest importance to this story are the Chippewa, or Ojibwa as they are also known.

In the early 17th century, the Chippewa were distributed across the northern shore of Lake Huron from Sault Ste. Marie as far east as Lake Nipissing, along the eastern shore of Lake Superior, and westward from Sault Ste. Marie into the eastern part of today's Upper Peninsula of Michigan. Not a numerous people, they lived in highly dispersed groups. The many names by which they identified themselves—names often linked to animals—suggest the early Chippewa were organized by clans based on a totem, or mythical progenitor of a clan. The "people of the bear" would be an example of such a name. To the French, however, these were the *sauteurs* or *saulteurs*, because the rapids of the St. Mary River, which flow from Lake Superior into Lake Huron, were the center of Chippewa activities. The Chippewa were drawn to the Sault by the abundant fish resources of the river, where spawning whitefish and sturgeon in the river and lake trout on the shoals of Lake Superior fell prey to their dip nets, spears, and gillnets. When the last of the autumn spawning runs was over, most of the

Chippewa then returned to their interior villages to harvest wild rice and to engage in trapping and subsistence hunting through the long and harsh winters of the region.

The scale of Chippewa activity seems to have grown, however, through the course of the century. For when Father Pierre Marquette set up his Jesuit mission at the Sault in 1668, he encountered not just a few Chippewa fishermen and their families, but a bustling community of a thousand or more people made up both of Chippewa and related or allied Indian peoples. It was not so much fish as furs that created these new circumstances. The Chippewa had, by this time, become deeply involved in the fur trade, both as trappers and as middlemen who took in pelts from various isolated groups and moved those pelts along to the east. As a result, summertime at the Sault became a time for the Chippewa and their allies in commerce to gather, trade, and engage in various ritual ceremonies. In particular, the Feast of the Dead, which honored ancestors, seems to have had the effect of drawing together more tightly the Chippewa and those to whom they were related by ties of kinship or commerce. In time, these interactions seem to have enhanced the Chippewa's sense of identity and increased their numbers by the addition of others to their ranks. This strengthened Chippewa nation soon began a significant push that extended their presence into lower Michigan, northern Wisconsin, northern Minnesota, and Canada as far as lakes Manitoba and Winnipeg. By the end of the 17th century, the Chippewa dominated the upper Great Lakes from their centers in Mackinac, Sault Ste. Marie, and La Pointe. For the most part this advance met little or no resistance, except in northwestern Wisconsin. There, the Chippewa bumped up against the Santee Sioux, and the two nations became rivals over rich hunting lands along and on either side of the Mississippi River. Intermittent warfare over this territory became a part of the pattern of life in that region. Ultimately, intervention by non-native people was needed to tamp down this conflict.

The same century that found the Chippewa establishing themselves across such a vast swath of the upper lakes region was also the century that Europeans first canoed into, and then set foot upon, this beautiful, resource-rich terrain. These European travelers included men such as Etienne Brule, who around 1621-23 became the first Frenchman to see Lake Superior and Jean Nicolet, whose exploration inland from Green Bay in 1634 almost certainly made him the first European to enter Wisconsin. Who led the way into Iron County? It is quite possible that the honor belongs to Pierre-Esprit Radisson and Meedard Chouart des Groseilliers. The journal of their voyage in 1659 along the south shore of Lake Superior mentions a "shallow river which was a quarter of a mile in breadth," (The context makes clear that this was the Montreal River; the river's name first appears on a map from 1688.) The journal is silent, however, about whether they actually stepped on shore at this location. For sure, the two men pushed on to Chequamegon Bay and then journeyed south as far as Lac Court Oreilles. There they spent a harrowing winter, fighting off imminent starvation among a village of Hurons, before pushing on westward.

Radisson and Groseillier represented a new turn in the French penetration of the upper lakes. Previously, allied Indian nations had, in effect, borne the brunt of the fur trade themselves— trapping, collecting, and transporting the furs to French *entrepots* (trading posts where goods were collected and then transshipped to France) in Quebec. In the second half of the 17th century, however, Frenchmen, some licensed by the government, some not, became an integral part of the trade. They ventured deep into Indian lands, living, trapping, and trading along with the Indians; and they even accompanied their Indian hosts on fur-laden voyages back to the east. These men were variously known as *voyageurs* or *coureurs de bois* (woods rangers). In all likelihood, the honor of being the first European to visit the interior of Iron County belongs to some unknown French *coureur de bois*. For certain, everything was in place for such a person: woods, fur-bearing animals, Indians interested in trade, and an established route—the Flambeau Trail.

The Flambeau Trail ran from the mouth of the Montreal River to the Indian settlement at Lac du Flambeau. The first hint of its existence can be found in Radisson's account of his journey. When the expedition reached the mouth of the Montreal River, a number of Hurons who had accompanied Radisson and Grossilliers struck out inland "to win the shortest way to their nation." Their destination was probably not Lac du Flambeau but somewhere near the source of the Chippewa River, where a remnant group of Hurons had taken up residence. Even so, the trail was ideally suited, leading as it did to the Manitowish and then on to the North Fork of the Flambeau. Undoubtedly, the Flambeau Trail predated the arrival of Europeans in the area, but by how many years, decades, or centuries will never be known.

The trail itself began with an arduous portage of some 45 miles, traversing the rocky terrain of the Penokee Range and numerous swamps and lowlands beyond. At Portage Lake (now Long Lake), travelers took to canoes—which during the height of the fur trade were cached there—and then wended their way by water to Turtle Lake (now Echo Lake). A brief portage took them to Little Turtle Lake (now Grand Portage Lake), from which they paddled into and directly across an unnamed lake (now Mercer Lake). At this point, they encountered the final and perhaps most difficult portage: a six-pause portage. (*Voyageurs* measured portages by the number of times they paused to rest; each pause came somewhere between 600 and 1,000 yards, depending on the difficulty of the trail.) This portage ended at the Manitowish River, just a few miles upstream from the Lac du Flambeau River (now the Bear River)—the final link to Lac du Flambeau.

The best information about the course of the Flambeau Trail comes from two 19th-century accounts and from surveyors' field notes and maps. James Doty's notes for the Schoolcraft expedition sketch the route in a general sort of way but contain no comments on it. By way of contrast, J. G. Norwood, a geologist who visited the area in 1847, precisely describes each stage of a trail that was still in active use by "the Fur Company for the transportation of goods to their trading posts in this section...." Norwood displays a keen eye for spotting changing vegetation along the trail—from sparse to luxuriant and back again. His description of the Manitowish River in the three miles above its junction with the Bear could be applied equally well today: "Where the bends of the river approach the margin of the meadows [where, he earlier notes, the grass stood from two to five feet high], the banks are from four to six feet high, and composed entirely of a yellowish coarse sand...." But his eye for the natural did not cause Norwood to hold back when it came to appraising the trail itself. "[It] is certainly one of the worst portages in Wisconsin," he writes of the first 40 miles southward from the mouth of the Montreal; and after pointing out that the final, six-pause portage passed mostly over a sand barren, he tells us that the last half mile "passes through one of the worst tamerack [sic] swamps I have ever seen."

The Flambeau Trail was still very much in evidence in the middle of the 1860s, when the first survey was made. A careful reading of the field notes, along with a review of the plat maps, makes it possible to locate the trail with some precision—especially where it crosses section lines. The trail may have been in active use up until the 1880s, when other means of transportation began to penetrate the area. What is for certain, though, is that a map prepared for the Wisconsin Geological Survey in 1876 plotted the trail across its entire length.

The actual course of the trail is one thing; the experience of it with two 80- to 90-pound packs is another. For that one can turn to the journal of Francois Victor Malhiot, a French-Canadian fur trader who passed over the Flambeau Trail on his way to Lac du Flambeau in 1804. The North West Company had sent Malhiot to Lac du Flambeau to set right a mess made by the incumbent clerk at the post, a man named Gauthier. Malhiot set out on the trail on July 28 with "a bale of merchandise, a roll of tobacco, 20 pounds of shot, 20 pounds of bullets, three quarters of a sack of corn, a barrel of rum double-strength, and all my baggage." He also had a toothache. He and his party made 40 pauses the first day, but they made only 20 the second when Malhiot's toothache intensified and the legs of his companions were tied up by cramps. Nonetheless, the party pushed on. At Long Lake they retrieved and gummed cached boats that awaited them and took to the water. The party, having negotiated successfully the final six-pause portage, arrived in Lac du Flambeau in midafternoon on the second of August. Some days later, after getting settled and recovering his health, Malhiot gave his verdict on the trail: "I will begin by saying that of all the spots and places I have seen in my thirteen years' of travels, this is the most horrid and sterile. The Portage road is truly that to heaven because it is narrow, full of overturned trees, obstacles, thorns and muskegs.... This vile portage is inhabited solely by owls, because no other animal could find a living there, and the hoots of those solitary birds are enough to frighten an angel or intimidate a Caesar." In his judgment, those who carried a pack over that trail "deserve to be called men." Malhiot's journal goes on to record the entirety of his stay at Lac du Flambeau, and in the process sheds a great deal of light on the nature of the fur trade at that time. In particular, his narrative reflects the devastating and degrading role that alcohol had come to play in the trade—

especially when rival companies vied for pelts provided by the Indians.

The Flambeau Trail comes just short of passing through the Turtle-Flambeau Scenic Waters Area. Even so, it has a proper place in this history. For it draws together the physical setting, including the two rivers that bring the Flambeau River into being; the wildlife of the area, especially the beavers that were at the heart of the trade; the many nations of Indians who found themselves either passing through or settling in hopes that this land would prove sustaining for them; and the people of European origin, who saw both the beauty and the rigors of this land, but who were ultimately driven by their cultural imperatives—the mastery of the physical world, the pursuit of gain, and their commitment to "civilizing" aboriginal peoples. None who traversed this difficult trail, and perhaps Malhiot least of all, could have imagined the shape of the future that would emerge from these modest movements of people and goods.

The fur trade, which had brought Malhiot to the Flambeau Trail, continued along established lines well into the 19th century—with one exception. Following the nation's independence, American fur-trading interests—especially those of John Jacob Astor's American Fur Company—strove to wrest control of the fur trade from established European hands. That struggle did not, for the moment, alter significantly the participation of Wisconsin's native population in that trade; they continued in their essential role as procurers of pelts. Nor did the struggle interrupt the growing dependence of the Indians on trade goods and their gradual integration into the market economy of the budding nation that this dependence fostered. But this overlay on their traditional lives as hunters and gatherers was not to last. As the number of fur-bearing animals declined in the state, so too did the trade in pelts. By 1830 Astor had signaled his concerns about the future of the trade, and in 1834 he sold out. Beneficiaries of a swing in fashion toward raccoon pelts, Astor's successors kept the company afloat for more than a decade, but they finally closed up shop in 1847. Deprived of their revenues from fur trading, Wisconsin's tribes found it difficult to pay for goods on which they had become dependent. The path ahead for them was to be rocky indeed.

Enter the United States

By this time, however, other resources—namely, minerals, timber, and water power—had caught the attention of Wisconsin's growing territorial population and of others back east looking for new business ventures. Lead mining in the southwest part of the territory brought about the first significant influx of white settlers into the area, and set in motion the gradual political organization of the territory. The discovery of copper along the shores of Lake Superior pointed toward yet another opportunity for mining in the state. Then there was timber, particularly the vast stands of white pine, a wood eminently suited to housing the nation's growing and spreading population. And finally, the timbered region of the state was rich in water power, which stood ready to assist in the exploitation of the pineries. In short, Wisconsin had resources aplenty to sustain and enhance the economy of the territory well into the future, but these differed in one important way from the furry resources that had been the mainstay of commercial life in the area for so long. Whereas the Indians had been an integral and indispensable part of the fur trade from its very beginning, by the first half of the 19th century they had become an obstacle to the exploitation of both subsoil and surface resources because of their ownership of the land. And the United States government had, from the Northwest Ordinance of 1787 on, committed itself to recognize the validity of Indian rights to their lands. As this seminal document says: "The utmost good faith shall always be observed towards the Indians; their lands and property shall never be taken from them without their consent; and, in their property, rights, and liberty, they shall never be invaded or disturbed, unless in just and lawful wars authorized by Congress...." That meant, by law at least, that no timber should fall, no plow should break the soil, and no mine shaft should be sunk until Indian lands had come into possession of the U.S. government and been duly transferred to its citizens. Negotiations with Wisconsin's Indians had consequently become the *sine qua non* for further economic expansion into the territory.

Treaties signed in 1825, 1826, and 1827 sought to delineate the territories occupied by the major Indian nations in Wisconsin: the Chippewa, Sioux, Sauk, Fox, and Menominee. By 1833, additional treaties, some of them calling for the removal of native peoples beyond the Mississippi onto lands designated "Indian Country," had transferred a good deal of Wisconsin south of the Fox-Wisconsin waterway into the hands of the U.S. government. Those transactions not only opened the southern part of the territory to mining and farming by white settlers, but they also set the stage for two major treaties, whose impact on the northwoods was to be both significant and lasting.

In 1837, at Fort Snelling on the Mississippi River, the Great Lakes Chippewa concluded what has come to be known as the Pine Tree Treaty with the U.S. government. As a result of this action, the Chippewa ceded 11 million acres of pine-rich land to the federal government. In return, the Indians were to receive annual payments in money and goods for a period of 20 years. In addition, the government was to compensate traders directly for outstanding debts that the Chippewa had run up. After calculating the total costs of the payments, one contemporary claimed that the land had been purchased at slightly less than 8 cents per acre. In addition to providing monetary compensation to the Chippewa for the cession, the treaty went on to state that "the privilege of hunting, fishing, and gathering wild rice, upon the lands, the rivers and the lakes included in the territory ceded, is guaranteed to the Indians, during the pleasure of the President of the United States."

At first reading, the basic features of the treaty seem clear: a complete transfer of land in return for payments of cash and goods and a promise of continued sustenance living. But careful analysis of the treaty suggests that it may have been interpreted differently by each of the contracting parties. For example, it seems quite possible that the Indians did not share the government's view of land as "property" subject to "ownership." According to this line of argument, the Indians understood that land existed to be used, and "ownership" simply determined who could use what resources on the land. If that premise is correct, the Indians may well have thought that they had conceded only the timber on the lands they ceded through the treaty of 1837. Whatever the merits of that argument may be, the Chippewa, heavily indebted to the traders and looking at the prospects of a declining fur trade, had ample incentive to strike a deal with the government. And the government, for its part, had good reason to acquire this land and a long legal tradition in common law to support its actions.

A scant five years later at La Pointe on Madeleine Island, a similar scenario played out. Only this time the government sought access not to forests but to minerals—at that moment believed to be primarily copper. In this so-called Copper Treaty, the Chippewa ceded 12 million acres that lay across northernmost Wisconsin and into what would become Michigan's Upper Peninsula. The compensation package of money, goods, and liquidation of Indian debts to traders mirrored that of the 1837 treaty, except that the annual payments were to be stretched out over a 25-year span. At a total cost of 7 cents per acre, the U.S. government got an even better bargain this time. The Copper Treaty, like its predecessor, spoke to the reserved rights of the Chippewa. "The Indians stipulate the right of hunting on the ceded territory, with the other usual privileges of occupancy, until required to remove by the President of the United States...." As the language of the treaty makes clear, the threat of removal hung over these deliberations in a way it did not in 1837. No doubt that threat helped to bring the parties to an agreement on the government's terms.

The Copper Treaty of 1842 did not, however, put to rest the notion of removal. In 1850 President Zachary Taylor issued a removal order for Wisconsin's roughly 3,000 Chippewa, an order that also revoked the usufructuary rights the Indians had secured in 1837 and 1842. The Indians vigorously resisted this order, not only because of their attachment to the woods and waters of the area but also because of their fear of being relocated in proximity to their longtime nemesis, the Sioux. With some skilled diplomacy of their own and with vocal support from progressive whites in the state, the Chippewa managed to stave off removal. In 1852 President Millard Fillmore rescinded Taylor's order, which in effect restored the Indian's treaty-given rights to hunt, fish, and gather in the ceded territories. Not content with this outcome alone and hoping to forestall another removal initiative, the Chippewa pressed the U.S. government for permanent settlements in Wisconsin. In 1854, a treaty negotiated at La Pointe created four such settlements, later to be known as reservations: Bad River, Red Cliff, Lac Court Oreilles, and Lac du Flambeau. Other Chippewa bands would have to wait until the 20th century before acquiring reservation lands.

The relationship between Wisconsin's Chippewa and the federal government experienced no significant changes in the coming years. Indeed, as of 1871 the U.S. government officially ended its practice of dealing with Indian people via treaties, though it left standing all existing treaties. This action meant that the cession treaties of 1837 and 1842, along with the reservation treaty of 1854, remained in force. By law, then, the Chippewa were secure in their reservation lands and in their usufructuary rights within the ceded territory. And their lives seem to have reflected the legal framework that had been established. That is, they hunted and fished both on and off the reservations, even as they lived and worked sometimes separately from, sometimes alongside, a growing white population that had been drawn to work in the forests and, later, in the mines. The creation of the state of Wisconsin in 1848 and the spread of its authority changed the political landscape for the Chippewa tribes. In the future they would have to deal with the state more often than with the federal government, and it was the state of Wisconsin with whom the Chippewa would eventually come into conflict.

By stripping them of millions of acres of land and rendering them wards of an ever more indifferent federal government, the treaties of 1837 and 1842 dramatically altered for the worse the lives and fortunes of the Chippewa. But in the eyes of U.S. government officials and of many inhabitants of the Wisconsin territory, the treaties of 1837 and 1842 clearly accomplished their goal of opening the area's resources for its steadily growing white population. It would not be until the third quarter of the century that the impact of the Copper Treaty would be fully felt (and ironically so, as it was iron ore that led the rush to the Penokee and Gogebic ranges); but the Pine Tree Treaty gave the green light almost immediately to those who had their eyes on the timber resources of the central and northern parts of the territory. Before, and even after, the newly acquired land had been surveyed and placed on public sale, entrepreneurs of fervent imagination contemplated monopoly control of the greater part of this pinery, while more practical types grabbed their axes and helped themselves to what they could cut and move. In time, the acquisition of timberlands became more orderly, if not less competitive; but government losses through illegal cutting proved difficult to eradicate.

From Pinelands to Papermaking

The push into the pinelands extended across the state from east to west, and gradually worked its way northward, using the state's waterways to move the buoyant white pine logs to sawmills, and from mills on to lumber markets. The Wisconsin and Wolf rivers certainly carried their share of pine, but for the purposes of this book it is the Chippewa River and its tributaries that must hold center stage. For not only did the Chippewa Basin contain approximately 40 percent of the state's white pine timber, but it also contained abundant water power of the kind that was essential to lumber processing before steam and electricity took over as the sources of power for milling and planing. Moreover, the Mississippi River afforded the lumber industry of the Chippewa Basin a ready water highway for moving its product to mills and lumber markets in river towns as far south as St. Louis. In these markets, the fabled trees of the Chippewa pineries helped to meet a growing nation's nearly insatiable demand for forest products.

A few isolated mills appeared in the Chippewa Basin in the 1820s and 1830s, some of them well in advance of the 1837 treaty. One such mill site, established (with the permission of the Indian agent) on the Red Cedar River in 1830, attracted a small settlement that grew in time into the town of Menomonie. The first permanent settlers of what was to become Chippewa Falls arrived in 1839; and the construction of a saw mill and dam on the Eau Claire River in 1845 or 1846 marked the founding of the town of that name. Both Chippewa Falls and Eau Claire, destined to become the two great lumber towns of the region, were formally platted in 1856. The push up the Chippewa River was on, but it would take place at a fairly measured pace for a decade or so. For this was an industry that could grow only as it brought into being the infrastructure essential to its operations (excepting, of course, the waterways, and even they were far from perfect). And this task had to be accomplished in a vast, sparsely populated, and not easily penetrable frontier setting. Put another way, in the mid-19th century, the distance between Chippewa Falls and Iron County was more than a matter of statute miles.

The lumbering industry in the Chippewa Valley took off in the years after the Civil War. Capital, which had been relatively hard to come by earlier, began to flow more readily both into the building of plant capacity and into the acquisition of land. The completion of government surveying in the headwaters areas triggered a race to acquire prime timberlands. Many entered the race as speculators, buying up timber-rich acreage in anticipation of the future appreciation of these assets. Perhaps the most successful of all these speculators was Ezra Cornell, the founder of the university in upper New York state that bears his name. In the 1860s, Cornell acquired 499,000 acres of Wisconsin timberland, 100,000 acres of which was in Price County. Cornell paid for the land with U.S. government scrip, issued pursuant to the Morrill Land Grant Act of 1862, which enabled universities to acquire land, the subsequent use or sale of which would help finance their founding and maintenance. Cornell's purchases, made on the advice of some skilled "land lookers"—known in the trade as "timber cruisers"— and with a little help from a land office official in Wausau, included some of the finest pine stands known, with some 40-acre parcels estimated to have as much as one million board feet. The price was right, too, ranging from 80 to 90 cents per acre. The university then gradually sold off its lands to the highest bidders. Cornell, of course, was but one of many who bought and sold timberland and profited greatly as a result. But there were also lumbermen who purchased large tracts of timberland to furnish their mills with a steady flow of timber. The Knapp, Stout & Company of Menomonie, for example, owned some 115,000 acres of pine land, timber from which the company milled some 5.7 million board feet of lumber in 1873. Naturally, there were lots of smaller players in the game—both speculators and lumbermen—who picked up land a "forty" at a time, and whose wins and losses were proportionate to their investments.

Improvements in technology also contributed to the mounting output of the industry during the second half of the century. The use of steam, created by the burning of wood waste, proved a superior source of power in the mills and enabled processors to replace the wasteful circular saw, which cut a wide kerf, with more efficient band saws. But it was perhaps changes in the organization of lumbering enterprises that played the lead role in boosting output. The most successful enterprises sought to free themselves from dependence on numerous independent contractors by placing the entire lumber-making process, from forest to market, under the control of a single company. Part of the genius of Frederick Weyerhaeuser, the German immigrant whose name is practically synonymous with the forest products industry, lay in his skill at restructuring the business. He parlayed the interests of mill owners along the Mississippi into the creation of a powerful organization, the Mississippi River Logging Company, which dominated the industry along the Big River and up into the Chippewa drainage area.

Wisconsin's burgeoning railroad system also contributed to the industry's growth. Railroads provided access to pine stands that were too distant from driving streams and rivers to move by water, and they made it possible to carry non-floating hardwood logs from forest to mill. And there was nothing quite like railroads for moving processed lumber to markets. By 1880 most of the cut lumber from the Wisconsin River valley moved to market via rail. The same process was at work in the Chippewa Basin, but at a somewhat slower pace. But like the rivers before them, railroads did not just haul timber; they moved people as well, one by-product of which was the appearance of small settlements along newly created rail lines. These settlements, in turn, were part of the pioneering activity by which Wisconsin's once formidable forests were peopled, however sparsely, and brought within the state's economic and political structures. Park Falls and Mercer, the two towns most closely associated with the Turtle-Flambeau Flowage, reflect this process.

In 1871, with the goal of linking Neenah, in the heart of the Fox River Valley, with Ashland, on Lake Superior, the Wisconsin Legislature created the Wisconsin Central Railroad. To help with the construction and operation of this route, the state provided the fledgling firm the opportunity to obtain land and timber through a federal land grant program designed to increase the nation's railway system. The program allowed the railroad to acquire 6,400 acres of land per mile by selecting one-section parcels from a strip of land 10 miles wide on either side of its roadbed. Others got to the timber first, however, and the railroad had to settle for the acquisition of 600,000 acres, a total less than the railroad had been entitled to. Nonetheless, the Wisconsin Central became an important landholder in some heavily timbered areas. The line was completed quickly, if somewhat shoddily, in 1877, and two years later Price County, whose territory had previously been parts of Chippewa and Lincoln counties, came into being. New villages, such as Ogema, Phillips, and Fifield had sprung up along the Wisconsin Central line, and there was a stop variously known as Gould's Siding, the Flambeau Crossing, or the North Fork Crossing, in the vicinity of a small settlement known as Muskellunge—or Muskallonge—Falls. In 1885 Henry Sherry, a

Neenah lumberman, purchased from Cornell University the land on either side of the falls, built a dam, set up a milling operation, and platted out a town. The name, Muskellunge Falls, soon gave way to the more urbane calling of Park Falls, and the town was incorporated in 1901.

The story is much the same for Mercer, except that it lacked the water power that was to drive the economic development and population growth of Park Falls. The location that is Mercer today had been an important portage point on the Flambeau Trail, as well as the site of a permanent Chippewa village from 1763 "to at least the reservation period," according to research done for the master plan of the Turtle-Flambeau Scenic Waters Area. But Mercer as a settlement of Americans of European background did not really come into being until the arrival of the railroad. In 1889, the Milwaukee, Lakeshore & Western Railroad Company built a line from Lac du Flambeau to Hurley, largely in support of logging, as the company's tracks had already reached Hurley from Watersmeet, Michigan, five years earlier. Four years later, Iron County was created *de novo* from pieces of Ashland and Oneida counties. It was one of the last Wisconsin counties to attain its present boundaries—a fact that can properly be taken as a measure of its remoteness. Thanks to the advent of the railroad, purchased by and renamed the Chicago and Northwestern in 1893, a sufficient number of settlers had arrived in the Mercer area to warrant construction of a school in 1894. The settlement grew steadily, but it would not be until 1908 that the town incorporated.

The confluence of increased capital, improved technologies, vertically integrated companies, and railroad development brought the Wisconsin lumber industry to its peak performance in the last decade of the 19th century. In 1892, the state produced some four billion board feet of lumber. That same year, the Chippewa Valley witnessed its greatest log-driving year ever, when 3.5 million logs—

the equivalent of 632,350,670 board feet of lumber—were moved to mills on its waters. The Wisconsin lumber industry would never again match those figures, but it remained the state's largest industry right through the first decade of the 20th century. That said, production began to taper off gradually, and between 1909 and 1912 a number of major companies, including Weyerhaeuser's Mississippi River Logging Company, closed down. The best of the pine had been harvested, and the high cost of getting out what remained cut into profit margins. In retrospect, it seems that Wisconsin's lumber industry might have enjoyed many more years of good business had the practices of the 19th century not been so wasteful. Lots of perfectly marketable wood was left in the woods, as only the biggest and best logs found their way to mills. Driving operations took their toll in water-damaged and sunken logs. Milling operations left mounds of waste. And fires, often an unwanted consequence of the presence of humans and machines (especially railroads), destroyed untold acres of forestland. Some scholars estimate that as much as 40 to 50 percent of the available timber never made its way to market. As tempting as it is to hold Wisconsin's lumber pioneers accountable for squandering and ultimately devastating a resource that had taken centuries upon centuries to create, the fact remains that they were operating in an era when the nation's bounty seemed practically limitless. The exuberant expansiveness of the era, not our contemporary notions of conservation, shaped their ethic. And so, Wisconsin's lumbermen wrested a resource from a difficult setting in a way that made a profit for themselves and that made that resource available to a growing nation at a price people could afford. It is no surprise that many of them held respected places in their communities and in the state.

For those lumbermen who were in business as the industry passed its peak and began its inevitable decline, a number of options remained open. One was to divest themselves of useless cutover lands with their annoying tax burdens. Several companies spun off real estate companies whose goal was to sell cutover property to would-be farmers. The Edward Hines Lumber Company of Chicago established the Edward Hines Farm Land Company, which marketed its properties using the somewhat boastful slogan, "Farm Lands in Upper Wisconsin—The Cloverland of America." Weyerhaeuser's entry into this field, the American Immigration Company, focused on attracting immigrants to the cutover. The company's success in that endeavor likely exceeded the success of the immigrant farmers in making a go of it on stump-filled and relatively infertile land. Another option for lumbermen was to take their capital and their knowledge of the industry elsewhere, as Weyerhaeuser did in 1900 when he acquired 900,000 acres in the Pacific Northwest and shifted his operations westward. But the Weyerhaeuser story was exceptional, in every respect. Many more lumbermen remained in the state. Some of them shifted their attention from lumbering to other industries, such as banking and insurance, while others stayed in the forest products industry, modifying their businesses to make use of vast quantities of unharvested hardwoods. Finally, papermaking and power generation beckoned to some entrepreneurs who had both experience in lumbering and access to water power. Thanks to changing technologies, more than half the paper manufactured in the state in 1900 used wood pulp. Moreover, water power provided the greater part of the power used in paper manufacturing. Wood and water—the resources that led to the opening of Wisconsin's north—were to loom large in the economic future of the region. The story of the Turtle-Flambeau Flowage is one that unfolds directly from the emergence of these two resources in Wisconsin's development from a frontier territory to an economically diversified state.

CHAPTER TWO

The Origins of the Turtle Dam

Conflicts Over Water Powers

The story behind the creation of the Turtle-Flambeau Flowage begins early in the 20th century amid a complex struggle over the use and control of Wisconsin's rivers. These rivers had played a crucial role for inhabitants of what was to become the state of Wisconsin from the time Paleo-Indians first arrived in this locale. For them and their successors, rivers were sources of food, means of exploration, routes of commerce, and avenues for seasonal migrations. The same could be said for early European explorers. Fur traders, whether French, British, or American, depended on rivers to move both furs and the trade goods that were exchanged for them over the course of nearly two centuries. And rivers, especially the Mississippi and the Wisconsin-Fox waterway, helped to knit together the Wisconsin territory politically and economically and, over time, to populate parts of it.

Initially, no laws governed the use of rivers in this remote and essentially ungoverned part of North America. But in 1787, the Congress of the newly independent United States issued an ordinance establishing a governing structure for the "Territory of the United States North-West of the River Ohio." Though its main purpose was to lay out guidelines whereby this vast region would ultimately be transformed into states and incorporated into the Union, the Northwest Ordinance laid out a number of principles that were to be part and parcel of governance in this region. Among them was a statement about the status of the territory's waterways: "The navigable waters leading into the Mississippi and the St. Lawrence, and the carrying places between the same, shall be common highways and forever free, as well to the inhabitants of the said territory as to the citizens of the United States... without any tax, impost, or duty therefor."

This doctrine, that navigable rivers are common highways free for everyone to use, was enshrined word for word in the Wisconsin Constitution in 1848, and remains a bedrock principle of the state to the present day. As straightforward as its language may seem, however, this doctrine was not to go unchallenged. For there are other uses to which rivers may be put besides simple navigation (to move timber to mills, to power saw, pulp, and paper mills, to generate electricity, and to store water for times of need). Those uses became more and more attractive as the Wisconsin economy developed and expanded over the last half of the 19th century and into the 20th. But unlike simple navigation, which did not affect the character and flow of rivers, these other uses, which required the construction of dams, booms and the like, did alter the nature of rivers—often to the detriment of other users. Battles over the exploitation of Wisconsin's rather prodigious water resources, which played out against the background of the Northwest Ordinance, became a major public policy issue in the first decades of the 20th century. The history of the flowage is inextricably intertwined with these conflicts and the efforts made to resolve them.

The first pressure to place dams on Wisconsin's waterways—apart from some grist mills established in agricultural parts of the state—came from the logging industry, which flourished in the post-Civil War era. The great white pine logs that fell to axe and saw were buoyant, and they were floated downstream on the state's bigger rivers for processing and sale. As the pursuit of this resource moved farther and farther north, the loggers had to make use of ever-smaller tributaries—some of them with limited or seasonal flows, or with their own natural obstacles such as rocks or sandbars—to move their logs. To enable these smaller rivers and streams to carry logs downstream, loggers made use of two kinds of dams: the driving dam and the flushing dam. The driving dam—placed so as to prevent logs from entering an extremely shallow chute—redirected and enhanced the flow in the main channel in order to keep logs moving along smoothly. Remnants of one such driving dam, at Island Rapids on the North Fork of the Flambeau River, closes navigation to the right of the island and forces canoeists to take the left fork of the river. Flushing dams served yet another purpose: they held back water until such time—normally spring—as the logging operation was ready to send a load downstream. At that time the gates were lifted, and the head of water that had built up behind the flushing dam surged down river along with the winter's logs. Most of these flushing dams, especially those on smaller waterways, were simple wooden constructions that were easily built and operated. Flushing dams in the Flambeau drainage area included the following: Shea Dam, Rest Lake Dam, Turtle Dam (on Lake of the Falls), Bear Creek (River) Dam, Spider Lake Dam, Rice Lake Dam, four small dams on Beaver Creek, and one on Swamp Creek.

By what authority were these dams constructed? Many were built by individuals who believed themselves to be exercising their riparian rights; that is, as owners of both banks of a stream or river, they felt themselves legally entitled to treat the waterway as they wished. Many small flushing dams, built in conjunction with the logging of a specific tract of timber, were the product of such individual initiatives. Other would-be dam builders turned to the state legislature for formal authorization—the only procedure by which dams could be legally constructed—especially when they anticipated some financial gain from the operation of the dam. Sometimes such acts of the legislature specified the precise location of the dam; in other cases the choice of location was left up to the recipient(s) of the authorization. For dams of some magnitude, the legislature stipulated what construction materials were to be used, how high the dam might rise in relation to the streambed, and the like. But in almost all cases, the legislature required that the dams be constructed in such a way as to make possible, and even enhance, the movement of logs downstream. The key words in these legislative acts were "improve" or "improvement." The essential meaning of this language was that dams should improve navigation—which was essentially equated in these legislative acts to the moving of logs—on the specified waterway. The idea of improvement of rivers persisted beyond logging days and expanded in meaning to include the evening out of flows along a watercourse.

It was an act of the legislature, published on March 23, 1895, that led to the creation of a dam across the Turtle River that forms what is now known as Lake of the Falls. "Henry Sherry and A.L. Maxwell, their heirs and assigns, are hereby authorized and empowered to construct, maintain and keep a dam or dams across Turtle river, on such part thereof as they may select in the county of Iron and state of Wisconsin, for the purpose of improving the navigation of said river and facilitating the driving of logs, timber, or lumber down same, and for hydraulic or manufacturing purposes...." The act went on to grant Sherry and Maxwell, "as compensation for the improvement of said Turtle river," the power to collect tolls in the amount of "ten cents per thousand feet, board measure, on all logs or timber sluiced or driven through or by the aid of said dam or dams or the waters collected therein." As was the case with all such acts, the state reserved "the right to alter, amend, or repeal this act."

Over time, flushing and driving dams proliferated throughout the headwaters country of northern Wisconsin, both on rivers and on tiny streams. However much these dams may have contributed to the efficiency of the logging industry, though, they posed both legal and practical problems. First, to the extent that these dams impeded navigation by boat and were often the basis for charging tolls, they could be said to conflict with the promise of the Northwest Ordinance that navigable waters would be "common highways and forever free." Of course, a few dams were on non-navigable waterways, but most were not, given the long-standing practice of the state's courts to define as navigable any watercourse on which a log could be floated. Second, and more important to future policy and practice, many flushing dams operated at the convenience of their owner/builders. They lifted gates when they had logs to move and left gates in place when they did not. Even those dams authorized by the state did not have to guarantee passage of logs at periods of low water. This haphazard management of dams created problems of flow for other users of the rivers and streams, whether downstream or up.

This man-made interference with the flows of water out of the headwater country of the state compounded the problem of naturally uneven seasonal flows of water along the state's two largest watersheds—the Wisconsin and the Chippewa. Both of these rivers flow basically from north to south. This means that their headwaters are located in the coldest region of the state, where winter precipitation is locked up in the snowpack and where summer river levels are often low because of heat and lesser amounts of rain. Finding ways to compensate for low flows during winter and summer became an urgent pursuit for those downstream users whose economic well-being depended on reliable flows of water.

This map shows the location of the Turtle-Flambeau Flowage in relation to the Chippewa River drainage basin. National Atlas of the United States

The rapid development of industry in late 19th-century Wisconsin brought forward two major water-dependent industries: electricity generation and papermaking. Indeed, the two go hand in hand, as most Wisconsin paper manufacturers not only used water for their industrial processes but also depended on hydro-generated electricity for their power needs. For both these industries, securing control over Wisconsin's waters—waters that had been declared common and free to everyone—became a major objective.

But the pathway to achieving this objective was not without its obstacles. In the first place, the Wisconsin Supreme Court handed down a ruling in 1853 that reinforced the principles on water use that had been laid out in the Northwest Ordinance and the state constitution. "If the stream is navigable, in fact, the public has a right to use it for the purpose of navigation, and the right of the owner of the streambed [riparian owner] is subject to public easement." Though this ruling left a lot of room for interpretation as to what activities did and did not impede public use, it did make clear that the public had a substantial interest in the state's waters. Then, in 1899, the state legislature declared that all fish and game in the state belong to the state. This act provided the basis for the management of the state's numerous fisheries—again, presumably on behalf of the public. These two actions, taken together, established a strong basis for government involvement in the fate of the state's waters.

A second obstacle to industry's pursuit of control over Wisconsin's water powers lay in a conservationist sensibility that was emerging both in the state and at a national level in the decades before and after the turn of the 20th century. A landmark moment in Wisconsin came in 1905 when the Weyerhaeuser Company, a giant of the timber industry, donated to the state the land that became the Brule River State Forest. The gift bore the condition that no dams be allowed on this beautiful and historic river. In the same year, the state began to involve itself directly in conservation matters when the legislature established the State Board of Forestry. By this time the vast pineries of the north were well on their way to depletion, but there remained for the board a substantial agenda of regeneration and conservation. In acting on this agenda, the board in 1908 created the Wisconsin Conservation Commission—the forerunner of the Department of Natural Resources. Interestingly, in its first report, the commission called for the protection of the state's undeveloped waters—an explicit recognition of the threats, already present or looming on the horizon, to these waters.

As Wisconsin entered the first decade of the 20th century, then, several forces converged to set the stage for what was to be a decisive battle over water powers. First, the rivers themselves were something of a mess as a consequence of the numerous uncontrolled dams that had been built in support of logging. Second, the growing hydropower and paper industries required lots of water, preferably water that flowed over the course of a year as evenly as possible. Third, the rising conservation movement, which had managed to attain representation within the very fabric of state government, sought to protect these waters from uses that would substantially transform them. Fourth, state law, constitutional and otherwise, had enshrined a public right to these waters, even as said law was interpreted liberally to permit certain water-dependent economic activities. These forces came together, not unsurprisingly, in the political arena. It was in Madison, then, that a characteristically Wisconsin resolution of the conflict would be worked out.

The question before the state's lawmakers and courts boiled down to this: how can navigable waters be managed so as to guarantee freedom of access and use to the public while meeting the needs of both old industries (logging and lumber) and new ones (paper and hydropower)? One answer would be for the state to build (or not to build in certain instances), own, and operate dams. Such a solution, according to its advocates, would provide consistent policy and practice, and, presumably, evenhandedness for all parties. Moreover, advocates of state ownership claimed that such arrangements would place a check on the rapacious treatment of the environment by powerful business interests. Quite a different answer to the question came from the riparian owners, who felt by virtue of their property rights that they had free rein to dam, divert, dredge, or otherwise alter waters that passed through their properties. In starkest terms, the conflict pitted notions of full state ownership against those of unrestrained private ownership.

In reality, however, this turned out to be something of a false dichotomy. For Chapter VIII, Section 10, of the state constitution clearly precludes state ownership of capital property. This section, which deals with "Internal Improvements," declares that "the state shall never contract any form of debt for works of internal improvement, or be a party to such improvement." It seems that, at the time of the drafting of Wisconsin's constitution, several states had recently gotten into financial problems because of expenditures related to improvements. It was to avoid such a fate that the Badger State's constitution contained this prohibition. Barring a constitutional amendment, then, the state of Wisconsin could not get into the business of building and operating dams.

Such an amendment was not altogether out of the question, however; for the state had already begun, in the early 20th century, to circumvent this broad limitation on government action by means of specific constitutional amendments. In 1908, for example, the constitution was amended to allow for highway construction, provided that the money be appropriated from the treasury or from taxes specifically to be raised for this purpose. Then in 1924, an amendment passed that permitted the state to acquire, preserve, and develop state forests. Amendments authorizing the establishment of airports, ports, and veterans' facilities followed decades later.

Water powers, however, are conspicuously missing from this list, though not for lack of effort on the part of those who wanted the state to directly control the waters within its boundaries. An amendment giving the state control over water rights did receive initial approval from the legislature in 1907; but the requisite second resolution never appeared before either chamber for a vote, and the attorney general subsequently ruled it null and void. The push for action continued, however. In January of 1911, Governor Francis McGovern made a strong case before the Senate and Assembly for a decision on water powers, and the legislature responded in July with a water powers act that dramatically strengthened the government's control over navigable waters of the state. It declared that the "beneficial use and natural energy of the navigable waters of this state for all public uses are to be held by the state in trust for all the people." Accordingly, it gave the state the authority to regulate and control power production, as well as the authority "to regulate, manage, and control the level of flow of all water" in all navigable waters. The law also provided extensive, uniform guidelines for those who would seek franchises to build dams or bridges. This law, which quickly fell under attack from water power owners throughout the state, proved short-lived (see pp. 78-79).

Ultimately, it was to take Progressive Era state policy to reconcile the public's interest in navigable waters with the requirements of economic development. This policy called for private companies to build and run dams—but to do so under the regulation of the state. In this case, the role of regulator fell to the Railroad Commission, which was the direct predecessor of the Public Service Commission. The most controversial aspects of this policy emerged clearly in 1907, when amid bitter political fighting between Robert La Follette Progressives and the Stalwarts, who were Republican supporters of business and development, the legislature authorized a private company, the Wisconsin Valley Improvement Company (WVIC), to build storage reservoirs (not hydro facilities) in the headwaters of the Wisconsin River and to manage water flows from them. In addition, the legislature stipulated that the company's activities were subject to regulation by the Railroad Commission.

The die had been cast, as it were, and in 1911 the legislature similarly bestowed upon another private company, the Chippewa and Flambeau Improvement Company (CFIC), "a perpetual right" to construct storage reservoirs in the headwaters of these two rivers. According to the act, the purpose of these reservoirs is to provide "a more even flow" of water throughout this large watershed. Like the WVIC, the CFIC fell under the regulatory jurisdiction of the Railroad Commission.

It remained for the state to provide some guidance for the Railroad Commission in its regulatory role over the WVIC and the CFIC. That guidance came in 1915, when the legislature passed a water powers law. This law, in effect, authorized the Railroad Commission to approve the construction of dams by private companies—under the condition that no harm come to lawful users of the affected waterways or to those who were the owners of regulated facilities on these waterways. These guidelines pertained essentially to economic uses of the state's waters; they were silent about possible environmental consequences of dam construction and operation. This silence ended in 1929, when the water powers law was amended in such a way as to allow considerations of aesthetics to enter into decisions about authorizing dams. Put another way, the Railroad Commission was empowered to deny permission to build a dam that would have an adverse impact on the character of a river. This amendment was a victory for conservation interests; but in terms of the history of the Turtle-Flambeau Flowage, it was water over an already built dam.

The Sherry Family Enterprises and the Chippewa and Flambeau Improvement Company

The protracted and heavily contested conflicts over Wisconsin's water resources not only played a major role in Progressive Era state politics, but they also provided the context in which the Turtle-Flambeau Flowage was conceived and built. This story begins with Henry Sherry, a Neenah, Wisconsin, businessman. Born in 1837 in East Mendon, New York, Sherry moved with his family to Columbus, Wisconsin, in 1846, making him part of the large flow of New Yorkers to the Badger State in the 19th century. In 1849 the Sherry family moved to Neenah, where they were among the first settlers and where Henry was to live until his death in 1919. Starting in 1868, Henry Sherry turned his attention to the lumber industry—both as a dealer in pine lands and as a processor of timber. During one winter in the late 1870s, Sherry's operations took 25 million feet of pine logs out of Wisconsin timberlands. He prepared his timber for market in mills that he owned in Oshkosh, Marshfield, and Neenah. In the mid-1880s, Sherry began to focus his entrepreneurial efforts on the Flambeau River Basin and its abundant timber and water. In 1885 he began buying timberland in Price and Iron counties; and from 1885 to 1888, he bought land and some existing lumber operations in the vicinity of Muskellunge Falls on the Flambeau River. These acquisitions set the stage for, among other things, the transformation of the village of Muskellunge Falls into the small city of Park Falls.

Sherry launched his operations in the Park Falls area on his own, but by the mid-1890s he was joined by his son, E.P. Sherry. The young Sherry was born in Neenah, Wisconsin, on April 12, 1870. After graduating from the University of Wisconsin, he promptly went to work alongside his father. While on a business trip to New York City, E.P. met Laura Case, an actress who had been born in Prairie du Chien and who was attempting to make her career in the big city. Sherry and Case married in Prairie du Chien in 1902, and took up residence for a brief time in Neenah. In a few years, however, the couple moved to Milwaukee, where the cultural scene better suited Laura's interests and talents—especially her leadership in the American Little Theater Movement. Later on, she served as drama critic for the *The Milwaukee Journal* and authored a book of poetry. What was good for Laura also turned out to benefit E.P. and the family's business interests. Milwaukee was the hub of the financial world in Wisconsin, and it was also close to Chicago and its dominant place in Midwest business.

Photo from the article announcing the death of E.P. Sherry. The Milwaukee Journal, *August 7, 1941*

According to a company history compiled by E.P. Sherry, the purchases his father made between 1885 and 1888 included "a saw mill plant, pulp mill plant, water rights, a dam, etc. on said lands." These various acquisitions set the stage for the creation of several companies that were at the core of the Sherry family holdings. First came the Park Falls Lumber and Pulp Company, which was incorporated in 1890. This company promptly purchased from Henry Sherry the productive assets cited above by E.P. Sherry. The next step came three years later, when the company was renamed the Park Falls Lumber Company, at which point the upper dam site (there were two dams in Park Falls), pulp mill, and canal were conveyed to the newly formed Park Falls Paper and Pulp Company (incorporated in Neenah Wisconsin on September 11, 1895). The language of its title signals Sherry's decision to add a full-fledged paper mill to his lumber and pulp businesses. This series of steps culminated on August 24, 1898, when articles of incorporation were filed for the Flambeau Paper Company (FPC), which, in effect, replaced the Park Falls Paper and Pulp Company. A paper machine was installed that year, and with it the Sherry family had entered the paper manufacturing business.

One other Sherry-controlled company, which was destined to play a significant role in the history of the flowage, also came into being at this time. On July 10, 1899, articles of association were filed in Milwaukee for the Wisconsin Realty Company. As was the case with other Sherry companies, the lists of initial officers and stock subscribers contained a number of businesspeople—many of them quite prominent—who were not members of the Sherry family. And, as always happened, within a few years the Sherry clan emerged as the controlling party. Henry, his wife, Abbie, their son E.P., and E.P.'s wife, Laura, all held various offices in these corporations and subscribed to varying amounts of stock. Other parties do show up as officers and directors, but never in a way to suggest they significantly challenged the dominance of the family. The Wisconsin Realty Company, as one might suspect, engaged in the purchase of land and timber of use to the Sherry's paper and pulp business, and it received the assets of the Park Falls Lumber and Pulp Company in 1907, when the latter company was dissolved. Wisconsin Realty also played an important role in the financing of the Sherry operations.

The Flambeau Paper Company suffered a major setback in May of 1900, when a devastating fire destroyed its paper mill and upper pulp mill. Financial hard times followed, and by 1902 the controlling interest in the company, as well as in the Wisconsin Realty Company, had shifted into the hands of the Milwaukee Trust Company, the trustee for the First National Bank of Milwaukee. It was not until 1907 that the Milwaukee Trust Company relinquished its hold over the two companies and the Sherry family reasserted full control.

E.P. Sherry's historical sketch of the first 16 years of the operations of the Flambeau Paper Company touches on every aspect of management, ranging from securing raw materials, to labor, to machinery, to sales. Not surprisingly, another major area of concern was securing an adequate flow of water to support papermaking and pulping operations and to generate the electricity that powered them. This need brought the company face to face with the problem of numerous small dams outside of its direct control. To deal with this situation, the company employed a variety of strategies. One dam of interest to Sherry was the Bear Creek Dam, located at the point where Bear Creek (now Bear River) exits Flambeau Lake on the Lac du Flambeau Reservation. The state had chartered this dam in 1887 to Charles Henry, and the dam itself had been constructed under the direction of Billy "The Beaver" England, a man known for his ability to construct long-lasting dams. In 1903, and apparently for several subsequent years, the Flambeau Paper Company shared with two other paper companies a lease on the Bear Creek Dam, which enabled this group to hold or release water as suited their needs. But there were problems, as Sherry's interest was the storage of water, whereas the others wanted to use the water for logging drives. In 1908, Sherry worked out an arrangement with the Indian agent to lease the dam.

At the same time that Sherry was trying to secure more control over the waters behind the Bear Creek Dam, he inquired, discreetly, whether the Rest Lake dam might be for sale—only to find that it was not. The following year an agent (Mr. Bruce) working for Sherry assessed the amount of head that could be built up behind the Turtle, Rice Lake, and Spider Lake dams. (Ironically, the Sherry family once had control over the Turtle River Dam at Lake of the Falls. Henry Sherry, along with A.L. Maxwell, had received legislative authorization to build a dam at that site in 1895. By the time E.P. Sherry sent Bruce on his mission, the dam was in the hands of its fourth owner.) Bruce concluded that there was more or less one continual flowage built up behind the Turtle Dam (on Lake of the Falls), and that the water stored there was adequate to move logs down to the point where the Turtle River flowed into the Flambeau. E.P. Sherry's reaction was that a lot of land (some of it his) was being flooded, probably without authorization, and that Sol Heinemann, the owner of the Lake of the Falls Dam, might be pressured into letting some water go to the benefit of the paper company.

Heavy rains and floods in September of 1907 led to a different kind of reaction from Sherry. As he saw it, water was being wasted, both at Bear Creek, which he had some say over, and at Rest Lake and Lake of the Falls, where he failed to persuade the owners to close gates on their dams to preserve water. Apparently the owners were letting water pass to facilitate a pulpwood drive down the river. His inability to prevent the waste of water prompted Sherry to contemplate the benefits of water storage. "This storage proposition [the need to capture and hold plentiful rains] was the prelude to the formation of Chippewa and Flambeau Improvement Co." Subsequently, he wrote, his company had failed to "secure any benefit from flood waters."

It would not be long, however, before the groundwork for a long-term solution to water problems—whether too much or too little—was laid. In late December of 1908, W.L. Davis, president of the Dells Paper and Pulp Company in Eau Claire, "arranged for a meeting at Chippewa Falls early in the following month to consider a possible storage reservoir system." No doubt Davis had the Wisconsin Valley Improvement Company in mind as he took this step. The meeting resulted in the creation of the Chippewa and Flambeau Improvement Company, whose articles of organization were completed and signed in Chippewa Falls on February 4, 1909. (The company moved to Eau Claire in December of 1919.) The signatories on behalf of the company were James T. Joyce, Angus McGilvray, and William Irvine, leading figures in the business communities of the lower Chippewa Valley. According to Article I, "The businesses and purposes of which corporation shall be to establish, create, maintain and operate a system of water reservoirs... for the purpose of producing as nearly a uniform flow of water as practicable in the said Chippewa and Flambeau rivers throughout all seasons, by holding back and storing up in said reservoirs suplus [sic] water in times of great supply, and gradually discharging the same in times of drought and scarcity, and thereby improving the navigation and usefulness of said Chippewa and Flambeau rivers and their tributaries throughout their entire length...." Sherry's Flambeau Paper Company and the Wisconsin Realty Company were initial subscribers to stock in the CFIC.

All the improvements to the rivers notwithstanding, the CFIC was a business, not a charity, and some means of remunerating its partners had to be found. They could not charge for the water per se, for it was a public good. But they could charge tolls for the water distributed for the benefit of rightful users. The charges would be based on the expenses incurred in maintaining and operating the reservoirs they would build or acquire. Article VIII allowed the company to raise revenues through tolls to cover these expenses and to provide a 6 percent return on the amount of capital actually raised by the corporation. When the legislature formally chartered the CFIC in 1911, it endorsed these arrangements for charges to users and for remuneration of the stockholders.

While awaiting legislative action on the CFIC, E.P. Sherry continued his quest for water. In 1909 he ordered a preliminary evaluation of the Beaver Creek, Swamp Creek, and Horse Shoe dams, and he attempted to lease the Rest Lake Dam. That effort having failed, he managed in May to persuade William Irvine, the manager of the Chippewa Lumber and Boom Company (a Weyerhaeuser-controlled company), to close the Rest Lake Dam to build up head for future use. In 1910 Sherry expressed an interest in the Lake of the Falls Dam—probably he had a purchase in mind—but found out that it was in poor physical shape and overvalued by its owner.

At the same time that Sherry was seeking to ensure adequate water for his operations in Park Falls, he was also fighting a bigger battle on the state front: namely, to prevent the state from taking full control of water powers. His platform for this fight was the Wisconsin Water Power Association (WWPA), a Milwaukee-based professional association for which he served as secretary. The association's target was the Water Power Act of 1911 (Chapter 652). For Sherry, as for other major users of the state's waters, this law was totally unacceptable and quite likely unconstitutional. As Sherry noted on August 25, 1911, in a general letter to water power users: "By this legislative act every charter heretofore granted by the state to erect and maintain dams, is repealed, and the present owners of such water power dams, are directed, under severe penalty, either to destroy such dams as a public nuisance or to pay an annual rental to the state for the use of the water powers." On July 28, 1911, the WWPA convened a meeting in Milwaukee of all water power owners of whom the association had knowledge. Legal counsel told those present that "the act was unlawful and unconstitutional, as well as unjust." The next step was litigation, and the WWPA, arguing that a single act of litigation was preferable to several, asked water power owners to agree to an assessment to cover legal costs. Apparently most owners went along with the assessment, but a few did not. One follow-up letter from the association was returned with this hand-written comment: "Gentlemen, Any time the state wishes to take over my little power plant it may do so. Yours very truly, Carl Vogel, Wilton Wis."

Whatever Mr. Vogel's sentiments may have been, the WWPA won the day in 1912, when the Wisconsin Supreme Court promptly ruled the act unconstitutional. A victor in this struggle, E.P. Sherry next turned his statewide attention to lobbying for a water powers bill that would be to his liking and to that of other water power owners. The outcome was the Water Powers Act of 1915. This legislation, though setting water power policy for the long term, was not, as will become apparent, wholly to the liking of major water power interests.

The Supreme Court ruling of 1912 and the Water Powers Act of 1915 brought a measure of order to what had been an unsettled segment of the state's economy: namely, water powers. The rules of the game were now clear for companies like the CFIC, and so it entered the field of play with some greater measure of confidence. That said, its initial actions were somewhat timid—

due in part to its weak financial condition and in part to some jockeying for power. The seven original capital subscribers made commitments in the total amount of $74,900 (749 shares at $100 each). The Flambeau Paper Company subscribed to 65 shares; the Wisconsin Realty Company to 38. But the stockholders were slow to come forward with the money. In fact, the records show that as of August 27, 1918, only 30 percent of the capital stock had actually been paid in by the nine stockholders of record at that date. E.P. Sherry was among those whose wallets were hard to open. When Wisconsin Realty received its first call for cash in the amount of $706 dollars, it remitted only $152. There was also some wrangling among the parties to this new corporation. Donald Boyd, who became secretary of CFIC early on, could not get the treasurer, D. Buchanan of Chippewa Falls, to release documents necessary for filing reports to the state government. In 1914 Boyd had to go to the Wisconsin Supreme Court to obtain the materials from Buchanan. Moreover, there were running disagreements early on about what level of tolls should be charged for the use of stored water. It seems clear that the principals of the corporation were in the process of feeling each other out, and that none of them was willing to part with any more cash—from which better returns could be expected in the short term—than was absolutely necessary. Nonetheless, in 1915 the CFIC declared dividends in the amount of $3,452.89 to be distributed to eight stockholders and two trustees, in proportion to the amount of stock paid in.

The first actions of the CFIC centered on the acquisition of existing properties. A directors meeting held in Chicago in late December of 1912 finalized "arrangements for the purchase of the Manitowish or Rest Lake dam," and looked into the advisability of authorizing the purchase of other dams, reservoirs, or riparian property. By December of 1916, the company had authorized "a complete survey of the proposed Reservoir System on the headwaters of the Chippewa and Flambeau Rivers." That survey appears to have directed attention to three sites for new reservoirs: on the Chippewa River below the junction of its west and east forks, at the junction of the Turtle and Flambeau rivers, and at the location of the existing Bear Creek Dam. Subsequently, the CFIC decided to act first on the Chippewa site. The reasoning behind this decision is not entirely clear. The Bear Creek Dam project seems to have faltered in the face of questions about ownership of tribal lands. And it may well be that the most influential downstream owners thought a reservoir on the Chippewa would be more immediately advantageous to them than one on the upper Flambeau. Whatever the case, work was under way on the site in 1922, and the Chippewa Flowage was filled in 1924.

Seeking Authorization for a Storage Reservoir

The road to the construction of the Turtle-Flambeau Flowage took a considerably more circuitous course. The main obstacles seem to have been financing, the reluctance of the directors of CFIC to move ahead with a second storage dam, and their opposition not only to state ownership of water powers but also to state regulation of them. These considerations can be found woven into the events that transpired from 1919 to 1925.

The first moves were straightforward. In 1919 the CFIC created two new corporations to establish and operate dams: the Chippewa Reservoir Company and the Flambeau Reservoir Company (FRC). The latter company, whose president was E.P. Sherry, was authorized to raise up to $500,000 in capital stock; in fact, stock actually paid in never exceeded $13,750. According to its annual reports to the Wisconsin Secretary of State, the sole activity of the company during its first three years was the making of surveys. From then until its dissolution in June of 1926, the FRC did not engage in business activities. The final product of the surveying work was an engineering map, surveyed in 1920 by John (J.W.) Harris and mapped in 1921 by C.B. Steward, a consulting engineer from Madison. The map, which demarcated the size and shape of the projected flowage at its high-water mark, is on display in the Mercer Ranger Station. At the same time that the CFIC created the Flambeau Reservoir Company, it also secured an agreement with the power owners on the two rivers that they would pay tolls to the "Turtle River Dam and Reservoir."

At this point, Sherry and the CFIC embarked on a new, more intricate strategy as they moved toward the building of this second storage reservoir. The first hint of something new came in 1921, when they managed to secure passage by the legislature of an amendment (Chapter 399, Laws of 1921) to their initial charter. This amendment replaced the words "to create, construct, acquire, maintain and operate" dams with "to create, construct, acquire by purchase, lease or otherwise." The crucial difference lies in the language that permits the CFIC to acquire a dam by means of a lease. That language opened the door to an innovative strategy for building and operating a storage dam that the CFIC was to pursue over the next several years.

It was to be a while, however, before this new strategy received its full and public elaboration. In the meantime, it was by no means certain that the construction of the dam would go ahead at all—if one is to take at face value a communication from E.P. Sherry. In a letter dated January 12, 1922, to C.M. Morris, an officer at First Wisconsin Trust Company in Milwaukee, Sherry remarks that "there is nothing definite about the Reservoir matter at the headwaters of the Flambeau River, except that the survey was completed some months ago, but the Directors have no plans under consideration at the present time for going ahead with the final plans for a dam, nor have they any idea as to financing it."

After noting that some have suggested that Flambeau Paper Company should undertake the project in its entirety and then lease it to downstream users, he rules out that course of action because of the present state of the paper business. In addition, he worries that the Chippewa Dam then under construction "may give sufficient storage capacity for the powers below the junction of the Chippewa and Flambeau rivers so that they will not be interested in our stream for some years." It is certainly understandable that Sherry, as the most upstream user of water, would worry that his interests might play second fiddle to those of the big downstream users. But after all this doom and gloom, he goes on to note that "we have been buying a few scattering lots of land which would be needed for this reservoir on a speculation that some time they would be needed for use."

Sherry's letter concludes with an offer of $5.00 per acre for land owned by one of Morris' clients. Whether this letter represents the actual state of affairs, or whether it is purposely drawn in uncertain tones to justify his bid price for the land, or some combination thereof, cannot be determined for certain. Other sources make it clear that his land acquisition program, an essential step if Flambeau Paper were to be the sole actor, was well under way by this time. Those land purchases suggest Sherry may have realized that if there were to be a dam on the Flambeau that he would more than likely have to be the one to build it.

Whatever Sherry meant to convey by expressing his uncertainty in 1922, he and his colleagues took decisive action in the following year. On the 26th of June, 1923, three individuals (whose qualifications, if any, for undertaking this project remain unknown) filed articles of association for the Flambeau River Improvement Company (FRIC). The purposes of this company were outlined in the broadest of terms: "the buying, holding, managing, leasing, selling, exchanging, pledging and disposing of and dealing in all kinds of real and personal property, tangible or intangible and wheresoever situated; the construction, building and erections of dams, plants, buildings and equipment of every kind and nature whatsoever...." The articles authorized a capital stock of just $1,000, none of which was ever paid in. E.P. Sherry was listed as its president in 1924, and Guy Waldo, his right-hand man at Park Falls, was vice president and treasurer. No business was ever transacted before its dissolution in 1925.

What was the purpose of yet another company alongside the CFIC and the Flambeau Reservoir Company? The answer: to eliminate the possibility that the state might one day take control of the dam. As noted earlier, the state constitution prohibited the state from building and owning capital property, and efforts to secure that power for the state had failed both as a constitutional amendment and as a legislative act. But the notion that such a power might someday come into being was enunciated in the charters to the WVIC and the CFIC; and it was firmly embedded in the Water Powers Act of 1915. According to Section 9 of the charter to the CFIC: "The state of Wisconsin shall have the right at any time, whenever it may have the constitutional power, to take over to itself and become owner of all reservoirs and other works and property acquired by the Chippewa and Flambeau Improvement Company pursuant to this act...." Compensation, of course, was to be paid. The Water Powers Act has similar language, except that the state must wait 30 years after a permit for the building of a dam becomes effective before acquiring the property.

Needless to say, the state's recapture policy cast a heavy shadow of uncertainty over the affairs of water power owners and was vigorously opposed by them in principle. In this case, Sherry and his fellow directors of the CFIC sought to subvert this policy with a corporate end run. What they planned to do was to have the Flambeau River Improvement Company build the dam and then lease it to the CFIC. (The 1921 amendment to the charter of the CFIC had enabled it to acquire dams by lease.) This strategy was implemented in December of 1923 when the CFIC submitted an application to the Railroad Commission asking approval for such a lease. The commission promptly held a hearing on December 27, and pursuant to that hearing, took the matter under advisement.

At virtually the same time that the CFIC was placing its case for a lease agreement before the Railroad Commission, it also took a major step toward resolving the issue of who was actually going to foot the bill for the construction of the dam. When the CFIC directors held a special meeting in Chicago on December 19, 1923, they gave unanimous approval to a motion to begin construction of the "Turtle Dam and Reservoir" as soon as conditions permitted. At that point, "Mr. Sherry stated that the Flambeau Paper Company interests have worked out a plan to finance and construct said project and then lease it to the Chippewa and Flambeau Improvement Company for an annual rental of $50,000." Having put that notion on the table, Sherry then seemingly reversed course by expressing his preference that the CFIC undertake the project and by promising that he would readily convey 18,000 acres of already purchased land to the CFIC at $7.50 per acre—"reserving the timber." Moreover, he expressed a readiness to contribute to the financing of the project, which he estimated would cost between $700,000 and $800,000. With these options before them, the directors responded by appointing a three-person committee to decide whether the CFIC or the Flambeau Paper Company would do the work, but there can be little doubt that Sherry's initial proposal to finance, build, and lease through the FPC was not in line with the directors' understanding of the way in which the CFIC should operate—

and had operated, up to this point. It is hard not to think that Sherry put this idea forward to put pressure on his colleagues, who had been somewhat reluctant to undertake another large reservoir project so soon after the completion of the Chippewa Flowage. And, like any good gambit, this one had the attractive fallback position by which the Flambeau Paper Company would sell the requisite land and help finance the project. Whatever may have been behind Sherry's maneuvering at this meeting, the result was that the CFIC ultimately decided to take responsibility for constructing the reservoir.

While waiting for formal action from the Railroad Commission to have a lease between the CFIC and FRIC approved in principle, the CFIC proceeded on two fronts. First, it secured in March of 1924 the agreement of the downstream power owners to the proposed scheme of construction and lease, as well as their commitment to meet their appropriate financial obligations for the use of the stored water. The parties to this agreement were the Eau Claire Dells Improvement Company, the Wisconsin Minnesota Light and Power Company, the Lake Superior District Power Company, the Chippewa Power Company, the Cornell Wood Products Company, the Great Western Paper Company, the Flambeau Paper Company, and the Flambeau Power Company. Second, the CFIC set about drafting a formal lease by which the Flambeau River Improvement Company would construct the dam and lease it to the CFIC. This lease was executed in September of 1924. As written, the lease was silent on the recapture clause as it is embodied in the CFIC charter and in the Water Powers Act. But there can be no doubting the intent of Sherry and his colleagues. In a letter to the Railroad Commission dated October 31, 1924, Paul Reiss, an attorney for the CFIC, put the case for his clients succinctly: "It is the desire of the Chippewa and Flambeau Improvement Company to have this approval based on the laws of Wisconsin under which the Company operates and not complicated with any reference to the General Water Power Act. The General Water Power Act... provides that the State may at any time after thirty years acquire the reservoirs built under the terms of said Act and it is to avoid this complication that approval is asked under the specific laws that pertain to the Chippewa and Flambeau Improvement Company." It was their contention that the authority granted to the company in its initial charter and in the amendment of 1921 was sufficient to warrant approval of a lease.

The Railroad Commission, whose regulatory powers placed it in the position of ruling on the activities of the CFIC, thought otherwise. In a ruling handed down January 20, 1925, it denied approval of the lease. The commission argued that the authority of the CFIC to build a dam was specific to its charter of 1911 and could not be legally passed on to others. Moreover, it found that any dam constructed under the terms of this lease would be "out of harmony" with the long-standing policy of the state to recapture water power facilities in the event of a change in the state's constitution. In short, the commission refused to permit the company's effort to evade the state's recapture policy.

This ruling came down at the beginning of the year that construction of the dam had been scheduled to take place. So many plans were in process and so much was at stake with the project that the CFIC had little choice but to abandon its scheme of leasing the dam from another owner. Its only route forward was to file a revised application that eliminated any role for the FRIC. The company submitted such an application on March 31, 1925, noting that the dam was to be built and operated by the CFIC but under the watchful eye of the Railroad Commission. The following day, the Railroad Commission set a hearing date for April 15 in Madison, notice of which was to be published in the

Park Falls Herald and conveyed by mail to each and every person affected by the construction of the reservoir, both water power owners and those whose properties would be taken or flooded.

The hearing took place as scheduled. The CFIC was represented at the hearing along with Northern States Power Company and the Great Western Paper Company. Eighty-seven property owners or their representatives also participated—including those for the Jerome Fishing and Hunting Club and the Merkle Lake Fishing and Hunting Club, two organizations that would be affected by the proposed dam. Once the hearing concluded, the Railroad Commission set about its deliberations. It should be noted that the commission, while it had regulatory powers over the CFIC, basically interpreted its role to be one of helping the CFIC achieve its goals in a way that did no harm to public or private interests. Since it was already familiar with the details of this project—based on the CFIC application of 1923—the commission's main tasks at this point were to make sure that the application attempted no evasion of the recapture principle and to assure itself through the hearings that the dam would do no harm. It comes as no surprise, then, that the Railroad Commission on May 27, 1925, approved "generally" the plans for the project. It set the maximum elevation in the reservoir at 1,572 feet mean sea level (MSL), and the minimum elevation at 1,539 feet MSL. Finally, the commission stated that it had set its benchmark, a bronze tablet, in ledge rock near the future dam site at an elevation of 1,558.72 feet MSL. As of this date, then, the legal authority for the construction of the dam was fully in place—and not a moment too soon, as a construction camp had already been established and work on the dam site had begun.

CHAPTER THREE

Of Cutovers and Virgin Stands: Sherry Acquires a Future Lakebed

The Sherry Strategy

L egal authorization was but one precondition for the construction of the Turtle Dam and reservoir. Acquiring the property that would be wholly or partially flooded by the reservoir was yet another—and a major one at that. Happily, the story of land acquisition for what became the Turtle-Flambeau Flowage can be reconstructed in minute detail through the copious records developed and kept by E.P. Sherry.

Three sets of circumstances combined to create such extensive records. First, the focus of the Sherry family's economic interests had shifted from the Fox Valley to the Park Falls area. Second, that shift, coupled with Sherry's decision to live in Milwaukee both for personal and business reasons, increased the physical distance between him and his main business activities, a situation that required regular communication between the two locations. And third, Sherry was a detail-oriented, hands-on businessman who made decisions only when he had solid information in front of him. Of course, telegraph and telephone connections did link Milwaukee and Park Falls and could be used for urgent business. But Sherry's preference was for written communications, both those conveying information to him from Park Falls, and those conveying his queries and instructions to his businesses in that area. For this long-distance micromanagement to work, Sherry needed a totally reliable surrogate who could not only handle day-to-day business on his own but who could also document, regularly and precisely, all aspects of the family business in the Flambeau Basin. Those needs were met, and then some, by Guy Waldo, the manager of the Park Falls Paper Company. A shrewd and precise businessman himself, Waldo wrote to Sherry on matters large and small—including each and every land purchase for the proposed reservoir. The thoroughness of the correspondence makes it possible to document this phase of the project from start to finish.

Acquiring lands for a flowage turned out to be a daunting and prolonged undertaking. Imagine a vast plat map, embracing some 25,000 acres, each square or partial square of which had to be assembled into a seamless whole before the gates on a dam could be closed and the waters raised. And imagine the complications inherent in each transaction—land of differing quality, owners with disparate views of the worth of their properties, the ups and downs of the Sherry enterprises, and on and on. It seems perfectly understandable, then, that the process of land acquisition, which began in 1917 when the Chippewa and Flambeau Improvement Company (CFIC) instructed Sherry to look into how this task might be accomplished and what it might cost, had yet to be completed when construction of the dam began in the late spring of 1925. Indeed, it would not be until 1942 that a settlement was negotiated on the final piece of property.

Without doubt, E.P. Sherry was ideally suited to carry out this task. To begin with, it was in his interest. From the moment that the Flambeau Paper Company (FPC) began operations, he had demonstrated an awareness of the critical role played by water power, and had spared no effort to secure the flow of water essential to the company. There could be no doubt that the construction of a storage reservoir immediately upstream from Park Falls would directly benefit his papermaking operations. It is hardly surprising, then, that Sherry became the principal advocate within the CFIC for the construction of a dam at the confluence of the Turtle and Flambeau rivers. Sherry not only had strong incentives to devote his considerable energies to this task, but he also had the corporate means to do so. The Wisconsin Realty Company and the FPC carried out the bulk of the land acquisition for the flowage; and they were abetted by the Winnebago Realty Company, another Sherry operation, and, in a few instances, by the Flambeau Reservoir Company.

Sherry also brought to the table his own personal style of doing business. He was clearly as comfortable with the nitty-gritty work of bargaining as he was with high-stakes financial transactions. Indeed, a great deal of his success can be attributed to his pursuit of knowledge—as much and as precise as he could attain. And when it came to land purchasing, he knew all the right questions to ask to secure that knowledge, such as: Where, precisely, is the parcel located? Has the parcel been logged? If it is timbered, what is the value of the timber? Does the seller want to sell the land and reserve the timber, or sell them both? Is the seller a seasoned lumberman or an inexperienced person with a single parcel? Is the seller reasonable, stubborn, deluded, or even downright kooky? Is the seller in some kind of financial difficulty? Is the title clear? What kind of deal is best—cash, or a land contract, or a down payment and short-term mortgage at 6 percent? Is there some unseen benefit lurking in the acquisition of this parcel? Answers to questions like these Sherry acquired from his numerous professional contacts—not the least of whom was Waldo—as well as from his agents, such as J.W. Harris, the surveyor, and Mr. Kilger, a timber cruiser whose systematic tramps through the woods provided knowledgeable estimates of the value of various timber stands, and from assessors, tax clerks, and anyone else with a shred of information. Once he was in the know, Sherry was in a position to push his advantage in every transaction. That said, he did not become a captive of his own calculations and goals. He could never have assembled 25,000 acres without demonstrating a considerable measure of flexibility.

Finally, Sherry recognized that a task of this magnitude required an overall strategy. The one he came up with had both financial and procedural elements that served as a broad guide for his actions. First of all, he worked up a financial schedule based on a rough estimate of the total cost of the project, which suggested how much he would be able to pay for varying kinds of properties. Early on, bolstered by a few inexpensive purchases, he hoped to average $5 per acre; and in keeping with that goal, in July of 1920 he set $8 per acre as the outside figure that he would pay. But when he got to the tougher cases, he was forced to extend the range of per-acre prices well beyond $8. That said, keeping the total cost of land acquisition as low as possible was absolutely essential, because this land would have to be sold, eventually, to the CFIC. Sherry knew that his colleagues in the CFIC would not look favorably at a bill for the land that far exceeded their sense of the fair market value of that land.

The second element of his strategy involved the sequencing of purchases. In January of 1920, Sherry received some advice from Charles McPherson, counsel for and a director of the American Public Utilities Company. McPherson urged Sherry to buy up the cheaper lands first, leaving higher-priced properties for purchase or condemnation only when those properties were about to be flowed. In this way, Sherry needed to pay only for the land actually overflowed, and not for surplus acreage. The record shows that Sherry took McPherson's words very much to heart.

McPherson's counsel bears directly on the three avenues open to Sherry for acquiring the requisite properties: outright purchase; purchase of flowage rights; or condemnation by means of eminent domain. The vast majority of parcels obtained by Sherry for the flowage were purchased outright, in fee simple (ownership without limitations or conditions), with or without their timber content. On occasion, however, he had to resort to the purchase of flowage rights on properties whose owners were reluctant to part with their land. In such cases, the deed would say, in effect, that the seller has given to the buyer the right to flow the land in question to an elevation of 1,572 feet MSL. The seller, however, retained fee ownership of the entire parcel, including its flooded portion. Reminders of flowed ownership can be seen even today on a plat map of the flowage where straight lines (other than section boundaries) run out into and across the flooded part of the flowage. The area encompassed by these lines is part of a parcel whose owner sold flowage rights and retained the fee. For example, the small-tract parcels along Kimmear Road in Mercer, Wisconsin, are one example of such a property. Were the plug pulled from the flowage today, the property owners along the shore on this road would find that, with the waters receded, their parcels extended as far as the southern boundary of the original parcel. A similar outcome would be the case for certain property owners in the Bastine Lake area and a few other parts of the flowage, including one fully flowed parcel in the amount of 35 acres in the Horseshoe Lake area. Farther to the south, the plat books show 1,046.28 acres belonging to the State of Wisconsin Land Commission. These parcels also fall into the category of lands whose flowage rights had been purchased.

Securing the entire 25,000 acres needed for the project would, in all probability, have been impossible to achieve had the CFIC—and Sherry as the principal purchaser—not had an ace in the hole: seizure by the right of eminent domain. Although this right had been granted to the CFIC in Chapter 640, the law of 1911 that authorized the formation of the company, it did not entitle Sherry and his companies to unilaterally condemn properties and assess values. Rather, it entitled them to pursue seizure by eminent domain within the framework of statutory law. In practice, this meant that the Railroad Commission, as the state agency supervising the CFIC, held hearings about and assessed value on land taken by this means. In light of this statutory framework, Sherry and his colleagues could, and did, warn stubborn sellers that unresolved disputes over prices would ultimately go to settlement before the commission—a commission that would insist that fair market values, and no more, be paid for land or for flowage rights. That said, eminent domain proceedings had their potential downsides; they were costly, and their outcome could not be predicted with complete assurance.

The Big Acquisitions

With his strategy set and a variety of tactics at his disposal, Sherry went about his task of gathering land. A certain caution, however, marked this early phase. For one thing, he needed to test the market to determine the lowest-going prices both for cutover lands and for timbered lands. And while doing so, he sought—with limited success—to keep a low profile, lest potential sellers get wind of the project and inflate the asking prices of their lands. For another, he was cautious about overcommitting his financial resources toward a project that might never come to fruition.

Indeed, the record shows that Sherry retained, and with good reason, doubts about the viability of this project almost to the moment when the first shovel went into the ground.

One of Sherry's first sorties involved the Wisconsin Central Railroad (WCRR), which had substantial timbered holdings in the area, many of which would be needed for the flowage project. Sherry took out options on 2,683.29 acres of WCRR land, but then he decided to let the options expire at the end of July of 1920. He blamed "construction difficulties" (whatever this meant) and a shortage of funding for his failure to exercise his options. Caution and uncertainty about the value of timber in the area are perhaps better explanations. He may also have been responding to attempts by the WCRR to get him to purchase parcels not connected with the reservoir. Whatever the case, Sherry decided to buttress his understanding of the situation by taking an in-person look at some of the timbered lands that lay at the center of the projected flowage. As he wrote in November of 1921 to W.H. Funston, the land commissioner at the Soo Line Railroad (a part of Wisconsin Central): "Mr. Waldo and I have recently returned from a trip down the Manitowish and Flambeau rivers with our woodsman and the engineer who made the reservoir survey [J.W. Harris]… nearly all of the land which can be seen from the river is low and swamp and a great part of it has been burnt and that it will be very many years before there will be any great call for it for agricultural purposes, or even for resort purposes." Sherry followed up these remarks by citing details of purchases he had already made. After subtracting timber values from the purchase prices, Sherry stated that he had purchased 922.92 acres from the Park Falls Lumber Company at $5.27 an acre, 1,050.47 acres from Lake Region Land Company at $4.53 per acre, and had a pending deal with American Immigration Company that would likely come in at about $5.30 per acre. He also mentioned a purchase where the timber value exceeded the purchase price—much to the detriment, it would seem, of one Mrs. McDonald, the seller. Clearly this recital of purchases was intended to inform Funston of where the market lay and what Sherry might be willing to pay.

In the following year, however, Sherry became a more active buyer. In March he acquired 1,147.93 acres of cutover land from Homeseekers Land Company at $5 per acre. Guy Waldo had endorsed this deal, even though it included 240 unneeded acres, as a step toward setting a price for cutover lands. It should be noted, however, that Sherry acquired some cutover lands for as low as $2.50 per acre. With this purchase accomplished, Sherry returned to the WCRR properties. At a minimum, he reasoned, he should buy the timber on WCRR lands to prevent others from acquiring the timber rights. For every buyer of these timber rights would become yet one more party for Sherry to deal with in acquiring lands for the flowage. Worse yet, with the word getting out about the proposed dam, Sherry feared the proliferation of development—whether cabins or resorts—that might raise the costs of acquisitions. Waldo concurred, based on what he could see happening in the north. "We believe that good roads and automobiles are advertising northern Wisconsin and that if some arrangement is not made soon with the Railroad Company that probably we will require quite a number of descriptions will be needed [sic] and will just add to the difficulties when the Reservoir Company is ready to go ahead." Waldo also worried that any significant development on what would become known as Big Island might force the CFIC to build a bridge to it. Acting on these concerns, Sherry had identified 4,526.59 acres of WCRR lands by November of 1922 that would be needed for the flowage, along with a little more than 1,029 acres of additional land. A deal was completed in January of 1923 when Funston sent Sherry two contracts, one for each set of lands. Sherry paid $5 per acre for the flowage lands and more for the others.

It is clear from their remarks about the WCRR lands that by 1922 Sherry and Waldo had learned to appreciate the benefits of pursuing large parcels of land in the possession of established timber and land companies. Though some of the sellers could be a bit on the prickly side, Sherry and Waldo knew the value of their lands and how to strike a deal. Those in possession of cutover land were more than ready to dispose of a depleted asset; and holders of timbered lands recognized that in the end they would have to make a deal with whatever entity built the flowage. They, like Sherry, preferred to avoid costly and unpredictable condemnation proceedings. There was, however, one notable exception to this rule. Sherry began dealing in 1919 with H.H. Heineman of Merrill, Wisconsin, the owner of the Heineman Lumber Company and the Hardwood Land Company. Their negotiations took a bad turn from the outset; and all of Sherry's stratagems—from attaining a favorable appraisal from Matt Plunkett, the local assessor, to threatening condemnation—fell on deaf ears. Finally, in late 1924, both parties yielded enough to conclude a deal. Sherry had to spend $11.70 per acre for 1,940.93 acres—reserving timber and mineral rights to Heineman. This was the last large parcel Sherry took into possession.

The Tough Acquisitions

If the large parcels were relatively easy to acquire, the same could not be said of many of the smaller ones—especially when they were located on or near existing lakes or rivers. The lands around Muskellunge and Turtle lakes (today's Lake Bastine area), the Lake of the Falls Dam and land below it, and both Merkle and Trude lakes would be cases in point. What made properties in these areas so difficult to come by was that people had already put these areas to personal use, or had plans to do so. In short, improvements, real or projected, rendered these properties a wholly different kettle of fish from isolated stands of timber or cutover—as illustrated by the following examples.

One of the largest files in the Sherry archives—54 pages worth—bears the name Ledvina. On March 23, 1892, the federal government General Land Office in Wausau, Wisconsin, issued a patent to Matias Ledvina, an immigrant from Bohemia, for 160 acres in Section 32, Township 42 North, Range 2 East. As the story has it, the Ledvinas then took the train to Butternut. There, for $10 and a ham, they hired an Indian familiar with the land to take them to their property. After one or two nights on the trail, the Indian disappeared with his payments, and the Ledvinas nearly failed to locate their homestead. But find it they did, and Ledvina successfully established a small farm. He did well enough to add to his initial holdings and to gain a reputation as a man who knew how to look after his own interests.

Ledvina first shows up in Sherry's files under the name Matt Lavina, in a letter from Waldo to Sherry dated October 29, 1919. In it, Waldo observes that "Mr. Lavina has as good a bunch of timber as there is anywhere in this part of the country." But timber was not their real concern. Ledvina had properties that would be affected by two of Sherry's projects. First, he had obtained from Wisconsin Central Railroad a parcel in Section 33 that was certain to be affected by the flowage. Second, Ledvina owned three other parcels that Sherry would eventually need for yet another of his proposed projects: the Island Power Dam. Once the flowage project was over with, Sherry planned to construct a hydropower facility at Island Rapids on the Flambeau River. (Canoeists will recognize Island Rapids as the next whitewater passage after the Notch Rock Rapids. At this location, the river splits apart around a

The United States of America,

TO ALL TO WHOM THESE PRESENTS SHALL COME, GREETING:

Homestead Certificate No. 2927

Application 4606

Whereas there has been deposited in the GENERAL LAND OFFICE of the United States a CERTIFICATE of the Register of the Land Office at *Wausau, Wisconsin* , whereby it appears that, pursuant to the Act of Congress approved 20th May, 1862, "To secure Homesteads to actual settlers on the public domain," and the acts supplemental thereto, the claim of *Matias Ledvina* has been established and duly consummated in conformity to law for the *South West quarter of the North East quarter, the South half of the North West quarter, and the North West quarter of the South West quarter of Section thirty-two, in Township forty-two North, of Range two East of the Fourth Principal Meridian in Wisconsin, containing one hundred and sixty acres*

according to the Official Plat of the Survey of the said Land returned to the GENERAL LAND OFFICE by the SURVEYOR GENERAL.

Now know ye, That there is therefore granted by the UNITED STATES unto the said *Matias Ledvina* the tract of Land above described: TO HAVE AND TO HOLD the said tract of Land, with the appurtenances thereof, unto the said *Matias Ledvina* and to his heirs and assigns forever.

In testimony whereof, I, *Benjamin Harrison* President of the United States of America, have caused these letters to be made Patent, and the Seal of the General Land Office to be hereunto affixed.

Given under my hand, at the City of Washington, the *twenty-third* day of *March* , in the year of Our Lord one thousand eight hundred and *ninety-two* , and of the Independence of the United States the one hundred and *sixteenth*

By the President: *Benjamin Harrison*

By *M. M. McKean* Sec'y.

J. P. Roberts , Recorder of the General Land Office.

1892 Land grant to Matias Ledvina, an early settler in the Bastine Lake area. Bureau of Land Management, General Land Office Records

long, slim island. Passage is had to the left of the island; on the right-hand side, remnants of a logging boom make navigation impossible.) The Island Rapids project would, among other things, build up a flowage of its own, especially up the Swamp Creek Basin. The negotiations with Ledvina, which spanned a three-year period starting in 1923, were to become more than a little complex.

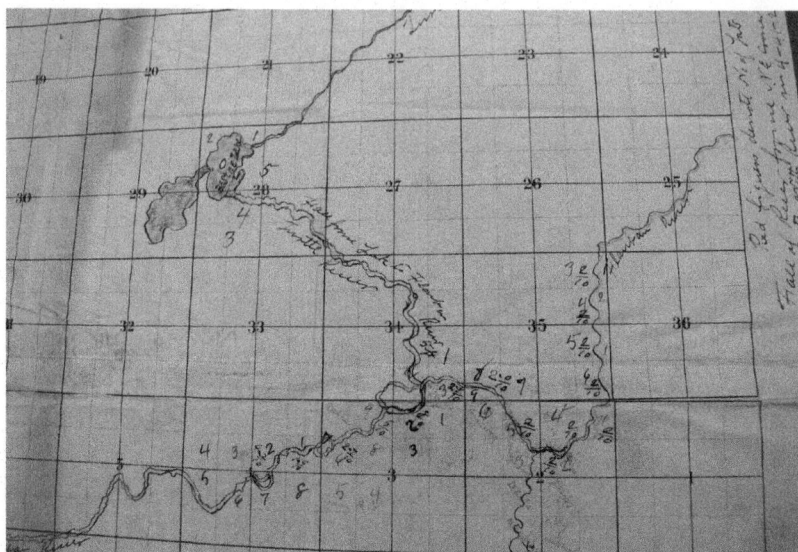

A working drawing that calculates the fall in the North Fork of the Flambeau River as far as the proposed (but never built) Island Dam site. Wisconsin Historical Society

As for the property needed for the reservoir, Ledvina initially said he would trade his land in Section 33 for a nearby parcel owned by the Roddis Company. But by the time Sherry had acquired the Roddis property, Ledvina had set his sights on a different piece of property: namely Government Lot 2 in Section 29. As Waldo put it, that lot "would give him [Ledvina] all of the shoreline on Minnow Lake and would also give him access to Muscallonge Lake." Sherry, however, objected to such a trade. He wanted to hold on to the Muscallonge Lake frontage, as "it may be valuable in the future." Sherry's reaction reflects his maturing thoughts about the long-term potential of flowage waterfront property—at least such property as would be located along the shores of the existing natural lakes. The premium in those cases derived from access to deeper water.

Negotiations for the land needed for the Island Power project did not fare much better. In July of 1924, Ledvina offered to sell all of his land except for the forty on which his home and farm buildings were located—but at a price of $70 per acre. Waldo rejected that offer outright, and from that time forward the Ledvina file goes silent on the Island Power project. But Ledvina's tough bargaining stand left its mark on Waldo. "Mr. Ledvina, we realize, is going to be a hard man to do business with particularly in view of the fact that he secured such a high price from the Lake Superior District Power Company for an easement across his land. Mr. Ledvina, being the nearest settler to the dam, can be of more or less service to us from time to time and we do not want to antagonize him, certainly not for a while... we think we can eventually work out some sort of a deal with him for the NE NE of Section 33 without giving him the land on Lot 2."

In the end, Waldo was right, but the deal was costly. Ledvina abandoned his pursuit of a trade for Lot 2 and agreed to sell the flowage rights on his forty for $60 per acre of land flooded. Timber rights would go to the buyer, except for white pine timber, which was to be reserved for Ledvina. In point of fact, the title abstract indicates that white pine timber on the property did not belong to Ledvina, but it amounted to so little that even the cautious Sherry thought title to it could be ignored. A survey of the parcel estimated that 20.6 acres would be inundated, leaving the CFIC with a bill for $1,236. In parsing out this expenditure, the CFIC booked $678 for flowage rights ($34 per acre), and the remaining $558 covered the estimated value of the timber on the 20.6 acres. Just to be on the safe side, Ledvina demanded a legal instrument that assured him payment of $60 per acre should more than 20.6 acres of his land be flooded. When this transaction finally closed on July 20, 1925, construction of the dam was in full swing.

The cost of the flowage rights on the Ledvina property far exceeded the norm that Sherry had established, but that purchase pales before another difficult case in the same area. Mrs. George Goellner was the owner of record of a two-acre parcel on the south shore of Turtle Lake. She had paid $200 for the land, and her husband had added a hunting cabin that, according to Sherry's estimator, could be replicated for $500 at the most. The Goellners had bought the land and improved it, knowing all the while of the flowage project and the likelihood that it would flood a portion of their land. Nonetheless, when approached about selling the land or the flowage rights, Mr. Goellner claimed that his wife had set a price of $2,500. Playing good cop to Mrs. Goellner's bad cop, he suggested that they might sell for $1,250—an offer that Waldo immediately rejected. In the wake of Mrs. Goellner's continued intransigence, however, Waldo and Sherry thought it the better part of wisdom to pay as much as $1,500 for the purchase of the fee lest the Goellners break the property into pieces and sell them off, which would complicate matters even more. That decided, Waldo employed a local friend, Ike Hermann, to see if he could get the Goellner's to agree to the $1,500 figure. He failed. The owner insisted she had been offered $1,800 for it already and would not settle for less than "$2,000 net to her." By the summer of 1925, Mr. Goellner began to support his wife's position, claiming that he was renting out the cabin and boats at the rate of $90 per month. Therefore, he argued, the property had extra value as a source of income. In response, Waldo then obtained from Mr. Tomkins in Ashland a copy of Goellner's tax return for 1923, which did not list any income from cabin rental. Waldo and Sherry figured this information might be helpful to their side if a condemnation proceeding became necessary. In the meantime, Goellner inquired of Sherry and Waldo what plans they had to clean up all the timber and brush that would litter the flowage after it was filled. Were it not cleaned up, Goellner claimed, his land would be rendered worthless. For obvious reasons, Sherry wanted to prevent this issue from coming before the Railroad Commission as a part of condemnation hearings for flowage rights. This tit for tat struggle finally came to a head in the summer of 1925, when Mr. Harris, the surveyor, drove some stakes in the Goellner property at the 1,572 feet MSL elevation. When the Goellner's saw how much of their property was at risk of flooding, they consented to an outright sale in the amount of $1,500. This is a case where condemnation might well have been to Sherry's financial advantage, but he obviously preferred to have this one behind him when the gates of the dam shut.

Lands along the Turtle River, from the falls on down through Lake Lindsey, a pronounced widening in the river, also turned out to be challenging and costly acquisitions. Here, as in the Bastine Lake area, improvements to, or plans for the improvement of, properties were at the heart of the problems Sherry and Waldo encountered—to say nothing of the personal idiosyncrasies with which they had to deal. Purchases from Warren Dewey, Ida Bormann, and Peter Dimmer, though relatively modest in size, illustrate the point.

Dewey, a resident of Chicago, owned two forties adjacent to Dead Horse Lake. In addition, he ran Camp Dewey—"Where the Lake of the Falls empties into the Turtle River," according to his letterhead—on land he did not own, but presumably rented. His first thought, in May of 1923, was to buy the land where the camp was located, but he could not make a deal with the owner. He then offered Sherry his two forties at $50 per acre. There was no timber, but the land, he claimed, was level. Negotiations went on at a leisurely pace until the summer of 1925, when it appeared that Dewey would accept payment for flowage rights on one forty and sell the other one outright. That was, until he went to town and talked with some locals. "I have visited Mercer and find that there is nothing sure about your reservoir not spoiling the road leading to my land and in fact may make an island of it." The local rumor mill had done its work, and Dewey decided that he wanted no part of a sale of flowage rights. In the end, however, he settled for $125 in payment for flowage rights to .84 of an acre on one parcel and $500 for the fee of the other. For Sherry, timberless land at $12.50 an acre could only be considered exorbitant, but in the summer of 1925, with dam construction under way, he needed the deal closed.

Sherry had been insistent on securing flowage rights to at least one of Dewey's parcels in order to set the precedent for a related acquisition. It seems that Dewey had sold five acres from the parcel in question to Hiram Craw, who in turn had sold it to Ida Borman of Chicago. For Sherry, purchasing flowage rights would surely be cheaper than the fee. Accordingly, in the spring of 1925 he wrote to Mrs. Borman's attorney with an offer of $25 for flowage rights. The lawyer responded with a request for 10 times as much. Then Mrs. Borman got in the act, writing to Sherry that "my attorney has not done anything for me" and requesting that Sherry deal directly with her. Mrs. Borman soon agreed to sell the flowage rights for one and a half acres for $125. But then Waldo made an uncharacteristic error. He sent her a deed with the usual language about the right to flow all land up to 1,572 feet MSL. Mrs. Borman spotted that and said she would not sign the deed unless it specified that no more than one and a half acres were to be flooded. The deed was quickly rewritten, and the deal sealed. Whatever Sherry and Waldo may have anticipated when they began negotiations, Mrs. Borman was certainly no Mrs. McDonald, who, as noted earlier, had sold a parcel whose timber value exceeded the sale price.

In the case of Peter Dimmer, it seems that Wisconsin Central Railroad slipped up and sold him a forty that was to be held for Sherry. This forty lay on the east shore of Lindsey Lake, just upstream of the narrows that today separate the Turtle River from the broader waters of the flowage. Dimmer had built a 16-by-24-foot log cabin where he lived with Octa Craw, variously described as "his common law wife," "his woman," or "Mrs. Craw." Dimmer worked at the Jerome Fishing and Hunting Club, but he was thought to have had plans to build some cottages on his land.

Waldo and Sherry were confident that Dimmer's property (15 acres of which was already in Lindsey Lake at the time Dimmer bought it) would be severely affected by the reservoir, but they were uncertain what value to place on his holdings. Meanwhile, Dimmer hired an attorney, George Barr, who was already representing a client on Trude Lake. The involvement of Barr moved things along promptly, and the parties reached an agreement in the fall of 1925 to pay Dimmer $1,600 for his property.

But that was not the end of the transaction. Consummation of the deal was held up by claims against the deed and by Dimmer's procrastinating ways; and so the matter dragged on into 1926, when the gates were shut and the water began to rise. In May of that year, Waldo stopped by to see Dimmer. The waters were already up to the front step of Dimmer's home, and Waldo figured it would not be long before the foundation posts would be undermined. Future prospects were even worse. "We measured and found that with the water at 1,572 that it would come nearly to the top of his screen door on the porch. Peter Dimmer's woman was there and both claimed she had been sick and was feeling none to [sic] good at the present time, but we think this is largely put on and the chances are that both of them have been drunk most of the time." Waldo, who was determined not to leave without a deal, rejected Dimmer's requests to have a few days to talk the matter over and finally secured Dimmer's mark on an agreement to buy at $1,600 dollars—$200 cash on the spot, the remainder to be paid by check in exchange for the deed. Needless to say, both Sherry and Waldo were relieved by this outcome, for they both thought that Dimmer might well have the basis for a costly lawsuit. It was not until July 21, 1926, that E.S. Hagen, cashier of the Iron Exchange Bank in Hurley, wrote to Waldo that he finally had been able, "after... three auto trips to Mercer, and several telephone calls," to deliver the check to Dimmer and receive the deed in return. The bank charged Park Falls Paper Company $5 for its services; but Mr. Hagen felt compelled to add a postscript to his letter. "Had it not been for auto and telephone service we can assure you that the charge would have been much less. These people are the hardes [sic] customers we ever dealt with."

Though the costs of the Dewey, Borman, and Dimmer settlements exceeded the amounts Sherry had planned for them, the total additional dollar amount was not that great. The same cannot be said for the outcome of his prolonged contest with Heinemann Land and Power Company over the Lake of the Falls Dam. At the conclusion of a number of white pine lumber drives, the various owners of the dam had allowed it to fall into disrepair. As of 1910, it carried only its dead head—4 feet (that is, it was not raising the water level behind its structure); and no upgrading of the facility took place in subsequent years. As the reservoir project moved forward in the mid-1920s, Sherry began to worry that the current owner of the dam might at some time attempt to raise the water level behind this deteriorated facility, which, in turn, could lead to an accidental discharge of a large volume of water into the projected flowage. Consequently, Sherry thought it advisable to secure control of the dam and make repairs to it in order to forestall a potentially disastrous event. It should have been an easy task to determine which properties to target for such a purchase. Indeed, Sherry thought he knew precisely which parcel of land described the location of the dam (his father had once owned it, after all). But when he began to look into the matter he found that he had poked a hornets' nest. Some cloud or other hung over a number of properties in the immediate vicinity of the dam. Either the descriptions were unclear, or the surveys were in doubt, or the interests were conflicting. In 1925, Sherry sent Harris in to do an exacting survey of the area. Harris reported that the dam was holding back "very little water" and that Lake of the Falls "is approximately as the lake existed in 1865." More to the point of Sherry's concerns, Harris asserted that the government survey was "fraudulent" and forwarded his own drawing of the area. These problems notwithstanding, a deal seemed to have been reached between Heinemann's Lake of the Falls Land Company and August Schmidt, a straw buyer whose role was to prevent the seller from knowing Sherry's identity.

Sherry's efforts to mask the purchase failed, however, as word soon reached Sol Heinemann, who was in Portland, Oregon, that Sherry was to be the ultimate recipient of the property. At that point, Heinemann, no doubt spotting a target with deep pockets, claimed that the proposed reservoir would inflict $80,000 in damages to his water power. Sherry countered with a report from J. William Lint, a hydraulic engineer. Lint asserted that developing hydro at this site was senseless as the head was not sufficient. The development of additional head, he pointed out, would require a large and costly land acquisition. Given the stalemate, Sherry decided to seek a ruling from the Railroad Commission on the value of the Heinemann property. Both sides presented their cases, and the Railroad Commission delivered its decision on November 25, 1925. The commission began its argument by noting that there was "a natural fall of 21 feet over a distance of 500 feet" where the river passed through the Heinemann property. The now inoperative dam, which stood at the head of the falls, had once been able to generate an additional eight feet of fall when the water behind it was at maximum elevation. The combined fall of 29 feet, the report went on to say, would generate 230 "theoretical horsepower... for 50% of the time," based on historical data about stream flow. When the flowage was filled, however, the fall would be reduced by about 13 feet, a situation that "renders the power site valueless for power purposes." The commission concluded by setting the value of the land and damages at $10,000. In effect, they authorized the CFIC to spend up to that much for the Heinemann land.

Heinemann's lawyers refused to accept this settlement, forcing CFIC to initiate condemnation proceedings. This time the commission fixed a value of $20,000, but even that sum was not to Heinemann's liking and the ruling was appealed. A final settlement was privately negotiated between the two parties for $23,000. The record of this settlement is contained in a supplementary order from the Railroad Commission, dated May 10, 1930. This outcome surely must have reinforced the standard wisdom that condemnation proceedings were to be avoided if possible.

Three Costly Acquisitions

Negotiations for the three most improved properties—those of the Merkle Lake Fishing and Hunting Club, Theodore Gerlach, and the Jerome Fishing and Hunting Club—have as much or more to say about the owners and their northwoods activities as they do about Sherry's efforts to gather up the land. They also contain incidental information relative to the flowage area.

In 1890, John Merkel of Ashland County secured a patent for five government lots in the amount of 164.60 acres that abutted a small lake, identified on some maps as Red Lake. The land eventually passed from Merkel's hands into those of E. Brumbough, but Merkel held it long enough to leave his name—slightly modified— on the lake. By the time Sherry learned the details of the property from Mr. Harris in 1920, it had come into the possession of the Merkle Lake Fishing and Hunting Club. Formally established in February of 1919 in Milwaukee, the club comprised some 25 members, each of whom is said to have put in around $1,000 for the land and its improvements. When Harris first saw the property, he reported that in addition to the renovated "Old Brombough house" (the dwelling of the previous owner of the property) there were three cabins, a guide shack, an icehouse, various small outbuildings, and a water tank and pump. Harris also provided the following assessment of the operation: "The location of the Merkle Lake Club is not the best from a sporting standpoint. There is not very good fishing on the Lake and it is some little distance to either the Flambeau or Turtle Rivers. The mosquitoes are especially bad due to marshes on the south side of Lake [sic]. I believe they want to unload their property and are entirely sick of the place."

Whether or not Harris got it all right—this author has heard from a descendant of a club member that the fishing was excellent—the members did seem quite ready to entertain an offer from Sherry for the purchase of the property. Even though it appeared that their improvements would not significantly suffer from a higher water level, they disliked the idea of being surrounded by a reservoir. It was their hope to realize enough from the sale of the property to start anew on another lake. The usual negotiations followed with Sherry claiming that the true value assessment of the property was $9,133 and with the club's lawyer asking for $35,000. The final settlement, concluded in September of 1925, came to $27,500—$25,000 for the land and improvements and $2,500 for personal property. Sherry must have been satisfied, as he had earlier expressed the view that this property could probably be turned around easily, quite possibly at a profit.

Theodore Gerlach was a successful and well-connected Illinois businessman and sportsman. In addition to being a member of the Jerome Fishing and Hunting Club, he owned Pine Island and a nearby smaller, unnamed island on Trude Lake. On the three acres of Pine Island, Gerlach had constructed a substantial lodge—60-by-54 feet by his calculation—with a large living room, five bedrooms, a kitchen, two bathrooms, housekeepers' quarters, running hot and cold water, and a 9-by-60 foot screened porch. There was, however, no electricity. Additional improvements included a guide's cabin, an icehouse, a chicken house, a root cellar and a boathouse "with a 27' gasoline launch, an Evinrude, four row boats, two canoes and a large scow." Another cabin, better winterized than the lodge, stood on the unnamed island. It was used as a hunting cabin in the cold months. The operation was of sufficient size to require a year-round caretaker. In a letter describing his property, Gerlach is at great pains to talk about how convenient it is to get to this location, one surrounded by 200 or 300 square miles of wilderness: "To me the beauty of the place has been very much enhanced by the fact that you can leave Chicago at 5 o'clock in the evening, or even seven, and have breakfast there [his lodge] the next morning. And you need not leave until 7:30 in the evening to be back in Chicago the next morning at 9:45...." Of course, there was an additional 50-minute, 11-mile drive from Mercer to the dock at the Jerome Club, from which Gerlach traveled to his island and back.

Sherry approached this deal cautiously, using a third party to make the initial contact with Gerlach. But the stumbling block remained money. Gerlach had claimed in 1920 that he had put $16,000 to $17,000 into improvements, and this was before he bought and built on the second island. He was certain to want to get his money out of a property at least part of which, the small island and its improvements, would be badly damaged by the waters of the flowage. Waldo, with more foresight and wisdom than he might have given himself credit for, had a different view: "In building a summer home, we do not believe that any man figures he can sell the property for what he puts into it." In the end, the $10,000 damage figure set by the Railroad Commission for flowage rights to Gerlach's islands proved unacceptable to the owner. Backed by his attorney, Mr. Barr, and by some pressure from the "Insull interests" in Chicago (Samuel Insull was a prominent Chicago businessman and national leader in the electric utility industry), Gerlach held out for a better settlement and got it: $24,000. The lodge still stands on Pine Island.

The Jerome Fishing and Hunting Club was both the costliest and the most storied acquisition that Sherry made. Beginning in 1907, the property had come under the control of Charles Comiskey, owner of the Chicago White Sox baseball club, and some 60 to 70 Chicago area outdoor types who were also shareholders in the JFHC. Every fall, Comiskey invited a number of men from his wide circle of acquaintances to spend a week fishing, hunting, feasting, and relaxing in this relatively primitive northwoods setting. Over the years, the guest list included baseball owners Garry Herman of the Reds and Jacob Ruppert of the Yankees; the legendary manager John McGraw of the New York Giants; White Sox pitcher Ed Walsh; Frank Chance and Johnny Evers of the Chicago Cubs trio, "Tinkers to Evers to Chance"; and the entertainer George M. Cohan—to name but a few of the luminaries who graced the shores of Trude Lake.

As would befit a club that could attract such star power, the JFHC was a big operation. It controlled almost half of the shoreline on Trude Lake, most of which was on the southern shore; and the club also had a farm on the north side of the lake. In addition, the club controlled considerable backland, though the word was that Jerome members preferred to hunt on non-club properties. It was the level of improvement, however, that accounted for the greater part of the club's value. An inventory taken in 1925 lists some 29 structures, ranging from a root cellar and a chicken house to numerous cabins, lodges, and the like. The club had also established its own wildlife preserve of native and not-so-native animals.

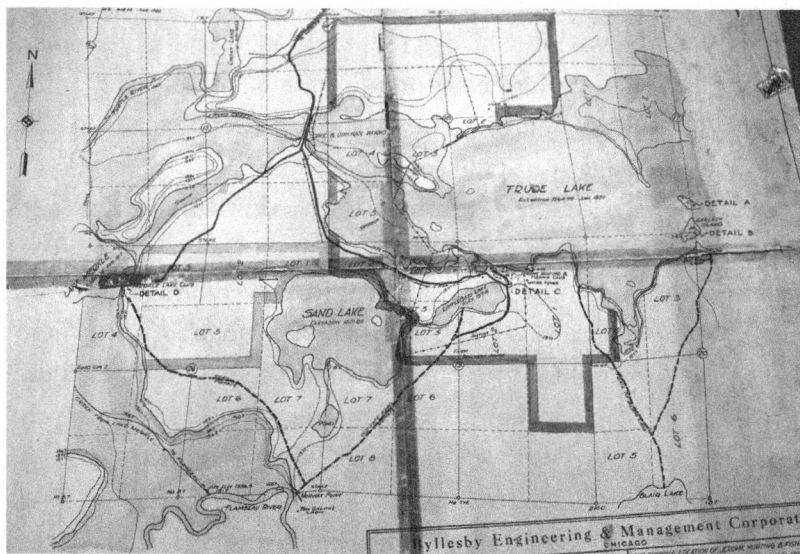

Byllesby Engineering's 1925 map of the Trude Lake area. The heavy line on both sides of the lake outlines the Jerome Fishing and Hunting Club property. Wisconsin Historical Society

By the time Sherry began work on the Jerome acquisition, Charles Comiskey had cut his ties with the club. In a phone conversation with Waldo, Comiskey said that "they got into a little trouble last year with some of their members and that he with quite a good many of his friends sold their shares in the club for $250.00 each." That left Sherry to deal with Comiskey's successors, who proved, on balance, to be a reasonable lot.

The central issue in the negotiations turned around water levels. The initial survey showed that Trude Lake would rise by 5.8

feet when the flowage was at full pond. Though such an elevation did not significantly threaten the club's improvements, the existing shoreline would be utterly destroyed and bank erosion would likely result from fluctuating water levels. This eventuality prompted Sherry and Waldo to contemplate the construction of a dike or dam that would prevent flowage waters from running into Trude Lake and so maintain the lake at its historical level. The volume of water lost to the flowage would be, in their view, trivial. Should seepage from the flowage into the lake occur, a pump system could be installed to return the unwanted water to the flowage. Harris was set to work identifying a suitable dam site on Sand Creek, which drained Trude Lake to the west. The obvious location was where the road crossed the creek, which today is the site of a newly constructed bridge on Popko Circle West that permits boat traffic between Trude Lake and the flowage. A visit from a high-level delegation of representatives of various CFIC companies, however, put an end to this notion. Any solution that involved a pumping system, they contended, would commit the company to long-term operating costs. Better to build a dike and indemnify Trude Lake interests if it were to fail. One member of the party, J.H. Sargeant, the land and tax agent of Northern States Power Company, took still another tack: Trude Lake would be much improved as a body of water if it were deeper, and so the flowage of it should go ahead.

Though acquiring flowage rights to the property remained on the table throughout the course of the negotiations with the club (the club wanted $40,000 for flowage rights or $75,000 for a fee sale), Sherry and Waldo became increasingly convinced that outright purchase of the property made the most sense. They felt they could turn it around fairly quickly as a resort property. In fact, they even had a potential buyer in mind: namely, Hugh Boyd, who had founded Boyd's Mason Lake Resort near Fifield. Boyd, it seems, was looking for a resort property for his two sons. On October 9, 1925, the Jerome Fishing and Hunting Club sold all the real estate and personal property for $70,000. It was a big sum, to be sure, but it may well have been one of the better bargains struck for property. Sargeant had expressed surprise at the club's initial asking price; he had thought owners of a property that extensive would have started at $150,000.

Small Acquisitions of Varied Historical Interest

Several additional transactions are worth noting, if only briefly, for the light they shed on place names, or for some unique set of circumstances. The Kimmear Road development, mentioned earlier, fronts on a long but narrow bay that was once known as Drott's Slough. It was named after Martin Drott, owner of the Wausau Timber and Stone Company, who in 1894 obtained a patent for 120 acres in Section 14, 42N R2E. When Waldo approached him in 1922 about a deal, Drott was reluctant to sell his land outright. He had built a cabin and loved to hunt the area, and he seems to have harbored the belief that his mineral rights might someday pay off—possibly because of the imposing rock outcroppings in the area. Finally, he was of the opinion—farsighted as it turns out—that land on the projected flowage would someday prove valuable. As it turns out, Drott had serious financial troubles and had been forced into an agreement with William Fordyce, president of the Ashland County Bank and a resident of Butternut, whereby Fordyce held title to the lands in question and Drott had the right to redeem them when he was in a position to do so. Both Drott and Fordyce placed an unrealistically high value on the lands, a situation that brought the Railroad Commission into the negotiations in 1925. When the CFIC finally obtained the property in 1928, flowing 80 acres and buying 40 outright, compensation was paid to William Fordyce and spouse, and to John Fordyce and spouse (either William's brother or son).

Schenebeck's Point, today a developed area of the flowage, likely takes its name from Leo Schienbeck, who in 1910 obtained a patent to two government lots and a forty in Section 30, 42N 3E. Schienbeck, who also went under the name Schienebeck, turned out to be a hard party for Sherry and Waldo to deal with, in no small part because his property and the cabin in which he lived were extremely remote and hard to access. (A hand-sketched map places the cabin at the juncture of Horseshoe Creek and the Flambeau River.) He also wanted a lot of money for his land. As a consequence, Waldo tried to persuade Schienbeck to sell flowage rights and remain at his cabin, which would stay high and dry. In doing so, Waldo played to Schienbeck the outdoorsman by noting how fabulous the musky fishing and duck hunting had become in the newly completed Chippewa flowage and by suggesting the same would be true for the projected flowage. "It is our intention to make a forest and game preserve on the big island between Merkle Lake and the Turtle, and to plant Horseshoe Swamp and several other swamps with celery and rice." That effort to entice failed, and Schienbeck sold the property outright. Sherry, ever the worrier, cautioned Waldo to make sure that the spelling of the man's name on the deed matched the spelling of the signature. In the end, Scheinebeck was the name of record. To keep matters straight, it should be noted that another Schienebeck, Joseph, obtained a patent in 1890 for a forty to the north and west of Island Lake, but that property is so far from today's Schenebeck's Point as to rule him out as the eponym.

The derivation of Bastine Lake is fairly straightforward, though it too involves several changes in spelling. Once again, the Government Land Office records provide the starting point. In March of 1893, Joseph Bastein obtained a homestead patent for five government lots in Section 28, T42N R2E, in the amount of 159.9 acres. A hand-drawn map from the Sherry files shows a "Bastien clearing," no doubt Mr. Bastein's homestead site, at the base of a peninsula of land that separated Turtle Lake from Muskellunge Lake. On today's plat map, this would roughly be the area marked with small tracts, north of the Flambeau Trail and west of Hiawatha Road. Another rough map shows the water as "Bastne Lake." A more formal drawing by J.W. Harris, dated July 1924, labels the lake, "Turtle or Bastien Lake." Precisely when both lakes, Muskellunge (its spelling had undergone a change as well) and Turtle, became a single lake is unclear; but a Northern States Power map from 1938 identifies that part of the flowage as Bastine Lake.

One of the few times Sherry seems to have lacked his usual shrewdness and tact came in his dealings with Cornell University in Ithaca, New York. Cornell owned 120 acres of cutover land that he needed. The land had been acquired in 1869 by Ezra Cornell, the founder of the university that bore his name, pursuant to the Morrill Land Grant Act of 1862. In keeping with the purposes of the act, the university had long since sold the timber to finance its operations. Sherry politely made his case for $5 an acre. The university wanted twice as much, arguing that the properties had nice sandy loam and that they had sold similar properties for $7.50 per acre. Sherry responded that there were only half a dozen farmers in the whole township and such a sale was unlikely. They finally agreed on $7.50; but before the deal was closed, Sherry asked to see title abstracts of the property, and he also hinted that there might be some unpaid taxes on the land, as this was often the case with cutovers. Moreover, Sherry mistakenly set the value of the sale at $750, not $900. At this point George Rogalsky, the university treasurer, decided to set this somewhat suspicious and mathematically mistaken Midwesterner straight. After pointing out that the deal was for $900, he wrote: "We have no abstract on any of our Western lands at all. We have owned these lands since 1869 and every purchaser of the same (and there have been thousands of purchasers) have been satisfied with our warranty. At the close of our last fiscal year, June 30th, 1922, the University had assets of $26,839,000, with total liabilities of $5,000. We will furnish you with a certificate to the effect that we owe no taxes on the property we will convey to you. Trusting this will be satisfactory, we are, Yours Very Truly...." Case closed.

One transaction stands out for its connection to international affairs of the time: namely, a 490-acre parcel owned by Anton Schreiner, an American citizen of German origin. It happens that his property was seized during World War I by the United States government and turned over to the Alien Property Custodian, an agency that took possession of and held property belonging to aliens with whose states we were at war. Why this happened to an American citizen is unclear; possibly it was because Schreiner had returned to Germany to live, which is where he was when Sherry tried to acquire his property. What followed was a frustrating set of negotiations with an extremely bureaucratic government agency, compounded by Schreiner's death and the need to deal with his son and family. It took four years for the process to play out and the land to be acquired from the government.

Perhaps the most curious and certainly the most impassioned single document in the Sherry files is a letter written in April of 1925 by Mary Rodgers of Mankato, Minnesota, to Adolph Kannenberg of the Railroad Commission. Rodgers, who owned several parcels of land abutting the northeasternmost part of Trude Lake, did not write to complain about the price being offered for the flowage of her properties. She wrote, instead, to defend not just her land, but earth itself, from the work of power companies and even to decry electricity itself. "I am very sorry to hear that those power trust people are about to gain a footing in Iron Co. The activities of this giant trust is like a great octopus and has tentacles fastened now on the vital forces of nature and our government don't consider the awful import of all the consequences to follow." She feared, among other things, that dammed-up water would put pressure on riverbeds and lead to earthquakes. "Start a ball rolling and prick it ever so little, even with a pin, and it is bound to shake." And as for electricity? "Storms rage and property is destroyed daily caused greatly by electrical currents concentrating gasses, etc. Electricity is the devil's own tool and lives of those in future wars who dwell in our cities will go out at the command of these wizards of the electrical trust." One can only wonder what reaction the serious-minded Sherry had to this letter when Kannenberg forwarded it on to him. Needless to say, Ms. Rodgers' properties went to condemnation.

⋯❀⋯

In a formal sense, Sherry's involvement in land acquisition ended on February 17, 1925, when two separate conveyances, one from the Flambeau Paper Company and the other from the Wisconsin Realty Company, turned over to the Chippewa and Flambeau Improvement Company all the properties they had gathered for the flowage. The price, in each case, was "One Dollar ($1.00) and other valuable considerations to be paid by the said grantee [CFIC]." The parties to the deal used this convention because at that moment the CFIC lacked the ability to pay the price in full. Sherry and Waldo did continue to play a role in working out the details of the properties still outstanding, but they did so alongside the RRC and the construction management firm in charge of building the dam. Under this regime, newly added properties went straight to the CFIC.

When all was said and done, Sherry and Waldo had acquired land or flowage rights to 673 separate pieces of property. In the process, they had dealt with 17 companies, at least 41 individuals, one university, two outdoor clubs, and the state of Wisconsin. The total expenditure for these properties, according to documents issued by the Railroad Commission, came to $358,629.64. In 1934, the Public Service Commission (PSC), the successor to the Railroad Commission, ruled that at full pool the waters flooded all or parts of an additional 140 acres, owned either by the Flambeau Paper Company or the Wisconsin Realty Company, and valued those lands at $1,050. The final settlement on record came in 1942, when Lee Doriot, who owned a forty just south of what is now the Flowage Landing Road near Schenebeck's Point, filed a claim against the CFIC for flooding some of his lands. The PSC assessed his claim at $400.

CHAPTER FOUR

A More Even Flow at Last

The Roddis Connection

E.P. Sherry might well have wished that his obligations to the flowage project began and ended with gathering the property for it. But he was not to get off so easy. For he and his associates in Park Falls were forced by necessity to add logging and railroad building to their already broad business portfolios. Their successful completion of these two undertakings was yet another precondition for the construction of the dam and flowage.

Although cutover lands and some poorly timbered lands together made up a sizeable portion of the properties Sherry acquired, there were plenty of parcels with marketable timber. These parcels had been put on the books at a low per-acre price for the purpose of turning over land as cheaply as possible to the Chippewa and Flambeau Improvement Company (CFIC). But the actual cost of these timbered lands had far exceeded the booked price. To come out whole, the timber assets had to be realized.

Indeed, it was critical to the financial survival of the Flambeau Paper Company (FPC) and the Wisconsin Realty and Winnebago Realty companies that this timber be harvested and sold.

By the fall of 1924 when the application to build the dam was before the Railroad Commission, Sherry, and especially Waldo, turned their attention to this matter with some urgency. In early October, Waldo wrote to Sherry that he had prepared a map of the timber that should be harvested in the coming winter. He limited his map to timber lying below the 1,572 feet MSL elevation, since, if it were left standing, it would be a total loss once the reservoir was filled. His calculations showed that lands owned by the three companies held an estimated 8,528,000 feet of timber. This estimate fell well below the 15 million feet that Sherry had earlier put forward, but Waldo's estimate did not include timber on state lands or on a few other parcels for which ownership was not yet settled. Waldo planned to hire a scaler who could sharpen up these estimates. In the meantime, he set about hiring jobbers for the logging operation itself, and decided to put his woodsman, Mr. Kilger, in charge of them. Waldo finished his letter on a cautious note. "This logging job is going to be quite a big job and mean a lot of work and worry due largely to the fact that we are not loggers and have had very little experience. We hope, however, to get in a few good jobbers and this will reduce our troubles somewhat."

Waldo's caution turned out to be justified, for the logging operation did not go as well as hoped. As a consequence, Waldo found himself in an awkward spot in the summer of 1925 as the manager of the FPC. The arrangements in place called for the company to purchase the timber from the Wisconsin Realty and Winnebago Realty companies. This meant, in effect, that the paper company had to pay stumpage fees to the two realty companies. Looking at a bill for $20,000, Waldo complained that Sherry, on behalf of Wisconsin Realty, was charging too much for stumpage, thereby hurting the paper company. The two men finally worked out a deal, based on an understanding that the paper company, given its role in the dam project, ought to have good books. In addition, they sought to avoid the appearance that the FPC was paying too much in the way of stumpage fees, thereby adding to the overall cost of the project. By comparison, if the realty companies suffered a hit to their bottom lines, the consequences would be relatively benign. Sherry therefore agreed to cut the stumpage fee by half, and Waldo promised to pay more than 50 percent should revenues make that possible. This arrangement appears to have persisted through the final phase of logging, which took place during the winter of 1925-1926.

Getting the trees down was one thing; getting the cut logs out of the forest and to mills for processing into sawn lumber was quite another. Hardwoods, like maple and birch, along with hemlocks and cedar, made up the greater part of the wood to be cut—though there were still some white pines scattered about. This makeup of the timber, with its substantial portion of non-floating logs, precluded the use of the Flambeau River as a vehicle for getting these logs to the mills. Nor could they be moved by means of the few roads in the area. In 1925, Guy Waldo observed that "the road from the Jerome Fishing & Hunting Club to a point near the dam site is strictly a Ford road," by which he surely meant that with a light-duty Ford truck and some luck one might get through. By process of elimination, then, railroads became the only feasible option. Indeed, they had proven indispensable to the second-stage logging that had sprung into being after the exhaustion of the greater part of the pinery.

In February of 1920, when the reservoir project was in its earliest stages, Sherry had already begun to think about getting the timber out of the affected area—as well as getting construction materials to the dam site. He quickly zeroed in on the railroad line nearest—

about six miles—to the dam site. This track belonged to a major player in the Wisconsin lumber industry, the Roddis Lumber and Veneer Company. Based in Marshfield, Wisconsin, the Roddis Veneer Company came into being in 1897, three years after W.H. Roddis took control of a troubled but innovative hardwood veneer company. Roddis made a success of the company, and in 1903 he expanded his operations to Park Falls. Roddis was attracted to this location by the vast hardwood resources that covered the landscape north of this budding mill town. In addition, he had his eye on the hemlock and cedar timber that grew abundantly in the area, as well as on the scattered but still valuable pine stands that had evaded the sawyer. Sensibly, Roddis set up sawmill and planing facilities in Park Falls to deal with the softwoods, and shipped hardwood to Marshfield for processing. To reflect its broader scope, the corporate name was changed to the Roddis Lumber and Veneer Company.

To provide a continuing supply of timber for its operations, the Roddis Company purchased land or timber rights to enough timber to keep the company going for decades. According to Harvey Houston, the author of a study of the Roddis rail line, these purchases embraced "an area northeast of Park Falls, which ultimately was about 25 miles long and 8 miles wide. These lands extended from Park Falls in the south to Island Lake in Iron County on the north, and were bounded generally on the east by the north fork of the Flambeau reaching upstream to the confluence of the Turtle and the Manitowish, and on the west by the east fork of the Chippewa."

To get the timber down to Park Falls for milling or for shipment on to Marshfield, W.H. Roddis arranged to have the Wisconsin Central Railroad build a 9.5-mile rail line running out of Park Falls in a slightly northeastern direction. Thereafter, responsibility for further expansion of the line lay with the Roddis Company—with the stipulation that it use Wisconsin Central rails. Over the years, that initial stretch of track became the trunk of a tree that was to move ever northward, with temporary branches extending east and west as the company systematically harvested its holdings. The Roddis line operated continuously until 1938; and the company went on harvesting timber until 1960, when it was absorbed by the Weyerhaeuser Company.

In 1920, the year Sherry began investigating rail links to his project, the Roddis Company underwent a major transition: W.H. Roddis died at the age of 76 and was replaced as president by his son, Hamilton Roddis. H.R., as the young Roddis was known, was 45 years of age and had ample experience, which included serving as treasurer of the family business. But he seems to have been either inexperienced at, or ill-suited for, making high-level executive decisions. This shortcoming contributed to seemingly endless negotiations with Sherry and Waldo over matters of mutual concern: namely, Roddis properties that would be affected by the flowage project, and the construction of a railway spur that would connect the flowage area with the Roddis main line. For Sherry, and particularly for Guy Waldo, negotiating with Hamilton Roddis proved to be frustrating, perplexing, and a bit sad.

Early in 1920, Sherry notified the Roddis Company that the projected flowage would flood wholly or in part some 284 acres of Roddis land, as well as six parcels of land that Wisconsin Realty owned but to which Roddis owned the timber rights. Sherry offered to purchase these properties and timber rights. His offer, however, was not to the liking of Roddis. A year later Roddis indicated that he was not in a position to log the timber but, at the same time, did not "wish to part with it." Even so, he went on to suggest a possible trade of lands that would be of equal value. Finally, Roddis said that "it seems a pity that this land should be overflowed before the timber is removed. It may be necessary to build a railroad into this timber to remove it." Needless to say, it was nearly impossible to discern Roddis' intentions from this communication, though the door seemed to have been opened a bit to a rail link to the area of the proposed flowage.

Sherry, of course, had already been thinking about how to get logs out of the project area. Tractors were ruled out for reasons of terrain; and although J.W. Harris, surveyor for the project, said a roadway would be possible, his own preference was for a railroad. Sherry followed suit, concluding that a spur or extension from the Roddis main line was the best solution. The costs of such a spur, he figured, might be borne equally by Roddis and by other timber owners in the flowage area. This spur would also be a base for extending a line to the Island Power project when it was time to build there.

Given the realities of the situation, the self-interests of the parties, and their prior history of reasonably satisfactory dealings with one another, these matters really ought to have been settled quickly. Roddis, for his part, knew he would eventually have to relinquish his lands and timber rights when the reservoir project went ahead, and he stood to profit from hauling on his main line timber cut from the future lake bed and construction materials for the dam. Sherry, for his part, could not achieve his objectives without acquiring the Roddis lands and without a useable rail line. But despite this congruence of interests, agreement eluded the two parties for a number of reasons. First, Roddis placed an extremely high value on his lands and timber, well beyond what was the norm for Sherry's land purchases. That valuation also made any swap of land impossible, though Waldo explored the issue seriously. Second, Roddis dragged his feet in negotiations on a railway extension. The sticking point here was his reluctance to spend money either to build an absolutely essential bridge over Swamp Creek or eventually to buy back a bridge that someone else built. Third, Roddis kept shifting tactics. Sometimes he claimed that any settlement would have to embrace both the land deal and arrangements for a rail line; at other times, he expressed a willingness to settle one issue at a time. Fourth, Roddis was not beyond introducing some tangential issues into the bargaining, such as his desire to buy land from Wisconsin Realty in Park Falls for an expansion of his facility there. And in 1923, he even raised the possibility that he might sell his Park Falls plant, and maybe even his one at Marshfield. Fifth, it was essential to commit everything to writing as Roddis, according to Waldo, "changes his mind so often and forgets what has transpired."

So frustrating were the negotiations between the two parties that Waldo, who early on described Roddis as "a rather peculiar man to do business with," eventually concluded that things were even worse. He noted as much in a letter to Sherry: "While our dealings with Mr. Roddis, as you know, have not been at all satisfactory we really believe that Mr. Roddis is honest and it is a question of whether we can get further with a crazy but honest man than we can with Mr. Coleman." Coleman, the manager of Roddis' Marshfield plant who had begun to represent the company in negotiations in 1925, had proved to be a hard bargainer.

The railroad extension was the first of the two main issues to be resolved, but not without a lot of going back and forth. On two separate occasions, once in 1923 and once in 1924, Sherry and Waldo contemplated an alternative solution—one which, by the way, Roddis endorsed at one point. The Park Falls Lumber Company, as an independent company, had built and pretty much finished using a railroad line from the town to its Camp A, which today would be in the southwest arm of the flowage. A relatively short extension of this line would connect it with the proposed dam site. Moreover, the lumber company was ready to do a deal. But there were problems: not only was this line in shoddy condition, but it was also quite long. Repair and maintenance might prove excessively costly. That said, Sherry kept lines of communication open with the lumber company even as he pressed Roddis for an agreement

Two considerations appear to have tipped the balance in favor of an extension from the Roddis main line. First, Sherry was prepared to build the spur at his own expense, whether or not Roddis would someday buy it from him for his future logging needs. Indeed, by May of 1924 engineering plans for the extension had been completed. Second, when Roddis heard that there might be as much as 15 million feet of timber to be hauled from the reservoir area, he realized that he could make a handsome profit by carrying these logs along his main line to Park Falls. In August of that year, Roddis sketched out what a deal would look like. Sherry would build the extension, and Roddis would charge by the car for logs hauled from the junction to Park Falls and for construction materials going the other way. Waldo responded in mid-September by sending off a contract along these lines, slightly tweaked to reflect his interests. No signed contract came back. With winter about to close in, Waldo simply went ahead with the first stages of the rail spur, as described in a letter to Sherry: "We are getting our equipment lined up and have three or four men brushing out the right of way at the present time, and Mr. Harris and helpers are busy on the survey...." Uncharacteristically, he dismissed with a wave of the hand the fact that he lacked all the easements—including one from Roddis. They could be secured, if needed, by getting the town to grant them. Waldo had also decided to get on with installing a phone line to the proposed dam site. Roddis finally signed the contract on October 6, and work on the spur picked up pace.

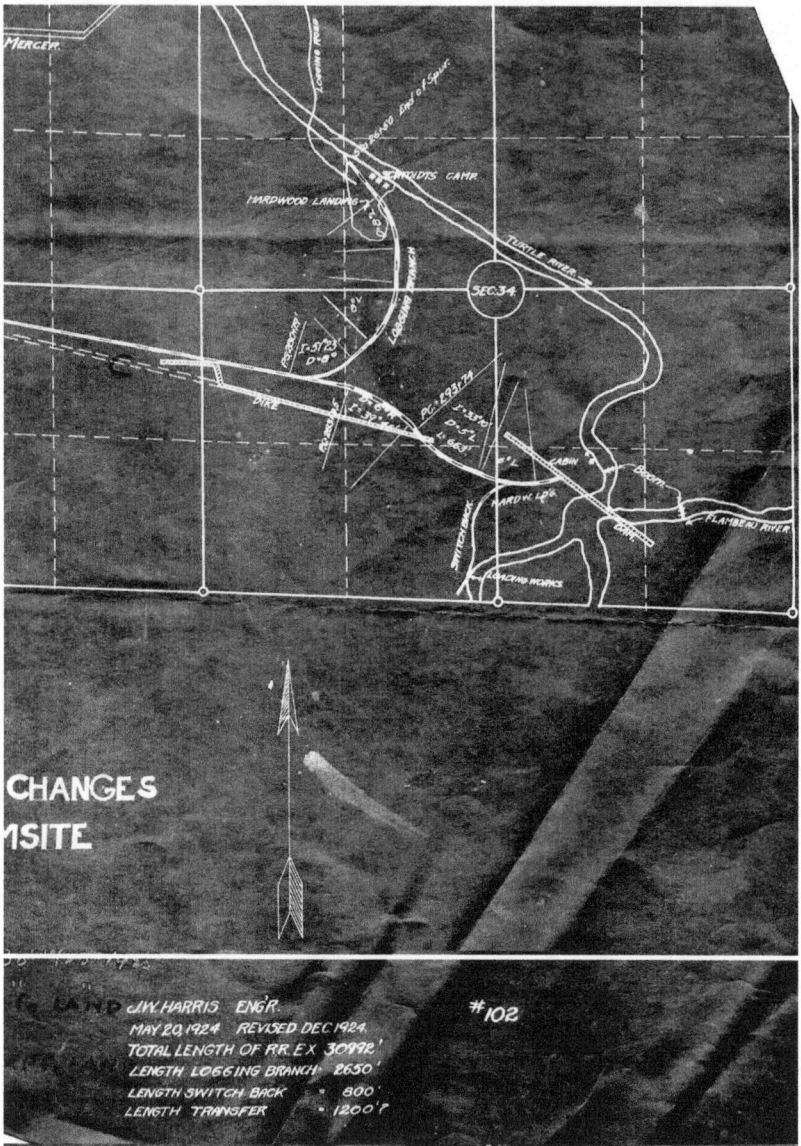

The terminal portion of "Map Showing Proposed R.R. Extension and Highway Changes Roddis R.R. to Reservoir Damsite. Flambeau Improvement Company. Prepared by J.W. Harris, Engineer." (December, 1924) Wisconsin Historical Society

Arguments over the Roddis Company's lands and timber rights continued into the summer of 1925. In the end, Roddis gave up his efforts to sell his holdings outright and settled on the sale of flowage rights. By this time the list of properties at issue had grown substantially from the time when Sherry first approached the Roddis company. It now comprised 324 acres of Roddis land and timber as well as 505.3 acres to which Roddis had timber rights. The Railroad Commission, which had been drawn in to help break the logjam, concluded that "the consideration to be paid to the Roddis company is understood to be $12,500, and it is understood that the Roddis company will retain all timber." And so ended this phase of a troubled relationship. Though Sherry and Waldo found it all trying, they must, in the final analysis, have realized their good fortune in having a major, responsible, second-stage logging company in the area. The Roddis Company entered 1925 with 18 miles of road and 5.5 miles of yard track. Its rolling stock included 100 flat cars or logging cars, four ballast cars, a steam shovel, and two engines. All of these assets were at the disposal of the CFIC to handle both timber and construction. The Roddis Lumber and Veneer Company was at the right place at the right time.

Construction Plans and Financing

While Sherry was working on matters close to his home base, the CFIC was setting the wheels in motion for the construction project that lay ahead. In 1924, the Madison, Wisconsin, firm, Mead and Seastone, Consulting Engineers, delivered to the CFIC a set of specifications for the dam. To be located just above an island that sat downstream of the confluence of the Turtle and Flambeau rivers, a concrete spillway dam would be approximately 100 feet in length and 34.5 feet in width at its base. This dam would be flanked on either side by earthen embankments designed to raise the elevation of nearby lowland. Additional embankments, rising to the same elevation, would also have to be constructed where the terrain was insufficiently high to prevent overtopping by the waters of the reservoir.

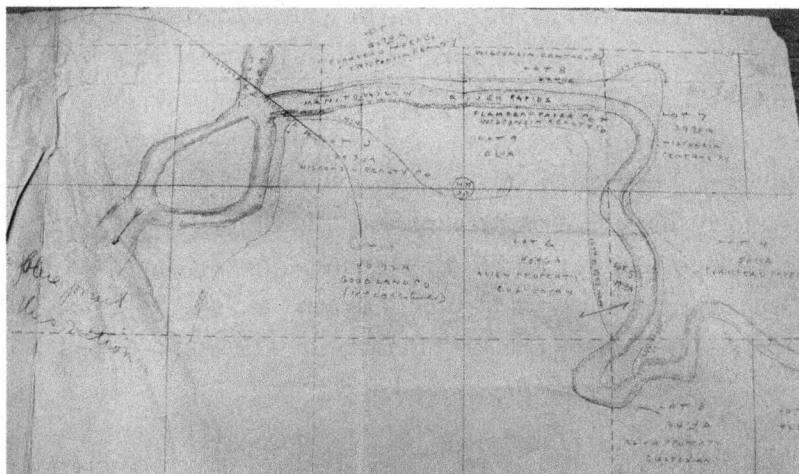

A working drawing that shows the confluence of the Turtle and Manitowish (Flambeau) rivers, the island that lies below, and the proposed location of a dam to create a storage reservoir. Wisconsin Historical Society

With a set of plans in hand, the CFIC promptly settled on a construction management firm: Byllesby Engineering and Management Corporation of Chicago. The choice of Byllesby was, as the saying goes, no accident. Its relationship to the CFIC can be most succinctly represented through the words of a Wisconsin Supreme Court decision from 1931. "The majority of the stock of [CFIC] is owned and controlled by the Northern States Power Company; that through successive holding corporations the actual control of said Improvement Company is vested in the Standard Gas and Electric Company [a Delaware Corporation], which control is exercised by H.M. Byllesby & Company." Byllesby, for its part, operated and provided general management for some 14 public utility companies as of 1923. From the moment Byllesby was retained, H.W. Fuller, the firm's vice president of engineering, took over direct responsibility for all aspects of the reservoir project including, as Sherry's records make clear, some of the outstanding land deals. Sherry was now playing in the big leagues.

On February 24, 1925, the Byllesby Corporation submitted to the CFIC a detailed cost estimate for the construction of the dam itself. The total amount came to $557,891.62. (In late March, Byllesby, after reviewing and modifying the Mead and Seastone plans, upped its estimate by $6,800.) Among the more significant items in the estimate were 6,909 pounds of structural steel, 1,120,000 pounds of steel sheeting, 164,000 cubic yards of material for the dikes, and 3,670 cubic yards of concrete for the core walls of the dikes— slightly more concrete than was to go into the construction of the spillway dam itself. The estimate also included $5,500 for the dam operator's cottage, $8,500 for a telephone line, and $15,000 for transportation of materials, supplies, and equipment from Park Falls to the dam site. In addition to construction costs, Byllesby's estimate showed that $178,063.51 had already been spent as of that date to acquire land and flowage rights, and that it was likely to cost $155,916.00 to secure land or flowage rights from an additional 23 parties. Taken together, construction and land acquisition costs brought the total estimated cost of the project to nearly $900,000. On March 25, Byllesby revised its estimate upwards substantially. It added to the cost of land purchases an additional $58,611.98 for taxes, legal fees, surveys, and changes to highways; and it added entries for legal fees and bond discounts. The final estimate came to $1,008,784.

With plans at the ready, cost estimates developed, and a construction management firm in control of the project, it remained only to hire a company to do the actual work. The CFIC accomplished this task on March 28, 1925, when it signed a contract with the L.E. Myers Company of Chicago "for the Construction of a Dam, Headworks and Dykes to form or create the Flambeau Reservoir." Myers had a large construction camp (Byllesby's estimate figured Myers' cost at $25,000) already in place in early May, and work crews seem to have been at work several weeks in advance of the final authorization of the project by the Railroad Commission.

Of course, all this had to be paid for. Heading into 1925, however, the CFIC fell woefully short of having the necessary resources. At that time, its authorized capital stock was a mere $75,000, and a trial balance of October 21, 1924, showed that the "amounts received and paid out on stock subscriptions" had a balance of $38,700. The balance also showed unissued capital stock in the amount of $36,300. To remedy this situation, the company applied to the Railroad Commission on March 31, 1925, for authorization to issue securities in an amount sufficient to complete the project. On May 13, the commission responded by authorizing the CFIC to issue "Ten Thousand (10,000) shares of its common stock of the par value of $100 each, making a total issue of $1,000,000, and $500,000 of its First Mortgage 5 ½% Twelve and one-half Year Gold Sinking Fund Bonds dated May 1st 1925, maturing November 1st 1937...." The CFIC moved quickly to market these securities. In a report to the commission dated May 23, 1925, the company reported that it had sold 400 bonds, at a par value of $1,000 each, and raised $362,013.90 from the transaction. It had also sold 5,500 shares of stock at par value, with $110,000 in hand and a balance of unpaid subscriptions in the amount of $440,000. The company chose not to issue the full amount of bonds authorized, pending future knowledge of how expensive the project would turn out to be. In 1926, it asked for and got permission from the Railroad Commission to issue the remaining $100,000 worth of bonds.

With funding in hand, the CFIC was finally in a position to see the reservoir project through to completion.

The Flow Stopped: The Flambeau Reservoir Dam

The relatively short northwoods construction season dictated that work proceed quickly. Under these conditions and given the scope of the project, it would be unreasonable to expect the project to unfold along a carefully developed linear timeline. Indeed, that was the case from the beginning when the Myers Company built its construction camp in advance of the final approval of the project. One part of the approval process brought Adolf Kannenberg and C.A. Halbert of the Railroad Commission to the area in the third week of May 1925 to familiarize themselves with the properties yet to be acquired and to look over the dam site. Guy Waldo proposed that they work out of the Jerome Club for a few days, and out of the Myers camp for the remainder of their stay. It may have been during this visit that the commission's benchmark was installed at the dam site. Whether this was the case or not, pre-authorization inspections and construction seem to have gone hand in hand. One matter that surely helped all parties during the spring of 1925 was the weather. Spring precipitation in Park Falls totaled just 3.47 inches, the lowest for that period on record between 1910 and 2001.

The pressures and complications of the construction process come through clearly in a letter that J.W. Harris, the surveyor, wrote to Fuller at Byllesby on July 25, 1925. Fuller had been pressing Harris to complete some surveys and maps of the Jerome Club property, which Harris had not been able to accomplish because he had been surveying for the dam project. "As it is, I have staked out and located four different locations on Dike two, five locations on the diversion channel, figured yardages of earth and made profiles of each one. The other dikes have been just as carefully located. In some places I have set in three sets of slope stakes, up to date on 9100 feet of dike." Harris goes on to point out the difficulties of working in "a cut over timbered region where locations are many times more difficult than in a prairie country," and he states bluntly that the inspectors assigned by Byllesby to help him were inexperienced in such circumstances.

But the problems Harris identified went beyond inadequate help for his surveying work: "Every time I have left the work here [at the dam site] for more than a day I have discovered many mistakes that would have [been] costly to the contractors as well as to the engineers reputation e.g. a foot in elevation on the concrete section, two times as much dirt about to be excavated in the diversion channel as was necessary, destroyed reference points which are absolutely necessary to the correct location of structures, mistakes in yardage, and many others." That said, he promises to "do my best to meet the situation."

In addition, this letter from Harris to Byllesby contains two pieces of information that bear on the progress of construction to that point. First, the "approximately 1100 cu. yds. of concrete poured to date" amounted to about 30 percent of the estimated amount for the spillway dam, and only 15 percent of the total concrete for the project. Second, he notes that "200,000 cu. yards of fill and excavation" remained to be done. The better part of this undone work surely pertained to the construction of the more than two miles of dikes. In the same paragraph, Harris pledges to convey this information to two of the project's subcontractors, a Mr. Collins and a Mr. Groves, "so that we may see to it that there is equipment here to finish the job November first." Though a great deal of site work had to be accomplished before the dam structure itself could be erected, it still seems that the project had a long way to go as of the third week of July.

Construction of the central portion of the dam. The tower at left elevates a bucket of concrete which flows through a tube to the forms. Mark Fort Photo Collection

The problems of completing the project on time were not limited to those connected with getting the engineering and surveying correct. The level of technology available to the contractors had a significant role to play as well. The first American patent application for a tractor with a front-mounted blade was not filed until 1923, and it would be years after the dam and dikes were built and the flowage filled that the now ubiquitous bulldozer found its way onto construction sites around the country. When it came to deploying heavy equipment for the building of the Turtle Dam and its lengthy dike system, the construction managers had no option but to bring in draft horses and wagons; and picks and shovels were the instruments of choice for digging the trenches that held the footings for the cement cores of the dikes. Given the limitations of such equipment, the builders' goal of completing the dam and dikes within a year strikes one today as being wildly optimistic.

Another problem, which did not substantially delay the project but which did increase its cost, had to do with material for the building of the dikes. When Harris surveyed the route for the extension, he came across a gravel deposit about two miles from the dam site and marked it on his map. Moving material from that point to the construction area would be relatively cheap, given that it would take place entirely on the spur that Sherry had constructed. Of course, the Roddis steam shovel would be needed to remove and load the material and Roddis ballast cars to haul it. As it turns out, this deposit did not contain the proper kind of material, and fill had to be excavated at a greater distance and hauled on some Roddis track. What was not so good for the CFIC was good for the Roddis line: its operating revenues jumped from $2,431.50 in 1924 to $74,061.25 in 1925. This figure includes revenue from both timber and construction materials that moved over Roddis tracks. As busy as the Roddis Company must have been during this year, Roddis found time to send Waldo a letter with the following request: "The S.J. Groves and Sons Company who are doing some work at the dam site have an account with us which is past due. Will you kindly let us know from whom we can look to for this money in case we are unable to collect this account." The amount was $2.20.

Though the timetable seemed pressed in July of 1925, there is no evidence to suggest that the entire project—both spillway dam and embankments—was not substantially finished on time. A complete description of the dam can be found in the first inspection report of the Railroad Commission of Wisconsin, dated October 12, 1930. The completed spillway dam had three sluice gates located deep in the dam. Each of them was four feet in diameter, adjusted by a threaded shaft and worm gear mechanism. Three tainter gates—rotating, curved gates that controlled the flow over the spillway—constituted the primary means of regulating the discharge from the dam. The hand-operated worm gear and chain mechanisms that worked the tainter gates were, in the judgment of the inspectors, difficult for one person to operate. The dam also contained a log sluice or chute to facilitate the discharge of floating timber. In addition to the central portion of the dam that accommodated the sluices and gates, there was also a concrete retaining section, without operating features, that completed the span of the dam. Nine separate dikes, totaling more than 9,000 feet, were distributed over a five-mile stretch that flanked the spillway dam. They ranged in height from 15 to 33 feet—though all topped out at an elevation of 1,577 feet MSL. Embankments with core walls—placed in the most critical locations—were 16 feet in width at their top; those without core walls were 12 feet in width.

Workmen dig a trench for the core wall of dike number 2, their backs and shovels substituting for backhoes. Mark Fort Photo Collection

A steam-driven piledriver installs metal sheeting for the core wall of dike number 3. A horse-drawn wagon waits for its next task. Mark Fort Photo Collection

The initial authorization permitted the CFIC to operate the dam between a maximum (full pool) of 1,572 feet MSL and a minimum of 1,539 feet MSL. The latter figure, because it turned out to be seven feet below the apron of the dam, essentially meant that the flowage could be drawn down as far as the sluice gates permitted—1,548 feet. The authorized minimum was later raised to 1,560 feet. When operating at full pool, the dam has a head of 22 feet, which, in turn, creates a reservoir of approximately 13,000 acres. Today the full-pool capacity of the flowage is 5.9 billion cubic feet of water.

Dams, of course, must be designed to withstand abnormal rainfall and snowmelt events. According to a 1978 report from the U.S. Army Corps of Engineers, the flowage dam had never been threatened by overtopping. Its total spillway capacity at full pool is 17,040 cubic feet per second (cfs). The maximum discharge on record is 3,440 cfs, reached on May 28, 1939, and from July 22 to July 27 in 1952. Routine discharges only occasionally exceed 1,050 cfs, and they hover between 300 and 400 cfs in dry years. Clearly, the Flambeau Reservoir dam and dikes, as originally designed and built, had a considerable margin of safety. That said, the report calculates that if the dikes were to be overtopped by one foot, the resulting breach would produce a flood wave nine feet high.

The Flow Resumes

On April 2, 1926, Paul Reiss, an attorney from Cummins et al., the legal firm that represented the Chippewa and Flambeau Improvement Company (CFIC), received the following telegram from the Railroad Commission: "We have made an engineer's inspection of the Flambeau Reservoir Dam and find its construction satisfactory to this commission." With these words, Northern States Power Company, the principal operator of the CFIC reservoir system, had the green light to begin filling the flowage. And so, at 8 a.m. on April 3, the operators ordered the first of the three sluice gates to be closed. At that moment, the elevation of the surface water at the dam was 1,557.2 feet MSL. By adjusting the three sluice gates, the operators were able to bring the water level to 1567.35 by May 31. For the next three months, the elevation hovered around 1,568, with the occasional slight rise or fall; and the filling of the reservoir appeared to have come to a halt. The reality, however, was that the reservoir was "filling down" during the summer. That is, the dammed-up waters were raising the groundwater levels throughout the flowage basin and in the low, swampy lands that abutted many parts of it.

The upward movement of the water level resumed in the early fall. In the course of September, the elevation rose 3.15 feet, and on October 6 the waters attained their maximum operational elevation—1,572 feet—with a discharge of 1,050 cfs. Once again, the project got a boost from Mother Nature. If the construction of the dam had been blessed by a spell of unusually dry weather, the filling of the reservoir was facilitated by extraordinarily wet weather. Annual precipitation at Park Falls set an all-time record high during 1926, as did the three months of fall when 17.34 inches poured down.

Mother Nature's blessing, however, turned out to have a downside. The engineers had estimated that it would take a relatively leisurely two years for the needed five and a half billion cubic feet of water to fill the reservoir. But when the water unexpectedly reached full pool during the very first year and showed every sign of continuing to rise, the engineers had to struggle, literally physically, to wrestle with the stubborn mechanisms controlling the heights of the tainter gates in order to prevent the flowage from exceeding its maximum elevation of 1,572 feet MSL. In the end, they managed to keep the water from directly overflowing the dam and its dikes. This was only part of the story, however. According to Clifford Wells, the son of the chief engineer at Flambeau Paper Company and a participant in the construction of the dam, the surveyors and engineers had missed some low spots in the dike system, and now water was flowing around the dikes and flooding the adjacent land. The situation was particularly troubling in the vicinity of the Lake Ten dike. The waters that had circumvented it were flowing in the direction of Lake Nine, which lies in the drainage area of the South Fork of the Flambeau River. This unintended diversion of the flowage's water was apparently stanched, in Well's words, by the erection of "wheelbarrow dikes." The rapidly rising flowage also had an unanticipated impact along the Turtle River below Lake of the Falls. At least five property owners found their lands flooded beyond what they had been led to believe would be the case. Lawsuits followed, and as the Sherry land acquisition records show, the CFIC was forced to make some settlements with plaintiffs.

The discharge waters from the dam attract anglers and observers in 1935.
Wisconsin Historical Society 82790

These problems aside, the Flambeau Reservoir had become a reality, and the driving figure behind it, E.P. Sherry, must surely have savored the moment—though he was not the kind of person to take time off work to celebrate this or that moment of good fortune. Sherry had at last secured an abundant and reliable supply of upstream water power for his Park Falls enterprises. But the path to that achievement had not been an easy one. Sherry was, after all, something of a geographical outlier in the CFIC, an organization whose center of gravity was farther down the Chippewa Basin in the cities of Eau Claire and Chippewa Falls. (It should be noted that Sherry attained a leadership role in the CFIC only in 1930, when he became the company's president.) As such, Sherry had to take the lead in bringing his colleagues into agreement on constructing a second major storage reservoir. And this he did. He directed the difficult task of land acquisition in a fashion that met the demanding expectations of the Railroad Commission, and his efforts to keep the costs of the project in line were well-received by the members of the CFIC. In fact, Byllesby's records for April 30, 1926, show a total expenditure for land acquisition and dam construction of $1,049,884.08, a number remarkably close to its earlier estimate. And, when the concrete had set and the gates had been closed, Sherry's dam afforded benefits not only to his own interests but also to the other operating companies in the CFIC: Northern States Power Company, Lake Superior District Power Company, Great Western Paper Company, Cornell Wood Products Company, and Eau Claire Dells Improvement Company. Indeed, the combined capacities of the Flambeau Reservoir and the Rest Lake flowage totaled approximately seven billion cubic feet of water. Given the operating instructions in place for both dams, the great bulk of this water could be accessed annually for downstream users—assuming, of course, adequate rain and snow to replenish these reservoirs. And though downstream considerations—that is, the needs of the operating companies— predominated in the strategy of the CFIC, the directors could hardly ignore the revenue-producing aspects of the new reservoir. Toll assessments for the period 1927 through 1930 totaled $827,817. After deducting operating expenses and taxes, the company netted $262,906, or an average of $65,727 per year.

That both water and revenues were flowing rather freely does not mean that the reservoir, once in place, was a trouble-free operation. And because there was no local management other than the dam operator, the office of Donald Boyd, the secretary of the CFIC, became complaint central for matters sometimes great but often small. On November 15, 1926, for example, Boyd wrote a lengthy memo to Flambeau Paper Company quoting extensively from a report of Lincoln Nissley (apparently the engineer responsible for checking on the newly completed reservoir), who had just completed an inspection of the reservoir. His report included the following assessment of the caretaker's cottage, which it seems had a wet basement and a wholly inappropriate heating system: "I would like to see your Board of Directors do something to better the living conditions of the caretaker's cottage, not from a utilitarian standpoint, but from the standpoint of making the living quarters of the caretaker and his wife comfortable, or you may have trouble keeping a caretaker on the dam. I would suggest you take out the present coal burning furnace and put in a suitable furnace for burning wood, and someway water-proof the basement."

Boyd's memo also spoke to the shortcomings of the telephone service linking the dam with Park Falls. It seems that Nissley and the dam keeper had ventured out onto the flowage where they found that the phone lines, which had been strung from tree to tree, had become submerged beneath the waters of the flowage. Relocating the lines above the water level, however, failed to rectify the situation. This led to an investigation of the lines that ran along the railroad spur, where the two men found that some lines had been run under the ties and had been broken under the weight of train traffic. Once these breaches were repaired, phone service to the dam resumed, but the sound quality was terrible. It was clear that some major work needed to be done. In keeping with the agreement between Roddis and Sherry concerning the rail spur, Boyd presumed repairs done on the phone line where it paralleled the spur would be paid for by the CFIC, and repairs on the line from the junction to Park Falls would be paid for jointly by CFIC and the Roddis Company. In his memo, Boyd took this issue head-on: resolving the problems of the cottage and phone were the business of the FPC, which, in effect, meant Waldo.

The CFIC may have been able, in this first year of the dam's operation, to shift onto the Flambeau Paper Company the obligation for fixing these relatively minor problems; but in the long run it was the CFIC that was the responsible party for the flowage. In

1927 the CFIC had to authorize an expenditure of $5,500 for work on the Flambeau Reservoir and directed Nissley to take charge of getting it done. The nature of the problem cannot be inferred from the communication authorizing the expenditure. The headworks might have required some modification, or perhaps one of the dikes needed reinforcement. It is even possible the expenditure was intended to rectify some unanticipated overflowing of the shoreline. Whatever the case, this event foreshadowed the long-term obligations of maintenance the CFIC had assumed.

One of the most persistent obligations—albeit a minor one—was the above-mentioned phone line. In October of 1930, a Railroad Commission inspection of the dam and adjacent area noted that a nearby logging camp had pulled out, leaving Mr. Boehr, the dam keeper, to snowshoe nine miles to mail in reports about elevations. Mercifully, the commission suggested that he might phone the data to Park Falls—assuming, of course, that the phone worked—where it could be mailed to interested parties. Once again, the onus for maintenance of this private line fell on the CFIC, as it would for some time to come. As late as 1955, the CFIC asked the Public Service Commission (PSC) for permission to abandon the line, which served only four parties: the dam keeper, Art Schmidt's Muskie Camp, Al's Place, and Joseph Ledvina. The latter three parties objected, no doubt because they had been free riders on this line almost since its installation. On December 16, 1955, the PSC dismissed the petition of the company, arguing that the commission lacked jurisdiction over a line that was never intended as a public utility.

Problems with the caretaker's cottage, the barely serviceable phone line to the dam, and an unexpected early need for maintenance were all matters that could be dispatched more or less expeditiously—though the phone line was still a troublemaker a decade later. But there was one issue, inherited from the land-acquisition stage of the project, which proved to be a persistent and steady item on the plate of Boyd and the CFIC: namely, the Jerome Fishing and Hunting Club property. As mentioned earlier, Sherry and Waldo had high hopes for the prompt resale of this property to some aspiring resort owner. This was not, however, to be the case; and until the right suitor came along, Sherry, Waldo, and Boyd could not escape the numerous obligations and costs that fell upon them as property owners. Protection and maintenance of the improvements required a caretaker—a position jointly held by Otto and Melanie Janzen at equal salaries of $62.50 per month. Supplies for them, mostly food, added to the costs—and to the business of M.E. Brandt, who delivered orders to the door in his Ford truck every few weeks. The telephone line from the club to Mercer, some of which was strung along now-flooded fence posts, had to be rebuilt. To beautify the property for potential buyers, a crew was sent in during the winter of 1927 to cut trees and brush along the shoreline. And finally, a section of the road from Jerome to Mercer, washed out by flowage wave action, needed repair. Ed Evenson, the Mercer town chairman, sent the bill to the new owner—the CFIC.

But the most unusual inheritance from the Jerome Club was its "game park," which at the time of the purchase contained some deer, six or seven elk, and three buffalo—one adult male, one adult female, and a juvenile male. Initially, the elk proved the most troublesome because of their propensity to escape through downed sections of flooded fence, swim about the flowage, and return to dry land outside their compound. In time, the buffalo learned the same trick, and some more. In September of 1928, Boyd recounted their errant behavior in a letter to Sherry: "The buffalo swim the lake and get out of our park. We drove them back once and it cost us $84.00 to do it. This was the first real expense connected with them. Then they got out again and the bull hooked a cow and pony owned by Mr. Voss who lives near Mercer. We will probably have to pay damages, but do not think they will be very heavy. The buffalo are now hanging around the farm of Henry Peters, but have done no serious damage. They broke some fences and dug up two or three little spruce trees which were in his front yard." According to Mitch Babic, a longtime Mercer guide, the culprit in this escape was his grandfather, George Schwarz, a caretaker and guide for the Jerome Club, who left a gate open.

As this account foreshadows, the matter of expense proved decisive in resolving the buffalo problem. All Sherry operations relentlessly sought to cut every cost and to realize the maximum gain on every asset. The buffalo, clearly, were well on their way from being assets to becoming liabilities, and so it comes as no surprise that the Chippewa and Flambeau Improvement Company moved resolutely in the fall of 1928 to divest themselves of them. The company contacted both the Brookfield and Lincoln Park zoos in Chicago as well as the zoo in Milwaukee for information on the value of the animals and for assistance in finding a buyer. Values ranged from $125 to $250 for the adult animals, and $100 for the calf. The company made at least two attempts at a direct sale, one to the Steuben Outdoor Club in the town of Winchester in nearby Vilas County, Wisconsin, and the other to Budd Small of Kankakee, Illinois; but both contacts failed. In the meantime, it seems that at least three of the elk were sold for $300 to a Mr. Klich of Mercer for his resort and park. Klich had earlier purchased four deer from the Jerome park. But the buffalo remained, and, as of October 5, CFIC officials were puzzling over the best way to get these animals into someone else's hands.

The end came swiftly. On November 12, Boyd wrote to Sherry, "We will have no more trouble with the buffaloes. Mr. Furgeson and Mr. Jones of this city [Eau Claire] went up to Mercer last Saturday, shot them and brought them to Eau Claire on a truck.

They will sell the meat through one of the local butcher shops and expect to have the hides for their profit." In the end, the CFIC realized $150 for the sale of the carcasses, an amount "which will just about let us out even on the damages we had to pay." The whole episode seems to have left the otherwise hard-boiled secretary of the company saddened and puzzled. Boyd concluded his letter, perhaps in ignorance, perhaps in condescension, as follows: "It seems strange to me that the people of Mercer and vicinity, knowing for a long time that we wanted to get rid of these animals, would let them go out this way instead of helping us to sell them alive, and thus keeping in that vicinity one of the best attractions for tourist trade that they can ever hope to get."

Meanwhile, the search went on for a buyer for the property. Not all the prospects seemed promising, as a letter dated February 25, 1929, from Charles Wolf of Mercer attests. In it, Wolf presents himself as someone experienced at acquiring and disposing of large properties to interested groups of fishermen: "I have a large following in my line all over the U.S. from Steel Trust officials R.R. Presidents down, and know hundreds of the fishermen that are worthwhile to know." After noting that he has done business with banks in Ashland and Hurley, Wolf promises that he "can give you references from hundreds of big men of business throughout the country and then also across the waters." Boyd responded by saying that Wolf's letter had been forwarded to Fuller at Byllesby, who would surely reply "in the near future." The CFIC finally sold the Jerome Fishing and Hunting Club property in early 1931 to Charles Lindquist, along with some "upland and excess" property (apparently backland in the Trude Lake area). From the perspective of the CFIC, the Jerome saga had at last come to an end— or so it seemed. For by 1939, title to the property had reverted to the CFIC and the company had to set about the task of finding a new buyer.

Regulating the Flow

Not only did the CFIC have to deal with a host of tangential matters subsequent to the construction of the flowage, but it also had to settle on a regime for the operation of the reservoir. Given that the Byllesby Engineering and Management Corporation had experience operating and managing at more than a dozen public utilities and the CFIC had a couple of years of experience with the Chippewa Reservoir, it might be expected that some fairly specific operating guidelines would have been developed prior to the flooding of the flowage. But that was not the case, as the minutes of a "Special Meeting of the Directors of the Chippewa and Flambeau Improvement Company," held on June 29, 1926, make abundantly clear. T.D. Crocker of Northern States Power and vice president of CFIC began the discussion by pointing out the absence of any "fixed program for the operation of the Chippewa Reservoir." Basically, the water was held back until July, when stream flows declined, and then released. Then the CFIC drew down the flowage enough to accommodate fall rains. At this point, Crocker noted, "The gates are again opened and set so that the water from the greater portion of the pond area will be discharged before January." Such a drawdown was intended to minimize the amount of flow-inhibiting ice in the reservoir. Generally speaking, Crocker acknowledged that management plans for the Chippewa Flowage boiled down to the following: keep in touch with the two principal users of this water—Cornell Wood Products Company and Eau Claire Dells Improvement Company—and "handle the reservoir in a matter satisfactory to them."

Guy Waldo, speaking for the interests of the Flambeau Paper Company, said that he would like to have water from the new reservoir in the winter. But he was also aware, based on his experience of winter releases of water from the Rest Lake Dam, of the probability that said water would freeze up and not be available until spring. According to the minutes of this meeting, the parties present agreed "that the greater part of the water stored in the Flambeau Reservoir shall be released so that it will be received by the operating plants before it has a chance to freeze."

At the same meeting, the directors tackled a somewhat different but equally complex operational matter: how to apportion tolls when one operator has an emergency and requires a sudden release of water. A breakdown of a steam generator in Park Falls and a request for extra water for power generation seems to have prompted this discussion. Questions abounded. Should tolls be spread around as in normal circumstances? Or should the operator who requires the water pick up the toll charges for others? And what if there is rain somewhere in the system that occurs simultaneously with an emergency release? How much is the flow attributable to rain, how much to the release? In the end, the directors did what all institutions do when confronted with a thorny problem: they formed a committee.

What is interesting about these two challenges—the basic, ongoing regulation of storage and discharge, and a formula for apportioning the costs of special discharges—is that the CFIC seems to have been inventing part of their business model on the fly, as it were. Why Byllesby could not tap its own experience for some more specific guidance remains unclear. Perhaps Byllesby saw its role as deferring to the needs and preferences of the operating companies; or it may have been struggling to work out the "water politics" of the CFIC itself. No direction came from another possible source: the Railroad Commission. In authorizing the project, the commission had given the CFIC the ability to draw water as low as the mechanisms of the dam allowed, and it remained steadfast in its support of the main operating principles as articulated in the law of 1911 that created the CFIC: that the CFIC should "so manage, operate, and maintain" the reservoir system as to assure "as nearly a uniform flow of water as practicable... at all times and at all points on said Chippewa and Flambeau rivers; and during the times when it may be found impracticable to maintain at the same time such uniform flow of water throughout the entire length of said rivers, the upper portions of said rivers shall be given preference." But the commission neither recommended nor ordered a schedule for raising and lowering elevations that would help to achieve such a goal. The commission seemed content— at least initially—to let the CFIC manage the water however it wanted, without regard for the consequences. The shortcomings of this approach were soon to become glaringly and awkwardly apparent.

The Flambeau River Lumber Company (FRLC), whose office and sawmill were located in Ladysmith, Wisconsin, cut, milled, and sold softwood lumber starting sometime around 1913. In the mid-1920s, it logged on its own lands along the Flambeau River in Sawyer County and floated the timber downstream to its riverside mill. FRLC employed about 450 people, including loggers, and its mill could turn out 100,000 feet of lumber every 10 hours of operation. It was, in short, an established and substantial enterprise.

In the winter of 1924-1925, the company had cut and assembled on and near the ice of the North Fork of the Flambeau River near Babbs Island (located in eastern Sawyer County, where County Road W crosses the river) 8,790,850 feet of logs in anticipation of driving them downstream in the coming spring. But when the ice left the river, the company found itself undertaking a log drive with an unusually low stream flow caused by the exceptional dry spell of that year. With great difficulty and over a prolonged time, the crew managed to get the logs below the junction of the north and south forks of the river, but little farther. The logs jammed up at Cedar

Rapids and had to be abandoned until the next year. In the winter of 1925-1926, the company racked up an additional 3,797,460 feet of lumber at the same location. When spring arrived, so did heavy rains, and all would have gone well for the combined log drive had there not been a new obstacle to the spring flow. Unbeknown to the lumber company, the CFIC had begun in April to fill both the Flambeau Reservoir and the Rest Lake impoundment, which substantially reduced their discharge rates. Once again, the FRLC struggled with its drive. It was only when the CFIC, in response to the complaints of the lumber company, raised the discharge rate to above 1,000 cfs for nine days in mid-May that the drive could be completed.

The reactions of the two companies to these events were predictably quite different. The CFIC made an informal request of its regulator, the Railroad Commission, for some instructions on how to operate the flowage in the event of a log drive. The commission held a hearing on September 1, 1926, and issued its ruling in early March of the following year. After acknowledging that the time for filling reservoirs coincided with the time for log drives and that conflict between the two practices was a likely consequence, the commission argued that providing a flow equivalent to "the natural and usual flood would, therefore... impair the ability of the Improvement company to conserve the water supply for equalizing the flow throughout the year as contemplated by the act." It then ordered the CFIC to discharge 621 cfs when a log drive is underway, with the stipulation that a timber company planning a log drive notify the CFIC and the commission five days in advance of said drive. The FRLC, however, did not find this order to its liking and sought a new hearing before the commission. Pursuant to this hearing, the commission came forth, in March of 1928, with yet another order. This time, it developed a complicated scheme for managing both the Flambeau and Rest Lake reservoirs, based on the notion that they should be filled during the course of a 95-day period. To accomplish this goal, discharge rates were to be reset every five days in response to the elevations of the flowages and the variations of the spring flood. But the bottom line was even tougher than that of its previous order: during a log drive, the discharge from the Flambeau Reservoir should not be allowed to fall below 150 cfs (a very low rate of discharge), and the water level in the flowage should never be allowed to drop during the spring storage period. This ruling was an unquestioned victory for the CFIC.

The Flambeau River Lumber Company not only tried— however unsuccessfully—to plead its case with the Railroad Commission, but it also sued the CFIC to recover damages for its losses. It sought reimbursement for extra expenses incurred in the drives of 1925 and 1926, for logs lost or damaged by prolonged immersion, and for profits foregone during the years 1927 to 1929, when the company did not attempt log drives. In total, it asked for $183,991 in damages. The Railroad Commission joined the CFIC as a defendant in the suit. A.H. Reid, the circuit judge in Rusk County, ruled that the CFIC bore no responsibility for the failed drive of 1925, but that the company had unlawfully withheld water in 1926. He awarded the plaintiff $7,400 in damages for the extra expenses of that drive. The judge refused to award damages for the years when the lumber company ran no drives. Finally, Judge Reid set aside the Railroad Commission order of March 1928, and he ordered the CFIC not to reduce the discharge of the Flambeau Dam below 1,350 cfs when a log drive was under way.

None of the parties to this case was satisfied with the ruling. The damages fell far short of the lumber company's claim, and the order on the rate of discharge was unacceptable both to the CFIC and the Railroad Commission. On appeal, the matter found its way to the Wisconsin Supreme Court. On May 12, 1931, the court issued interrelated rulings on two cases: *FRLC v. CFIC,* and *FRLC v. Railroad Commission of Wisconsin.* The Supreme Court affirmed the lower court's ruling on damages, as well as the decision to deny damages for the years when no drives took place. More importantly, the court also affirmed the decision to set aside the March 3, 1928, order of the Railroad Commission.

This latter judgment of the Supreme Court takes us to the heart of the case. In writing the opinion for the court, Justice Marvin Rosenberry turned the spotlight directly on the actions of the Railroad Commission. First, he cited language in Act 640 (the legislative charter of the CFIC), according to which the "commission... shall have supervision and control of the time and extent of the drawing of water from the reservoirs...." Second, he argued that said power should be used to advance the declared purposes of the act, which he found are "(1st) to improve navigation for log-driving purposes, and (2d) to maintain as nearly as practicable a uniform flow of water...." Third, the facts of the case show that the commission's order of March 3, 1928, would essentially make log driving impossible. As the justice wrote, "it is not sufficient to furnish water enough to float a cedar fencepost." In effect, he argued that the commission had set up its rules to favor hydropower rather than log driving. But the law, as written, put navigation first. "If with the passage of time," he observed, "navigation has been of decreasing importance, a new situation has arisen which must be dealt with by the legislature." Until then, he concluded, the Railroad Commission had an obligation to revise its rules in conformity with the principles laid out in the court's rulings. In short, the Railroad Commission had put its thumb on the scales on behalf of those it regulated and been caught out by the courts.

Neither the CFIC nor the Railroad Commission (as of 1931 it became the Public Service Commission) could have liked this outcome. Economically speaking, however, theirs was the forward-looking view. Log driving, for all intents and purposes, was a thing of the past, and hydro was the future. Yet, ironically, both the company and the commission had fallen victim to this very past. The right of the public to use navigable streams was well-embedded in the law, and the notion of "improving" waterways had been closely tied, from the beginning, to navigation for logging. In drafting Act 640, the legislature had simply adopted the well-established notion of improving waterways into its language on the creation of dams, even as it hid its real purpose behind this euphemistic language. The closest the act came to linking a uniform flow of water to the purpose of generating hydropower was the phrase, "improving the usefulness of said streams for all public purposes." The courts had no choice but to fall in line with the traditional view of improvement as it related to navigation.

In addition to his legal ruling, Justice Rosenberry also offered some friendly, common-sense advice to all the parties. "It is suggested that a spirit of reasonableness and cooperation would go far in solving the problems presented by the conditions which exist on many of the interior navigable waters of the state, to the end that the natural resources of the state shall be made available to the highest extent reasonably possible for all public purposes." This advice may have paved the way for a less-than-formal resolution of the next potential conflict between logging and hydropower. As of August 1933, the Public Service Commission, perhaps hoping that the whole problem would go away, had yet to act at all on the court's request that it prepare a new operating order for the Flambeau Reservoir. On the 22nd of the month, however, the commission revealed that the Flambeau River Lumber Company had reported its intention to conduct a drive in the spring of 1934, and had asked the commission to "make an order in conformity with the decree of the Supreme Court...." The commission set a date for a hearing at which the lumber company, the CFIC, and any other interested parties could present their views. The records of the Public Service Commission contain no formal order pursuant to that hearing, which may indicate that the matter was resolved informally with some "reasonableness and cooperation." Whether or not this was the case, in subsequent years conflicts over log drives disappear from the PSC reports, at least as they pertain to the CFIC. In the end, a new regime for Wisconsin's water powers emerged, one that was no longer accommodating of the traditional log drive.

The presence and operation of the Flambeau Reservoir had posed serious obstacles to longstanding practices on the river and confronted the CFIC with some awkward moments. Nevertheless, some redress for the aggrieved parties had been available through the courts, the Public Service Commission, and through direct negotiations. The same cannot be said for those who considered the erection of the dam to be nothing short of an offense to nature itself. The Flambeau had long been regarded by many—conservationists, hunters, anglers, trappers, and local residents among them—as the quintessential northwoods river. For eons, its copper-colored waters had run free, tumbling over rocky riffles and coursing smoothly past forests of mighty white pines, hemlocks, and yellow birch. Now these free-flowing waters had been interrupted by a dam at the river's very headwaters—a dam that subjected the river's downstream course to the manipulation of water levels for purely commercial purposes. Even worse, perhaps, was the fact that the upper Flambeau's replacement, as it were, was an aesthetically challenged storage reservoir, dotted with patches of standing timber and awash with floating logs and slash. Moreover, the ever rising and falling water levels in the flowage had killed shoreline vegetation and left exposed and eroded banks.

This epic transformation of the landscape was ably recorded in a short, silent film made in 1930—probably by the Conservation Commission, though the film carries no attribution. The power of the film lies in its visual images, as well as with the accompanying subtitles that reinforce these images in no uncertain terms. "The Flambeau Turtle Flowage—the greatest destruction of nature's beauty in the State of Wisconsin.... Where at one time there was a fine stand of beautiful white pines and hardwood, now the dead trees stand as a monument to destruction.... When the water is down to lower levels, numerous pot holes are created in which millions of fish of all sizes and descriptions are landlocked and die. This is an annual occurrence." There was no doubt in the minds of many Wisconsinites that a state treasure had been ruined. In their eyes, the barons of industry had destroyed a precious river, and the land adjacent to it, beyond repair.

And so it was, amid controversy in the courts over the impact of the dam on traditional logging practices and within public opinion over the loss of a natural treasure, that the Turtle-Flambeau Flowage began its existence. But neither the proponents nor the opponents of this new impoundment were aware of history's joker in the deck: the unintended consequences of intended actions. The immediate future, as it turns out, was to be shaped less by conscious human action than by Mother Nature's prodigious powers to heal and to multiply. In fact, her transformative hand was at work from the minute the dam gates closed and the waters began to rise. But no one seems to have seen what was coming, let alone recognize how quickly it would arrive.

CHAPTER FIVE

Lands and Waters of the Turtle-Flambeau Flowage: The Early Years

The CFIC and the Lands of the Flowage

A witty friend once remarked, in reflecting on the long-term demands of child-raising, that "once you have children, you have them." And so it is for those who create flowages. To be sure, the leaders of the Chippewa and Flambeau Improvement Company (CFIC) had a deep and abiding interest in managing the buildup and discharge of flowage water on behalf of both their operating companies and their shareholders. And, as we have seen, E.P. Sherry remained dedicated to closing out the remaining handful of contentious land purchases and, in the case of the Jerome property, disposing of an expensive liability. But it was to the bigger issues pressing on the CFIC, such as the lawsuit with the Flambeau River Lumber Company or working out a sensible flow regime, that Sherry and his colleagues directed their greatest efforts in the first years of the flowage's existence. Once those issues were resolved, Sherry seems to have refocused his attention on his own business interests and on the management of the CFIC, whose president he became in 1930. These preoccupations drew little public notice, and Sherry's name all but disappears from the scant public record on the flowage during these years. After his death in 1941, executives from Northern States Power Company—often also serving as officers of the CFIC—became the spokespersons for the corporate interests of the flowage.

As a consequence of these developments, it seems fair to say that the CFIC had little interest in the property as a whole apart from actually operating the dam and tidying up incomplete land acquisitions. Almost all of the merchantable timber had been harvested before the dam gates closed and the waters rose, so there was no near-term need for forest management. Public use of the land and water had virtually no bearing on the company's essential interests, nor could such use easily be curbed. As long as there were privately held parcels here and there, the public could hardly be kept off the water (and anyhow, the water itself was not the property of the CFIC); and policing the land to stop such activities as camping, hunting, or berry-picking could only cause headaches and costs for the folks in Eau Claire. On occasion the company did sell or lease a piece of land here and there on the flowage, but it was not company policy to actively divest itself of its holdings or develop flowage shoreline. The term "benign neglect" might well be used to describe the approach of the CFIC toward its flowage shorelines and islands.

Perhaps the only kind of occurrence that might have drawn the attention of the CFIC to these properties was fire. The possibility of fire was always high in slash-filled cutovers of the kind that were left after the hasty pre-flowage logging, and the sources of ignition, whether from nature or from the unregulated presence of campers and picnickers, were many. But in the early years of the flowage, even fire did not seem to provoke a response. In July of 1933, for example, some 20 to 25 fires broke out in the region supervised by the Park Falls fire warden. The most serious of these burned along a six-mile front about 10 to 12 miles to the west of Mercer and, according to an account in the *The Milwaukee Journal,* was bearing down on the "Forest Wanderer Lodge" (no doubt the reporter had in mind Forest Wonder Lodge, a property located on Swamp Creek Road). The fire, blamed on "campers and berry pickers," raced through slash and dried-up marshes and appeared to pose a threat to Mercer as well. Both the lodge and the town were spared, however, when a shift in wind direction and a light rain helped firefighting crews to control its spread. But this fire left its mark both on the landscape—some charred stumps and snags can still be seen in lower reaches of Four Mile Creek—and on the memory. A youthful Mitch Babic, later to become a well-known Mercer guide, barely escaped with his life while fighting this fire. He and several others had been using an abandoned logging shack near Four Mile Creek as a base for their work. As the fire drew near, they evacuated the structure—and just in time—as some dynamite, which an earlier logging operation had stored in the shack and left behind, blew up and demolished the building. No accounts of CFIC reactions to the fire appeared in the press.

In October of 1948, a period of severe drought and low water, a fire broke out among the dry, woody debris on an exposed portion of the lakebed. It took 50 to 60 men four days to squelch the blaze, but not before it had torched 100 acres. Fortunately, they were able to save Rudy's Resort on Trude Lake, which had been in the initial path of the fire.

Ten years later a major fire—the worst in the state in 10 years—

directly affected the flowage. It broke out in late May on an island in the Beaver Creek area when a campfire burned out of control. Soon after breaking out, the fire leaped 300 feet to the mainland and took hold there. Despite vigorous efforts to control it by Bob Tietgen, a forest ranger, and Everett Seifert, the area fire warden, and two fishermen whose boat they had commandeered, the fire took on new life when a gust of wind carried flames onto a pile of cedar driftwood. As described by the noted outdoor writer, Dave Duffey, "the dry wood went off like a gasoline explosion, blasting out sheets of flame 100 yards long.... Conifer trees became torches, heavy smoke obscured all details, and firefighters on foot bumped into trees as they fumbled through the smoke." The already substantial problems posed by a fire in a cutover were compounded by the difficulties of gaining access to it through boggy areas. At the peak of the firefighting operation, 200 high school youth from Mercer, Park Falls, Hurley, and Woodruff had joined 100 men (40 of whom had been dispatched by St. Croix Rods, a fishing tackle manufacturer in Park Falls) on the fire lines. When the fire was finally suppressed four days later, 500 acres had burned. According to Duffey, crews doing the final mopping up had to extinguish two additional campfires that had been left burning by anglers, one on an island and the other on the mainland. The whole experience left a bad taste in the mouth of Ranger Tietgen, who felt that there had been enough anglers on the flowage the day the fire broke out to have put it out with water from their minnow buckets. Instead, he grumbled, they motored up to the scene, watched the initial four firefighters frantically at work, and motored off.

This fire, and the obvious potential for others like it, finally moved the CFIC to action. In March of 1959, company officials met with the Iron County Forestry Department to talk about setting up "cookout" campsites on islands and other places on the flowage. The goal was to restrict fires to areas where they could be controlled. Shortly thereafter, Stuart Willson, president of the CFIC and of Northern States Power, announced a new company program to protect northern Wisconsin resources and to enhance public usage on all of the company's lands and waters. The program called for "tree planting, new and better access roads to company-owned shoreline, picnic areas, and shore dinner points for fishermen." In addition, he noted that "agreements have been reached with the majority of area resort owners to assist in developing the area for both public and resort use," though no specifics on these agreements were forthcoming. There is little reason to doubt that this initiative was driven by the company's concerns about fire and the liabilities that were likely to follow in its wake. Indeed, Willson acknowledged directly that fire prevention was an objective of the program. "We believe that, by providing specified areas for campers, picnic groups, fishermen and others, fire hazards will be reduced." Whatever its motivation may have been, the CFIC had, after more than 30 years of inaction, committed itself to ensuring that the flowage was both more accessible to and safer for outdoor enthusiasts.

A New Fishery in a New Body of Water

If the CFIC displayed little, if any interest, in the land surrounding the flowage—at least until 1959—it had even less incentive to bother itself with what went on beneath the surface of the flowage's waters. As it turns out, however, what was taking place in waters deep and shallow would prove decisive in creating a distinct identity for the flowage—an identity that quickly attracted people from far and near to its shores and waters, and that subsequently elicited both private and public efforts to sustain its unspoiled character into the future. At the heart of this identity was a rugged body of water with an abundance of fish.

Once anglers got out on the flowage, they found themselves in an unaccustomed environment. The flowage was anything but a typical northwoods lake, where an angler's attention was invariably drawn to weed beds, points, and the occasional deep rock pile. The flowage, by contrast, had relatively few weeds (especially deep ones), much of its complex structure could not be inferred from shoreline features, and it was choked with wood, both standing and floating. It was clear from the beginning that anglers would have much to learn about its waters and how to pursue their quarry. But what most differentiated the flowage from other north country lakes was its overall visual impact, an edgy blend of the primordial, the adventurous, the dangerous, and the mysterious. Fred Losby, a Springstead area guide and resort owner, said as much in reflecting on the flowage in this earlier era: "I wish you could have seen the flowage in them days. When they flooded the flowage, they didn't cut the trees down like they have to do now. Them trees and stumps stayed there. The only way they ever got removed was by the ice taking them out in the wintertime and then the spring when it thawed out. And, oh, that was a mess with all them logs floating around and of course there wasn't very many motors in them days for the boats. We rowed."

Setting aside the problems of floating wood, navigating just the standing timber was no easy task, and guides and others often tied flags or ribbons to emergent trees to mark channels from shore to open water and back. Furthermore, in the right circumstances, the whole scene could become downright eerie. Some of Losby's clients, particularly women, found the atmosphere more than a little discomfiting. "That was a dreary, dreary place," Losby recalled. "It was misty and you know horrible weather. And all these dead trees sticking up and that. A lot of them women they see that, they say 'my god, this is a haunted place there. I don't like to be here... it give me the shakes.' 'Ah,' I says 'that's nothing.'" Another woman told him that the flowage "looked more like a graveyard with all them dead trees" and insisted that Losby take her home. Ever the sensitive guide, Losby sought to dispel such unease with his own brand of dark humor. "I've had a lot of women specially say 'Fred, what would you do if we fell into the lake?' Well, I says I usually throw them an anchor, then I know where they're at. They got a good laugh out of that, they did, they thought that was something."

The flowage as viewed from the dam in October of 1926, the flowage's first autumn. Mark Fort Photo Collection

That the flowage proved difficult, and perhaps a bit unnerving to those who initially plied its waters, seems to have been a matter of utter indifference to the fish below. They had been adapting to the waters of this area for millennia, and the construction of a dam was not about to bring this to a halt. To be sure, the creation of the flowage did not introduce species previously unknown to the waters of the area, but it did liberate all the native species from the confines of their home lakes, rivers, and streams, opening up for them a vast and varied playground in which to act out their respective genetic heritages. In October of 1926, when the flowage first reached full pool, these fish may have been dazed by all the empty water around them, yet they seem to have quickly seized upon the new role that had fallen upon them—to colonize every useable nook and cranny of the flowage. It is probable, in the view of Lawrence Eslinger, a fisheries biologist with the Wisconsin Department of Natural Resources (WDNR), that the flowage fishery "got rolling almost immediately.... Primary production likely skyrocketed shortly after the flooding of the terrestrial habitats and vegetation, which would then proceed to stimulate fast growth and expansion of the fishes." The vegetation was plentiful: it included sunken tops, stumps, and smallish standing trees, all remnants of pre-flowage logging, and then there was the abundant forest understory that was inundated when flowage waters rose. In short, the very physical messiness inherent in the creation of a reservoir in this type of setting primed the pump for a burst in fish populations.

The Turtle River below Lake of the Falls in the early years of the Turtle-Flambeau Flowage. Mercer Historical Society

Nature's initial "stocking" populated the flowage and Trude Lake with some 25 distinct species of fish—including game fish, panfish, minnows, and a handful of others. Rather quickly, the fish sorted out their relationships with one another, and what emerged was a predator-dominated fishery. Walleyes, northerns, muskies, and black bass controlled the waters and, not surprisingly, drew the most attention from anglers. The flowage fishery has retained its predator-dominated character to the present day. This is not to say, however, that no other fish are there in sufficient numbers to draw the attention of anglers. Yellow perch, a Wisconsin table favorite, have their advocates among flowage anglers, as do black crappies, a species that prospered greatly after the creation of the flowage. Indeed, photos of large strings of crappies have a distinct place in the lore of the flowage. Several other species—bluegills, pumpkinseeds, and rock bass, for example—play supporting roles, especially when it comes to helping fill up the skillet. But at the end of the day, it is the toothy critters and the relentlessly aggressive bass that have most shaped the character of this north country fishery.

As the fish populated their new home, the anglers were not far behind. Fred Losby remembered it this way: "When the flowage was put up in '26, boy, that brought the people up here. The fish [especially]...." The flowage's reputation as an extraordinary fishery seems to have been well established in the mid-1930s, if not sooner. Not surprisingly, it was the flowage's top predator species—the muskellunge—that initially drew the greatest attention and publicity beyond the local area. Starting in 1933, Bert Claflin, an influential outdoor writer for the *Milwaukee Sentinel* and avid musky fisherman, championed musky fishing on the flowage in a number of enthusiastic articles. In addition to the standard fare of recounting types of covers fished, lures used, and fish taken, Claflin had a sharp eye for the overall appeal of the flowage, something that he captured in a column published in the *Sentinel* on March 20, 1937: "Talk about wild country! You seldom meet another human being, but you see all kinds of wild animals and you hear big muskies flop at intervals. The fresh air, the beautiful scenery, the sweet odor of unpolluted water, the goodfellowship [sic] that prevailed, the old clothes we wore—those are the things that make a trip to virgin country so enjoyable. It isn't just the fish. I recommend this water to you who would get out into nature at her best. There is no better muskie fishing in the state." These are words ideally suited to March, when, even as winter drags its departing feet, anglers begin to sense a certain flow of adrenaline that fuels anticipation of spring and summer days on the water. But more important, Claflin puts his finger on the very essence of the flowage: it is not just an excellent body of water in which to catch fish—most notably, muskies—it is also a special kind of place to be fishing. This sentiment has endured to the present day, and it regularly resurfaces in the words of anglers and guides.

The frequent press coverage given to musky fishing in the early days of the flowage is understandable, as this topic gave outdoor writers a chance to expound on a dramatic fish in a spectacular setting. But muskies were not the prime target for the majority of anglers who took to the flowage's waters either then or now, notwithstanding the current boom in ultra-serious musky hunting. What drew most anglers to the flowage were species of fish that provided far more consistent action, as well as good table fare—walleyes, bass, crappies, perch, and northern pike. From the beginning, then, the flowage was seen as a place where one could go to fill a stringer, sometimes with a single targeted species, other times with a mixed bag of tasty fish. It was, in short, a "fried fish and potatoes" fishery, where anglers got down to the basics of working hard for fish they wanted to keep and eat. Of course, the odd trophy fish was welcome, though it was rarely the main object of pursuit. It would, however, be a serious mistake to see the flowage as just some northwoods variant of a fish market; it was also, as we have seen, vast, rugged, awesome, sometimes forbidding, and often challenging. Ultimately, then, it was the combination of good fishing and a captivating wilderness that was to shape the popular view of the flowage for generations of anglers and non-anglers alike. Life could not be any better than a day spent on its waters, whether acquiring the makings of a hearty fish fry or simply reveling in its beauty.

As noted earlier, the flowage contained from the beginning all the species of fish present in it today. But the relative abundance of any given species has been subject to change over time. This fact is most evident with walleyes, which have been the signature fish for catch-and-keep anglers for the bulk of the flowage's existence. Although anecdotal evidence makes it clear that some walleyes found their way onto anglers' stringers in the early days of the flowage, Art Schmidt Jr., the son of a pioneering resort owner, once told an interviewer that there were "no walleyes in the flowage for the first years after its creation." The dominant fish, in his memory, were muskies, bass, northern pike, and crappies. Schmidt may well have exaggerated a bit to make his point, but he was on target in seeking to distinguish the early flowage fishery from what followed. Nor was he alone. Writing in 1937, Burt Claflin noted the excellent bass fishing, especially toward evening. Whether these were largemouth or smallmouth, he did not say; but both fish were present in good numbers in those days, and, in contrast to today's catch-and-release fishing, bass mostly went on the stringer. These bass, it seems, continued to play a large role in the flowage, even as the walleye population became more numerous. In 1940, Dan Vickers, the postmaster in Park Falls and an active promoter of the flowage, wrote that "our bread and butter fish on these waters are the walleyes, bass, crappies, etc. You can always catch 'em."

It was that promise of catching lots of fish to eat that attracted anglers to the flowage in the wartime summer of 1945. In a July 3rd article in the *The Milwaukee Journal* titled "Meat Hungry Anglers Seek Answer in the North," Gordon McQuarrie pointed out that a war-weary population, whose meat intake had been limited by rationing, was on the hunt for meat—in this case, fish. People from Milwaukee and Chicago told him that once they got to the lake they were "living on meat [i.e., fish]... and we'll take home all the law allows." (Before portable coolers became standard household items, Art Schmidt's resort packaged fish for transit in cedar boxes filled with flowage ice, sawdust, and, of course, fish.) It was not just dedicated, lifelong anglers who showed up; whole families piled into boats and headed for prime water. Al Koshak, another early resort owner, told McQuarrie that his guests were putting pressure on the flowage to get something into the frying pan, although he went on to observe that "bass, walleye, and crappie" were present in abundance. Indeed, some "locals" claimed that the flowage had, in effect, rested during the early years of the war and was consequently primed for a heavy harvest. McQuarrie was skeptical of this notion, and rightly so. The better explanation may well be that the flowage was continuing to evolve into an ever more productive fishery.

What is for certain is that the physical character of the flowage was gradually changing, and as it did new types of fish habitat came into being. Floating timber, drifted or blown toward leeward shores, built up into rafts, which often became anchored to the land. Standing trees eventually rotted off at the waterline, although their trunks were still firmly rooted to the bottom even as their separated tops floated toward the shores. In time, vast logjams built up, some of them extending 100 yards or more from shore—city blocks, some people say. The greatest concentration of logjams lay along the east side of the "Big Water" (the large southwestern arm of the flowage), but there were other jams, large and small, throughout the flowage. Finally, some wood, saturated at last, simply sank to the bottom.

This gradual rearrangement of the flowage's wood had a profound impact on fishing. First, it facilitated access to mid-lake structures. Second, it distributed bits and pieces of wood across across the bottom in such a way as to provide good cover for fish. Third, the truncated standing trees, especially those that leaned substantially ("leaners," as they are locally called), proved to be excellent places to fish. And finally, and most importantly, the logjams became attractive refuges for fish, especially light-averse walleyes.

It also seems likely that this transformation of the physical character of the flowage contributed in some manner to the emergence of the walleye as the flowage's most prolific and most sought-after denizen. This phenomenon became increasingly clear in the years following the extreme low water of 1948. As longtime flowage guide Joe Golomb told Don Johnson of the *Milwaukee Sentinel*, that disastrous summer marked a turning point in the fishery: "Before that, bass were the big thing here. After the water was raised again, the walleyes really came on strong." Whether and by what means the low water level might have influenced the relative abundance of bass and walleyes remain matters of speculation. But the walleye's burgeoning presence was incontestable; and the outdoor press, not surprisingly, was more than ready to put its stamp of approval on this change. An article in the *Milwaukee Sentinel* edition of June 30, 1957, declared that the flowage offered "some of the state's best walleye fishing from June well into July." Similar praise followed, from time to time, right into the early 1980s. Writers described bringing copious numbers of walleyes to the boat, and not a few to the skillet, as they fished, and fished again, with various area guides. From the 1950s on, then, the word was out: the Turtle-Flambeau Flowage meant walleyes, and vice versa. Just how important the walleye was to the reality and image of the flowage would become abundantly clear in the 1980s, when Wisconsin's Chippewa tribes sought to reclaim hunting and fishing rights that had been negotiated in 19th century treaties.

During the years when the walleye was on its way to becoming synonymous with the flowage, a new assessment of the overall aspect of the flowage's waters gained what proved to be a lasting foothold. In May of 1966, Tom Guyant of the *The Milwaukee Journal* chronicled a trip on the flowage with Park Falls guide Len Urquhart. They caught the makings of a fine walleye shore lunch while fishing jigs on gravel bars at the tips of islands. Guyant was taken not only by his time spent catching and eating fish but also by his surroundings, which, with the disappearance of so much standing timber, had assumed a new visage. "The Flambeau Flowage is wild real estate, a region which is seldom crowded. It reminds a man of Canada's canoe country," he wrote. Indeed, by that time the comparison to Canada was well on its way to becoming a much-used description of the flowage, and has remained so to the present.

The First Interventions

And so the flowage fishery emerged and evolved. The indigenous fish of the rivers and lakes that were incorporated into the newly created Turtle-Flambeau Flowage carried out—on their own and quite successfully—the task of stocking the broad expanse of this new body of water. The predator-dominated fishery that they and their progeny brought into being drew anglers in great numbers, which in turn led to the creation of a local resort industry that gave enormous satisfaction to generations of visitors. But for all the spontaneity and serendipity that marked these events, the fact remains that the flowage fishery was not some fixed, self-regulating system, impervious to forces for change, whether internal or external. From very early on, it turns out, flowage fish both needed and benefited from human intervention on their behalf. This intervention had three basic aspects: efforts to rescue flowage fish from naturally occurring emergencies; spontaneous and somewhat disjointed citizen initiatives to enhance the fishery; and the establishment by the state of regulatory regimes designed to protect the fishery from overharvest by anglers.

The flowage was but three years old when its finny inhabitants faced their first severe crisis: a string of low water years that began in August of 1929 and ran well into the middle of the next decade. The resultant conditions imperiled the budding fishery and raised alarms among fishery professionals and citizens alike. A report in the November 23, 1929, edition of the *Iron County News* spoke of a "fish rescue and stock experiment carried out... in the head waters of the Flambeau River at the junction of the Turtle and Manitowish rivers." The problem, it seems, was that the water in the flowage (unnamed, even in the local paper!) created by the dam at that location had fallen to such a low point that "many fish were stranded in landlocked pools which were rescued by the department of fisheries men and planted in nearby lakes." Whether these were some of the natural lakes that had become part of the flowage or totally separate pockets of deep water is not clear from the news account. B.O. Webster, the state's superintendent of fisheries, reported that they had worked five miles up the Turtle River in their efforts at rescue and restocking. Webster went on to speculate that this rescue operation might herald a new technique in fisheries management: "New flowages should give more food for the fish because of the great amount of vegetable matter submerged. Consequently, if we could plant extensively in flowages and later take the fish out after they have had advantage both of natural water and good food, it should certainly help in our program to distribute larger fish." For its part, the Wisconsin Conservation Commission found the operation to have been of sufficient merit to recommend that it be repeated the following year. Whether there was a follow-up is unknown.

In a related story, the December 16, 1929, edition of the *Eau Claire Daily News* contained an Associated Press report that noted that the state's attorney general had given the Conservation Department the "legal power to start action against power companies operating dams to the detriment of fish life." The article goes on to say "... where there are no suitable sluices or other means of escape for fish around or past dams in Wisconsin streams there are many thousands of them killed. Raising and sudden lowering of the waters above or below the dams also leaves many fish stranded that have been carefully reared by the Department." Some action was expected from the Conservation Commission, but for the moment the attorney general's ruling was said to be under review. Though the idea of constructing means by which fish could move to safety either above or below dams was to appear later in connection with the flowage, nothing ever came of it. The Rest Lake Dam, however, did have such a capability: a ladder invented in 1931 by Henry Barr of Ironwood permitted fish to pass from the Manitowish River into Rest Lake. According to an article in the July 4, 1931, edition of the *Wakefield News*, the intent of this structure was to permit some of the healthy brood stock that came up the Manitowish River from the flowage to propagate in the Rest Lake flowage and enhance its fishery. The ladder was still in operation in 1942.

A lone observer stands on the dry lakebed of the flowage during a drought year (date unknown). Mercer Historical Society

During the first half of the next decade, there were certainly occasions for rescue operations of the kind Webster had undertaken in 1929. On June 10, 1931, the flowage water level measured 14 feet below full pool, a number that was matched in late September of 1934; in October of 1933, the water level fell to a mere 12.6 feet below full pool. There is no record of action taken on behalf of the fish populations in these years, and one can only speculate as to whether any efforts were made to mitigate the damage. For certain, however, these potentially disastrous circumstances made a powerful impression on opponents of the reservoir and its management regime and figured in their critiques of the flowage. The official records of water levels (prepared by the CFIC and later Northern States Power) show that the flowage reached its all-time low for the open water season on October 10, 1948, when it measured 1,557 feet MSL, or 15 feet below full pool. That year is enshrined in the collective memory of area residents and longtime visitors, though they do not always get the year right. Mitch Babic recalled that the low water exposed abandoned railbed from the logging era in parts of the flowage, to say nothing of the huge amounts of standing timber still firmly rooted to the bottom. As historically interesting as such a sight may have been, it paled in relation to the desperate situation for the fish. In an attempt to save as many as possible, volunteers dug trenches to connect stranded groups of fish; and they seined fish in shallow pockets and moved them to deeper water.

After 1948, the flowage never again fell so low as to threaten the fishery. In fact, the lowest levels did not exceed seven feet below full pool, and that on only a few occasions. In 1957, it fell to 1,565 feet MSL and in the following year the water level hovered around 1,566 or a shade lower until July 1, when it rose sharply thanks to 12 inches of rain that fell in June and July. The last episode of significantly low water took place in 1976, when the level dropped a bit below 1,666 feet MSL from late September through mid-December. If the fish got a pass in these years, boaters did not. The hazards to navigation that lurked just under the surface, as well as those exposed to view, left lasting impressions on many a flowage user.

The management of the flowage fishery by WDNR scientists and technicians has never taken place in a vacuum. Local and faraway anglers, guides, resort owners, merchants, and civic organizations have always had a stake in the success of the flowage fishery. These interested parties—today grouped under the bureaucratic rubrics of "stakeholders" and "partners"—have never been hesitant to voice their concerns and complaints, whether from a barstool podium or through direct conversation with fishery biologists. Nor have they been shy about offering a slew of recommendations for surefire solutions to problems. When it comes to action, these groups and individuals have occasionally operated independently, but far more often they have established some type of working relationship with the WDNR.

Perhaps the first attempt of the public to influence the development of the flowage fishery was undertaken by the Mercer Chapter of the Izaak Walton League of America—one of a number of conservation groups that emerged in the first decades of the 20th century. In a letter dated February 28, 1931, M.E. Brandt, the chapter secretary, wrote to Donald Boyd, the secretary of the CFIC, stating that "we wish to close a small part of the flowage area to fishing during the month of June each year to help the breeders and afford protection for a short time after spawning. The area we have in mind is on the west side of the Turtle—and takes in all of Four Mile Creek from its source to where it joins with the Turtle." Brandt concluded by asking the CFIC to provide a map showing the parcels that would be involved in creating such a refuge. Boyd sent Brandt's letter along to E.P. Sherry with the following comment: "I believe we should send this so as to appear to be co-operating. Does this meet with your approval?" Sherry's archives contain no reply to Boyd's query, but the notion of "appearing to be co-operating" is something that one would not be surprised to find in the tactical arsenal of the CFIC or of Sherry's various companies.

The first large-scale and consequential effort to enhance the flowage fishery began in 1934 when the Mercer Lakelands Association, which described itself as "a Civic Organization," held a benefit dance at Camp Roosevelt to raise money for the construction of a fish hatchery. Potential donors were attracted to the event by the promises that "a good orchestra will play and the admission will be nominal." Construction, which seems to have been carried out by the Mercer Rifle Club, began that summer, and the project, located at the Lake of the Falls Dam, was completed in 1935. Mercer businesspeople then donated hatchery jars. The facility began operation the following year, and in 1937 the hatchery raised and stocked 167,040 musky fry in the flowage. Walleye stocking from the facility began the next year, and by 1940 the hatchery produced 6 million walleye and musky fingerlings.

The waters of the Turtle River swirl around Mercer's citizen-sponsored fish hatchery. Mercer Historical Society

What prompted local leaders to establish a hatchery remains unclear. It seems likely that the previously noted episodes of extremely low water in 1929, 1931, 1933, and 1934 had a good deal to do with it. For a body of water that averages between 10 and 15 feet in depth, such low water levels were bound either to isolate some fish populations in shallow pockets or to concentrate them in deeper river channels and old lake basins. Considerable mortality could be expected in either instance. Whatever the cause for its construction, the hatchery swung into full production, and the stocking of walleye and musky from it continued until the facility closed in 1942.

A rather more quixotic effort to improve fishing on the flowage took the form of a petition, dated October 20, 1936, addressed to the Wisconsin Conservation Commission and the Public Service Commission: "We the undersigned, sportsmen, citizens and/ or taxpayers, interested in the general locality adjacent to the Turtle-Manitowish River in Section 34, Town 42 North R.2 East, Iron County, Wisconsin, having in mind the statutory policy once in force in this state, the great benefits to fish propagation and conservation, and knowing of the existence of a dam, commonly named Flambeau Dam, on and across said river, respectfully petition and request that a Lock Type Fish Way be installed in said dam." The petition was signed by Frank Vaughn of Mercer and 279 other signatories—some of them local, others from elsewhere in Wisconsin and beyond. The reference to Section 34 clearly relates to the dam site, but the rationale for the petition can only be described as opaque. There are no clues to which "statutory policy" the petitioners had in mind, nor are the "benefits to fish propagation and conservation" spelled out. It is possible that the petitioners, having experienced the adverse consequences of the severe drawdowns of the early 1930s, felt that the river might be a source of fish to replenish the flowage. Conversely, they may have felt that river fishing could be improved by making it possible for fish to descend from the flowage into the North Fork of the Flambeau—though it seems unlikely the river had such a numerous set of advocates at that time.

The Public Service Commission (PSC), acknowledging its responsibility to review "the reasonableness of equipment for any dam in Wisconsin," duly scheduled a hearing on the petition for December 8, 1936, in Madison. Notice was sent to the *Iron County News* in Hurley for publication in advance of the hearing. On the day of the hearing, two representatives of the CFIC and one representative of the Conservation Commission appeared before Adolph Kanneberg and one other member of the Public Service Commission. But for reasons unknown, not one of the 280 petitioners showed up. Kanneberg asked G.E. Laughlin of the CFIC if he had anything to say. "No, we don't know what it is all about," Laughlin responded. "It is about a fishway," Kanneberg said. "I know, but let's see what the others have to say first," replied Laughlin. Kanneberg then announced that "we will hold the matter open," and the hearing closed. No follow-up communications or decisions appear in the public records of the PSC. In the end, this citizen initiative failed even to make its case before the proper authorities, let alone secure its objectives.

Enter the State of Wisconsin

As well-meaning as these various citizen-driven interventions were, they were sporadic, and on some occasions totally ineffectual. In the end, this fishery, like all others in the state, stood in need of the kinds of ongoing protection that could only be provided by state-administered fish and game regulations. When the flowage opened in 1926, its waters were subject to regulations set by the state legislature and uniformly applied throughout the state. Although some bag limits of the time seem in retrospect to be truly excessive—30 trout per day, for example—the size and bag limits pertinent to flowage predators appear to be reasonably protective, especially given the state's ample water resources and the limited pressure on them. According to the 1928 regulations, both largemouth and smallmouth bass had to be at least 10 inches in length with a bag limit of 10; walleyes had to be 13 inches with a bag of 10; the minimum length for northerns was 16 inches and the bag was 10; muskies had to be at least 30 inches in length and the bag was one. Clearly, those who set the rules were well aware of the value of the fabled musky to the state, a value that the one-fish limit helped to underscore. Setting length and bag limits were the first acts of human intervention in this newly created ecosystem, but they were far from the last.

As it happened, the early years of the flowage coincided with profound changes in the way sport fishing regulations were made and enforced in the state. The year 1927 witnessed the creation of the Wisconsin Conservation Commission, a policy-making body, and the Wisconsin Conservation Department (WCD), its executive arm. In the early 1930s, the WCD was authorized by the legislature to open and close seasons, prescribe bag limits, and regulate the methods of harvesting fish and game. This action brought about a major shift in responsibilities from the hands of the legislature into those of fish and game professionals. In 1934, another partner—the sporting public—came to the table of fish and game regulations with the introduction of county game committees, which in 1939 became known as the Wisconsin Conservation Congress—the name it bears today. By statute, the Conservation Congress is an "independent organization of citizens of the state and shall serve in an advisory capacity to the Conservation Commission" (later, to the Natural Resources Board). As it turned out, these developments set into motion, quite on purpose, an ongoing, working tension between citizen consumers of resources and fish and game conservers of resources. The former helped to set goals; the latter strove, if not to meet the consumers' fullest expectations, then at least to assure them satisfying days in the woods and on the waters. The Wisconsin Progressive solution took on its own, particular shape: private outdoor enthusiasts and public servants, working side by side, on behalf of resources they both treasured but nonetheless wanted to see utilized.

It was, of course, but a small step in aspiration—though a big one in practice—to move from conserving resources by means of protecting them to their outright management. But management was in the air, from the mid-1930s on, having been given a boost by the publication in 1933 of Aldo Leopold's influential book, *Game Management*. That work laid the groundwork for a more aggressive, science-based approach to natural resource issues, an approach that sought actively to shape natural communities— including those beneath the water. It would not be until the mid-1950s that the term "fish manager" gained traction among Wisconsin fisheries personnel, but the process of managing fish populations had been gradually maturing for some 20 years. The effects of this maturation could be seen in three areas: increasingly focused studies of fisheries, more elaborate regulations, and targeted stocking. The Turtle-Flambeau Flowage was to be front and center in each of these.

Fish Under Surveillance: The First Comprehensive Study of the Flowage

"Knowledge is power," one of the wisest of adages reminds us. And nowhere is this adage more appropriate than in fisheries management, where inadequate data or faulty assumptions can lead to useless, or even harmful, initiatives. Yet it is no easy task to obtain solid, reliable knowledge of what goes on in a complex world that is mostly hidden from our sight. Fortunately, the Turtle-Flambeau Flowage has been the object of well-conceived and carefully executed research for more than 60 years, and the data and conclusions of this research make the flowage perhaps the most thoroughly studied body of water in the state.

The first efforts to study the flowage fishery took the form of two voluntary creel censuses that were carried out in the summers of 1950 and 1951. The researchers distributed cards to anglers—mostly people from Milwaukee and Chicago staying at resorts on the flowage—and asked them to fill out and return the cards with information on their catches. The data gathered enabled the researchers to determine how many fish of each species were caught, how many man-hours it took to catch them, and what the size range of each species was. The data from the 1950 census was based on just 92 cards. In terms of numbers of fish, northern pike, at 472 fish, topped the survey. They were followed by crappies at 442, and walleyes at 349. Only 13 muskies were caught, but the largest was 50 inches. Northerns ranged in length from 18 to 28 inches, walleyes from 13 to 26. The researchers calculated that the catch per man-hour for all species (10 made the list) was .37. The data base for the 1951 survey was substantially larger—266 valid cards. Northerns, at 2,230, far and away topped the list, which also included walleyes at 583, and crappies at 311. Eighteen muskies turned up—including one 54-inch fish. The estimated number of fish caught per hour was .28—lower than that of the previous year. Fish sizes were similar to those of the previous census. Aside from the strong showing by crappies, which historically have done well in the early decades of artificial impoundments, the results were pretty much what one might suspect. The 1950 report confirms this, noting that "the low catch per man hour of .37 probably reflects the type of fish comprising the creel. It is dominated by predator groups of fish, the northern pike, walleye, and muskellunge. Under the circumstances it would not be expected to be large." Though nothing dramatic showed up in these two censuses, they provided what is now called baseline data—data against which subsequent information can be compared. The scientific study of the flowage was under way.

A second and far more substantial study took place in 1975 and 1976, when WDNR fisheries personnel conducted the first survey of the fishery in the flowage and Trude Lake, along with a companion creel census. By this time, walleyes had established themselves as the dominant fish in the flowage, and the work of the survey and the bulk of the subsequent report (written by James Lealos and Gerry Bever of the WDNR bureau of fish management and published in 1982) centered on them. The data gathered during spring and fall fieldwork were analyzed by means of a known research algorithm to produce population estimates for walleyes and northern pike during each of the two sampling periods. The survey also developed data on the size structure and growth rates of walleyes, northerns, and muskies. The creel survey conducted during the open water season of 1975 and the ice fishing season of 1975-1976 provided extensive data on angler harvests for a full year of fishing.

The survey (which combined data from the flowage and Trude Lake) found the walleye population to be both dominant and robust, apparently unaffected by the decision made more than a decade earlier to drop the 13-inch minimum length requirement for this species in the flowage. The population estimate for walleyes of all sizes for the spring of 1976 was 165,739, or 11.6 fish per acre; this number grew to 196,401, or 13.7 fish per acre, by the time of the fall survey, thanks in part to a very large class that year. Data from the spring sampling showed that an estimated 74,000 walleyes, 13 inches and larger, were available to anglers during the open water season. Northern pike population estimates were 23,154 for the spring and 36,243 in the fall. Data on muskies were not sufficient to permit a population estimate. Black bass turned up in even smaller numbers: 34 largemouth between 3 and 6.4 inches in length, and just 17 smallmouth, which ranged up to 15.4 inches.

The analysis of the creel census data showed that fishing pressure on the flowage was 14.8 hours per acre for the open water season, a number that, according to the report, "could be considered light by national, statewide, and regional standards." By way of explanation, the report cites the flowage's "distance from major population centers, unattractiveness for other water-related activities (water skiing, swimming, scuba, etc.), and the low species diversity of the fishery. This latter item probably influences pressure to the greatest degree, since angling for species other than walleye, muskellunge and northern pike is limited in scope. The walleye is intrinsically a hard-to-catch species and thus the casual, tourist angler may become discouraged fishing here." That said, the report estimates that anglers harvested some 35,525 walleyes during the course of the study. The exploitation rate, a ratio of the estimated harvest to the estimated spring population, was 21 percent for the entire year. Put another way, roughly one in five of the flowage's walleyes ended up on someone's stringer. Still, it took some time on the water to take these fish, as the open water harvest rate came in at 0.15 fish/hour; that is, it took slightly more than six and a half hours of fishing to catch one walleye. During the open water season, an average of 74 percent of the walleyes harvested were 13 inches in length or greater, and the average size of walleyes caught in the open water season was 14.6 inches and 1.2 pounds. Data derived from fin-clipped fish confirmed some suspected migration patterns: namely, that post-spawn walleyes remain near spawning sites for a while, slowly move away during mid-summer, and then return to areas near spawning sites in the fall. The creel survey also confirmed some popular wisdom that was solidly rooted among area anglers: most notably, that almost 50 percent of the open water harvest occurred in May; and that local anglers and those using guides enjoyed the most success when fishing for walleyes.

One of the report's most important passages dealt with the adequacy of walleye spawning habitat. Striking a positive note, the report asserted that "major spawning areas for walleye have been identified;" and it went on to argue that if protected from disturbance these areas should provide the flowage with adequate year-classes of walleyes. As a consequence, no stocking of hatchery-reared fish should be needed in the future. This conclusion called, in effect, for a sharp departure from past practice, as walleye stocking in the flowage had begun in the second half of the 1930s when fingerlings from the Mercer hatchery were planted in flowage waters for four consecutive years (1938 to 1942). From 1945 to 1948, only muskies were stocked, and walleye stocking resumed in 1950 with additional stocking in 1952, 1953, and 1956. No walleye stocking took place during the 1960s and 1970s.

In addition, during years when flowage walleyes were stripped of spawn and milt for hatchery operations elsewhere, a percentage of the resultant fingerlings were "planted back" into the flowage. In spite of the conclusion of the report from the 1975-1976 survey that no walleye stocking should be needed, the WDNR resumed the practice in 1980, 1982, 1983, 1991, and 1992. The last recorded stocking of walleyes in the flowage took place in 1994, at which point the stocking of hatchery-raised walleye ceased to be an active management tool. It should be noted that the WDNR moved promptly after the publication of the report on the 1975-1976 survey to protect critical spawning sites by setting up temporary refuges each spring at three locations: the waters immediately below the Lake of the Falls Dam, the waters around Sivert's Point, and on the Flambeau River below the flowage dam (a location where a variety of game species spawn). This practice, which is regarded as a major policy tool for sustaining the walleye population in the flowage, has continued to the present day.

Data on northern pike as gathered in the 1975-1976 survey turned out to be somewhat less definitive, largely because the catching and harvesting of northerns seems to have been an incidental by-product of fishing for other species. Few anglers specifically targeted northerns in the flowage because of their limited size. The creel census showed the average open water northern to have been 17.9 inches in length, and those caught through the ice averaged a fraction of an inch smaller. Indeed, only two northern pike captured during the population estimate phase of the study exceeded 27 inches. The northern, it seems, had become something of a problem child for the flowage. It had been protected by minimum length requirements—initially 16 inches in 1928, rising to 18 inches in the late 1940s—and it had been stocked in 1940 and 1941. In 1955, however, the minimum length requirement was eliminated, though a five-fish bag limit remained in place. Neither changes in size limits nor stocking, however, yielded northerns of a size attractive to anglers. The remarkably candid conclusions of the 1975 survey reflect on this reality: "Northern pike offer, in terms of size, a poor quality fishery to the angler. Protection of this species with season and bag restrictions while attempting to manage for muskellunge in the same water is unsound at best." The report recommended completely deregulating northerns on the flowage.

The survey report has the least to say about muskies and asserts that they do not appear to be overharvested. The creel survey found that anglers harvested 24 muskies that ranged from 30 to 47 inches and measured out "well above the state average." Moreover, these anglers reported returning 40 fish, both legal and undersized. Naturally reproducing muskies grew less well than stocked fish, which led the report to recommend continued stocking of this species. Muskies had been regularly stocked from 1937 through the end of the 1940s, irregularly for the period from 1950 to 1960, and again annually from the late 1960s. Despite the limitations of natural reproduction and the corresponding reliance on stocking, the musky fishery received an endorsement in the survey report that could have been taken from a chamber of commerce brochure: "The flowage offers a unique, almost pristine setting to the musky angler and continued management for this species is desirable." That management would require continued stocking and steadily high water levels during the spawning season. The report concludes by noting that "several large specimens are caught from its waters each year, and the possibility of a state record muskellunge living here cannot be discounted."

The comprehensive survey of 1975-1976 was the first study of its kind undertaken on a northern Wisconsin lake. As such, it served both as a model for work that would be done elsewhere in the state and as a possible starting point for continued monitoring of the flowage. That said, this study, carried out on such a large body of water, was quite costly and therefore unlikely to be repeated any time soon. But even as this information was being collected and analyzed, a chain of events had been set in motion that would render both the results of this survey and the experience gained in conducting it critically important to the future management of the flowage.

By the time the flowage marked its 50th anniversary in 1976, it had established a reputation as a first-class fishery, providing opportunities for anglers seeking top-of-the-hierarchy predators as well as those looking for a good dinner. The rough edges of its tree-studded beginnings had been worn off by time, and its various natural characteristics more and more resembled those of the fabled Canadian Shield with its ruggedly beautiful lakes and forests. Those who were drawn to it either to fish or simply to appreciate its natural setting treasured their moments on its shores and waters. During these 50 years the flowage also attracted the attention of those who wished, in one fashion or another, to shape its future. In 1926, the interested parties were but two: the CFIC and its overseer, the Railroad Commission. But soon the number grew to include citizen volunteers who came forward in times of crisis, organized citizen groups with an interest in enhancing the fishery, and, of course, the state of Wisconsin acting on behalf of the state's resources and citizens. To this point, the parties acted more or less in isolation from one another, but the stage was set for more and more vigorous interactions—and even for additional players. Valued assets do not go uncontested.

CHAPTER SIX

A Place to Rest Along the Way: The Resort Era

Resorts on the Rise

The 1989 movie *Field of Dreams* enriched our discourse with the famous line: "If you build it, he will come." What came to pass for the mythic ball field also held true for the flowage, though the anglers did not appear from the pines as rapidly as did the ballplayers from the corn. But come they did, and their growing presence increased the demand for boats, guides, and places to stay. Unfortunately, gaps in the sources make it difficult to date with precision the exact sequence by which various services came to the flowage. Still, it is possible to get a general sense of how a thriving resort industry came into being on this vast new body of water.

Before the construction of the Turtle Dam in 1926, the resort industry had only a modest presence in the general area of what was to become the Turtle-Flambeau Flowage. An undated advertisement for Al Seifert's Glennwood Resort on French Lake indicates the presence of only three other resorts within a six-mile radius of his property—the Jerome Hunting and Fishing Club on Trude Lake, and the Flambeau Lodge and the Feely Resort, both on Springstead Lake. One principal reason for the paucity of resorts in an area with an abundance of lakes is not hard to find: only two roads appear on the advertisement. One, labeled the "Road to Powell," starts at the Glennwood Resort and disappears off to the east, roughly along the course later to be followed by County Trunk G (still later to become State Highway 182). The other road, scarcely visible, heads northwest from the Jerome property. The map shows no way by which the three resorts in the Springstead area could be approached from the west, though a road from Park Falls to Stone Lake—the so-called East Road—was in existence at that time. Nor was there road access to most of the natural lakes that were to become part of the flowage, lakes such as Townline, Horseshoe, Bass, Rat, Musky (Muskellunge), Turtle, Baraboo, and Trude. All connections between and among these lakes and others are described in the advertisement as "trails," most of them having had their origins in logging or firefighting.

As if the absence of roads were not hindrance enough to the development of recreational facilities in the area, the few roads that did exist were in rough shape in good weather and impassable in bad. Here's how Fred Losby, a longtime Springstead resident, described them: "Boy, I'll tell you, the roads were all sand and ruts. There was no blacktop or gravel anywhere. It was something what tires [were like] in them days, the tires on the cars weren't made to travel very far. You had to carry casings with you and plenty of patches to patch up the tubes." In winter, the lack of plowing effectively shut down most all roads. In short, automobile travel in this area in the 1920s was a northwoods adventure of a special kind. But it was an adventure that dedicated anglers would never let stand between themselves and their quarry.

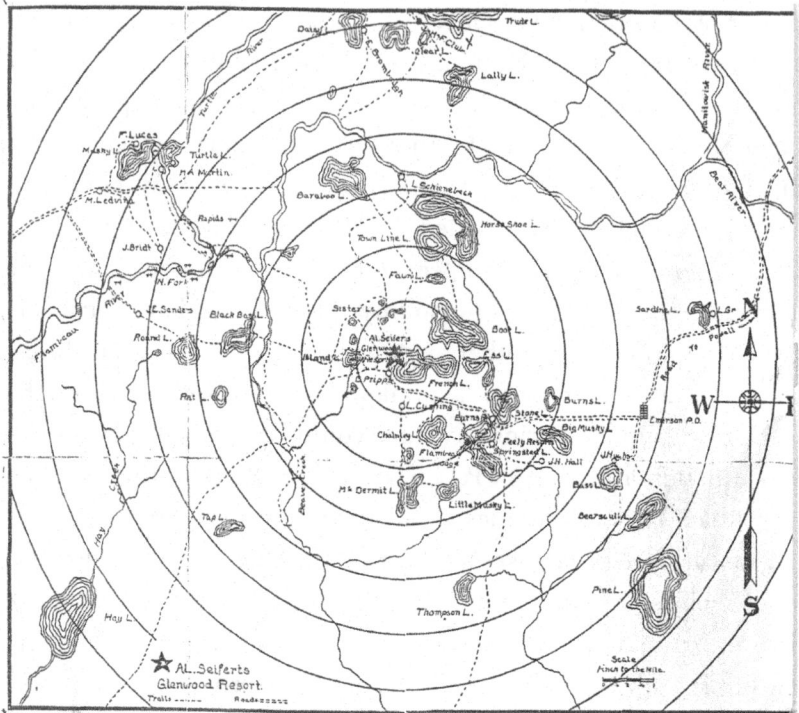

An early promotional map for Seifert's resort on French Lake. Of particular interest is the limited development of the road system in the area during the early 20th century. A member of the Turtle-Flambeau Flowage and Trude Lake Property Owners' Association

"A Map of the Famous Flambeau Flowage," prepared in 1938 for Northern States Power Company, shows the locations of five or six boat liveries, four resorts, and the Jerome Fishing and Hunting Club. The locations of these establishments are telling. Six of them—Jones Boats, Pemble Boats, the Popko Cabins, an unlabelled site (possibly Lacy's Boats), Trails End Resort (the former Merkle Lake Fishing and Hunting Club), and the Jerome Club—were all easily accessed by the road (today's Popko Circle West) that had served the two fishing and hunting clubs well before the flowage was built. By 1938, this road intersected a now completed road (today's County Highway FF) that linked Mercer with Butternut. Two other liveries, Schienebeck's and

An Accidental Jewel. Wisconsin's Turtle-Flambeau Flowage Flowage

Seifert's, were located on two points of land on the flowage that today bear their respective names, though with changed spellings. By this same year, these liveries could be reached using a road that ran from the tip of the peninsula (Schenebeck's Point) south to County Highway G, which was, in effect, an extension of the old Powell Road westward so as to link Manitowish and Park Falls. The remaining two resorts on this map of 1938 were Art Schmidt's Muskie Camp and Al's Place—both in the Bastine Lake area. A relatively short access road connected these two locations with the road from Mercer to Butternut. It seems safe to say, then, that the emergence of resorts in three distinct locations—along the road that paralleled the Turtle River, on the peninsula that divides the main arms of the flowage, and in the Bastine Lake area—depended to a large extent on improvements in a slowly maturing road system in the area. Subsequent expansion of resort facilities on the flowage was largely confined to two of these three areas—Bastine Lake, and the Turtle River and adjacent land on the flowage proper around to Norway Point.

The years just prior to WWII witnessed a rapid increase in the number of flowage resorts. An advertisement that appeared in the *Iron County Bulletin* in 1941 listed nine resorts, and a Chippewa and Flambeau Improvement Company map of the same year placed the total number of resorts at 11. Both sources identified seven resorts in the Bastine Lake area. Growth continued after the war, and it would seem that the flowage resort industry reached its peak in the early 1950s. A Mercer promotional brochure from 1952 listed 15 resorts on the flowage itself, and 74 resorts and 37 businesses for the Mercer area as a whole. At least one operating resort, Joe Miller's Cottages, did not appear on that list, and it is quite possible that others might not have been on it as well. With good reason, then, the early 1950s might be considered the beginning of the golden age of flowage resorts.

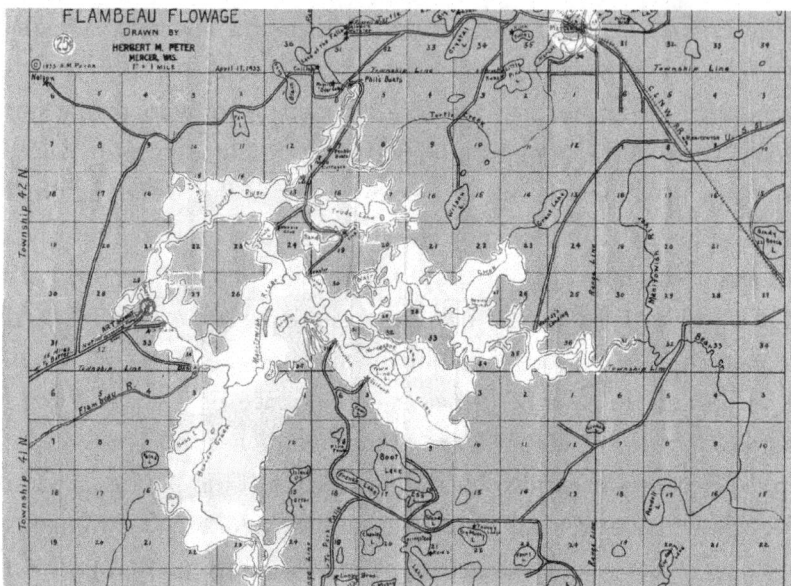

The full title reads "Map of the Famous Flambeau Flowage." Prepared in 1933, it is the first map to show resorts on the flowage. Wisconsin Historical Society

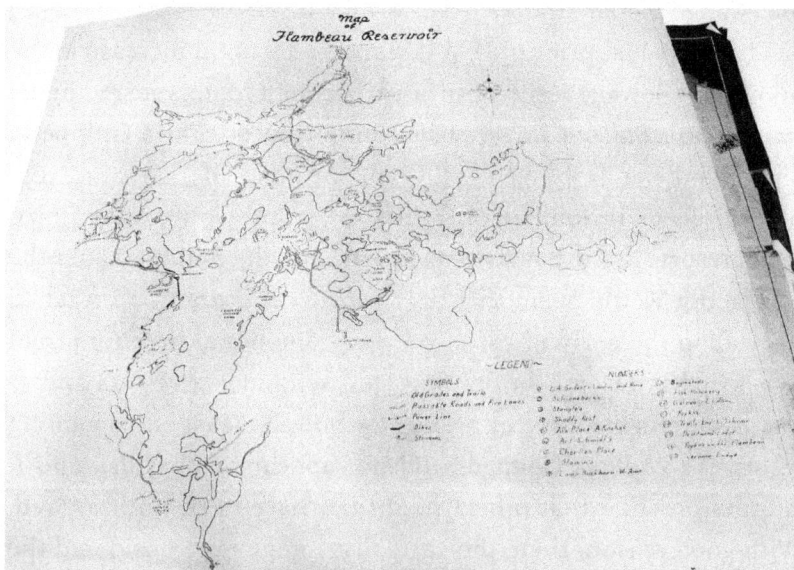

Map of Flambeau Reservoir prepared for the Chippewa and Flambeau Improvement Company by R. Thompson in 1941. Wisconsin Historical Society

An Accidental Jewel. Wisconsin's Turtle-Flambeau Flowage Flowage

The steadily growing reputation of the flowage as a prime fishery, passed on by word of mouth from satisfied anglers to their friends, certainly played a major role in the growth of the resort industry on the flowage. But other, larger social forces contributed to this growth as well. The whole pattern of recreation in Wisconsin, as in America, underwent dramatic changes in the first decades of the 20th century as a consequence of significant improvements in transportation—more and better passenger rail service and a burgeoning network of highways that helped to usher in America's automobile culture.

Early on, railroads seem to have been the preferred means of travel for those who vacationed at some of the American Plan lodges (American Plan hotels and resorts included three full meals in the room rate) that had sprung up during the teens of the 20th century. Most of these lodges, according to a study of vacationing "up north" by Aaron Shapiro, were within easy traveling distance of Minocqua or Hayward, towns with rail service. These resorts tended to cater to a fairly affluent clientele who could afford both the relatively costly train travel and the amenities of an American Plan resort. In time, demand for such service led the railroads, which had historically run lines to the north primarily for hauling freight, to introduce fast passenger trains to northern tourist hubs. In 1936, for example, the Milwaukee Road introduced its Northwoods Hiawatha route that ran from Chicago to Minocqua via a spur that branched off at New Lisbon, Wisconsin. Service under the Hiawatha name continued on this route until 1955. It was not until 1970 that the Milwaukee Road discontinued all passenger service to Minocqua. The Minneapolis, St. Paul and St. Ste. Marie Railroad, operating in part on tracks belonging to the Wisconsin Central Railroad, ran the Laker, an overnight passenger service from Chicago's Grand Central Station to Duluth-Superior, with service also to Ashland. This train passed through Park Falls and

Butternut. And the Chicago and Northwestern Railroad ran the Ashland Limited, later renamed the Flambeau 400, a train that passed through Mercer. The travel time from Chicago was nine hours. The latter two trains carried many a flowage visitor, who were picked up at northwoods stations by personnel from resorts.

Passenger rail proved to be a convenient and attractive means of travel, and trains like the Hiawatha, the Laker, and the Flambeau 400 carried thousands of vacationers to the northwoods well into the post-World War II decade. But it was the relatively inexpensive automobile, more than anything else, that made vacations away from home affordable and accessible both to middle- and working-class Americans. Already by 1923, some 700,000 tourists annually visited Wisconsin resorts and other tourist facilities, and the bulk of them arrived by car. Indeed, Model A and Model T Fords are mentioned so often in the records of northern Wisconsin that it would seem that scarcely any other automobiles were manufactured in the country. And as people hit the road during the period between World Wars I and II, the demand grew for a wider variety of tourist accommodations than had existed in the teens, a demand that the resort industry met in a variety of ways. Some American Plan resorts adapted by adding a handful of housekeeping cottages, that is, cottages equipped with kitchens, cookware, and eating utensils; but most of the additional capacity came from newly established resorts. Some new resorts comprised a modest lodge with restaurant facilities and a few cabins, while others consisted only of housekeeping cabins. The latter two types of resorts, because of their smaller scale and the possibility of incremental growth, required far less capital than did large American Plan resorts. As a consequence, the field was open, as the stories of many flowage resorts make clear, to some adventurous and talented entrepreneurs.

Pioneering Resorts

The first resorts on the flowage were established in the early 1930s, just a handful of years after the Turtle Dam had been put in operation. That they should appear so quickly, given the deficiencies of transportation in the area and the ragged condition of the wood-choked waters of the flowage, is testament both to the rapidly growing reputation of the fishery and to the foresight of the men and women who built and ran them. In 1931, two young area men, Art Schmidt and Al Koshak, secured long-term leases from the Wisconsin Realty Company for separate, but relatively close, parcels of land in the Bastine Lake area of the flowage. There, with the aid of their equally young wives, they set about to create resorts aimed at the growing number of anglers coming to the area.

The beginnings of their resorts were humble. Art Schmidt's Muskie Camp, as it was named, initially comprised a number of tents, a couple of cabins, one of which had a bar, and a few rental boats. In 1933, an advertisement for Al's Landing, soon to be renamed Al's Place, boasted of a boat landing, a bar, and hamburgers. As modest as their assets were, however, both owners evaluated their prospects highly enough to replace their leases with outright purchases of flowage land from Wisconsin Realty—Koshak in 1935, Schmidt in 1937. Year by year and board by board, these two resorts grew incrementally with the addition of cabins, main lodges, more boats, and staff. Schmidt financed his resort in part by reselling some of his flowage frontage and hired carpenters to do most of the work; Koshak built his cabins by himself, roughly one a year, while working in the woods during the winters to supplement his income. In the summer of 1937, Koshak built a new lodge that could serve 100 meals a day; and a few years later, Schmidt enlarged and remodeled his lodge to include a magnificent stone fireplace and bar, built by Carl Nove, a well-known area artisan. By 1947, Al's Place had a lodge, 13 cabins, a "girls'" cabin for the housekeepers and dining room workers, a laundry, an icehouse, a garage, 20 boats, and about a dozen motors. All that, and a small home for the owner and his wife and son.

There are way more trees standing in the flowage than on the grounds of the resort. Wisconsin Historical Society 67452

Though these resorts served the basic needs of their clientele for shelter, food, liquid refreshments, boats, and the like, they were far from luxurious. Windmills generated low-voltage, direct current electricity for the cabins; and gasoline-fired generators provided 110-volt electricity to the lodges. In time, guest cabins were outfitted with running water (at first water was delivered to each building by cabin boys), but most continued to have outside toilet facilities, which served both guests and owners alike. Full "modernization" of plumbing in these resorts took place only after the end of World War II. Phone service arrived sometime in 1935, but it was barely adequate. Limited amenities, however, do not seem to have diminished the experience for guests or prevented many of them from returning year after year.

Another of the pioneer resort owners located on or near Bastine Lake was Joe Miller. Originally from the Chicago area, this farmer from Agenda, Wisconsin, purchased 141 acres in 1939 from the Wisconsin Central Railroad and set about clearing the land—with axes, shovels, and grub hoes—for his future resort. Using wood from this land along with some salvaged from the area, Miller promptly erected an icehouse, a residence for his family, and a guest cabin. Joe Miller's Resort welcomed its first guests in 1942. In the 1960s, the fifth and final cabin was built, bringing the total number of buildings at the resort to five cabins, a house for the owners, and assorted outbuildings. The cabins had two bedrooms each and a living space equipped with all the necessary items for housekeeping. Each cabin could accommodate four to five people, or more, such as when guests arrived with children. Over time, the older cabins were fully electrified—Rural Electric Association lines got to the area in 1948—and retrofitted with indoor plumbing. To add to their ability to attract guests, many of the area's resort owners obtained liquor licenses, but not all did. Joe Miller's Resort operated successfully for more than four decades without a liquor license, though it did have a common area where guests could congregate.

Two other resorts that had similar beginnings in the 1930s were established by Joe Popko. His first resort, Pine Trees Hideaway, consisted of some 11 cabins Popko had built along the Turtle River portion of the flowage, on land that must have been leased from the CFIC or Wisconsin Realty. In 1938, Popko not only added quite a substantial house of his own to the property, but he also put up four cabins on the Norway Point area of the flowage. After selling

The pier at Popko's Resort juts out into the wood-filled waters of the Turtle River area of the flowage. Mercer Historical Society

Art Schmidt, Al Koshak, Joe Miller, and Joe Popko can be taken as representative of resort owners who built their establishments from the ground up by their own labors; and the process of resort creation they followed—that is, a modest start and an incremental expansion—was repeated over and over again on the flowage, though just how many times cannot be easily determined. A list of resort names, compiled from advertising materials, newspapers, and personal memories of longtime area residents, exceeds 30, but many resorts underwent name changes when ownership changed. Art Schmidt's resort, for example, had at least 11 changes of ownership between its founding in the early 1930s and its demise in 1998; and it operated under three different names, Hiawatha Resort being the final one. Turnover of the Schmidt resort was certainly higher than average, but six or more owners of a given resort property was not uncommon. As a consequence, opportunities for name changes were ample. Taking this fact into account, it seems likely that the overall number of flowage resorts must have been in the low to mid-20s.

Latecomers

There never seemed to be a shortage of eager buyers when resort properties went on the market. Without a doubt, the attraction of owning a business in the magical northwoods exerted a powerful allure on those individuals and families who had some personal experience with the area and who were eager to escape the urban grind. But that does not mean that everyone who succumbed to the call of the north was ready for the demanding tasks that lay ahead. As a former Minnesota resort owner who observed the rush to buy resorts in the immediate post-World War II years noted: "Most of the new owners now buying resort property have no more business to be in that business than the man on the moon." Although these newcomers did not have to build their businesses from the ground up, they nonetheless faced significant challenges of a different kind: either sustaining the momentum of a well-functioning operation or breathing new life into a faltering one. The stories of the Lodge of Lakeview and Pine Trees Hideaway illustrate how two new pairs of owners, their families with them, stepped mid-career into the resort business, beat the odds, and attained their goals.

In October of 1976, Rodney Brown and his wife, Maryann, purchased the Lakeview Resort on Bastine Lake from Frank and Josephine Strach. The facility comprised four housekeeping cabins and a home. In so doing, the Browns, who were from the Chicago area, became the sixth owners of a resort that had been established in 1942 by Frank Stamm. When the couple opened up shop in 1977, they tweaked the resort's name a bit, calling it the

Lodge of Lakeview. This was at least the fourth name in the then 35-year history of the resort.

To make a go of their venture, the Browns undertook some modest upgrades of the property, acquired a liquor license in 1980, and turned the basement of their home into the resort bar and gathering site. Starting in 1987, they decided to remain open through the winter to cater to a growing population of snowmobiling families. In 1994, however, the Browns bowed to the changing realities of the resort business and turned the four original cabins into a condominium. As of 2015, the Lodge of Lakeview property comprised the condo, the owners' house, and two rental units. Though changed in character, the resort had been under the control of the Browns for more than four decades.

On Memorial Day weekend in 1971, Pine Trees Hideaway, the resort founded by Joe Popko along the Turtle River, opened its doors under the management of Ernst (Ernie) and Aranka Both. The Boths' road to resort ownership had much in common with others who took over existing businesses, but it was certainly longer. Born in Hungary, they were displaced to Germany in the aftermath of World War II. By 1954, they had married and settled in Milwaukee. They came to know Wisconsin's northwoods through family vacations at a cabin belonging to one of Ernie's uncles. When they learned that a resort on the flowage had been placed on the market, the Boths needed little persuasion. With characteristic conciseness, Aranka recalled her arguments for this new venture: "I can cook, Ernie can bartend, we both can work, and the kids love the northwoods." And so it was that the Boths became the Hideaway's sixth owners.

The Boths found themselves in possession of a resort whose facilities had badly deteriorated. The previous owners had been unable to undertake necessary maintenance, leaving the cabins, fairly primitive to begin with, badly in need of an upgrading.

Moreover, the Boths intended to serve the snowmobile crowd, which meant that the buildings had to be insulated against the winter. Ernie took on the construction tasks, and Aranka took over the kitchen and restaurant in the basement of the owners' residence. Her food soon gained a reputation well beyond the Mercer area, and it became the distinguishing feature of the resort. The demands of ownership proved wearing, however, and the Boths sold the resort in 1979. Two subsequent owners failed to make a go of the Hideaway, though, and in 1986 it was back in the Boths' hands. Once again it flourished under their management until they sold it for the final time in 1990.

Whoever's name was on the deed of a resort property—husband, husband and wife, or other combinations involving family, friends, or business acquaintances—the fact is that these were in the main very much family businesses. Katherine Schmidt and Charlotte Koshak fully participated in the operations of the resorts that bore their husband's names. They picked up guests from rail stations, secured supplies, tended bar, handled reservations, supervised staff, and did so much more. Maryann Brown managed the Browns' resort business and tended bar while her husband continued to work in Chicago for many years. Aranka Both cooked while Ernie carpentered. And children in all these families, from surprisingly early ages, were able helpers who responded to requests from guests for assistance, waited tables, cleaned cabins, and performed numerous other tasks. The best exemplar of ongoing family ownership is Joe Miller's resort—officially known as Joe Miller's Resort and Campground. As of 2017, the resort had been continuously owned and operated by family members for some 75 years.

Guests

There were many satisfactions for those in the resort business: the sense of accomplishment that comes from creating something from nothing; the confirmation that hard work really makes a difference; the self-expression involved in applying one's talents to a broad range of tasks; the victorious feeling that follows turning around a failed operation; and, of course, the everyday happiness that attends living and working in a location of special beauty and meaning. That said, however, interactions with guests proved for most owners to be far and away the most rewarding aspect of resort ownership.

Who were these guests who clearly meant more to the resorts than just sources of a revenue stream? The guests shared a couple of revealing traits. Almost all of them, in one way or another, had succumbed to the mystique of the northwoods. And the greater number of them—especially the men—considered themselves outdoor enthusiasts (though some colossal novices showed up as well). Beyond this, variety ruled. Celebrities like entertainers Dennis Morgan and Jack Carson, as well as the jockey Eddie Arcaro, visited Art Schmidt's Muskie Camp. And some "shady" types, linked to the underside of the Prohibition Era, showed up here and there along with some serious gamblers (slot machines were legal in the early resort era). One gambler, whose fortunes rose and fell on a two-year cycle, would show up one year at Al's Place in a Cadillac, the next year in a run-down Chevy. Predictably, however, the great bulk of the resorts' clientele fell between these extremes of fame and infamy. Within this broad group of guests, social class may have played a modest role in the choice of resorts. Housekeeping resorts seem to have catered more to a working-class clientele while resorts with restaurants were favored more by professional people, although this distinction can hardly be taken as a rule.

"People from all walks of life" is the phrase the author encountered most in interviewing those knowledgeable about resorts. For example, guests over the years at Joe Miller's included trades people as well as "firemen from Oak Park, members of the Chicago Board of Trade, doctors, undertakers and ministers." In addition, the president of General Mills stayed at Miller's, as did Tommy Thompson in the 1970s when he was serving in the Wisconsin State Assembly. There was even one priest, whose name was Joe Miller, who stopped by just long enough to have his photo taken by the "Joe Miller's Cabins" sign. "Good people" and "good family people" are two other phrases frequently used to describe guests at the flowage resorts. Geographically speaking, a large proportion of these people came from the Milwaukee and Chicago metropolitan areas, but there were plenty who came from more distant locales, even "from coast to coast." Almost all were white and from Christian backgrounds.

It seems altogether likely that owners and staff, on the one hand, and guests, on the other, were drawn to one another by a quite understandable mutual curiosity. For the owners, hearing, whether across the bar or in the boat or in casual encounters on the resort's grounds, about the triumphs and trials of their guests' lives provided them with an opportunity to walk a while in many different moccasins—some of which were pretty big. For the guests, an exposure to the various practices, skills, and arts essential to making a living so close to and so dependent on nature was an awesome education in and of itself. And then there was the ever-present likelihood of hearing some brisk, quasi-aphoristic, and not always printable words of northwoods wisdom about everything from politics to the price of gas to casting techniques. More often than not, these exchanges between owners and guests led both parties to broadened visions of the world and toward a sense of their common humanity—though it is doubtful that those who talked about the world while chasing walleyes or who participated in late-night conversations in resort bars would ever choose to use such language to assess their experiences.

Whatever was at play in the relationship between owners and guests, the outcome was friendship, plain and simple. "We became friends, such good friends." This refrain, or some variant of it, shows up over and over again in the language both of resort operators and of their guests. A week or two at a resort did give both parties ample time to get to know one another. And friendships struck up then only deepened as guests returned year after year. Some of the longer-standing resorts have been hosts to as many as four generations of a single family. In 2011, three men opened the spring fishing season at the Lodge of Lakeview, as they had done every year since the Browns opened shop in 1977. Families who became friends with one another while staying at a resort sometimes coordinated bookings for subsequent years, which contributed to an overall camaraderie of friends getting together with friends. For the Boths, an annual Fourth of July pig roast, free to all guests (except for drinks; the Boths were, after all, prudent businesspeople), stood out as a particularly convivial tradition. In some circumstances, returning guests seemed like family, according to Carol Zilinger, the granddaughter of Joe Miller. "As a young girl, I used to call a lot of the guests 'uncle' or 'aunt.'" Moreover, owner-guest friendships endured well beyond the time when some of the resort owners had left the business. Letters, Christmas cards, and the occasional visit kept and keep these relationships alive. In the final analysis, friendship lay at the very core of the resort business.

Reaching Out for Customers

To reach their growing pool of potential customers, resort owners soon recognized that word-of-mouth endorsements, as powerful as they often were, did not spread their messages widely enough. And so they quickly turned to active promotion of their resorts by means ranging from printed matter to direct person-to-person contacts with potential clients. Advertising had come to stay, and vehicles for spreading it proliferated. In addition to the efforts of individual resorts, local booster groups, regional promotional organizations, big-city newspapers, and the state government all had a hand in pushing up-north recreation.

Who could resist this imaginative piece of advertising? Image courtesy of Neil Koshak

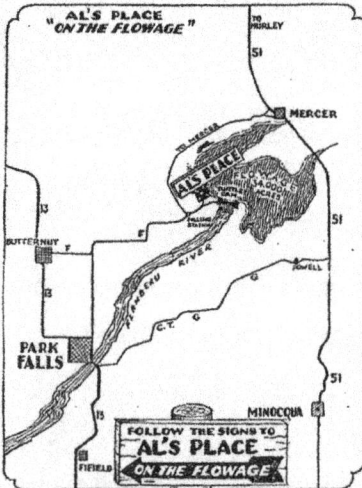

FISHING and HUNTING

You may have your meals served in the Lodge, or our housekeeping cabins are completely furnished to do your own cooking, with screened in porches, ice boxes, good beds and electric lights.

Located on the Turtle-Flowage, at the junction of the Turtle, Flambeau and Manitowish Rivers, the home of the King of Waters, the fighting Tiger Muskie, as well as many pan fish such as bass, pike, crappies and perch.

"There are over 175 miles of shore line, and every mile of it is an ideal fishing spot. There are two wonderful river spots to make—one is about seven miles long and the other is over twenty miles. We have experienced guides, capable of cooking those good old delicious shore lunches; and of course, they are all experts when it comes to handling boats, motors, etc. Plan now to spend a few weeks at Al's Place and enjoy fishing at its best. Also hunting in season."

LODGE and FURNISHED CABINS
WITH ELECTRIC LIGHTS

Housekeeping Cabins, Including One Boat, Ice, Fuel and Linen

Cabin with one double bed, per day_____$2.75 Per week____$16.50
Cabin with two double beds, per day_____ 3.25 Per week____ 19.50
Cabin with three double beds, per day_____ 4.00 Per week____ 23.50

Discount on cabins for two weeks, 10%—for one month, 20%—for two months, 25%.

Meals at the Lodge—Breakfast 40c; Dinner 70c; Supper 70c.
Meals by the week—per person $12.00.

Boats—Resort model, per day_____$1.00 Per week_____$ 6.00
Boats—Flat bottom, per day_____ .75 Per week_____ 4.50
Motors—with gas and oil, per day_____ 2.00 Per week_____ 12.00

Guides—per day, $4.50
Fishing Tackle, Line, Bait, Fishing Licenses.
Meals, Lunches, Refreshments.
Free Camping Grounds.

Two Big River Trips for You to Make

Here is real sport—one trip is about seven miles long, and the other is over twenty—on the famous "Flambeau River." — We furnish the boats and transportation to and from the river. The charges for this service are:

7 mile trips, 1 boat_____$3.75   Two boats_____$5.25
20 mile trips, 1 boat_____ 5.25   Two boats_____ 7.00

A businesslike brochure promises good roads, tasty food, excellent fishing, and electric lights—at prices that would be hard to beat. Neil Koshak

Michael Hittle

A portion of a vividly designed brochure for Art Schmidt's Muskie Camp. The original is in red, white, and black. Art Schmidt Jr.

Owners of flowage resorts made use of all these means to spread the word. Al Koshak, the founder and initial operator of Al's Place, distributed informational brochures, handed out matchbooks with essential information about the resort on the covers, and sold postcards of the lodge and cabins. Al also gained publicity in bigger markets, such as Milwaukee, by giving interviews with outdoor writers and by attending annual outdoor shows. Guests at Downey's Shady Rest Resort could send home postcards with a picture of their preferred cabin, presumably accompanied by glowing words about both the fishing and the overall vacation experience. Art Schmidt placed ads in Milwaukee papers for "Wisconsin's No. 1 Fishing Camp" and, for his customers' convenience, promised to "meet trains at Butternut and Mercer." Schmidt also used outdoor advertising—namely ads painted on barns along downstate highways that touted his "famous rock bar"—to call attention to his Muskie Camp. A large-format brochure for this same establishment—which dates to the mid-1950s when the resort was under the ownership of Glenn and Mavis Greiner—touches all the bases. The graphics highlight the size of the flowage and its iconic fish, the musky. The text describes Art Schmidt's Muskie Camp as "A Home for Outdoor Men and Women," and makes it clear that children are welcome—and sure to be safe on the gradual swimming beach. The pitch here is clearly aimed at families rather than all-male parties of fishermen. There is plenty of information about cabins, amenities, and various rental arrangements—including rates. The brochure also lists the driving distances from three major population centers—Milwaukee, Chicago, and St. Paul—and includes travel instructions and a map that seem to make getting there, whether by automobile or rail, a piece of cake. And as Neil Koshak, Al's son, remembers, once highway travelers were in the vicinity, they did not lack for additional guidance: "Between Butternut and the flowage there must have been at least a 100 8-inch by 48-inch arrow-shaped signs pointing the way to each resort, mostly Al's and Art's. Every intersection was plastered."

In addition to their own promotional efforts, individual resorts received help from a variety of organizations dedicated to promoting Wisconsin's recreation industry. Founded sometime in the early 1950s, the Mercer Resort and Businessmen's Association stepped forward as the principal advocate for the flowage, promoting local businesses and supporting activities to keep the flowage healthy and attractive. Renamed the Turtle Flambeau

Association (TFA) in 1976, it remains an active organization today. In its early years, the TFA began printing small advertising brochures on an annual basis. Each contained an attractive photo of some outdoor activity, as often as not fishing, as well as information about some particular attraction of the area, and a fairly comprehensive listing of resorts and businesses that might serve tourists' needs. Once in a while, the association's well-meaning optimism stretched the limits of credibility, as it did in a brochure from 1956 which promised the ultimate in mosquito control: "Even better results are expected in 1957 as the Association is planning an all out campaign to control this insect and earlier sprayings will be made to eliminate the early hatch and thereby hopefully result in a 'mosquito-less Mercer.'" The brochures also provided space for resorts to place small advertisements describing their facilities and giving contact information. The majority of the advertisements identified the owners by name—a practice designed to emphasize the personal and homey relationship between guests and owners that constituted the great appeal of these small resorts. A couple of resorts included in their advertisements the phrase "clientele restricted." This phrase, a part of the code language of discrimination often used in the pre-civil rights era, meant no African Americans or Jews. Most of the ads, however, had no such restrictive language.

The work of the Turtle Flambeau Association was supplemented, with varying degrees of emphasis and enthusiasm, by the Mercer Chamber of Commerce (formed in 1949). The latter group tended to focus on Mercer itself and the lakes immediately around it, although in recent years it has given greater prominence to the flowage in its promotional materials and overall marketing approach.

As effective as the promotional activities of individual resorts and local business organizations may have been, there were limits to their scale and scope. Not surprisingly, organizations of wider compass emerged to fill the need for more far-reaching publicity. In the late 1930s, the Wisconsin Greater Recreational Association (WGRA) took the lead in organizing major events. The association was an umbrella group comprising "official representatives of Wisconsin vacation areas; owners and operators of summer resorts; [and] organizations engaged in drawing vacationers from other states into Wisconsin...." Interestingly, individuals from towns surrounding the flowage dominated the leadership of this statewide organization. In 1940, Dan Vicker, the Park Falls postmaster, was president; Charles Lacy of Mercer was executive vice president; H.W. Parker of Lac du Flambeau was secretary; and Florence Evans of Mercer was treasurer. The WGRA was more than ready to act on its own in promoting the state's recreational industry, but it soon forged what turned out to be a beneficial alliance with the Wisconsin Conservation Department, an agency with growing experience in advertising.

In 1936, the Wisconsin Conservation Department created its recreational publicity division and began a program to spread the word about Wisconsin's great outdoors. At that time, only five other states actively promoted outdoor recreation through governmental agencies. In July 1938, the division set up Wisconsin displays in both the Union and the North Western stations in Chicago. Originally intended as temporary displays, their popularity gave them an unanticipated longevity. In 1941, the contents of the displays rotated to reflect the changing seasons of the year. Some 275 viewers per hour stopped to give these two exhibits a once-over.

The Conservation Department's recreational publicity division also made a number of motion pictures about Wisconsin outdoor sports and conservation activities. The *Wisconsin Conservation Bulletin* (*WCB*) of January 1939 reports that these films had been shown to audiences in 167 cities in 28 states and one Canadian province. By the time of the International Sportsmen's Show held at the Chicago Stockyards amphitheater in 1942, the Conservation Department showed only sound pictures with such enticing titles as *Siren*, *Muskies of the Future*, *Fetch*, and *Tight Lines*, as well as two color movies on canoeing and wildflowers.

In 1941, the division began the production and distribution of articles "pertaining to the vast and diversified recreational attractions and facilities of Wisconsin." These were sent to more than 600 out-of-state newspapers. Article No. 8 in the series, titled "Wisconsin's Famous Recreational Regions," contains the following spirited write-up of the Mercer-Springstead area:

"'Haven of wildlife and home of the fighting muskellunge' they call this Iron County region of far northern Wisconsin.... This is up in the Wisconsin iron-range country, with Indians, forests, trout streams, great iron mines, muskie waters, and some of Wisconsin's wildest woodlands." The article goes on to praise the fishing on the flowage and other area lakes, as well as the "naturally excellent resorts and camps in this region." It concludes by noting that the area is served by the "Chicago and Northwestern railway with the 'Flambeau' and other fast trains from the south." Highway 51 also gets a mention as well, but without any claims as to its speediness.

The Conservation Department's recreational publicity division and the WGRA demonstrated what a public-private partnership could accomplish when they combined forces to put on the Wisconsin Outdoor Life Expositions at Chicago's Hotel Sherman starting in 1939. In effect, the Conservation Department brought the dazzle and the WGRA brought the recreational professionals. For three years, from 1940 to 1942, the Conservation Department provided a miniature waterfall, fresh trees and plants (ferns) from northern Wisconsin, game fish specimens (live and mounted), and animals and birds from the state game and fur farm at Poynette. According to the June 1942 issue of the *WCB,* the animals for the

1942 show were placed under the care of "Alfred Korth, of Poynette, long known in outdoor show and animal handling circles as 'Bring 'Em Back in Good Condition Al.'" The conservation folks also had a chance to delight new audiences with their promotional movies, shown in what was described as a "sylvan" theater, and with their presentation of Lac du Flambeau tribal members who displayed native crafts and danced for the spectators.

The Conservation Department's contributions, however, were only part of the story. The *WCB* noted in June of 1940 that the WGRA had assembled representatives from "31 regional organizations, resorts, and vacation centers" to provide a personal touch to the exposition. Guides lured customers, no doubt with endless tales of monstrous muskies, voracious walleyes, tasty and prodigious shore lunches, and the promise of putting the prospective angler on secret patches of water that never fail to produce. Resort owners and representatives of regional tourist associations handed out literature and assured potential clients that a northwoods experience was there and waiting both for experienced anglers and for vacationing families seeking fun and sun. Writing in the *WCB* of May 1941, C.L. Coon, the assistant superintendent of recreational publicity for the Conservation Department, summed up the 1941 show in an ebullient fashion: "Visitors found in the huge exhibition hall the answer to many a vacation problem and the inspiration for fulfilling that Wisconsin vacation dream. Trips to fit every size of budget, and suggestions for fun, outdoor activity, sightseeing or complete relaxation were found in the many beautiful displays, movie films, literature and helpful vacation talks by outdoor guides and knowing resort operators." Coon was hardly a disinterested party, but the growing crowds from year to year, which had already necessitated an expansion of the exhibition space, suggest that his comments were pretty close to the mark.

Al Koshak in his Sunday best at the Hotel Sherman in Chicago. Neil Koshak

Interestingly, World War II did not seem to interrupt Wisconsin's efforts to promote tourism, in spite of limited gasoline supplies, the large number of men and women in the military, and the general hardships faced by the civilian population. The Chicago show went on at least through 1943, and the Conservation Department continued to encourage vacationers to come to the state through articles in the *Bulletin*. Indeed, it was about this time that the department came up with a new sales pitch: the desirability of taking a vacation during wartime to recharge the batteries for more war work. In an issue of the *Bulletin* in 1943, the department urged its readers to "Relax, be fit, do it!" (In neighboring Vilas County, the town of Boulder Junction encouraged people to "Buy bonds first, then vacation in Boulder Junction.") Apparently these patriotic pleas fell on fertile ground. At least this was the case for one flowage resort. According to Art Schmidt Jr., his father's

An Accidental Jewel. Wisconsin's Turtle-Flambeau Flowage Flowage

resort, after having struggled somewhat during the 1930s, had a substantial influx of visitors in the war years, many of whom were newly employed in the munitions industry in the Chicago area. These people were making good money for the time and were ready to spend some of it on a vacation that got them away from the wartime drabness of the big city.

When the war was over, a new but still war-related message emerged to lure tourists north. In the June 1946 issue of the *Bulletin*, Coon called on people to take a "Victory Vacation" in Wisconsin. A rush was expected, he noted, and accommodations were only slightly more numerous than they had been during the war years. It behooved interested parties to be sure they had confirmed reservations before setting out for the north. And, in the event that there were no summer openings at the resorts of their choice, prospective tourists might want to consider autumn vacations.

An article in the March 22, 1953, edition of the *Milwaukee Sentinel* captures well the atmosphere of the outdoor sport shows: "Resort owners, experienced fishing guides and leaders of the many tourist agendas throughout Badgerdom are talking and selling the gospel of 'See Wisconsin First.' Many families look forward to the Sports Show each year for it offers the chance of renewing friendships which so many people enjoy with resort owners who have contributed so much to past happiness." The Turtle-Flambeau Flowage area was represented by the Mercer Resort and Businessmen's Association, Art Schmidt's Muskie Camp, Al's Place, and Cedar Lodge.

Limited sources make it impossible to create a comprehensive list of those who attended the shows on behalf of flowage or regional resorts, but it is clear that owners of at least two of the earliest resorts recognized the value of being present at such shows—Al Koshak and Art Schmidt. Koshak attended himself, and also took advantage of these trips to talk with local journalists who covered outdoor activities. Art Schmidt sometimes dispatched others to the shows on his behalf. His son, Art Jr., was sometimes absent from school for a two-week period when assisting his aunt and uncle, George and Mary Ertl, at the Chicago and Milwaukee shows. Mitch Babic, a guide from Mercer, managed the Iron County exhibit at sport shows in Milwaukee for some 14 years. Another Mercer guide and active promoter of the area, Leonard Scheels, represented Iron County at the outdoor show in Chicago in February of 1958. These examples are but the tip of the iceberg, as there were countless others who worked the exposition circuit. It would be hard to overestimate the value to a resort of having representation at these events. For the personalities of the men and women who owned resorts, as well as of the guides, played a pivotal role when it came time for people to choose where to stay and with whom to fish. Most of the resorts offered roughly comparable facilities, and nearly all the guides could get fish for their parties. It was the personal touch that attracted tourists initially, and that kept them coming back. As a consequence, publicity with a personal touch was, from the very beginning, an indispensable tactic for most successful resort owners.

Resorts in Decline

The number of flowage resorts appears to have held fairly constant well into the 1960s and early 1970s. A flyer published by the Mercer Chamber of Commerce in 1967 listed some 13 flowage resorts, and the one from the following year included at least two long-standing resorts that had not been present in the previous year's list. But significant change was in the offing. The number of resorts listed in brochures gradually diminished in the 1980s and 1990s (it is impossible to give exact figures as functioning resorts sometimes chose not to pay for a listing in years when they were well-booked), and this trend has continued right to the present day. Currently, only four resorts still own all of their original property and improvements. The rest have been broken up, wholly or partially, for the creation of condominiums, or their owners have sold some or all of their units or have sold everything to a developer.

The declining number of flowage resorts was not an isolated phenomenon: it reflected a broader statewide trend that became clearly noticeable in the 1960s. A study by Lawrence Monthey turned up a 14 percent drop in the number of resorts across the

The Rise and Decline of Resorts on the Turtle-Flambeau Flowage

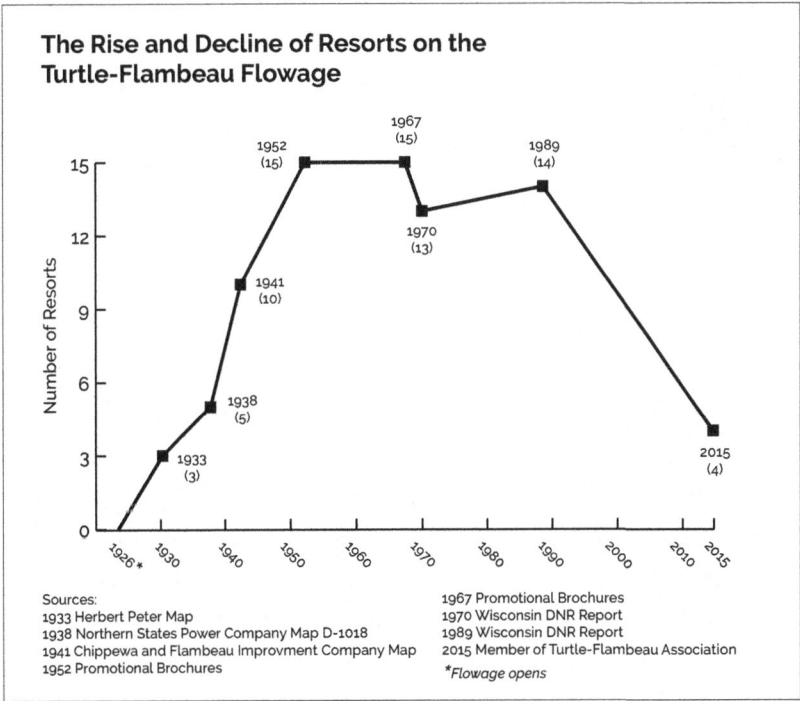

Sources:
1933 Herbert Peter Map
1938 Northern States Power Company Map D-1018
1941 Chippewa and Flambeau Improvment Company Map
1952 Promotional Brochures
1967 Promotional Brochures
1970 Wisconsin DNR Report
1989 Wisconsin DNR Report
2015 Member of Turtle-Flambeau Association
*Flowage opens

state from 1961 to 1968; and the fall-off for Iron County during the corresponding period was an even more precipitous 36 percent. Cabin colonies and cottage resorts took a particularly hard hit—especially those with somewhere between five and 19 bedroom units. The causes for this major change in the tourist industry fall roughly into four categories: the relentless burdens of resort operations, financial difficulties, changing recreational preferences among potential patrons, and new patterns of family life.

Small though most of the resorts were, their operations were complex and extremely demanding on the time and energy of their owners. During the season, the needs and wants of patrons—for matters big and small—laid almost continuous claim to owners' time. Requests for assistance followed one another in an almost endless stream. "Do you have an extra landing net?" "Can you fix the heater in our cabin?" "How do I start this motor?" "Could you draw me a map of where that rockpile is?" "Have you got a small screwdriver to work on this reel?" And on and on. The personal touch that was so important to a successful operation required that these customer requests be met, and, if at all possible, met promptly and with a smile.

Then there were the demands of maintenance—mostly buildings, boats, motors, and electric supplies, all of which entailed a considerable amount of work. Maintenance was particularly time-consuming for those resorts that consisted primarily of old "fishing camp" cabins that needed ongoing care, or, worse yet, major renovation bordering on rebuilding. Fortunately, most owners were, by necessity if not by training, jacks-of-all-trades and were able to tackle the bulk of the maintenance work; but it was an exhausting addition to the requirements of daily operation. Finally, there were some built-in operational limitations that eventually diminished the attractiveness of the small resort. These limitations showed up in the fairly restricted number of services they could offer their customers: lodging, boats and motors, bait, and for some, a bar and/or restaurant facilities. As recreational tastes diversified, most of these small resorts had little additional to offer.

On the financial side of things, the basic fact is that resorts did not take in all that much revenue. Short seasons, relatively few rental units, and low rates severely limited income. In the mid-1950s, flowage housekeeping cottages—depending on amenities such as inside plumbing—rented for $35 to $45 per week, an amount equivalent to $284 or $362, respectively, in 2010 dollars. According to Monthey, Wisconsin resort owners took in, on average, a gross income of approximately $700 per cottage per year in the early 1960s. Adjusted for inflation, this would be $4,845 in 2010 dollars. Accordingly, a five-cabin resort would have brought in, before any expenses were paid, the equivalent of $24,000. Expenses depended in part on how diligent an owner was about upkeep and improvement, and in part on the owner's ability to do the work with a minimum of help from outside contractors. But if expenses could be highly variable, taxes could not. And as time went on, property taxes on resorts mounted substantially in response to ever-increasing assessments. The latter, of course, were driven by escalating demand for lakefront property. So, in the final analysis, net revenue for most resorts was not all that great—particularly for those owners who sought to support whole families. Revenue from other sources—such as winter jobs, investments, and retirement pensions—was more than helpful, if not absolutely critical. Maryann Brown, a resort owner with nearly 40 years of experience, says that she "doesn't know of any resort that was totally self-sustaining. They had to have income from other sources." In her case, the survival of the Lodge of Lakeview depended on her husband's full-time job at Lever Brothers in Chicago.

Perhaps the biggest challenge to long-term resort ownership was the aging of their proprietors. To be sure, some resorts—like Art Schmidt's and Al Koshak's—were founded and run by relatively young families until such time as it made sense to them to sell the business and move on to other pursuits. But examples of long-term ownership are few and far between. More often than not, resorts passed from hand to hand at a fairly brisk pace. Oftentimes the new owners had just retired from jobs and businesses "down south," and many envisioned resort ownership as a retirement project, an investment of sorts, and a way to live and work outdoors. Such attitudes tended to relegate to the background the notion of the resort as a source of income, or even as a potential cash drain. As the years went by, however, the relentless work wore on them, expenses mounted to unanticipated levels, and taxes steadily rose. Faced with these conditions, and with a market that placed ever greater value on their lands, older resort owners yielded to the call of the marketplace and realized some handsome financial gains. Some sold off cabins one at a time, in effect turning their properties into condominiums. Others sold outright to developers who had various plans for the property and buildings. According to Monthey's study, sales of resorts in northeastern Wisconsin brought, on average, "prices equal to about twice the owner's total investment." The endgame for many a resort owner was a winning one, but the victory often came at the cost of broken initial dreams.

If the difficulties of running a resort contributed to their gradual disappearance, so too did the changing recreational preferences of those who had been their patrons. Camping, for example, burgeoned in popularity in the 1960s. It had, of course, always been an alternative to staying at a resort, and as such was considered a competitor. "Damn campers" were the words that I remember being uttered by an otherwise mild-mannered and cheerful resort owner as a prelude to complaining about people who stayed in tents, brought all their food from home in grocery bags and coolers, and contributed little to the local economy beyond the purchase of a few gallons of gas and a dozen minnows.

Her hostility notwithstanding, camping was on the scene to stay by the mid-1960s. But the phenomenon was not limited to tent camping. The advent of towable camping units not only "took the ground out from under" a night in the woods; but it also began the never-ending process of refinement of these units, a refinement that led to self-propelled "camping" units that often exceeded in features and luxury the standard rental cabin—and even some year-round homes. Moreover, camper units radically enhanced the mobility of vacationers. Why stay for a week on one lake when it was easy to visit several lakes for a night or two each? The phrase, "cottages on wheels," is all too apt, and the irony is too blatant to miss. The automobile that brought increasing numbers of tourists to resorts from the 1920s to the 1960s had, by the mid-1960s, begun to carry them away.

The growing interest on the part of Americans in having vacation homes of their own also contributed to the declining patronage of the state's resorts. Between 1960 and 1966, the number of vacation homes (seasonal dwellings) in Wisconsin increased by some 74 percent. In yet another ironic turn of events, it was as if Wisconsin's lakeside resorts had done their jobs too well by turning erstwhile guests into would-be buyers of cabins or land— sometimes from the very resorts they had visited. This process, which seems to have peaked on the flowage in the early 1990s, can be seen at work on the flowage on properties that once belonged to the following resorts—Fort Flambeau, Shady Rest, Lodge of Lakeview, and Birch Point, among others. In some instances, old cabins have been renovated or expanded; in other cases, they have been torn down or moved, only to be replaced by newer structures. Outright demolition of resorts and the subsequent creation of new building sites was yet another option. In 1998, the original lodge and most of the remaining cabins at Hiawatha Resort (originally Art Schmidt's Muskie Camp) were torn down and the property platted for building sites. All that could be salvaged from the lodge's famous fieldstone fireplace was the head of an American Indian created by Carl Nove, an area stonemason of considerable talent and repute. Had one been able to hear it, the collective din of decades of conversation, tall tales, laughter, and high spirits that bounced off those fieldstones over the course of seven decades would easily have drowned out the noise of demolition.

If some potential patrons of the flowage's resorts became avid campers and others acquired their own cabins, there was a substantial percentage who, in response to new patterns of family life, simply stopped taking conventional summer vacations of one to several weeks' duration. This was particularly true for the families who accounted for the great majority of bookings in the high summer months. According to Maryann Brown of the Lodge of Lakeview, the clientele of resorts traditionally fell into two groups: dedicated anglers who showed up in early spring and in the fall, and families who filled the long summer calendar. Successful resorts were family-oriented either from their founding or shortly thereafter—which also meant that they were family dependent and as a consequence vulnerable to changes in family life. And this life did change. As women entered the workforce in ever-greater numbers, spouses found it difficult to coordinate both the timing and lengths of their respective vacations. A mere week at the lake became harder and harder to schedule. Divorce took its toll as well; a family vacation minus one spouse was no winner. Children, for whom the appeal of a resort had traditionally consisted of a mix of swimming, chasing minnows and crawfish, fishing, and spontaneous games, found themselves participating in ever more structured summertime activities, whether sports or crafts or specialty camps. And then there were those children for whom the wonder of the outdoors had been replaced by that of personal electronic devices. Why head north only to sit inside and wiggle a joystick? And so for certain segments of the population, young and old alike, the traditional summer vacation fell prey to complex and crowded adult lives and to new versions of what was once called childhood.

Just as the rise of flowage resorts can be attributed to bigger trends in national life, the same can be said for their decline and, in so many cases, disappearance. The resorts blossomed at a time when their offerings matched a social demand; and when the match was no longer as compelling, they struggled. But in their prime, the resorts provided their patrons with a range of experiences that translated in later years into rich, indelible memories.

As of 2014, just five resorts remained on the flowage, and some of them were operating in limited fashion. Nonetheless, fish were being caught, families were swimming and boating, friendships were being formed, and good times were being had. But it is important to remember that the surviving resorts are the heirs of a great tradition started by a handful of pioneering types, and sustained for several generations by men and women dedicated to giving others a special kind of experience in a magnificent setting. The history of flowage resorts is all the more remarkable in that they took root in the Great Depression and hung on through World War II when ordinary living was so constrained. That they flourished, numerically, in the growing post-war boom seems only just reward for surviving and thriving through two decades of trying times. That they began to decline numerically so quickly after reaching their peak hardly seems fair, but it is understandable in our age of ever-accelerating change. The good things in the end, though, are the joys the flowage resorts brought to people and the memories that people brought home from them.

CHAPTER SEVEN

The Voigt Decision and Its Aftermath: The Past as Present and Future

With the 50th anniversary of the Turtle-Flambeau Flowage (TFF) in 1976, both the flowage itself and the human activities associated with it were still tracking on courses that had begun the moment the dam gates had first closed. The flowage's ever-changing fishery had by this time become dominated by its walleye population, a fact made abundantly clear by the exhaustive Wisconsin Department of Natural Resources (WDNR) study of 1975-1976 and by the full stringers that so many anglers brought off the water. The flowage's reputation as a special location to fish had never been stronger or more widespread. The resort industry—though signs of challenge were faintly visible on the horizon—was flourishing to the evident delight of resort owners and patrons alike. And then there were the various advocates. For in addition to the Chippewa and Flambeau Improvement Company (CFIC), which owned the dam and most of the shoreline, numerous other parties had come forward to stake their claims of interest in the flowage. These parties included the WDNR, regional tourist associations, the Turtle Flambeau Flowage Association that represented the resorts, and local groups and individuals interested in promoting fishing. For the most part the relationships between and among these parties were ones of parallel play, and no significant conflicts emerged during these first five decades of the flowage's existence. In short, as the flowage evolved, human activities and natural changes had moved forward in a fairly leisurely and mostly harmonious manner. This harmony, however, was soon to be interrupted by events that had their roots in the 19th century and that were influenced by America's Civil Rights Movement of the 20th century.

The Voigt Decision: The Courts Speak

The issue here turns on the efforts—eventually successful—of Wisconsin's Chippewa bands to reassert their "retained" usufructuary treaty rights—literally, the rights to use something that does not belong to one. The rights in question, articulated in the treaties of 1837 and 1842, and restated (in a somewhat ambiguous context) in the Treaty of LaPointe in 1854, allowed the Chippewa to continue to hunt, fish, and gather on lands they had ceded to the United States. Though initially the Chippewa appear to have exercised these rights in full, by the late 19th century these rights had eroded substantially. When fishing or hunting, tribal members were expected to follow the same regulations as other residents of Wisconsin, and the handful who continued old practices were regarded as violators. This situation continued until 1974, when Fred and Mike Tribble, members of the Lac Court

Oreilles Band, purposefully spearfished through the ice outside reservation boundaries. When the warden showed up, they handed him a copy of the 1837 treaty in defense of their actions, but they were arrested anyway. The Lac Court Oreilles Band then sued the state, claiming its treaty rights had been violated.

The case slowly wended its way through the court system over the course of 17 years. Early on, the tribe suffered a major setback in 1978 when U.S. District Court Judge James Doyle Sr. ruled that the Treaty of 1854 had brought an end to the rights at issue. In 1983, however, the Seventh U.S. Circuit Court of Appeals in Chicago, in a case known as *Lac Court Oreilles Band of Chippewa Indians v. Lester P. Voigt, et al.*, (Voigt was the secretary of the WDNR) overturned Doyle's ruling and declared that the tribe's rights to hunt, fish, and gather on *public* lands in the ceded territory were still operative. The court then charged Doyle with the task of defining these rights. The state of Wisconsin promptly decided to challenge this appellate court ruling by asking the U.S. Supreme Court to review the so-called Voigt decision. The Supreme Court refused, and so it fell to Judge Doyle in Madison to carry out the charge of the Court of Appeals.

The appeals court set three tasks before Doyle. He had to define the nature and extent of Chippewa rights; he needed to determine to what degree the state of Wisconsin could regulate these rights; and he needed to settle on damages owed the tribe for infringement on its rights. In February of 1987, Doyle issued a decision that focused on his first task. Finding that the Chippewa had a right to "a modest living," he went on to assert that, with certain exceptions, they "have the right to exploit virtually all of the natural resources in the ceded territory as they did at treaty time." Moreover, they could use all traditional and contemporary methods of harvesting—including gill nets for fish. And, based on the historical record of Chippewa trading in natural resources,

Doyle ruled that they could trade or sell to non-Indians what they obtained through the exercise of their usufructuary rights. The decision also permitted the state to regulate tribal rights "provided the restrictions are reasonable and necessary to conserve a particular resource." Precisely what such restrictions might be was left to a subsequent phase of the litigation.

Shortly after issuing his decision, Doyle resigned for health reasons, and the case landed in the hands of Judge Barbara Crabb of the U.S. District Court for the Western District of Wisconsin. Over the next few years, Crabb tackled the second and third elements of the case as set out by the appeals court: the scope of state regulation and damages. To the state's right to regulate for the conservation of a resource, which Doyle's ruling had called for, she added the state's right to regulate for the purposes of public health and safety, though she concluded that "effective tribal self-regulation... precludes concurrent state regulation," which left the door open to tribal supervision of its own members with respect to exercising their treaty rights. She next declared that there were not enough resources in the ceded territories to assure the Chippewa the "modest living" that Doyle had sought to provide them when he ruled in favor of their right to "exploit virtually all of the natural resources... that they did at treaty time." That being the case, Crabb qualified Doyle's ruling by asserting that the tribes were entitled to 100 percent of the harvest that was consistent with sound conservation practices. Subsequent to that general ruling, Crabb turned her attention to the technical means that should be used to determine what levels of harvest would protect muskellunge and walleyes over the long run. In 1989 she concluded that the notion of total allowable catch, a formula then in practice, should be replaced by a more complex but more conservative formula: the safe harvest level. Nonetheless, she left in place the tribes' right to harvest up to 100 percent of the quota permitted under the new formula. But in the following year, in a case dealing with tribal hunting of deer and small game, Crabb ordered that "all of the harvested natural resources in the ceded territory are declared to be apportioned equally between the [tribes] and non-Indians." It was not, at this point, entirely clear whether Crabb intended this statement to apply to the fisheries, which had been dealt with in her 1989 ruling. In February of 1991, Crabb denied the claim of the Chippewa that the commercial harvest of timber was among their usufructuary rights.

The final judgment in this lengthy judicial proceeding was handed down on March 19, 1991. In it, Judge Crabb summarized all of the court's orders to date, and made it unambiguously clear that all the resources were to be equally shared by Indians and non-Indians alike. Finally, to the consternation of the plaintiffs in this case, she ruled that the defendants—the state of Wisconsin and various individuals—"were immune from liability for money damages for their violations of plaintiffs' treaty rights." Though neither party was satisfied with the outcome of this lengthy process of litigation, both agreed in writing not to appeal this ruling, in effect committing themselves to working things out within the framework of Judge Crabb's decision.

The State of Wisconsin Responds

While attorneys and judges struggled for eight years, within the rarified confines of the judicial system, to determine the late 20th-century meaning of 19th-century treaties between sovereign states, two additional conflicts played themselves out: one between the WDNR and the Chippewa, and the other between residents of northern Wisconsin and their Chippewa neighbors. The Voigt ruling of 1983 made it clear that the tribes would soon be spearing and perhaps netting. But it was certain to be some time before any judicially sanctioned guidelines would be in place for the exercise of these newly reaffirmed rights. Having failed in its effort to secure a full review of the matter by the United States Supreme Court, the state had little choice but to begin negotiations with the tribes to work out some temporary arrangements while awaiting more permanent and detailed guidance from the courts.

To carry out the negotiations on behalf of the state, WDNR Secretary C.D. "Buzz" Besadny selected George Meyer. Meyer had earlier served as legal counsel to the agency, and at the time he became chief negotiator with the tribes he held the position of director of law enforcement at the WDNR. Like Besadny, Meyer understood that the Voigt decision had ushered in "a life-changing moment," and he recognized the urgency of the situation. But initially he lacked a negotiating partner. If each of the six tribes took a separate direction, the resulting negotiations ran the risk of being widely divergent, if not chaotic. Fortunately for the sake of the negotiations, the Chippewa moved forward promptly to create an agency that would parallel the WDNR. In April of 1984, building from the existing Great Lakes Intertribal Fisheries Commission, the tribes drew up a constitution for the Great Lakes Indian Fish and Wildlife Commission (GLIFWC). By May, this new commission had been authorized by 11 Chippewa tribes in Wisconsin, Michigan, and Minnesota. In addition to its existing biologists, GLIFWC immediately began to hire more wardens in anticipation of its law enforcement responsibilities as outlined by the court. As it turned out, GLIFWC gave Meyer and his team what they were looking for: namely, tribal counterparts with whom state biologists could ascertain common facts and understandings about the resources that would be subject to tribal harvest. Science would provide a useful measure of common ground in a setting that had the potential to be extremely divisive.

But one big issue stood above all the others. As Meyer later put it, "Who had the responsibility in the ceded territory for the actual management of the resource?" When the tribes had attained the necessary biological and law enforcement resources, the court had concluded, they would be able to implement and manage the exercise of their rights. But these capabilities did not embrace the totality of resource management. For example, again according to Meyer, who "issues permits for activities that affect the resource," such as stocking or conducting surveys? After all, the legislature had long ago asserted the state's right to ownership of all the fish in Wisconsin waters. Surely, then, the state had a legitimate interest in managing this resource. In the ensuing debate, the tribes and GLIFWC called for "co-management," but the state found that notion unacceptable because it would mean surrendering its sovereignty over those activities not specifically reserved for the tribes. This struggle between conflicting sovereignties was resolved when the two parties agreed to engage in "co-operative" management. This semantic compromise enabled the two parties to get together to split up management work, which included deciding such matters as who was going to survey, and where and when. At the same time, this compromise enabled the state to hang on to its claim to sovereignty with regard to big-picture management of the state's fisheries. This claim was subsequently reinforced, at least in part, by Judge Crabb's final ruling, which stated: "In the event of a dispute in determining the safe harvest level for any lake that cannot be resolved by the parties, the determination shall be made by the Department of Natural Resources."

At a more concrete, managerial level, Meyer and his team worked with GLIFWC and tribal leadership to hammer out preliminary regulations for seasons and allowable harvests. Open water agreements for 1984 came too late in the season for tribal spearing, but an agreement reached in April of 1985 set the stage for the exercise of tribal rights that spring. It allowed each tribe to spear six lakes, which had to be 500 acres or greater. Spearers were limited to 20 walleyes each, with a 20-inch maximum size limit, and one fish over 20 inches. Negotiations in subsequent years modified significantly the terms of this initial agreement, in part in response to partial declaratory judgments by the court and in part in response to pressure from the tribes to expand annual harvests. These were not easy negotiations, as the two sides had to work together against the backdrop of widespread public disagreement with the court ruling, as well as heated animosity directed toward the tribes.

By 1989 tensions and concerns had risen to the point where the state seemed to have felt the need to push back, in defense of the resource, against tribal aspirations. First of all, the tribes and the state agreed that any lake speared two years in a row must get a one-year rest—if the harvest exceeded 60 percent of the safe harvest threshold (the tribe had sought 100 percent, the state 50 percent). Second, in May, just before the opening of the fishing season, the Natural Resources Board passed an emergency resolution giving the WDNR power to set the bag limits of non-Indian anglers on 254 lakes from one to three walleyes—depending on the size of the spearing harvest on these lakes. This was done in response to an assertion by the tribes that they would take 100 percent of the total allowable catch if they were again to be threatened by protesters. Third, later in 1989 the state attorney general, Donald Hanaway, proposed that the state purchase for $50 million a 10-year lease of the treaty rights of the Lac du Flambeau Band—by far the most active spearers of the six Chippewa bands. This initiative failed, however, when the Lac du Flambeau Band voted 439 to 366 to retain its treaty rights. With this action, the lease option was essentially dead. It was within the context of these troubled negotiations and the social conflict that accompanied tribal spearing that Judge Crabb's final ruling of 1991 came down, allowing the state to retain a management role in the event of an unresolvable dispute over safe harvest levels. There was still much work to do, but it must be said that the state and the tribes had established a track record of negotiations from 1983 onward—there had been more than 40 interim agreements—that had seen them through an extremely trying period. The two parties would build on this record in future years.

Lines in the Sand of the Landings

Though the outcomes of state and tribal negotiations made the news from time to time, it was what happened at the boat landings and on the lakes where spearing took place that became the public face of the exercise of tribal rights. And what took place at these locations set the stage for years of confrontation—both civil and ugly. By several accounts, the sight of tubs of walleyes, spear marks evident, turned the stomachs and inflamed the passions of many of the non-Indians who witnessed the end product of a night's spearing. As word spread, people of varying perspectives turned up to observe the activity and to express their feelings about it. Some were anglers and other outdoor advocates who found spearing an ethically objectionable means of harvesting fish. Some were conservationists who feared for the future of the resource. Still others, with business interests in the area, feared that spearing would adversely affect tourism, one of the precious few mainstays of the northern economy. And there were those—some of whom might also fit into one or more of the preceding three groups—who just plain did not like Indians. This opposition to Chippewa treaty rights soon found expression in two local groups. Protect Americans Rights and Resources (PARR) led by Larry Peterson, a Park Falls resident, was an organization founded on the premise that all residents of the state (and country) should enjoy the same rights. PARR sought the abrogation of treaties, which they regarded as giving unequal rights to the tribes, through the political process. PARR members also held rallies and demonstrated at boat landings— though in 1987, at least, state officials credited them with help in "reducing the number of people and trouble at landings." Another organization, Stop Treaty Abuse (STA), headed by Dean Crist, the owner of a Minocqua pizza establishment, was also dedicated to fighting treaty rights through the political process. To that end, STA marketed its own brew, Treaty Beer, whose cans contained images and text that vividly conveyed the group's goals. Profits from the sale of Treaty Beer were to be used to finance candidates favorable to STA's position. In time, however, STA became known more for its aggressive protests and acts of civil disobedience at landings, as well as for its propensity to attract individuals of a coarser nature. Both PARR and STA would remain active players on the treaty rights scene for a number of years.

Confrontations at landings between Chippewa spearers and those opposed to them began in 1985, the first year of the exercise of treaty rights. During the last two nights of that season, wardens and supporting deputy sheriffs were hard put to maintain order between tribal spearers and opponents at two sites. According to the *The Milwaukee Journal*, George Meyer, administrator of the division of law enforcement at the WDNR, thought that the intensity of these confrontations exceeded what was reported in the press and that violence most likely would have ensued had the season run longer. Of course, not every expression of opposition to the treaties rose to the level of near violence. Sometimes protesters stood silently and watched. Other times they carried signs demanding the same rights for everyone, or some variation on that theme. But there were also crude signs with racist messages, often accompanied by shouts and taunts. For sure, race was not the only card played at the landing; there were other, wholly independent reasons why someone might protest. But the racism that manifested itself cast its shadow over the protests and protesters, whether fairly or not, and helped to shape perceptions of the events.

It was but a short step from some of the extreme forms of verbal hostility to treaty rights to actual harassment of those who were exercising those rights. The Chippewa—and sometimes law enforcement personnel assigned to maintain peace—found themselves targets of rocks, golf balls, or missiles fired from wrist rockets. On occasion protesters showed up with baseball bats. Angry opponents took to the water, using their boats to scare fish, to impede the course of tribal spearers, or to attempt to swamp tribal boats with heavy waves. Protesters also built cement walleye decoys and placed them in the shallows in hopes they would shatter Chippewa spears. And there were occasional fireworks or gunshots, close enough to jangle everyone's nerves, and in one instance sufficiently well-aimed to bring a few overhanging branches down among tribal boats. Throughout these troubled years, the one persistent response of the Chippewa to such harassment, however intimidating it may have been, was to keep on with the exercise of their rights. In time, though, they spoke back to their opponents in a manner of ways. There was, of course, some tit for tat, as when Chippewa supporters of the treaty showed up at the Balsam Lake landing with signs containing obscene comments about the protesters. T-shirts emblazoned with "Chippewa and Proud" and baseball caps with the legend "Walleye Warrior" asserted both tribal allegiance and a readiness to fight for treaty rights. But the signature response of the tribes to harassment involved practices that linked spearfishing to their traditional culture. They brought ceremonial drums to the landings; they chanted a number of songs; and they sometimes sprinkled tobacco on the waters on which they were about to fish. Whether such ceremonies won many converts to treaty rights cannot be ascertained; that they irritated quite a number of treaty opponents is a matter of public record.

Faced with acts of harassment and the ever-present possibility of large-scale violence, the Wisconsin Division of Emergency Government (WDEG) developed elaborate plans to coordinate varying assets to be used for peacekeeping—including local law enforcement officers, deputy sheriffs and wardens from around the state, members of the Wisconsin State Patrol, and equipment from the Wisconsin National Guard. The WDEG set up command centers from which assistance could be directed to locations deemed potential powder kegs or where confrontations had already turned ugly. All that said, peacekeeping duty was difficult, dangerous, and psychologically demanding, as the officers had to protect everyone's rights, even as they struggled to prevent matters from getting out of hand.

Confrontation Comes to the Turtle-Flambeau Flowage

The Turtle-Flambeau Flowage was bound to play a major role in tribal harvest plans. It was one of the largest lakes in the ceded territory; it had an excellent reputation for walleye fishing; and it was conveniently located just a few miles from the Lac du Flambeau Reservation. That the tribes would draw heavily on its abundant walleye population was evident from the first years of legal spearing. For example, on the night of April 26, 1986, 54 tribal spearers took 1,192 walleyes from flowage waters, a number that amounted to 86 percent of the permissible catch under that year's negotiated agreement. With no protesters at the scene, the rather substantial harvest seemed, to one observer at least, fairly benign. Terry Koper, an outdoor writer for the *Milwaukee Sentinel,* watched as young Indians girls and friends listened to traditional music at the landing and waited eagerly to see what success the men had experienced during their night on the water. Koper, who felt the flowage could safely give up that many walleyes, found a kind of historic charm in the evening. "The Indians' activities at the Turtle-Flambeau Flowage that night certainly seemed an important part of Wisconsin's culture." But in the same article in which he expressed these thoughts, Koper went on to note just how quickly actions and perceptions could change. Two nights later, Lac du Flambeau spearers took almost four times their quota from Star Lake in Vilas County, an action that Koper felt badly undermined efforts by tribal leaders to assure area residents that they could regulate the harvest on their own. Whether it was a response to a rally and march of treaty protesters in Minocqua and Woodruff or was simply a mistake, the Star Lake overharvest, coupled with another one earlier in the season at Squirrel Lake, went over badly with WDNR officials who had to rely on the tribes to police their own members. And of course news of the overharvests, coupled with the fact that the Lac du Flambeau Tribe alone harvested 5,743 walleyes during the season, fed the flames of those opposed to the treaties. The 1986 season ended on notes of unhappiness and anger among all parties—hardly a good omen looking forward.

The 1987 season played out under the auspices of Judge Doyle's ruling, which had opened the door to even larger harvests. The allowance for the flowage, for example, was set at 5,900 walleyes. Though protesters were a regular presence at landings throughout the flowage, the bulk of the season went without incident. For example, 88 Chippewa spearers took 2,954 fish from the flowage on

April 19, bringing their total take to just 714 fish shy of their season allowance on the TFF. Press reports indicated that some (unnamed) state fisheries technicians were concerned about possible damage to breeding stock caused by the one large walleye each spearer was allowed to take each night. James Addis, director of the WDNR Bureau of Fish Management, traveled from Madison to Minocqua to deny that spearing was threatening future fish populations. "As far as our professionals are concerned, we believe they are responding with their hearts instead of their biological sense." In a report he prepared later in the year, however, Addis stated "in at least some lakes, the disproportionate harvest of larger fish raises major biological questions about the long-term reproductive and genetic viability of certain fish stocks, such as walleyes and bass. New studies are needed to answer these questions."

But conditions deteriorated in the next week or so; and when four Lac du Flambeau boats, containing nine or 10 tribal members, set out on the flowage on April 28, some 100 white men, women, and children were present at the Springstead Landing. Although some protesters claimed that the mood was tense but the crowd was quiet (many were drinking beer), press reports say that the protesters were verbally challenging Tom Maulson and other tribal members who were waiting for the spearers to return. According to these reports, a number of outbursts were heard, such as: "Who paid for the landing?" "Indian boats have no registration stickers and no running lights." "If the Indians are citizens, don't they have to obey by the laws?" While all of this was going on, the crowd of approximately 100 people stood behind barricades that law enforcement officials had erected to limit the number of protesters at the landing. When one protester violated the barricade, he was arrested by Sheriff Don Bugni. Two others were also arrested that night, and Bugni later indicated he would charge them with disorderly conduct. "There was a lot of screaming and hollering,"Bugni said, "and we acted to prevent something more serious from happening." The sheriff's actions did keep matters under control that night, but they did not prevent Iron County citizens from putting together a petition, which had some 700 signatures by May 19, to recall Bugni.

Concern over potential violence led the state to strengthen peacekeeping arrangements still further in advance of the 1988 season. One change, the use of a standardized form for nightly situation reports (SITREP), not only provided uniform documentation for those involved in the operation but it also made it possible to reconstruct events with some degree of precision. The following excerpt from a SITREP on April 19, 1988, is a case in point. (The log uses military time.)

> "The largest gathering was at Turtle/Flambeau Flowage where there were 67 permits issued (to Chippewa spearfishermen). It is estimated that there were approximately fifty (50) non-Indian demonstrators/onlookers present. A mild altercation occurred between Sheriff Bugni and two young individuals. No arrests were made. The following is a log of events from the Turtle/Flambeau Flowage landing.

> 1958   Iron County Sheriff had the altercation with the young individuals.

> 2018   Iron County Sheriff called for mutual aid [sheriff's deputies and police officers on standby in the area], as well as support from the State Patrol, due to the altercation. Mutual aid officers from NW area were dispatched to the scene.

> 2020   Mutual aid personnel on the scene.

> 2045   State Patrol was at the landing with two officers. There were approximately fifty personnel on the landing, both pro and anti-treaty, with word that more anti-treaty were coming.

2130 State Patrol advised that all was calm at the time and the additional non-treaty persons did not come as thought."

The report does not specify the number of mutual aid officers who showed up, but it does indicate that a total of 35 law enforcement personnel were available in Iron County that night. Whatever the number, the effect was clear: lots of people departed from the landing. Richard Risler, the Dunn County sheriff, was to later describe this operation in a memorandum summing up his peacekeeping experiences for the year: "...I watched from the air as the West Central units flowed into the landing and saw that within minutes a lot [sic] of cars were leaving the area. My personnel advised later that once they arrived the people started leaving and appeared awed at the amout [sic] of squads and officers that arrived." Risler had flown in a Wisconsin National Guard helicopter on loan to the WDEG.

spearing starts with clash
ıke 1,352 walleyes in first night

Spearers from Lac du Flambeau, the most productive of all Chippewa bands, started their 15-day off-reservation season Monday by taking 1,352 walleyes using the method depicted by this photo from the Turtle-Flambeau Flowage. Two protesters were arrested at Butternut Lake in Ashland County. --Staff Photo By KURT KRUEGER

A tribal spearer takes a walleye in April 1988. Vilas County News-Review. Wisconsin Historical Society

The flowage drew the attention of tribal spearers for another nine nights before the season ended. On April 22, with 70 permits issued to the Lac du Flambeau Tribe, 25 mutual aid officers from Ashland and Price counties were on hand to assist Sheriff Bugni. Nonetheless, according to the SITREP for that evening, there was one incident: "A tribal biologist in a spearfishing boat reported a rock-throwing incident. Even though there was a quick response and search of the area, no apprehensions were made." The next night, Sheriff Frederick of Bayfield County, backed by more than a dozen deputies, manned the landing while 21 tribal boats were accompanied by wardens in a patrol boat. The cold weather limited the number of protesters. By the 25th, Bugni reported that he did not anticipate needing any assistance, and no personnel were assigned. And by the 28th, Alan Shanks, who headed up the WDEG command center, made the following observation: "I personally believe the Indians are tired of the hassle, and Maulson indicated just plain tired. I also believe the public is wearing down. They have so many Wisconsin State Patrol troopers in Price County, that the sheriff stated they [Price County residents] are walking to the drive-up bank." Strict enforcement of traffic regulations, it should be noted, was one part of the government's strategy for dealing with the situation. Sheriff Bugni's last report for the season, on May 3, noted that all was quiet at the flowage.

The Flowage Sits
Out a Critical Year

The quiet ending of the 1988 season at the flowage stood at odds with the kinds of reports coming into the command center from various departments involved in peacekeeping. "The issue is no longer fish, it's Race.... The tension is so thick you could cut it with a knife.... The explosion will take place when the weather warms." The explosion did not take place, but the intelligence that led law enforcement to anticipate it lingered in the minds of emergency government officials and shaped their preparations for the coming year. And as indicated earlier, 1989 did indeed turn out to be a high point in what came to be known as the "Walleye War." But the Turtle-Flambeau Flowage stood on the sidelines, as it were, while the conflict raged. It was one of 15 lakes closed to spearing because the spearfishing harvest in the preceding two years had exceeded 60 percent of the total allowable catch. One can only speculate what might have taken place at its landings had the flowage been open during the year.

What did happen elsewhere in 1989 was an intensification of the conflict as more extreme elements on both sides threatened to take over the agenda. Whereas PARR continued to press its case for a political resolution of the conflict, STA, bolstered by what law enforcement described as "redneck" supporters, sought more aggressively to disrupt spearing activities. A split also took place on the Lac du Flambeau reservation where the Wa-Swa-Gon Treaty Association, under Tom Maulson's leadership, took a more militant stance toward the exercise of treaty rights than did many other tribal members. At the landings, the language of protest escalated as signs reading "Spear an Indian, Save a Walleye," appeared alongside familiar ones such as "Equal Rights for Everyone" or "Stop Treaty Abuse." And in one instance, protesters used an effigy of "Indian Joe" to taunt the Chippewa. Arrests, which had been few in number in the preceding years, mounted rapidly: 35 at various lakes on the nights of April 26 and 27; and 109 at Trout Lake on May 5. As the confrontations increased in intensity, state officials feared that a continuation of spearing into the opening weekend for angling would lead to situations beyond the control of available law enforcement resources. This fear prompted the governor to ask the attorney general to seek a restraining order that would close the Chippewa spearfishing season the night before open water angling began. The request went to Judge Crabb, who ruled against the state. In her decision, the judge noted that the state "is seeking an injunction against the tribes solely because persons opposed to the lawful activities of the tribes are engaging in illegal and wrongful acts against tribal members.... As a matter of law, the fact that some are acting illegally and creating justified fears of violence, does not justify abridging the rights of those who have done nothing illegal or improper." It was the Chippewa themselves who terminated spearfishing two days later. Once again, the northwoods had escaped the violence so many feared, but only by a whisker.

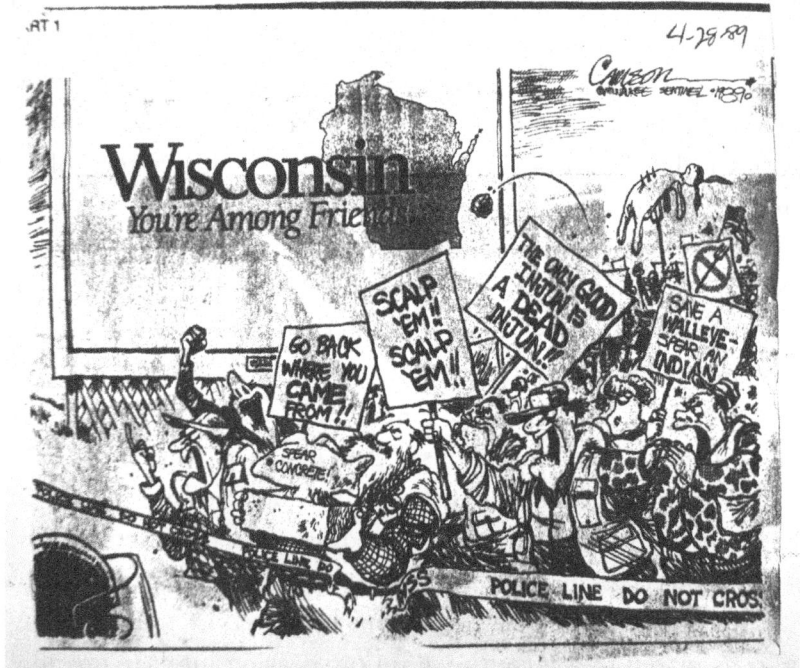

A Milwaukee Sentinel *editorial cartoon plays on the state tourism department's slogan: "Wisconsin. You're Among Friends." Division of Emergency Government Archives. Wisconsin Historical Society*

When the 1990 spearfishing season opened, the press was present in force—three television stations each from Minneapolis and Green Bay, NBC national news, *Time* magazine, and others— no doubt hoping for some headline-catching action. But the situation had perceptibly altered. A STA rally drew one-third the crowd it had drawn a year earlier; and on the night the Lac du Flambeau Tribe took to the waters, STA members passed out flyers on landing etiquette: no racism and no violence were among the admonitions. Crowds at two PARR rallies during the season fell way short of expectations. If the protest movement appeared less vigorous and a bit tamer, the balance of forces was further altered by the emergence in full force of pro-treaty groups, such as Citizens for Treaty Rights, Honor Our Neighbors' Origins and Rights (HONOR), and Witness for Non-Violence and Treaty Rights (sometimes referred to as Witness for Peace). These groups came out in support of the Chippewa wherever protesters appeared; and Witness, which seems to have specialized in worst-case assessments, tended to see media conspiracies as hiding ugly realities where others saw reduced tensions. Yet another pro-treaty presence in 1990 was the American Indian Movement (AIM), an Indian civil rights organization looked upon with some concern by law enforcement officials because of its record of militant actions. The growing presence of treaty supporters shows up clearly in the record of the 1990 spearfishing season.

The Flowage Returns to a Gradually Dimming Spotlight

After being on the sidelines in 1989, the flowage was front and center in 1990, at least if one judges by the preseason tribal declarations (the Lac du Flambeau and Bad River bands declared a total of 5,531 walleyes on the flowage) and by the number of law enforcement officers assigned to it. When the season opened on the flowage on April 20, 105 officers were present at Springstead and an additional nine state troopers showed up to help out. Six warden boats reported observing 14 tribal boats and three protest boats on the water. Crowd numbers—80 supporters, including 40 AIM members, and 350 protesters—were later determined to have been seriously inflated, but the proportions were roughly correct. Some pushing and shoving led to the arrest of one tribal member, and the record sheet indicates a rock-throwing incident. All in all, however, it was a fairly calm night. As the situation report notes: "Friday evening, Bill Hudson, WCCO-TV, Minneapolis called the Media Center by satellite link from the Turtle-Flambeau Flowage inquiring 'Where is the action tonight?' PIOs [Public Relations Officers] replied 'You're there.' And Hudson indicated nothing was happening."

As the season went on, progressively fewer incidents occurred. On April 21, 87 officers were present. Four boats with wardens, 13 treaty boats, and one boat of protesters plied flowage waters. Fifty supporters of the Chippewa and 90 protesters were counted. The situation report notes that supporters formed a tight circle to protect the Lac du Flambeau drum, "which has become an object of protesters' anger." One arrest was made for disorderly conduct. The following night, the police presence was down to 51. Eleven treaty boats and two protest boats were shadowed by just one warden boat. The 70 treaty supporters substantially outnumbered the 30 protesters, and there were no incidents. When the Bad River Band speared the flowage on the 23rd, just 21 officers were present. Ten protesters and one protest boat were on site; there were no treaty supporters. The situation was about the same the following night: nine officers, two warden boats, two protest boats, three supporters, and four protesters. When the two bands got around to Trude Lake, there were a total of four protesters over the course of three nights. To be sure, there were a few bigger crowds and some more tense moments at other locations in 1990, but the season as a whole passed much less contentiously than had been the case in the previous few years. The Walleye War was not over, but the energies that had sparked it were steadily dwindling. That said, this change in circumstances was not without cost. State appropriations for the peacekeeping operation added up to $2,558,922.79. Counting both walleyes and muskies, the cost per fish speared was $97.92.

Prior to the 1991 season, emergency government personnel had begun to discuss ways to gradually wind down their heavy presence—assuming that nothing unpredictable arose. They were to be assisted in achieving this goal by three situation-altering factors. First, in 1990, the state legislature passed the so-called hunter harassment bill. It had been intended to protect state hunters, anglers, and other outdoor enthusiasts from various anti-hunting and fishing groups, although its applicability to the spearfishing situation had come up during its movement through the legislature. In April of 1991, Chief Wisconsin State Conservation Warden Ralph Christensen made it clear that the law would be invoked in the event of harassment of Chippewa spearers. Second, in a ruling handed down on March 15, 1991, Judge Crabb enjoined STA, Crist, the founder of STA, and others from participating in a number of activities that constituted interference with the Indians' exercise of their rights. And third, four days later Judge Crabb issued her final ruling on the main treaty case. Short of appeals to higher courts, all the main issues had been resolved in a definitive manner. In light of these developments and the gradual tapering off of hostilities over the last two years, there was reason to expect an even quieter season in 1991.

Events at the Turtle-Flambeau Flowage bore out that

expectation. A large Lac du Flambeau presence on the flowage on April 20 brought out just 11 officers and three boats with wardens. The five protesters who showed up were vastly outnumbered, especially early in the evening, by 170 AIM members before the latter headed off to another lake. In subsequent nights, less than a half-dozen officers patrolled the Springstead Landing, and the few protesters who showed up, nine one night, seven another, indicated that they were flowage "landowners who were not happy with the spearing." No incidents were reported at the flowage, and only one arrest took place anywhere during the first two weeks of the season. The records for this year reveal, for the first time, a lighter side here and there—no doubt a sign that tensions were abating still further. One situation report, for example, notes that "Iron County sheriff advised he received a phone call from pro-treaty people this afternoon demanding that he put lights on the landing tonight, because they didn't want to be there in the dark. [Emergency government authorities had begun withdrawing lights from the landings during this year.] He advised caller that if they don't like the dark they shouldn't come." As Karl Marx wrote, "History repeats itself, first as tragedy, and second as farce."

In many ways, 1992 witnessed a transition to what was to become the new normal for spring in the northwoods. Emergency planning activities were minimal. Peacekeeping was turned over to local authorities—principally sheriffs—with modest backup from the State Patrol. Wardens were instructed to return to "their traditional enforcement duties," as opposed to shepherding spearing boats or just waiting around landings in readiness should some need arise. GLIFWC wardens, some of whom had been cross-deputized at the height of the conflict so that they could engage in law enforcement, were expected to be at the landings to monitor catches and to play a broader role in enforcement. GLIFWC was also charged with informing local law enforcement in advance what lakes would be speared and by which bands. This task had previously been handled by WDEG command posts. In short, emergency government sought to recede into the background as much as possible.

As far as the flowage was concerned, these decisions and actions proved to be the right ones. When it was heavily speared on May 2, there were no problems anywhere—even though the open water angling season had opened that same day. Tribal spearers subsequently took to flowage waters four more times, again without incident. All told, just four arrests took place across the northland in 1992, three of protesters, and one of a tribal member accused of shaking off small fish. It is little wonder that the final report for the 1992 season, written by Rick Risler, director of emergency police services, began with these words: "The spearfishing season passed in a quieter mode then [sic] even we had hoped for."

Short-Term Reactions and Long-Term Impacts

The preceding overview reflects the place of the flowage in the broader course of the Walleye War, but it does not capture the experiences of those who found themselves drawn, willy-nilly, into the fray. In particular, resort owners, guides, and local businesses could not help but see the spearing, and the conflict it created, as a serious threat to their livelihoods. People phoned resorts to ask, among other things, whether it was safe to bring their children to the flowage; and most resort owners reported some reductions in the number of their guests—bad news given the narrow margins of their businesses. The question for all involved parties was where to turn for help—and help for most of these parties meant either an end to, or a substantial curtailment of, the exercise of treaty rights by the Chippewa. Though a federal appeals court had played a critical if momentary role, the matter (and the lawsuit that prompted it) was really a state one. While the state did respond, effectively, to threats to public order, no executive or legislative action to address the larger set of issues raised by the court's ruling was forthcoming—perhaps because the issues involved were too politically sensitive. And the magnitude of the situation seemed beyond the powers of local government. So what to do, as the National Guard helicopter hovered annoyingly overhead near resorts (or in the case of one citizen complaint, threatened to produce aberrant behavior among the animals at a fox farm), as guests cancelled out, as the media seemed always to be fanning the flames, as rumors and speculation ran their course (might it be that the state, which was buying the flowage, allowed spearing to take place so as to encourage resort owners to sell out)? The answers ranged, of course, from glum resignation to active participation in protest groups and activities, depending on personal preference or abilities.

One interesting set of responses came from Maryann Brown of the Lodge of Lakeview. With a long record of involvement in promoting the flowage and its businesses, she was accustomed to taking an active stance on behalf of local economic interests. Early on during the spearfishing struggle, she recognized that the number of people—whether business owners or residents—with vested interests in the flowage was limited, and so she reached out for support to people in the tourism business in nearby areas, such as Boulder Junction. The Chamber of Commerce in Boulder Junction, to judge by a communication it sent to Governor Tommy Thompson, was a moderate and thoughtful voice in seeking to defuse the tensions in the area. In her search for support, Brown also joined PARR, presumably attracted by its goals of treaty revision. But her support for a major protest organization did not prevent her from actions of quite a different kind. As one of a delegation of people recruited by the Wisconsin Department of Tourism, Brown visited the Lac du Flambeau reservation to engage in a discussion with tribal elders about the impact of spearing on the economy. She remembers a moment of some tension before their first meeting convened when Tom Maulson, adorned with his Walleye Warrior cap, came striding into the room only to be promptly ushered out by some of the elders. As the participants introduced themselves, Brown noticed that she was sitting next to an elder named G.W. Brown. When it was her turn to speak, she pointed out that her father-in-law's name was G.W. Brown and that she and the elder must be related. The ensuing laughter helped to break the ice. These meetings were to continue on a regular basis for some time. If nothing else, they showed that divisive issues could be discussed civilly and that the outcomes of these discussions could last beyond the moment. Indeed, as Brown relates, at some later date several members of the Lac du Flambeau Band, who were unsuccessfully spearfishing in front of her resort, hailed her and laughingly shouted: "You were right, Maryann! There aren't any walleyes here." Brown's responses to the situation, though they might appear outwardly contradictory, could also be seen as complementary ways to an end—though none of them was a "silver bullet." In short, the spearing controversy was extremely complex, as was the path to its resolution.

"In the darkest days of past seasons everyone thought that this too shall pass. It took sometime [sic] but yes it did pass!!" These words concluded Rick Risler's report in 1992. Written by a law enforcement officer who had helped to prevent potentially tragic violence, the words ring true. And yet, even after the tumult of the struggle had abated and peace had returned to the landings, a lingering and often poisonous residue remained. For what had passed was the crisis, not the thoughts and feelings it had generated. For many non-Indians, legacies of sadness, regret, or anger haunt their memories of the episode. To some, the onus for what they see as an assault on and a degradation of the fishery falls squarely on the Chippewa. One longtime resident of the flowage area bitterly noted the contrast between Indians he had once seen harvesting wild rice on the flowage and the Indians he had witnessed spearing and who he holds responsible for wasting fish. For him, it was as if a romantic image had been shattered, only to be replaced by an in-your-face approach to spearing by the Chippewa. Others blame all that transpired on a judicial system that, in enforcing 19th-century treaties, failed to give sufficient credence to the realities of the second half of the 20th century. But the naysayers were not without their critics. One veteran flowage area resident claimed some of the most vituperative critics of tribal spearing could be heard in local taverns boasting of their own double- and triple-bagging of walleyes, only to follow up such boasts with accusations that the Indians were ruining the fishery—with no apparent awareness of the hypocrisy of their words. There are, of course, some local residents and regular visitors who either have made their peace with the new order of things, or who have welcomed outright the vindication of native claims; but their numbers are not large, nor their voices loud. Change, especially that which challenges a complex web of cultural, social, economic, and political views, does not go down easy.

Tribal reactions to this turbulent time and its aftermath were, in spite of a definitive victory in the courts, far from uniform. After all, the tribal government and Wa-Swa-Gon were not always, as noted earlier, on the same page; and the Lac du Flambeau members narrowly split their vote on the state's offer to buy out their treaty rights. That said, reactions from the Indian side tended to be more positive than those of non-Indians, and certainly lacked the apocalyptic tone that so often infused the latter.

An early assessment of the initial years of spearing appeared in a 1994 book, *Walleye Warriors*, written by Rick Whaley with Walter Bresette. This work, based on personal involvement of the authors, focuses on the formation and activities of Witness for Non-Violence for Treaty and Rural Rights in Northern Wisconsin, an organization of Indians and non-Indians who actively supported the Chippewa in the exercise of their newly reaffirmed rights. The authors argue that Witness drew on the experiences of individuals and organizations who had been involved in various other movements, such as "Wounded Knee, Black Hills, southern civil rights, anti-Vietnam war, women's and environmental movements." More broadly, Witness also associated itself with efforts to assist oppressed, largely rural indigenous populations in countries around the world. In short, this book seeks to elevate what appeared to some to be a limited, regional conflict in Wisconsin's northwoods into an exemplar of larger national and global movements for human rights.

Bresette and Whaley, while celebrating the nonviolent process by which the Chippewa and their allies attained their goals, do not consider the outcome of the struggle to be an unqualified success. The tribes failed in court either to achieve timber rights in the ceded lands or to secure damages for the years in which their reserved rights had been denied. Moreover, tribal governments found themselves in the awkward position of policing their members with respect to laws and policies that originated outside the bounds of tribal sovereignty. Nevertheless, in the authors' view, the end result amounted to much more than a legal judgment on the tribes' behalf: "Chippewa spearfishers and tribal governments had secured the sovereignty [sic], treaty right to off-reservation harvesting, and, in doing so, had reestablished the right to what was really an ancient cultural and religious practice—the intertwining and honoring of spring's bounty and our survival."

A subsequent scholarly examination of the spearing controversy appeared in the spring 2011 edition of the *American Indian Quarterly*. In an article titled "After the Storm: Ojibwe Treaty Rights Twenty-Five Years after the Voigt Decision," Patty Loew and James Thannum identify several factors that contributed to the explosive reaction to the court's affirmation of native rights and the tribes' exercise of these rights. A nationwide recession had hit Wisconsin hard, sending its unemployment rate to 11.7 percent in 1983. The tourist industry, already suffering from aging facilities and a failure to meet changing demands from their clientele (the great majority were drawn to the state for activities other than fishing), took an added hit from the recession. Moreover, in spite of the declining percentage of tourists who came to Wisconsin to fish, pressure on northern Wisconsin fisheries, especially for walleyes and muskies, had grown to the point where these resources were in some jeopardy. Not surprisingly, then, when the courts gave the green light to spearing, many area residents and resort owners feared that the practice would lead to unlimited tribal harvests, which in turn would destroy fish populations and ruin business. To this core concern must be added poor communication between the tribes and their neighbors, popular perceptions that the Indians were recipients of disproportionate government assistance, and racist attitudes among some opponents of spearing. For Loew and Thannum, these various conditions and attitudes came together in "a perfect storm."

Such a reading of this period of conflict, in which preconceptions, misunderstandings, and ignorance of other people's interests and concerns played an important role, suggests that the road to resolution of the conflict would need to be paved with education and cooperation. And this is the case the authors make. Education entailed informing all interested parties about procedures in place for setting harvest limits and making public hard numbers about actual fish harvests by Indian spearers and anglers alike. It also took the form of efforts to educate Wisconsin youth about tribal history, culture, and sovereignty. As for cooperation, the article points to the positive role played by the Great Lakes Indian Fish and Wildlife Commission in monitoring fish populations and in cooperating with the WDNR in the management of fishery resources in the ceded territory. Once this perfect storm abated, the article concludes, tourism remained strong, the fisheries benefited from cooperation, and race relations improved, if modestly.

A more recent perspective on the events surrounding the initial exercise by the Chippewa of their reserved rights, as well as the long-term consequences of this transformative time, comes from a 2016 interview by the author with Tom Maulson. As noted earlier in this chapter, Maulson actively lobbied Lac du Flambeau tribal members to reject a state offer to buy out their treaty rights, and his leadership of Chippewa spearers at the boat landings placed him at the center of the storm of opposition to treaty-based fish harvests. Subsequently, he has served as a tribal judge, as tribal president, and as a member of the Voigt Intertribal Task Force.

Reflecting on the early days of spearing, Maulson attributes the hostile reaction of so many people to sharply different perspectives on the nature of the tribal harvests. For the tribes, taking large numbers of fish in a short time was a deeply historical practice that had supplied their communities with life-sustaining food. Sports anglers, however, were accustomed to taking a few fish, time and again, over a long season, to satisfy more limited, short-term needs. As a consequence, their first encounter with traditional tribal harvests "was a new experience for sports anglers," Maulson contends, one that was difficult to understand given their own sense of what fishing was all about. Not surprisingly, then, when sports anglers saw or learned about the extent of the tribal harvests, which were so concentrated in time and place, they concluded that the fishery was under threat of overharvest. This was not, however, necessarily the case, Maulson argues. To illustrate his point, he recalls that during one of the early years of spearing, the tribes' season take from the flowage was 3,500 fish. But that same spring, on one day alone during opening weekend, a creel check of sports anglers at one landing on the flowage counted some 3,000 fish. Such data clearly support the conclusion that angler harvests over the course of a year exceeded tribal harvests many times over. (To corroborate Maulson's point about the disparity in numbers between tribal and angler harvests, one might cite a WDNR report from 1990, which estimates that sports anglers took 839,000 walleyes from lakes in the ceded area between 1986 and 1989, whereas the Chippewa tribes took 70,283 fish during the same period.) Finally, in defense of tribal restraint, Maulson points out that under the initial—if rather imperfect— rules for tribal harvests the Lac du Flambeau spearers could have taken 55,000 fish. That they did not do so, he notes, is indicative of a cautious approach to a highly valued resource.

This difference between tribal and angler traditions and perceptions, Maulson believes, created a level of misunderstanding between the parties that lay at the heart of the conflict. In an effort to counter this misunderstanding, the tribes engaged in extensive outreach to schools and clubs in the hope that explanations of their cultural traditions and of the limited impact of their harvests on the fishery in the ceded territories would ease tensions. How much these educational initiatives contributed to the eventual dissipation of overt hostility toward the exercise of treaty rights cannot easily be assessed, but Maulson contends they were of value, so much so, in fact, that he continues to place his trust in the education of the young as the best way to bridge social and cultural gaps between Indian and non-Indian communities in the future.

With respect to his experiences with the Turtle-Flambeau Flowage, Maulson remembers that when the tribe first speared it in the 1980s there were "fish aplenty." Now, however, he contends that fish numbers have gone down, and he worries that the flowage may be subject to overharvest, either at the present or in the future. The issue, from his perspective, turns on fish population estimates that are used to set both tribal and sports angler harvests. Whereas the number of fish the tribes harvest is a precisely known quantity, as their take is monitored, fish by fish, at the landings, sports angler harvest levels are derived from creel censuses that are based on current sampling techniques. Maulson has serious reservations about the validity of these numbers. Do these numbers reflect how much catch-and-release fishing affects musky survival, or motor trolling increases the take of walleyes? In short, he argues that the WDNR angler harvest numbers may not be calculated rigorously enough to base policy on. This concern about the validity of the numbers becomes all the more worrisome given the recent introduction of three-fish limits on all lakes in the ceded territory.

Ultimately, Maulson's views put him at odds with the WDNR, which, of course, would not be the first time in his life. But his current position, interestingly enough, places him in the role of protector of the resources in the ceded territory while at the same time facing off against the agency that has a similar role in protecting the state's natural resources. To some extent, this situation may stem from a number of ongoing disagreements between the tribes and the WDNR that have severely eroded trust between the two parties. It may also be attributed to the fact that, as he puts it, "everyone wants to be boss." This latter observation reflects a basic truth about the flowage that will become increasingly evident in subsequent chapters. These issues aside, the fact that Tom Maulson is willing to entertain the notion that harvests on lakes in the ceded territory may have to be significantly limited to the benefit of future fish populations suggests that his concerns for the resources are genuine, as is his commitment to seeing the natural resources of the northwoods preserved for everyone's children and grandchildren.

Fisheries Management Under the New Court Rulings

Whatever opinions people may have held in the wake of the court rulings and the Chippewa's exercise of their treaty-based rights, tribal harvests were on the scene to stay. Spearing on the Turtle-Flambeau Flowage began in 1985, and it has continued annually with the one exception—noted earlier—the year of 1989. During the 1980s, the tribes harvested an average of 3,594 fish annually—with a low of 21 in 1985 and a high of 6,056 in 1988. In the 1990s, tribal harvests on the flowage averaged 3,004 fish annually—with a low of 2,147 in 1992 and a high of 5,048 in 1990. In the 2000s, the average was 1,942 fish annually—with a low of 1,063 in 2001 and a high of 3,100 in 2000. More walleyes have been taken from the flowage by tribal spearers than from any other single lake they have chosen to harvest within the ceded territory. Indeed, somewhere between 7 and 9 percent of the total tribal harvest in Wisconsin's ceded territories has come from the flowage. These numbers are certainly eye-catching, and they make it clear that spearing on the flowage is no casual phenomenon. That said, the impact of tribal harvests is certainly diminished by the following statistic found in the *Fisheries Management Plan of 2007*: "Tribal harvest [on the flowage] has averaged only 3.6% of the estimated adult walleye population in any given year."

That tempering percentage notwithstanding, it is fair to ask just what impact tribal harvests have had on the flowage. Unfortunately, there is no perfect way to assess their impact. Even data showing declining walleye numbers cannot be attributed directly or solely to tribal spearing, given the number of variables that can affect these numbers. Beyond these problems of interpretation, there is the longer-term reality that the flowage fishery has been ever-changing from the day the dam gates were first closed. What has been altered by human activities cannot easily be sorted out from what has been transformed by nature's subtle hands. Absent the perfect, then, we must be satisfied with the good; and this means that the best insights into the evolving flowage fishery come from the work of WDNR fisheries biologists, whose surveys provide a series of snapshots that, within the limits of scientific accuracy, can show what changes have occurred, even if they cannot always identify the causes for these changes.

Thanks in part to the WDNR survey of 1975-1976, fisheries personnel responsible for the flowage were in a relatively good position to deal with the demands of a new regulatory regime that began, in effect, in 1985. To be sure, their data were a decade old, and the formulas were not yet in place for determining what percentage of a population would constitute a safe, total allowable catch for tribal spearers and anglers combined. That said, WDNR fisheries biologists had anticipated the need for even more data, and in response produced in 1984 a fall walleye recruitment index. The index measured the size of each year's class; that is, the number of fish that had survived from spring spawning. Preparing this index continues to be an annual event, though today the actual work is carried out not by the WDNR but by the Great Lakes Indian Fish and Wildlife Commission. The additional information gathered by this index was to prove especially useful in setting bag limits in the early days of spearing, when protocols were still being worked out.

Flowage fish managers also made use of another means to assure that the spearing harvest did not threaten the target species. In response to concerns about the potential harmful impact of spearing on the future of the fishery among both anglers and some fisheries experts, the WDNR decided in 1989 to introduce "sliding" bag limits for walleyes for anglers in ceded territory lakes. Sliding bag limits worked as follows. Each year the tribes "declared" in advance their maximum intended harvest from a given lake. The simple act of declaration immediately resulted in an adjustment of the bag limit from the statewide limit of five fish down to three. If the lake was not speared, the limit could return to five. If the declared number amounted to a high percentage of the total allowable harvest, bag limits for anglers were adjusted. The closer a declaration came to the total allowable harvest, the more severely the bag limit for anglers was reduced. In the case of the flowage, which was speared annually, bag limits were adjusted downward from three, dependent on the percentage of the total allowable harvest the tribe actually took. This regulation, by recognizing the unpredictability of angler success over the course of the long open water and ice fishing seasons, sought to prevent an unintended over-harvest by combined tribal and sportfishing efforts. The following table shows how this regulation has affected flowage bag limits since its inception.

Year	Limit	Year	Limit	Year	Limit
1985	5	1995	2	2005	3
1986	5	1996	2	2006	3
1987	5	1997	3	2007	3
1988	5	1998	3	2008	3
1989	5	1999	3	2009	3
1990	3	2000	2	2010	3
1991	3	2001	3	2011	2
1992	3	2002	3	2012	3
1993	2	2003	3	2013	2
1994	2	2004	3		

The sliding bag limits were introduced in part as a precautionary measure, before significant new data had been gathered on the actual impact of tribal harvests on the flowage. But these data were soon to be gathered in a succession of comprehensive fish surveys undertaken in 1989, 1992, 1997, and 2009. The latter two surveys, conducted 22 and 34 years, respectively, from the initial comprehensive survey, provide the best vantage points from which to assess continuities and changes among the various flowage fish populations. The 1997 study, in particular, was written in such a way as to facilitate the comparison of its data with those of the three previous surveys. This, in turn, made it possible to gain some insights into the effects of spearing on the fishery.

Walleyes were front and center in the analysis of the data gathered in the 1997 survey, both because of the dominant role of the walleye in the fish community and because of the pressures put on them by angler and tribal harvests. The study estimated the total walleye population (on the flowage only, not including Trude Lake) to be some 186,486 plus or minus 26,605 fish—a number that falls in the same ballpark as the estimate from 1975. Fishing pressure remained about the same as it had been in earlier studies, at 14.1 hours per acre for the open water season. The study's author, Jeff Roth, concluded that "above average densities, slow growth, and an adequate size structure continue to characterize this [the walleye] population." But the report was not without its caveats. It found that the number of mature walleyes and fish of unknown gender greater than 12 inches in length per acre had dropped from 7.1 fish per acre in 1975 to 5.7 in 1989, and then to 4.7 in 1992, and to 4.8 in 1997. Moreover, it turned up a "moderate deterioration in size structure," specifically, a statistically significant decline in the number of walleyes greater than 13 inches in length. This decline was not deemed sufficiently great or long-lived to prompt any recommendations for changes in walleye regulations, but it did put walleye size structure on the agenda for the future.

When it comes to explaining the origins of the aforementioned changes in the flowage's walleye population, the report lists a number of "evident" explanations, without attempting to rank order them. These include the pressures on the walleye fishery from the newly instituted tribal harvests; enhanced angler harvests made possible by new fishing technologies and increased angler knowledge; and changing natural conditions, such as fluctuations in natural recruitment or a maturing flowage (declining woody cover, for example). There being no obvious ways to control for these variables in the scientific assessment of the fishery, "all of the above" seems the only satisfactory explanation, though each of the explanations put forward in the report has attracted its own vigorous advocates.

The 1997 study contains both good and bad news with regard to the muskellunge—another fish subject to tribal harvest. More people were fishing for them than ever before—fully 10 percent of all anglers were targeting muskies exclusively; and they were catching more fish more quickly than anglers previously had. It took 27.6 hours to catch a musky in 1997, which is a decided improvement over the 71.4 hours it took to boat one in 1989. In 1997, anglers spent an average of 61.3 hours to land a musky that they harvested, as compared to 200 hours in 1989. The average length of harvested muskies, 42 inches, represented an increase of 1.3 inches over the decade. The report notes, however, that insufficient time had elapsed to assess the impact of a 40-inch minimum length regulation that had been put in place in 1993. On the negative side, the report concludes that "natural musky reproduction is lacking in the flowage and Trude Lake." Negative interactions with northern pike, or inadequate muskellunge densities, or both, may be implicated in this failure. Whatever the cause, the inability of muskies to naturally propagate in the flowage makes stocking absolutely necessary if the fishery is to be sustained. Toward that end, the report recommends that stocking take place in locations of the flowage with favorable musky spawning habitat, and that the locations rotate annually. Such a practice had apparently helped natural reproduction in some small lakes. In contrast, the report called for annual stocking of Trude Lake from its public landing.

Northern pike fare no better in the 1997 survey than they did in previous ones. Though the second most numerous game fish in the flowage, the size structure of their population remained poor; and their tendency to early mortality persisted. Whether the problems northerns have can be attributed to habitat—the flowage has fairly warm water—or genetics is still unknown. What is clear, according to the report, is that changes in fishing regulations are unlikely to alter the condition of the northern fishery. In striking contrast to its findings on northerns, the survey documents the steady rise in both numbers and lengths of smallmouth bass. Some 250 smallmouth were sampled in 1997, up from a meager 17 in the 1975 survey; and lengths ranged up to 19.4 inches. The average length of harvested smallmouth in 1997 was 15.7 inches, a substantial increase from 1989, when the average length was 12.0 inches. The report surmises that the 15-inch minimum length and two-fish bag requirements, instituted in 1995, may have contributed to the increased size of harvested fish.

On balance, the results of the 1997 survey make it clear that the fishery on the flowage and on Trude Lake had not been severely degraded by the exercise of Chippewa tribal rights, as so many people believed to be the case. Within the limitations inherent in the science of fish management, the numbers simply did not support such a negative conclusion. At the same time, however, there were signs in this study that the flowage was not the same body of water that it had been two decades earlier. The decline in density of mature walleyes and walleyes of unknown gender above 12 inches was real, as was a growing diversity in the gamefish population brought on by the surging smallmouth population. As the report concludes, "it is unlikely that exceptionally high walleye densities [as had been the case in the 1970s and 1980s] will occur in the flowage within the near future." The days of the Turtle-Flambeau Flowage as an almost totally walleye-dominated fishery appeared to have come to an end.

CHAPTER EIGHT

The Shaping of a Long-Term Vision for the Flowage

B eginning in the early 1970s and continuing well into the next decade, there slowly took shape, in fits and starts, a vision of the Turtle-Flambeau Flowage and its future that differed from early perceptions of it as a big and rugged body of water with lots of fish. This emerging vision drew on many sources: recreational users of the flowage, a wide range of natural resource professionals, and the Chippewa and Flambeau Improvement Company (CFIC), the company that owned and controlled this property. As we have seen, the many anglers, hunters, campers, canoeists, bird-watchers, and other outdoor enthusiasts who were drawn to the area accorded it a special status as a place where they could carry out their activities in a semi-wilderness setting. These dedicated, one might even say entranced, individuals passionately sought to convey the aura and allure of the flowage to anyone willing to listen. And so it was for folks within the natural resources community, whether they worked in the field or in the office. As Wisconsin Department of Natural Resources (WDNR) field biologists became ever more knowledgeable about the flora and fauna of the flowage property, they gained a deepening appreciation of its overall biotic richness and seized upon opportunities to enhance this richness through assistance to scarce or endangered species. For them, the flowage stood out as an ideal location for science and science-based resource management. And for the office-bound WDNR staff whose responsibilities involved taking in the big picture, the flowage stood out, within the state, as a rare, if not unique, property, one that could provide outdoor lovers with a special kind of experience in a semi-wilderness setting.

The respective enthusiasms of the knowledgeable public and the WDNR reinforced one another and pointed in the same direction: namely, the need to preserve this setting as much as possible. The onus of securing this objective fell, of course, on the WDNR managers, who had to take on the challenging task of defending the flowage and the flowage experience against the many threats that loomed on the horizon. This was no easy task, however, for the flowage belonged to a private company whose essential interest was storing and releasing water. But as it happened, the CFIC proved to be a surprisingly amenable partner. Steadily mounting recreational use, especially that which involved camping and picnicking, had raised significant problems with regard to shoreland owned by the CFIC—problems that called for a systematic and workable management program that would enhance the recreational experience even as it protected the property from degradation. Concerns of this sort led the CFIC to be a willing participant in discussions with other parties about the regulation and management of recreational activities on the flowage. As it turns out, what enabled the parties to work together toward a sustainable future for the flowage was the incremental evolution of a long-term vision for the flowage that protected the unique value of the resource, facilitated public use, and respected the fundamental business needs of the CFIC. This, and some dedicated and far-sighted individuals who acted on their convictions.

The Flambeau Flowage Recreation Plan of 1970

The 1959 decision by the CFIC to create designated fire sites for camping or picnicking (see pp. 160-161) constituted a clear departure from the company's early hands-off policy with regard to its flowage properties. As of 1970, the company had created "twelve island campsites and five picnic table sites." Other facilities open to the public at this time included some other island campsites and picnic areas established by Iron County (with permission from Northern States Power), a county park and a camping area at Lake of the Falls, and six public access points around the flowage.

This inventory of public facilities on the flowage comes from a groundbreaking, indeed prescient, document: the Flambeau Flowage Recreation Plan. The impetus for this plan came jointly from the WDNR and the CFIC, though the task of putting it together fell to the WDNR. In the draft of the plan, which was completed in February of 1970, the agency assessed the character of the flowage, identified threats to its essential character, and laid out concrete measures by which it might be preserved and even enhanced. The plan was to be submitted to the CFIC for comments and suggested changes, and then, after agreed-upon modifications, to be approved by both parties.

The document begins with a straightforward statement of objectives: it is "absolutely necessary" to preserve the undeveloped shoreline to maintain the flowage's "characteristic wilderness aspect"; and any "changes should be limited to improved maintenance and a slight increase of supporting facilities on established recreation areas." With the bottom line firmly drawn, the authors of the plan then move on to flesh out their argument.

Following a brief sketch of the various vegetative, fish, bird (including waterfowl), and four-legged animal communities present on the property, the plan turns to public use of the flowage. Fishing, of course, leads the list of activities—especially the flowage's "excellent walleye fishing," which, along with the additional attraction of muskies, northern pike, and panfish, draws anglers from near and far. (Bass, interestingly, are not mentioned, an omission consistent with flowage's evolution into a walleye-dominated fishery.) To illustrate the breadth of the flowage's reputation, the document cites a user study made during the opening weekend of 1968, which showed that about 20 percent of the "203 vehicles counted at landings and recreation areas... were from out-of-state (mostly from Illinois)." An equal percentage hailed from central Wisconsin, and about 10 percent came from the Milwaukee area. Obviously, the flowage was not a local secret. Hunting on the flowage property also received its due. Waterfowlers could find "good" hunting for puddle ducks and geese; upland hunters could pursue deer and grouse; and trappers could go after furbearers. Whatever quarry hunters, anglers, and trappers sought on the flowage, they had a number of choices of where to stay or how to access the land or water. In addition to the aforementioned campsites, picnic areas, and access points maintained variously by the county or the CFIC, there were 13 resorts ready to provide shelter, drink, and often food. In other words, there was no shortage of recreational facilities, public and private, to support flowage users.

Given this positive assessment of flowage resources and

recreational possibilities, one might ask why the WDNR took the time to develop the plan. The answer lies in the following paragraph, one that warrants quotation in full given its keen insights into the future:

A growing population, increased mobility, and intensification of resource utilization are factors which will directly affect the demands placed on the Flambeau Flowage in the coming decades. There will be greater pressure placed on the Company to sell shoreline for development purposes. Recreators crowded out of other resource areas will focus their attention on the Flambeau and demand more recreation facilities, more roads, stable water levels, removal of stumps, logs, and rampikes [standing dead trees], and leasing of new cottage sites. Industry on the Flambeau and Chippewa Rivers may expand and require larger quantities of water and greater drawdowns. Local communities will sponsor and support proposals that promise an increased tax base. And, finally, there will be a growing number of preservationists and sportsmen pressing for public acquisition and protection of the flowage.

In short, the social, economic, and political pressures that loomed on the horizon in the near-term threatened to transform the flowage beyond recognition, and as a consequence deprive the state of an outdoor treasure. Implicit in this litany of threats, of course, was the notion that steps needed to be taken, sooner rather than later, to prevent such an outcome. Toward this end, the plan identifies four possible courses of action that the CFIC might take, singly or in combination, with respect to the future management of the property. First, it could "continue present management and operation policies." Second, it could "accelerate the development of recreation facilities available to the general public." Third, it could "sell or lease all or a portion of the projects [sic] uplands to a unit of government." And finally, it could "sell or lease shoreline homesites to private individuals and developers."

After reiterating that ruination of the flowage's semi-wilderness character (which the document asserts to be of comparable value to the state's wild rivers) would be an "immeasurable" loss, the plan goes on to discredit some of the courses of action that it had just laid out. Selling or leasing of shoreline on various flowages had rarely worked well, in large part because owners and lessees often found themselves at odds with the controlling company over matters of water levels. For this reason, most flowage owners had ceased such practices, including the CFIC, which in 1970 had a policy of leasing only to government entities. Indeed, its five outstanding leases had been granted for purposes of public access only.

The plan also rejects the possibility that the company might substantially expand recreational facilities on the flowage. In the first place, usage did not, as a matter of record, seem to outstrip existing facilities; and, in the second, the county and northwestern Wisconsin had plenty of "suitable public (and private) land elsewhere" to accommodate "needed developments." (That the latter phrase was placed in quotes in the draft of the plan suggests that its author(s) entertained a certain measure of skepticism about the advisability of emasculating the wilderness to make it user-friendly.)

Having identified the problem and dismissed some possible remedies, the plan reaches its conclusion about the proper course of action: "The greatest public benefit in the long run would be achieved by retaining the present undeveloped shoreline on as much of the Flambeau Flowage as possible. This would not necessarily result in the maximum number of users. However, recreation should not be a numbers game, with the sole objective of serving maximum numbers of people with an insipid, meaningless outdoor recreation experience." A whiff of elitism might be detected in this statement, but it is elitism of a defensible kind. That is, the WDNR seems here to be endorsing opportunities for those who wish to immerse themselves in a wilderness setting with as few of the trappings of modern society as possible. Such recreation is not the preference of everyone, or even a possibility for some. But it is an experience of high quality that should be a part of a full spectrum of recreational options available to the public. All the state need not be an inviolate wilderness, but neither should it be the second coming of the Wisconsin Dells. That said, the plan's conclusion does speak to improved access to the flowage, to be achieved through better maintenance of access points and greater publicity of their existence and location.

The concluding section of the plan makes specific recommendations to preserve the flowage's wilderness character. All island properties owned by the company are to be left essentially untouched. No construction will be permitted on them except for rudimentary facilities needed for "primitive camping and picnicking"; and no alterations of vegetation— such as clearing, tree planting, or logging—will be allowed. Any exemptions to these restrictions must be "mutually agreed upon by the Company and the DNR." As for the company's unleased mainland shoreline, the plan calls for the creation of a shoreline zone, the depth of which is to be determined by multiple sight lines from the flowage as deeply into the woods as the eye can see at times of low vegetation. This zone is to be subject to the same restrictions as island properties.

A separate paragraph deals with leased land. Its most important recommendation is that "no leases for new private cottage or resort development should be issued." The remainder of the paragraph seeks to regulate existing leased property: fees should be raised to reflect the actual value of the properties; buildings should be painted to blend in with their surroundings; no new construction should be sited within 100 feet of the shoreline; changes in vegetative cover should be approved in advance by the company; and some control should be exercised over the type and size of signs on leased land. The overall goals of these recommendations are clear: to prevent additional development on the company's flowage property and to render existing private facilities as inconspicuous as possible.

As concerns current operating practice, the plan calls for no change in the water-regulation regime, unless it turns out that some change in this regime would improve fishing. But it does have something to say about the maintenance of public facilities. After noting that "trash pickup has proved troublesome," particularly on company-sponsored island campsites, the plan places on the company responsibility for "regular trash pickup, facility repair, and site renewal."

Finally, the plan gives voice to concerns about the presence of endangered species on the flowage—most notably the bald eagle. After noting that the flowage in 1970 was one of only a handful of locations with active eagle nesting sites remaining in the state, the plan asserts that all measures possible should be taken to protect this bird's favored habitat. To this end, "no activity" zones should be created within 500 feet of nesting sites; vegetation within a quarter mile of a nest should not be altered during the breeding season; and efforts should be made to identify older white pines that might be suitable candidates for artificial nesting sites. As will become apparent, this section of the plan foreshadowed significant efforts to support rare and endangered species on the flowage.

In April of 1970, Arthur Doll, the acting chief of the planning section of the WDNR, forwarded a copy of the draft plan to Jerry Kripps, general manager of the Chippewa and Flambeau

Improvement Company. In his cover letter, Doll observed that the plan had been "generally OK'd by our field personnel, although not by our top administration. It's now your turn to tear it apart. Any comments, suggested changes, etc. will be welcome." Kripps replied on May 22, 1970. He suggested only two changes: first, replace the name Northern States Power (NSP) throughout the document with Chippewa and Flambeau Improvement Company "to reflect true corporate ownership of this flowage"; and second, include a paragraph "to describe briefly the purpose and financial structure of the Chippewa and Flambeau Improvement Company." The letter closes with praise for the "report" and expresses a strong desire to see the document "carried to its final form."

On receipt of Kripps' letter, Doll sent a memorandum, dated May 26, 1970, to L.P. Voigt, secretary of the WDNR, bringing him up to date on the plan's development. In prefacing his remarks, Doll reminded the secretary that this matter initially arose in 1966 when a member of the Natural Resources Board had expressed an interest in seeing the WDNR obtain an easement from the CFIC for Big Island in the flowage, "and was given further push by NSP following the successful completion of the Chippewa Flowage plan and agreement." Now that the company had so readily given the draft plan a thumb's up, however, Doll and at least one other WDNR official had some misgivings about the failure of the plan to push harder for WDNR easements on company property. (Such easements would correspond to the third option presented in the draft plan: see p. 267.) Doll encouraged his boss to sound out a friend at NSP as to the possibility of discussing easements. His memo concludes with the following thought: "We could just incorporate NSP's comments and make it another mutually adopted plan. But if we could get something more, I think we should." Obviously, Doll could see the advantages of an easement, with its contractual dimension, as opposed to a mutual agreement, and hoped matters might be pushed in that direction.

Regrettably, a total lack of evidence brings the story to an abrupt halt at this point, leaving a host of unanswered questions. Did Voigt discuss easements with his contact at NSP? If so, what reaction did he encounter? Was the plan revised in keeping with the company's recommendations? Was it signed off on by the WDNR and the CFIC? If so, what steps did the two parties take to put the plan into action? Nothing could be found in the files of the WDNR in Madison with regard to these questions, and a spokesman for Xcel Energy (Xcel is the parent company of Northern States Power, which, in turn, has a controlling interest in the CFIC) stated that no documents on this matter could be found, possibly because they had been discarded in keeping with the company's records retention policy. Viewed from a historian's perspective, then, this promising joint initiative for a flowage management plan seems to have been swallowed up in an evidential black hole.

Mark Fort: Caretaker and Catalyst

Whether the two parties ever reached a formal agreement on the Flambeau Flowage Recreation Plan becomes a question of secondary interest, however, given what followed half a dozen years later when the CFIC took a step that could be seen as a direct response to the issues and recommendations raised in the draft of the 1970 plan. This step occurred in 1976 when the company hired Mark Fort, shortly after he graduated with a degree in forestry from the University of Minnesota, to serve as forester and reservoir manager at the Turtle-Flambeau Flowage. In hiring Fort, the company seems to have been looking for someone knowledgeable about the outdoors who could establish the company's presence at the facility, look after any structures and the property itself, and see to it that the trash was picked up from campsites—responsibilities that were all consistent with the thrust of the 1970 plan. Along with these duties, the CFIC in 1981 added the position of dam keeper to his responsibilities. Fort's interests and enthusiasms clearly qualified him, and then some, for this position. As his obituary in the December 3, 2002, edition of *The Chippewa Herald* noted, "He had a special bond with the outdoors. There were few fields he hadn't crossed, few waters he hadn't fished." Fort quickly became a keen observer of the entire flowage scene and, as will become apparent, a key figure in expanding the scope of management of the property for 11 eventful years.

By 1983, Fort had become sufficiently familiar with the property to prepare a comprehensive inventory of its facilities and their condition. According to the document, the CFIC and Iron County jointly maintained four boat-launching sites: Baraboo, Norway Point, Murray's Landing, and Trude Lake. All four had ramps, parking areas, and trash containers—in varying states of improvement and repair—but apparently no toilets. Yet another launching site, today known as Sportsman's Landing, was cared for by the CFIC and a local club. Additional access points included the launching site at the Iron County campground at Lake of the Falls and two little-used and unmarked landings. So it would appear that the company followed through on its commitment to make the flowage more accessible to all users.

The situation with regard to campgrounds is not so clear. The inventory notes that "there are twenty established island and natural shoreline campsites. Development in these campsites ranges from almost nothing to a picnic table, hand pump for drinking water, a simple fire ring, outhouse and trash barrel, or any combination of those mentioned above." Fort attributed the creation of these campsites to work done jointly by the WDNR and the Boy Scouts, though he could find no documentation showing that the CFIC had negotiated agreements for such work with either entity. It may be that Fort, or local legend, confused the Boy Scouts with another organization, the Wisconsin Youth Conservation Corps (WYCC). According to the April 21, 1963, edition of the *Racine Bulletin*, youngsters from the Statehouse Lake Camp of the WYCC had removed brush and enlarged campsites and picnic areas at Lake of the Falls, Murray's Landing, and Baraboo Landing. They had also developed four campsites on the flowage, including a one-acre site on Big Island. But that sole reference hardly accounts for the creation of the other 16 campsites that the report mentions.

No matter whose hands built them, the 20 campsites that were on the scene when Fort arrived showed "no signs of formal maintenance other than that done by campers themselves in the last 10-15 years." In the words of John Olson, one of Fort's friends in the WDNR, "Mark looked around and was pretty dismayed." In fact, Fort had concluded that his employer, the CFIC, had been doing nothing—no campsite maintenance, no timber management, no trail building, and the like. Such inaction was unacceptable to Fort, who was a man of strong opinions and high energy. He "liked to manage things," Olson noted, and manage them he did.

Right away, Fort set about bringing the campsites up to speed. His overall goal was to make them fully functional, but at the same time to minimize or eliminate those human impacts that diminished the natural quality of the camping experience. To this end, garbage pits—an unsightly presence as well as an undesirable attraction to various forest critters—were eliminated and, at the most-used sites, replaced by barrels and a routine of weekly trash removal during the summer months. Water pumps were repaired or replaced with new ones built by Bill Carrol, a WDNR staff member from Mercer. Open-pit toilets supplanted deteriorated outhouses. New picnic tables graced both campsites and picnic areas. Rustic wooden steps were installed to help curb erosion at steep-banked campsites. Fort also set up signboards to introduce campers to the CFIC and to post fishing regulations and other WDNR notices. Much of this work went well beyond the company's expectations of him.

Not surprisingly, given his background as a forester, Fort also turned his attention to the timber resources on the company's flowage properties. Fifty years had passed since they had been logged, and the cutover had been transformed into true forest. The CFIC had recognized this transformation, and in 1974 hired Walter Nicewander, a consulting forester, to make an inventory of the company's timber resources. Working from Nicewander's report, Fort identified stands of overaged timber—mostly aspen and white birch—and set up a plan to harvest them systematically over the next several years. Along the way, he worked with resort owners, letting them know what was going on and dealing with their concerns. Once again, the company's past pattern of indifference to its flowage properties gave way to active management.

Management and Science

If Fort edged beyond the limits of his assignment in his work on campsites and forestry, he left these limits totally in the dust where his interest in wildlife management was concerned. He recognized from the outset, as had others familiar with the flowage, that the property held a unique place in Wisconsin both for its high-profile birds—eagles, ospreys, and loons—and for other, less common species such as the yellow-headed blackbird and black tern. Securing their place in the ecology of the flowage quickly became one of Fort's most treasured goals. And, as fortune would have it, he was soon to have two equally dedicated collaborators who set up shop at the Mercer Ranger Station: Jeff

Wilson, a wildlife technician who arrived in 1978; and John Olson, the station's first wildlife biologist, who took up his duties in 1979. With Fort smoothing the way with the CFIC, the three men set out to learn as much as possible about the bird life of the flowage, and on the basis of this knowledge to actively intervene on behalf of those species in need of a helping hand.

To gain a general sense of what birds were present and how they were getting along over time on a lake with fluctuating water levels, Olson and Wilson chose to test out a survey technique that had been developed for studying wildlife on large bodies of water. Beginning in 1980, they organized and ran an annual, one-day survey of the flowage, staffed by WDNR personnel and others with more than a passing familiarity with bird life. The surveys were conducted in late June, at a time when the young of the year had been hatched and could be counted along with mature birds. Survey participants followed six prescribed routes, from roughly 5:00 a.m. to 1:00 p.m., and recorded their observations. Loons were the primary focus of these early surveys, but the survey teams recorded other birds as well—ospreys, eagles, and various waterfowl. After the completion of the 1990 survey, the investigators, now in possession of a baseline data set comprised of 11 years of observations, decided to run subsequent surveys on a five-year schedule. The survey technique seems to have worked best for loons, whose young accompany their parents closely on the water. But reliable data on eagles and ospreys, whose nests often could not be located, or, if located, not observed from lake level, could only be gained through aerial surveillance. These limitations of the survey did not, however, prevent Olson, Wilson, and Fort from taking action on behalf of the flowage's signature birds.

Ospreys drew their attention first. Like other raptors, they had begun to rebound from the ravages of various environmental contaminants and had been showing up at the flowage in greater numbers. The question was whether there were adequate nesting sites for them. Around 1970, Mark Pittman, an ornithologist from Wausau, had built some nesting platforms for them on the flowage. But the big push would come about a decade later. In 1978, Fort mapped existing nests and noted that many of them were in total disrepair owing to the deterioration of the trees on which they were located. When Olson arrived on the scene the next year, even more nests were gone. Prompted by this information, the WDNR initiated a program to build and place platforms around the flowage. Olson and Wilson learned how to scale trees and install nesting platforms. This was no easy task: it required hauling up 2-by-6-inch lumber, strap iron, and lag bolts, and then assembling the materials in the winter cold. Rather than use snags left over from the making of the flowage, the men chose sturdier old but very much alive pine trees on which to locate the platforms. The WDNR supported the program through its endangered species fund. In the program's first year, four platforms went up on Trude Lake, and the pace picked up in subsequent years. According to Fort, 24 platforms were erected in the winter of 1983, and eventually the total number rose to 50. The target audience seems to have approved the program, for in 1989 the flowage could boast of 25 nesting pairs of ospreys.

Eagles, it turns out, take less well to subsidized housing, and so Olson, Wilson, and Fort set a more modest goal: "to place artificial nesting platforms only in areas where a historic natural site is lost (due to some natural cause)." John Olson remembers one such occasion when a nest site south of Hot Dog Island blew down. On the advice of Charles Sindelar, a specialist on eagles, Olson and his helpers selected a white pine with a good canopy and installed a platform well below it. They then had to haul up bundle after bundle of brush with which to fashion the nest itself—while Margaret Levra, who was covering the project for the *Ironwood Daily Globe*, suffered in the cold below. The builders must have done their job exceedingly well, as eagles successfully raised a family that spring and summer. Olson remembers this achievement to have been a "first" in eagle management.

As important as work with ospreys and eagles was, it was loons, whose haunting cries are virtually synonymous with the northwoods, who received the greatest attention around the flowage during the 1980s. Flowages, with their rising and falling waters, pose unique problems for loon nesting. In particular, the spring filling of a flowage can easily flood a nest that has been located on land exposed by a winter drawdown. To combat this problem, Fort and his WDNR associates began, in 1981, to construct floating platforms that could be put in place near traditional loon nesting sites. Within two years, the flowage was home to some 13 platforms, fashioned of cedar posts, mesh wire, and polystyrene foam. Installing these platforms turned out to be a learning process for all involved, and the results were not conclusive. Nonetheless, the project continued as field surveys helped to identify more precisely locations where loon nests had a good chance of producing young.

In the latter part of the 1980s, flowage loons became the object of scientific study by Jerry Belant, a graduate student from the University of Wisconsin-Stevens Point. Working under the supervision of Professor Ray Anderson, Belant sought some basic information about loons, in particular, where they winter and what migration routes they take. To gather data on these behaviors, he set about to capture loons and to fit them with radio transmitters. Olson remembers that Belant's initial attempts to capture loons proved quite challenging, but in time he got better at the task. In 1987, Belant successfully banded 28 loons out of 22 nesting pairs on the flowage. This experiment in using telemetry to follow loons was the only one under way in the country at this time.

In addition, Belant was one of the earlier users of sonographs—visual representations of particular bird calls or vocalizations—to identify individual loons. Based on his work at the flowage, Belant published seven scientific papers, including "Winter Recoveries and Territorial Affinity of Common Loons Banded in Wisconsin" (with R.K. Anderson and J.W. Wilson) and "Chick Fostering by Common Loons, Gavia-Immer" (with John Olson).

Mark Fort, left, and John Olson transport juvenile Canada Geese for release in remote areas of the flowage. The birds came from Green Bay and Crex Meadows Wildlife Area. John Olson and Jeff Wilson

Work on bird habitat, however, was not limited to the "big three" species. A group of youth from the Iron County Conservation Corps removed willows and tag alders from potential upland nesting sites to accommodate the needs of mallards and geese. In the Murray's Landing area, black tern nesting received a boost from the placement of platforms that kept their eggs above rising spring waters. Another effort targeted wood ducks through the placement of some 200 nesting boxes in appropriate locations around the entire flowage. The WDNR provided the boxes while the CFIC contributed the pipe on which the boxes were mounted. Each winter WDNR personnel visited the boxes, cleaned them out, and did some "detective work" to figure out who had occupied them. What the WDNR staff learned during the first three years of these inspections was that they had one percent wood duck use (two boxes) and 30 percent merganser use (60 boxes). Fort, who was an avid duck hunter, responded to these skewed results by threatening to nail boards over the openings of the boxes used by mergansers. The nest box program, which could hardly be termed a raging success, became less and less relevant over time, as some of the shoreline timber matured to the point where an adequate supply of natural nesting cavities was present. Old, deteriorated boxes were pulled down, although a few of the original boxes can still be seen in secluded portions of the flowage. Finally, Olson was all prepared to undertake a project to reintroduce goldeneye ducks to the flowage—he had found some ideal habitat and the right nest box design—but the birds were commandeered by the United States Forest Service for a similar project on the Chippewa Flowage. It failed.

During these years when birds were atop the WDNR agenda, the four-legged creatures that call the flowage home pretty much got a pass from the wildlife people—though they were not totally ignored. John Olson, and especially Jeff Wilson, were avid trappers, and they kept their eyes and ears open for information on the beaver and muskrat populations. But they undertook no systematic surveys of furbearers, or any other mammals, for that matter. The animals, however, seemed to be doing well on their own. Fishers in the flowage area had become sufficiently numerous to be eligible for trapping when the first, though geographically limited, fisher season opened in 1985. And, of course, wolves were coming back as well. In 1985, Olson found himself on the WDNR wolf recovery team, and later on the wolf science team. The trapping and relocating of nuisance bears that showed up from time to time at the Lake of the Falls campground and around Lake Bastine resorts constituted the only "management" of mammals undertaken at the flowage during the period from 1976 to 1989.

All in all, these years had been highly productive ones for the Mercer wildlife people, and they knew how much they owed to Mark Fort and his energetic commitment to being a good steward of the land. In John Olson's view, "He was the reason why we were able to do so many things out there [on the flowage]." And Fort, for his part, benefited from the relative indifference of the CFIC toward the way he spent his time on the job. As he remarked so often to his WDNR colleagues, "My bosses in Eau Claire don't give a hoot about what I do on the land, so long as there are no negative repercussions from the public." That said, Fort had sufficient credibility in Eau Claire to draw on CFIC resources to aid his colleagues in the WDNR, and the resulting synergy of private and public entities earned some feathers (presumably not eagle) for everyone's caps.

Taking the Long View

Mark Fort's contributions to the flowage were not limited to his work on user facilities, forestry, and wildlife management: he also helped to lay the groundwork for the long-term future of the property. This story begins in the mid to late 1980s when the WDNR had entered negotiations for the purchase of Northern States Power properties on the Chippewa Flowage—negotiations that were concluded in 1988 with the state purchase of 6,862 acres from the company. During these years, Fort confided in Olson that he thought Northern States Power (the controlling shareholder in the CFIC and the operator of the dam on the Turtle-Flambeau Flowage) was likely to divest itself of its property on the Turtle-Flambeau Flowage as well. Both men agreed that the sale of the flowage to some private entity would put at risk all that they had worked for—minimal but adequate campsites, protected shorelines, access for local recreational users, and enhanced wildlife habitat. At that point, Olson remembers, he bounced a thought off Fort. "What do you think about us developing a management plan, identifying things that have been done and things that are important for the future. If agreed to [by the company and the WDNR] maybe the plan could go to the new owner, like a deed restriction." Fort immediately concurred. But the two were treading on shaky ground. Because the state did not own this huge property, there was no formal basis for Olson to be working on a plan for a private company unless requested to do so from the top of the agency; and Fort, for his part, had no assurances that such a company would have any interest in one. But supervisors for both men, "in their wisdom," gave them the green light to work up such a plan. In January of 1986, Olson sent Northern States Power a lengthy letter calling for "integrated management," essentially a sharing of responsibilities for the flowage between the company and the WDNR. In March of that year, he received from A.G. Schuster, vice president of power supply at NSP, an expression of interest on behalf of the company and encouragement to move forward. The process of developing a plan was under way.

Olson next recruited the fisheries, forestry, and law enforcement staff at the Mercer Ranger Station—in particular, Marko Hanson, a WDNR forester; Dennis Scholl, a WDNR fish manager; and Don Peterson, a WDNR forester-ranger—to contribute materials appropriate to their areas of responsibility. According to one source, however, Olson wrote the bulk of the plan with some additional assistance from Fort. Moreover, to judge by some correspondence from 1988, both Olson and Fort worked diligently to keep their respective organizations informed of the process and to establish in the developing plan the proper balance of responsibilities between the WDNR and the CFIC. In 1989, the final draft rolled off the station's old electric typewriter that printed on a continuous roll of paper. It measured out at 26 feet in length.

The 1989 Olson/Fort plan certainly qualifies as a lineal descendant of the 1970 recreation plan, but it is neither a simple restatement of nor a point-by-point elaboration of its predecessor. Whereas the earlier plan had systematically argued its way to the conclusion that the flowage was severely threatened and therefore in need of protection, Olson and Fort stated outright in the plan's introduction that the flowage is "a most unique and valuable resource in northern Wisconsin," and that both the CFIC and the WDNR "share a concern for this precious resource." It was their hope that this document, as "a product of our cooperative effort..." would "...be of value in understanding, protecting and enhancing this unique property." The new plan also brings forward aesthetic considerations to a far greater degree than its predecessor. This emphasis is clear from the outset when it sets as its goal "to manage an industry-owned, 22,515-acre semi-wilderness property for the benefit of fish, forest, wildlife, recreation, outdoor education, and protection of endangered or threatened species, *while maintaining an aesthetically pleasing environment.*" [author's italics] But the really big difference between these two plans lies in the greater volume and precision of information about the property that finds its way into the 1989 plan, and that give its recommendations added heft. This distinguishing feature can be attributed directly to the almost two decades of hands-on experience with the site by Fort and the many WDNR professionals who had been present during these years. Science and its application to natural resource management clearly and persuasively drive this plan.

Under the heading "Recommended Management and Development Program," the plan identifies four basic areas of activity: "[1] Continue upland management for forest-wildlife, waterfowl, and unique raptors, especially bald eagles, ospreys, and merlins; [2] maintain and improve the fishery through harvest regulations, aquatic habitat management, and stocking; [3] protect and manage wetlands for fish spawning habitat, waterfowl use, and endangered and threatened species; [4] continue existing level of management for camping and picnicking with emphasis on site quality, safety, and erosion control."

What follows is a thorough examination of these four areas. After a brief look at past management of each of them, the report inventories the current status of the resources pertinent to each area and identifies appropriate management goals and techniques. In the case of upland forestry, for example, the document lists existing forest types, specifies the acreage each occupies on the property, and then prescribes what means should be pursued—such as even-age cuts or all-age cuts—to achieve the desired management goal for each type. Not surprisingly, forested areas receive the lion's share of attention, in part because of the intimate connection between forest communities and wildlife, and in part because of the importance of some forest types to the aesthetics of the property. Fishing receives the least attention, probably because of the extensive surveys (some of which are cited in this book) that had already been carried out by WDNR fisheries staff. Recommended actions—namely, to manage primarily for walleyes and muskellunge—are consistent with these surveys and their evaluations.

Nowhere is the seriousness and professionalism of this plan more apparent than in its description of a management planning system. The basis of this system was to be an already completed "forest community inventory of the property." This inventory had divided the property into 32 units and had assembled on maps and overlays basic information for each unit. This information included: "timber type, condition, and age; presence and location of eagle, osprey, great blue heron, or common loon nests; existing structures such as trails, boat landings, or campgrounds; and special management activities." Future management initiatives "will be planned, identified and recorded on these reconnaissance maps and overlays." Of course, these activities will require funding, and it is to this necessity that the plan turns next. Without saying so directly, the plan implies that the WDNR and the CFIC will be the principal contributors to the budget for property management; but it also identifies potential partners that might provide some financial assistance. The list ranges from Pittmann-Robertson and Dingell-Johnson governmental funding to more focused sources, such as the Ruffed Grouse Society, Ducks Unlimited, and the Wisconsin Waterfowlers Association. Finally, the plan estimates the costs of specific actions, such as trail seeding, maintenance of openings, and monitoring of waterfowl nest boxes, and suggests possible maintenance intervals. Taken together, the management planning system and the discussion on budgeting provided the target audience, the WDNR and the CFIC, with a precise picture of what ought to be done with the property and how it could be accomplished.

The second part of this plan contains extensive background information about the flowage—from geology to topography to ownership—all organized by categories that suggest it is designed to meet WDNR project outlines. It concludes with a bibliography of references cited in the plan—mostly scientific papers. At 32 pages single-spaced, the Olson/Fort plan is more than three times larger than the 1970 recreation plan, but its force lies less in its length than in the specificity of both its data and its plans for action. It is hardly surprising, then, that the plan quickly received the blessing of the CFIC. But it is also possible that its warm reception may have been influenced by the fact that the plan's content meshed well with "quiet" discussions the company had recently initiated with WDNR to determine whether the agency had an interest in buying the flowage.

The next step followed, as if scripted, when in 1989 Olson received a call from Dave Jacobson, who was the northwest district director for the WDNR. Jacobson had played a major role in the state's purchase of CFIC lands on the Chippewa Flowage. Jacobson informed Olson that he would be coming over from Spooner "tomorrow" and wanted to look around the Turtle-Flambeau Flowage in the company of Olson and Dennis Scholl, the ichthyologist at Mercer. The next day, as the three men motored about the flowage in an old fiberglass "washtub," a reject law enforcement boat, Olson and Scholl introduced Jacobson to everything they thought essential to understanding and appreciating the flowage. Toward the end of their tour, Jacobson observed that "it would be so good if you guys could put all this on paper." At that point, Olson reached beneath the steering wheel and pulled out a copy of the plan that he and Fort had created, held it out to Jacobson, and asked, "You mean something like this?" Jacobson was ecstatic. No matter that the plan had been developed without his knowledge. What counted was that the plan documented thoroughly what the flowage was all about, as well as what it might become—features that meshed perfectly with Jacobson's desire to have the state purchase the flowage. The plan not only precisely fit the moment, but it also fit into a series of events pointing in the direction of state ownership. With a helping hand from Mark Fort and the CFIC, the wildlife scientists had moved from their customary domain of knowledge and understanding into the arena of policy. It was a step well taken.

CHAPTER NINE

From Storage Reservoir to "Crown Jewel"

The Big Buy

For big things to happen in the realm of public policy, lots of smaller pieces need to fall into place. And this was to be the case with the state's acquisition of the Turtle-Flambeau Flowage (TFF). To begin with, Northern States Power, in selling its landholdings on the Chippewa Flowage, had demonstrated a willingness to part with flowage shoreline on at least one of its major reservoirs. It also seems likely that Mark Fort's concern that the company might divest itself of the TFF sprang from something more than pure imagination. For sure, something was in the air with regard to the company's thinking about its flowage properties. Second, the idea of a purchase by the state had its advocates on the scene in Mercer and elsewhere in the northwest region of the state. For Olson, Wilson, and others associated with the WDNR in Mercer, state action was far preferable to seeing the flowage gobbled up by a development-minded private entity. Fort, of course, concurred with this view as well. Paul Gottwald, the

WDNR area wildlife supervisor in Park Falls who had strong ties with numerous flowage users from that city and the surrounding area, thought the time was right for a state purchase, and he strongly made this case to Dave Jacobson, the WDNR northwest district director who was based in Spooner. Jacobson proved to be the right person at the right time and place. As noted earlier, he had a personal commitment to acquiring the flowage for the state; he had experience as a principal negotiator among the parties to the Chippewa Flowage purchase; and he had the jurisdiction and authority to move things forward. Third, the broader political climate was favorable to such a deal. First-term Governor Tommy Thompson was seeking re-election in 1990, and was, to judge from the press, much in need of shoring up his environmental record. He had, however, garnered praise, even from some of his critics, for the purchase of the Northern States Power land on the Chippewa Flowage. Fourth, there was money available for a state acquisition, thanks to the Warren Knowles-Gaylord Nelson Stewardship Fund. The legislature had passed and Governor Thompson had signed legislation creating this fund in 1989, and $23.1 million dollars had become available as of July 1, 1990.

The sequence of events began to play itself out in the second half of 1989, when Jacobson set up meetings with the town chairs of Mercer and Sherman (the entirety of the flowage fell within the jurisdiction of these two towns) and affected local citizens to discuss the implications of a state purchase of the flowage. Olson and Gottwald joined in some of these meetings—though neither of these men would participate in the process through to its conclusion. In 1989 Olson transferred to Eau Claire and Gottwald retired, though not before strongly urging Jacobson to press on with the case for purchase. But reports of Jacobson's advocacy and his case for purchase clearly reached Madison during the year; and, if Fort is to be believed, some "quiet" discussions had already been under way between the Chippewa and Flambeau Improvement Company (CFIC) and the WDNR. By the end of 1989, the issue of purchasing the flowage had worked its way near the top of the respective agendas of the WDNR and the governor.

The public first learned of the negotiations in early 1990. On January 5, *The Milwaukee Journal* reported that Governor Thompson had telephoned Edwin Theisen, president of the Chippewa and Flambeau Improvement Company and Northern States Power, to talk about the possible sale of the flowage to the state. Following the call, the paper reported, Thompson had given the green light to Carroll "Buzz" Besadny, secretary of the WDNR, to move ahead with a land appraisal and with further discussions with the CFIC. Judging by his reaction, Besadny appeared fully on-board for the program. "It's the most magnificent property that I've observed in the more than 30 years I've been employed here [WDNR]. It's like being in the Canadian wilderness right... in northern Wisconsin." Apparently no price had been discussed at this point, but the article does go on to note that Stewardship Fund support would be available as of July 1. That the two indispensable principals to this deal—Thompson and Theisen—were ready to speak publicly about negotiations suggests that lower-level conversations had been under way for some time, and with more than a little progress. Not one to let his point slip by with just a single headline, two days later Thompson declared, at a Capitol ceremony, that 1990 would be "Earth Year" in Wisconsin. Not only that, but he also stated that his top environmental goal for the year was to purchase the land along the Turtle-Flambeau Flowage.

News of the possible acquisition of the flowage by the state posed some problems for critics of Thompson within the ranks of environmentalists. A spokesman for the Wisconsin Environmental Decade responded positively to the idea in principle, but then sniffed that "purchasing land is politically a very easy thing to do in terms of the environment." He wished that Thompson would pay as much attention to clean air and water as to buying property. The Sierra Club, for its part, found it possible to give the governor a "B" grade for his intent to buy the flowage and for his commitment to long-range planning for the purchase of other "environmentally sensitive land," though it dealt him a "C" for failing to tackle various forms of toxicity in the environment. But the press reaction was much more favorable. An editorial in the January 9 issue of *The Milwaukee Journal* had nothing but praise for the proposed purchase, arguing that it saved the flowage from being "chopped up" by development. The paper singled out Thompson, the state legislature (for approving the stewardship fund), and Dave Jacobson, "who championed the acquisition and helped bring the parties together." "Applause to all of them," the editorial concluded, "for an investment that will yield recreational dividends for generations to come."

There is every reason to believe that 1990 was a pressure-packed year for all who were involved in working out the terms of sale of the flowage. The precise boundaries of the sale had to be established, valuation set on lands of differing types and qualities, and a final price agreed upon. The expectation was that the overall price per acre to be paid for the TFF would be less than the $1,000 per acre that the state had paid for CFIC land on the Chippewa Flowage—mostly because the TFF was located in a more remote part of the state where property values were lower. Working out these matters and others might have stretched out over months and months, perhaps even over a year, had there not been strong pressure from the governor's office to get the deal closed sufficiently in advance of the November election to enable the governor to get some political mileage out of it. Without a doubt, politics and environmental progress were intimately linked, but it was politics alone that set this particular timetable. All signs pointed to late summer as a target date for the consummation of the deal, and, as it turns out, everything fell in place in the last week of August.

Money matters were not the only ones that had to be negotiated. Even more important, for the long term, would be an agreement on the management of water levels in the flowage. According to the terms of the proposed sale, the CFIC was to retain ownership of the dam and to be the operator of its gates. But the flow regime under which it had been operating, initially supervised by the Public Service Commission and then after 1967 by the newly created Wisconsin Department of Natural Resources, gave the company wide latitude in setting water levels—though it should be noted that in the years leading up to these negotiations the CFIC had been managing water levels more conservatively than it had earlier. Clearly, some formal change in the operating regime would be necessary in order to protect the ecosystem that the WDNR was about to spend precious stewardship dollars to acquire. Discussions over this matter led, in time, to the preparation of a memorandum of understanding between the Wisconsin Department of Natural Resources and Chippewa and Flambeau Improvement Company.

The MOU, as the document is known, begins with a series of "whereas" statements that affirm the CFIC's statutory powers and invoke the history of cooperation between the two parties (including mention of the co-management plan of 1989). Then after expressing a commitment to consultation between WDNR and CFIC on all relevant issues, the MOU lays down two "major principles of reservoir operation." Winter drawdowns are not to exceed eight feet from full pool, and summer drawdowns are not to exceed four feet from full pool. At no time during the year are discharges ("stream flows" in the language of the document) from the flowage into the waters below the dam to fall below 300 cubic feet per second (cfs). The affected stream, of course, is the North

Fork of the Flambeau River. These principles are followed by a list of "modifications," which can be implemented as long as they do not "conflict with the Major Principles." The most important of these is a commitment to filling the reservoir earlier than in the past. The CFIC commits to an "attempt to refill the reservoir to a level of 1571.5 or more by April 20 each year or within one week after ice-out conditions are present on the reservoir, whichever is later. Such a refill will normally be accomplished without lowering flow below 300 cfs."

The WDNR and the CFIC had, indeed, reached an understanding, but the document that embodied that understanding was not without some problematic elements. First, regulating streamflow is the principal means of water level management. Accordingly, the minimum stream flow of 300 cfs that is established in the major principles becomes a critical number. How this number was arrived at—there is no evidence that it was based on science and one secondhand account suggests that it was an off-the-cuff decision— is unclear; but if it were proven to be unnecessarily high—that is, higher than needed to maintain the health of the Flambeau River— it would seem to be an impediment to management of the flowage in low-water years. Second, the last sentence of the modification bearing on spring refill poses a problem of logic. It clearly implies that in certain unspecified instances discharge flows could be allowed to drop below 300 cfs, although such an action would clearly contradict a major principle. Third, the very instrument employed to define the relationship between the two parties, a memorandum of understanding, is, as used here, a kind of legal odd duck: that is, it is more than a handshake but something less than a contract. For it sets out expectations but remains wholly silent on what actions might be taken or what sanctions might be invoked should the conditions of the agreement be violated. These aspects of the MOU would become sources of contention in coming years.

The two parties affixed their signatures to the MOU on August 23, 1990. On the same day, the Natural Resources Board, at a meeting in Dodgeville, approved the purchase of the flowage. The price was set at $9,131,000 with payments to be made over a two-year period (half in 1990 and half in 1991). An interest payment to the CFIC in the amount of $290,200 brought the total purchase price to $9,421,200—pennies short of $400 per acre. The press release indicated that the state would be acquiring 114 miles of mainland shoreline, 150 islands, 11,395 acres of water, 8,477 acres of woodland, and 3,700 acres of wetland. The total, 23,572 acres, would make this the largest purchase of recreational land ever by the state. (The master plan of 1995, for reasons unknown, sets the purchase at 22,343 acres.) Some 260 private owners and 13 resort owners would retain full ownership of their properties—which amounts to somewhere between 5 to 10 percent of the mainland shoreline. The purchase did not cause any reduction in tax revenues for the towns of Mercer and Sherman for the simple reason that the CFIC was exempt from paying municipal taxes. Instead, the CFIC, which was classified as a "conservation and regulatory company," paid to the state an ad valorem tax (meaning "according to value") on its flowage property. This money went into the state's general purpose revenue, some of which found its way back to the municipalities under its shared revenue program.

Just two days later, Governor Thompson and Secretary Besadny traveled to Mercer to formally sign the deal with the Chippewa and Flambeau Improvement Company. In his remarks, the governor invoked a phrase that has become associated ever after with the flowage, even though he made clear that the phrase is inadequate. "'One of Wisconsin's Crown Jewels'... 'A Nature Lover's Juliet.' These are the descriptions that this magnificent territory has evoked in various observers of the past few months. Seeing it now, and especially after that canoe trip on the Flambeau, I don't believe they are adequate. No description is adequate to convey the beauty and magnificence of these trees, these lakes, this wildlife. The only sufficient response to it is to preserve it for future generations... so that they do not need to rely on descriptions." The governor then went on to mention some of the flowage's iconic wildlife, from eagles and ospreys to muskies, and to hail the boaters, campers, fishermen, and "explorers of every variety" who use the flowage. Before finishing, he graciously thanked "the people who have maintained this area before us.... On behalf of all the people in Wisconsin today and generations to come, I applaud you all and recognize the efforts of the Chippewa and Flambeau Improvement Company, the many nearby landowners, and the people of Iron County for watching over this special place." With these words, a governor with a modest environmental record turned over to the protection of the state, on behalf of "our children

Governor Tommy Thompson about to release a rehabilitated eagle at the dedication ceremony for the state's purchase of the Turtle-Flambeau Flowage. The festivities were hosted by Fort Flambeau Resort following a tour of the flowage by the governor and an attending flotilla. Sandra Gitzlaff.

and our children's children—to preserve... to honor... and to cherish," a flowage once reviled by conservationists for the damage it had done to pristine headwaters country. The "Crown Jewel," secured in a setting of historical irony, now belonged to the citizens of Wisconsin. It was a good moment for the governor, for the residents of the flowage locale and nearby communities, and for the citizens of the state; but it must have been an especially sweet moment for Paul Gottwald, Dave Jacobson, John Olson and his colleagues at the Mercer Ranger Station, and, of course, Mark Fort. Ironically, Fort, whose love for the flowage had inspired so many fruitful initiatives, died 12 years later in an ice fishing accident near the flowage dam.

Making a Master Plan

The Wisconsin Department of Natural Resources requires that all properties it intends to hold and manage, whether large or small, have a master plan. Accordingly, work on a master plan for the Turtle-Flambeau Flowage began soon after its purchase, and, as might be expected with almost any undertaking by a state agency, politics quickly found its way into the process. Some environmental groups, sensing an opportunity to create a wilderness-type reserve, pressed for limitations on access, timber harvests, and use of outboard motors. According to one source, these notions initially received a fairly warm reception in Madison and emerged in at least one preliminary version of the plan. This wilderness-oriented direction in management, however, received strong pushback, especially from those within the WDNR who had taken part in pre-purchase meetings with local citizens. They had been on the receiving end of a clear and consistent message from folks in Mercer, Springstead, and Butternut. Lisa and Dick Daly, owners of Cedar Lodge Resort, represented the views of many area residents and businesspeople. They supported the state's goal of preserving the area, but they also worried about possible restrictions that might interfere with the accustomed activities of flowage users. Similarly, Maryann and Rod Brown of the Lodge of Lakeview, who were all in with saving flowage lands from development, opposed any regulations that would limit the use of motors to access all parts of the flowage. Dick Sleight, the noted fishing guide, put his case succinctly: "Most of the people around here want the place unchanged. Just leave it. Leave those islands the way they are. It's a piece of wilderness." He then went on to claim—as if wholly unaware of efforts by the Mercer Chamber of Commerce and the Turtle Flambeau Flowage Association to trumpet the area's attractions far and wide—that more people did not know about it (TFF) because local people discouraged publicity. Another, somewhat more dispassionate participant in some of these meetings summed up the gist of the local message this way: "We want you to keep it [TFF] the way it is. Don't over-develop it; don't lock it up. This is a fishing flowage. It's shallow, it's got stumps, it's not a great big power boat recreation area. A lot of people's history is coming and fishing." In fact, it was to this vision of the flowage that Dave Jacobson, as district director, had committed the WDNR during these pre-purchase conversations. In the end, resistance from within the agency persuaded the WDNR to step back from its initial position and, instead, to endorse a plan that would be more consistent with local interests and aspirations—though the tensions among alternative approaches to flowage management seem to have persisted through the entire process.

The actual preparation of the master plan took place largely at the Mercer Ranger Station. Initially, Dennis Scholl, fisheries manager and interim property manager, headed up a master planning task force made up largely of local WDNR officeholders and supplemented by a few specialists from the area and from Madison. In addition, Scholl was charged with the task of obtaining input from the public. Toward this end, he appointed a citizen advisory committee to assist throughout the process of developing the master plan. The committee was chaired by

Perry Reas, an avid angler from Park Falls and owner of a flowage residence. Other members were Ed Borgiasz and John Raabe, town chairmen of Sherman and Mercer, respectively; Doris Cihak of Bastine Lake Resort; Mary Burns, a camper, canoer, and wildlife watcher from Mercer; and Bill Peterson, a retired WDNR forester/ranger with a cabin in the Springstead area and a frequent user of the flowage. Maryann Brown, from the Lodge of Lakeview, was an alternate on the committee.

In pursuit of still broader public input, Scholl held a number of public meetings for interested citizens from the area and around the state. On August 9, 1991, for example, Scholl hosted an open house at the ranger station. The public was invited to speak with WNDR personnel about the planning process and to leave written comments expressing their concerns about and aspirations for the property. Scholl then followed up by sending each participant a summary of the comments. A rough, thematic grouping of these comments breaks down as follows: camping–19; fisheries–9; development–9; amenities–8; boats and motors–7; sanitation–5; and water quality–5. The wide variety of comments within any given category—such as limiting motors to 25 horsepower, not limiting horsepower, not allowing motors in some areas—makes further generalizations impossible, which is indicative of the challenges posed to those who were drafting the plan.

In 1992, Roger Jasinski left his post as a senior water regulation and zoning specialist in Park Falls and moved to Mercer to become the property manager of the TFF. At the same time, he also assumed leadership of the master plan task force. As Jasinski recalls, responsibility for writing the master plan fell largely on himself and the various specialists in Mercer. He wrote the sections on recreation; Dennis Scholl those on fish and fish management; Christine Paulik those on forestry; and Greg Kessler those on wildlife. Jody Les, a landscape architect from the Madison

WDNR, assisted in editing and consolidating materials and in the making of maps. As fate would have it, everyone who was involved in the preparation of the plan had access to a tailor-made resource: namely, the co-management plan drawn up by Olson and Fort. Although their plan did not meet the formatting requirements for a WDNR master plan, much of the information it contained and many of its principles ultimately found their way into the master plan. The effort and commitment that Olson, Fort, and their colleagues had put into drafting the co-management plan paid off in the long run—though not in precisely the circumstances they had anticipated.

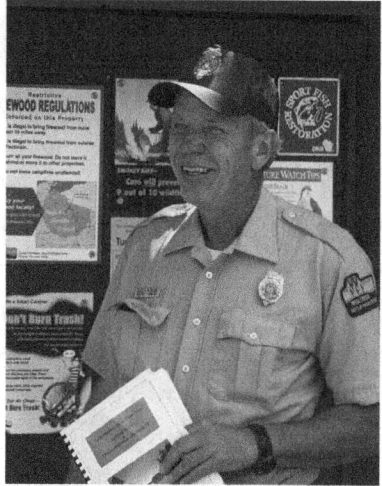

By late summer of 1994, successive versions of the master plan had been reviewed and revised, and the WDNR was ready to seek public comment on the current draft. And so, from mid-September

Roger Jasinski, the first property manager of the Turtle-Flambeau Scenic Waters Area, holds a copy of the master plan. WDNR

through early November, the agency conducted listening and informational sessions in Mercer, Park Falls, Stevens Point, Madison, and Milwaukee. At these sessions, the strongest and most persistent critique of the plan concerned its failure to create a non-motorized wilderness area, some 2,800 acres in size, out of the eastern part of the flowage. The supporters of this idea, including 10 conservation organizations, argued that Wisconsin was woefully short of wilderness land, especially in comparison with Michigan and Minnesota, and that the addition of a portion of the flowage to the adjacent Manitowish River Wilderness Area would create a 9,200-acre parcel of river wilderness. At an earlier stage in the deliberations, the citizen advisory committee had rejected such a proposal; and its opposition continued in force in 1994. The municipalities of Mercer, Springstead, and Park Falls, as well as the Iron County Board of Supervisors, also opposed any restrictions on use of the flowage—as did a citizen petition. When the committee convened on November 30, 1994, to discuss comments from the recently held public meetings, it once again turned thumbs down on a wilderness area. As the *Ironwood Globe* noted, "There is strong local opposition to any regulatory restriction on motorized craft, especially on the flowage where fishing and snowmobiling are popular uses." Questions of local sentiment aside, the WDNR did not think it appropriate or practical to block off part of a river system: boaters who enter a river system, the argument went, have reason to expect that they can continue their journey without encountering artificial barriers to their progress.

On March 23, 1995, the Natural Resources Board gave its approval to the master plan. The document (73 pages plus maps) calls for the creation of the Turtle-Flambeau Scenic Waters Area (TFSWA), based initially on the lands purchased from the CFIC and other scattering state holdings that predated this purchase. The express rationale for this new state scenic area is "to protect, maintain, and enhance the TFSWA's scenic qualities, outstanding water and wetland resources, plant and wildlife communities, and diversity of outdoor recreational opportunities." To make sure the scenic area could achieve these goals, the plan proposes to supplement the initial holding of 22,343 acres through the acquisition, over time, of an additional 20,386 acres of land surrounding the flowage, bringing the potential total size of the scenic area to some 48,941 acres. (The plan exempted from purchase subdivided lands or lands with capital improvements.)

Having established the basic contours, both geographically and programmatically, of the TFSWA, the plan then outlines a set of management objectives—and the means to achieve them. These objectives include land acquisition, land classification and management, wildlife and fisheries management, aesthetic management, water quality protection, and recreational management and development. Development, however, is to be strictly limited. The plan commits to 60 campsites, including two group sites and one that meets standards set by the Americans with Disabilities Act; and it promises maintenance of six existing access points. Other proposed management activities, such as closing roads and trails to motorized traffic or the removal or burial of utility lines, have the goal of enhancing "the wild scenic" character of the area. Toward that end, the plan states that "no new snowmobile or ATV trails are planned." In response to calls for the creation of a formal wilderness area, the master plan offers a compromise solution—or so the press labeled it: namely, "a voluntary quiet area" in the eastern one-fifth of the flowage. Persons using the area "would be asked, not required, to observe slow-no-wake operation of power boats and pursue quiet camping and fishing activities...." The notion of voluntary quiet would apply only during the open water season, leaving the designated area open to snowmobiling in the winter.

On balance, the master plan gives comfort to those who wanted the flowage to retain its traditional character. Time-honored recreational activities, such as island camping, fishing, canoeing, and wildlife viewing, stand at the heart of the plan, and the aesthetic considerations embodied in it promise the preservation, and even enhancement, of the area's northwoods feel. Moreover, the master plan offers some assurance that its vision for the flowage will be more than words on paper. The plan is, in effect, binding on WDNR personnel, and any proposed departure of significance from its principles, whether that be securing a variance or initiating a new rule or practice, must be approved according to agency protocol. Furthermore, the master plan promises some continuity; it was not to be revised before 10 years had passed. In fact, the plan has been in effect 20 years—and counting.

The final act in the master plan story took place on September 9, 1995, when Roger Jasinski, officiating at a ceremony on a flowage island, awarded the members of the citizen advisory committee with plaques honoring their volunteer work. The group, Jasinski noted, had met six times a year, starting in 1991. Their recommendations had ranged across a full spectrum of issues, including "boat access, property acquisition goals, recreation and

The citizen advisory group that assisted in drafting the master plan. From left to right: Jody Les (WDNR), John Raabe, Maryann Brown, Bill Peterson, Doris Cihak, Perry Reas, Mary Burns, and Roger Jasinski. Maryann Brown

campsite development, exotic nuisance controls, roads and nature trails, and informational items like brochures and trail guides." Beyond this, he noted, "The group also showed interest in water

quality protection, land classification, and aesthetic management."
Jasinski's remarks make clear that the guidelines by which the
state would exercise its authority over this valuable resource were
partially, and beneficially, shaped by the participation of
knowledgeable and dedicated citizens working alongside natural
resource professionals. The process of developing the master plan
brought the right parties to the table; and the end product, though
not to the liking of everyone on every point, nonetheless sought to
reconcile as reasonably as possible a broad range of recreational
uses to which the public had become accustomed with the science-
based needs of resource management. The master plan appears in
retrospect not only as a blueprint for the future of the flowage but
also as a useful model of cooperation between an agency of state
government and the public that it served.

The Flowage Under
the Master Plan

From its approval in 1995, the master plan shaped the early years
of WDNR management of the Turtle-Flambeau Scenic Waters
Area. In addition to setting broad, long-term goals, the plan also
laid out a fairly extensive agenda of activities in need of immediate
attention. Indeed, Roger Jasinski, the property manager, did not
have to look beyond the first paragraph of the plan to find one item
large enough to fill his plate: purchasing as many pieces of land as
possible toward the objective of increasing the overall size of the
TFSWA by 20,386 acres. In undertaking this task, Jasinski made
use of a WDNR program, payment in lieu of taxes (PILT), which
had been put in place to compensate local units of government
for revenues lost when the state purchased private real estate and
took it off the tax rolls. Lands purchased after January 1, 1992, were

subject to state statute 70.114, which in effect paid the towns the full value of taxes on the land based on either the purchase price or the assessed valuation. This latter arrangement actually yielded a higher rate of return than, for example, managed forest crop land. Finally, procedures were in place by which such a purchase could be developed and executed. Proposals for purchases first had to work their way up through the WDNR hierarchy and then receive approval from the Natural Resources Board. In this manner, the scenic area could be expanded without serious damage to local revenues. Jasinski worked on this land acquisition diligently and with marked success. As of the spring of 2014, nearly 14,000 acres had been added to the TFSWA by him and his successor, Christine Paulik, bringing its total size to 34,971.38 acres.

Securing additional land to fill out the TFSWA area was but one of the tasks before the property manager. The plan also detailed, and set budgets for, a number of specific projects designed to maintain or enhance the existing property and its facilities. These included work—some of it major—on five of the six landings that were to be maintained in the future. Only a new landing that had recently been constructed at Trude Lake escaped the list. Fisherman's Landing was totally refurbished in 2003 with a new ramp, toilet facility, and parking lots. The ramp had to be redone the following year because the previous job failed to meet specifications. Both Murray's and Sportsman's landings were renovated in 2003. Maintenance projects included the construction of new picnic tables for a number of sites, and the installation of metal fire rings and open-pit toilets at all campsites. Enhancements to the TFSWA included the placement of rustic entry and directional signs around the flowage and the construction of an interpretive nature trail at the Fisherman's Landing site. All of these improvements upgraded the overall flowage facility without significantly changing its traditional character.

The master plan also called for improving "navigation at three

bridge/culvert crossings by removing or upgrading the structures."
Two of these projects, though not actually described in the plan,
were intended to facilitate boat or canoe passage between the
flowage and two other waters: Trude Lake and the Little Turtle
River. Such expanded access was to be attained through the
replacement of the present culverts by enlarged culverts or bridges.
In the fall of 2014, after years of discussion, planning, and delay,
a bridge was finally erected on Popko Circle West, which opened
the way for boat traffic between Trude Lake and the flowage. The
Little Turtle project, however, remains an unfinished master plan
objective. The third navigation project, the budget for which was
included in the plan, tentatively called for the removal of an old
bridge (built in 1978) from the mainland to Big Island and the
restoration of that site. This part of the plan was set aside, however,
when it became apparent that adequate bridge access would assist
WDNR land management on the island, even as it would provide
a safe and convenient route for hunters and hikers. Consequently,
in 2008 the WDNR removed the old bridge and replaced it with
a more substantial structure. In the process, the abutments were
reworked to afford improved navigational clearance for boaters
moving between the Turtle River area and Merkle Lake.

In the course of carrying out his responsibilities as property
manager, Roger Jasinski came across two situations that had
not been addressed by the master plan: the diminishing stock of
driftwood along the shores of the flowage, and the increasingly
heavy use of the two existing group campsites. Great rafts of
driftwood had been one of the defining features of the flowage
over the years, both for their scenic appeal and for their ability to
attract walleyes seeking relief from the bright summer sun and,
of course, anglers seeking the walleyes. But driftwood stocks had
fallen victim to natural deterioration, to campfires, and to removal
for commercial purposes, such as for lawn ornamentation or for

the construction of craft items. To put a stop to the latter two practices, Jasinski resorted to an addition to the state administrative code, which, in part, read: "Driftwood or other dead and down wood located below the ordinary high watermark of the Willow, Turtle Flambeau and Chippewa flowages is considered a natural feature that may not be removed or destroyed without written authorization from the department [WDNR]."

The flowage had long enjoyed a reputation as a place to camp, and the two established group sites had always done a brisk business. But the publicity that attended the purchase of the flowage by the state further enhanced its reputation, and the pressure on these sites—each of which was designed to accommodate around 20 persons—grew accordingly. Instances of groups of 40 or more were not uncommon, and one group of over 80 stayed at one of them. Not surprisingly, one outcome of this increased use was that many groups of canoeists found themselves stranded on the water with nowhere to spend the night. This kind of predicament led the American Camper Association Wisconsin to formally ask the WDNR to provide additional opportunities for group camping on the flowage. The heavy pressure on these campsites also posed maintenance problems, particularly where sanitation was concerned. New pit toilets had to be hand dug at least once, and sometimes more often, each summer. To deal with these problems—downsides of the flowage's popularity—Jasinski had to seek a variance from the master plan. Accordingly, the WDNR set up a citizen advisory committee to discuss the matter and invited the public to attend its two scheduled meetings. The committee concluded its work by recommending that the existing group sites continue to be available on a first-come, first-served basis to parties of 15 people. To supplement these sites, the committee called for the construction of two "cluster" sites, each of which would accommodate three parties of 15 people. These sites would be operated on "a system of reservations and fees" that would guarantee the availability of sites to groups that signed up in advance. Finally, the committee agreed that the new cluster sites, though accessible to campers only by water, should have road access for the purpose of maintenance. These recommendations were included in a formal request for a variance that Jasinski submitted to the WDNR in July of 2005.

After the request wended its way through the WDNR and received approval, Big Island was selected as the best location for the two new group sites. It had suitable water frontage and land contours for campsites, and the existing road system could easily be modified for purposes of construction and maintenance. The choice of Big Island, it should be noted, contributed significantly to the decision to rebuild the bridge from the mainland, rather than remove it as the master plan had suggested. When construction was completed, late in October of 2009, each of the new sites had the following features: a pitted, vault toilet for men and women, both handicapped accessible; a boat docking area; gradual, wheelchair friendly approaches to the camping areas, as well as a wheelchair-accessible fabric that extended into the water. In short, not only did the new sites provide additional accommodations for groups but they also made camping available to those with physical limitations. As such, these campsites more than met the objective laid out in the master plan of providing "one site that meets Americans with Disabilities Act requirements." The new group sites welcomed their first visitors in the summer of 2010.

When Roger Jasinski retired in June of 2009, the greater part of the agenda set by the master plan had been accomplished, and then some. Only the two navigation improvements at Trude Lake and the Little Turtle River remained unfinished. The TFSWA had pretty much taken the shape envisioned for it by the advisory committee that worked on the master plan and by the WDNR.

This was the situation that greeted Christine Paulik in August of 2009 when she set aside her role as forester at the Mercer Ranger Station to assume the position of property manager of the TFSWA. As a result of her former position and her role in the preparation of the master plan, Paulik was intimately acquainted with the property and fully knowledgeable of the document that defined its character. This body of experience, however, could hardly have prepared her for the first challenge that landed on her doorstep.

The Big Blow

In the early evening of July 27, 2010, campers on the islands of the flowage and residents on its shores knew for certain that a storm was brewing. Some watched and listened from the shelter of tarps or porches as distant thunder rolled and the skies darkened. Others kept in touch with weather radio, which predicted a time of arrival for the storm over the flowage area. Soon, as the sky turned an ominous yellow and the winds suddenly mounted, some campers dove for safety under the king-size picnic tables at their campsites, while others took shelter in their tents. Then came the roar and the devastation as the storm uprooted some trees, snapped others off 15 to 20 feet above the ground, and turned once majestic pines, hemlocks, and spruces into a deadly mix of flying and falling projectiles. One tent moved some 30 feet with its occupants in it; a tree crashed across a shelter tarpaulin seconds after two campers had abandoned it; and some boats were smashed and submerged. Meanwhile on the shore, residents watched in awe as unknown objects flew past their windows, trees hit houses and flattened outbuildings, and roofing was blown away.

The National Weather Service Office in Duluth later identified the central perpetrator of this devastation as an EF-1 tornado, one with peak winds between 86 and 110 miles per hour. It was one of three tornados spawned by a passing supercell; a second one hit the Morse area, and a third cut through eastern Ashland County. The Turtle-Flambeau Flowage tornado began at 7:20 p.m. and ended at 7:26. During these six minutes it cut a path 4.8 miles long and about 660 yards wide at its maximum width. Although this tornado wrought the most severe damage, it was not the sole force at work. As the National Weather Service put it, "...This tornado path was embedded in a swath of rather substantial non-tornadic wind damage caused merely by intense thunderstorm wind gusts." The storm's larger path of destruction was approximately eight miles in length and ranged from one to three miles in width. It began near the Turtle Dam and ended about one-half mile east of Murray's Landing. Patterns of damage varied with the nature of the winds. Straight-line thunderstorm winds downed trees in a uniform direction, whereas tornadic winds snapped them off and left debris scattered every which way.

Trees, blown down or snapped off, devastate a one-time island campsite in the wake of the 2010 tornado. Michael Hittle

Response to the disaster came promptly, thanks to the fact that Iron County, the towns of Mercer and Sherman, and the WDNR all had emergency plans in place. In this case, the Mercer Fire Department, the first government entity to learn of the severity of the storm, assumed initial authority over the emergency response. Although it ascertained that Fisherman's Landing afforded the best site from which to carry out search and rescue activities, the Mercer response team nevertheless had to cut its way into the landing. Emergency personnel from the Mercer Fire Department, along with crews and ambulances from Winchester, Presque Isle, and Manitowish Waters then converged on the scene. Cell phone calls from some of the campsites where there were serious injuries set the immediate priorities. Josh Komrowski, the flowage ranger, a member of the Mercer ambulance squad, and a deputy sheriff headed off in a ranger boat to campsite C3 where these three rescuers located and evacuated a seriously injured camper. The camper was then transported by ambulance to Howard Young Medical Center in Woodruff. This initial response set the pattern for subsequent search and rescue efforts.

Within an hour after word about the storm had gone out, Stacy Ofstad, the Iron County emergency government director, arrived at the landing, and Chris Paulik joined him shortly thereafter. With rescue efforts now under way or even completed for some of those cases where distress calls had been received, the task became the broader one of checking the entire flowage. Ofstad and Paulik spread out a flowage map on the hood of a vehicle and worked out a strategy for sending search and rescue personnel to every campsite. Boats from the WDNR and Mercer Rescue were staffed with three persons: a driver, an EMT, and a spotter. Each boat was equipped with a radiophone and a cell phone so that the rescue party could report its findings and receive its next assignment. Rescuers brought a total of eight injured campers to the landing, where waiting ambulances transported them to the Howard Young Medical Center. Rescue boats also brought back a number of stranded but uninjured campers. Other campers, some injured, found shelter and assistance on their own. Though some of the injuries were quite serious, there were, amazingly given the devastation, no fatalities.

Ofstad then turned his attention to coordinating the efforts of all the responders—the towns of Mercer and Sherman, the Iron County Sheriff's office, the WDNR, and the ambulance services of nearby towns—in an effort to reach locations around the flowage that had been isolated by debris. A number of campers, including a few with injuries, had found their way off the flowage to Murray's Landing only to discover that the road out was blocked. A bureaucratic dispute over jurisdiction delayed a response to this situation, leaving Jim Cox of WDNR the lone sawyer attacking the mess for over an hour. Help eventually arrived from Mercer, and the road was finally cleared by midnight and the stranded campers rescued. Other town of Mercer crews worked through the night to open at least one lane on Flowage Dam Road, while crews from Sherman fought with the tangle of trees that had virtually isolated the Springstead Point and some first responders who resided there.

The search and rescue operation ended around 3:45 a.m. when all campers were believed safe and there were no reports of missing people, and when it had become clear that no flowage residents had sustained injuries. But a full appraisal of the damage would have to await daylight. And so at 7:30 a.m. on the 28th, a systematic search of the flowage began anew. With scarcely a respite from their labors of the night, Mercer Fire Department and WDNR crews set out again. They revisited first the most heavily damaged campsites, in part to make sure that no campers had been overlooked and in part to determine which sites would have to be taken out of service permanently. They then went on to investigate and inventory damage to all the remaining sites, here and there cutting trees that posed particular dangers. In addition, the crews escorted some campers who wanted to retrieve personal belongings from their campsites.

On the mainland, Wednesday the 28th was also a day to inventory the damage and to make plans for recovery and restoration, just as it was a day to begin the slow and difficult process of clearing trees and limbs to provide access to roads and homes and to enable the restoration of power. Some affected homeowners on the flowage found out, amid the debris, just how many trees had been on their lots. Others marveled at near misses. On Schenebeck's Point, simply opening up a lane to serve as the driveway for a few residences took a crew with a small loader at least three hours. Even with power machinery, the full cleanup took weeks. But people responded calmly to the tasks before them. Jim Golomb, who had lost a home to the Park Falls tornado of 1985, surveyed the downed trees, smashed garage, and crushed boat on his flowage property and remarked stoically: "We get to work. We'll be fine."

Chris Paulik, as flowage property manager, faced a challenge of a somewhat different kind: namely, to provide late summer and fall vacationers with as many safe, fully functional campsites as possible. Aerial reconnaissance on the 28th gave the WDNR a sense of the extent of the storm, and the second round of visits to the campsites revealed the severity of the damage. About half of the 66 campsites had sustained some level of damage, and, as it turned out, almost 75 percent of them required the removal of at least one

Chris Paulik, the property manager who dealt with the 2010 tornado and its aftermath. Chris Paulik

tree. The on-site inspections also revealed that 10 campsites were totally devastated, with nearly every tree broken or blown down. Of these sites, Paulik said, "There is just nothing left." These campsites—among them some longtime camper favorites such as Hot Dog Island, Fourth of July Slough, and the Narrows leading into Horseshoe Lake—had to be closed permanently.

With the assessment complete, WDNR crews then set to work on those campsites deemed salvageable, clearing them of fallen trees and debris and making them both safe and usable. Cut up wood was left for campers, who found no shortage of firewood near affected sites. By August 6th, the WDNR announced that 52 of the 66 campsites on the flowage had reopened. Four more followed in the next couple of weeks, including the two original group sites, which had suffered heavy damage. This prompt triage of the damaged sites allowed many vacationers to keep their plans for late summer and fall trips on the flowage. Even as the saws were whirring, however, Paulik and others from the ranger station were at work identifying spots where replacement campsites might be placed. As it turned out, eight former campsites had to be permanently closed and relocated elsewhere. By July 4, 2011, the flowage once again had its full assemblage of campsites: six reserve-only group sites and 60 first-come, first-served sites.

Although campers were fully back in business, many flowage islands and pieces of shoreline remained devastated. Public reactions to this situation varied. Some found the mess unsightly and urged that it be cleaned up; others welcomed uprooted and partially submerged trees as a potential benefit to fish habitat. In the end, the WDNR followed the prescription laid out in the master plan for the shoreline vegetative zone: "In the event of a natural disaster (e.g., tornado or insect infestation) the trees will be left lying and not salvaged or cut." The intent here was clearly to let nature take its course, but other considerations were at play as well. Salvage lumber, because of damage to fibers, had diminished market value. Moreover, there was not all that much of it, and the risks to logging operations of using the frozen flowage had to be balanced against a limited financial return on the wood. A different approach, however, was taken with lands beyond the 300-foot shoreline "no-cut" zone. There, WDNR Forester Heather Berklund contracted eight salvage sales—the most conspicuous of which was in the hard-hit area adjacent to Fisherman's Landing. The terms of sale called for the removal of marketable timber, but the logging operation left ample snags and den trees for wildlife as well as tops and miscellaneous debris for soil enrichment. The approximately 770 acres harvested in the salvage sales yielded about 16,800 cords of pulpwood and 434,000 board feet of sawtimber. These timber sales essentially wrote the final chapter in the story of the tornado, and TFSWA began the slow process of healing its wounds the old-fashioned, natural way.

"It's an ill wind that blows no good," as the saying goes, but this ill wind did give a push to some much-needed work on the flowage. The attention focused on the campsites in the aftermath of the tornado reinforced an existing concern about the effects of long-term erosion at some of the sites. This led, in turn, to an agreement between the WDNR and the Iron County Land and Water Conservation Department to embark on a five- to 10-year project to combat erosion at a dozen or more campsites. Projected remedies included the simple relocation of landings; the planting of trees, shrubs, and grasses; the installation of erosion control blankets; and the removal and replacement of deteriorated stairs. Work began in 2012 at a handful of the less challenging sites and was projected to continue annually. Campsite 26 was one of the first to receive treatment. Under the watchful eyes of MaryJo Gringras of ICLWCD and Chris Paulik, a group of Mercer High School students planted black-eyed Susans and little bluestem plants, put a coconut erosion barrier in place, and erected a rustic cedar fence to discourage campers from trampling the newly restored slope. The same year, the ICLWCD, utilizing funds from two grants, assisted the Birch Point Condominium Association with a 600-foot shoreline restoration project along the Turtle River shore of the flowage.

Restoration projects of the kind carried out in 2012 depend, in the last analysis, on the availability of funding. Such funding, however, became scarce beginning in 2008, when the Great Recession and the distressed fiscal condition of the state of Wisconsin combined to put a crimp in the budgets of all state agencies, including those dealing with conservation. Even funding for relatively inexpensive projects such as campsite restorations became scarce. As it happens, though, the flowage enjoyed—and will continue to enjoy—a modest hedge against the vagaries of governmental funding. According to a 2006 publication from the Natural Resources Foundation, "an anonymous donor created a permanent endowed fund to provide a perpetual source of support for the purpose of preserving, protecting and enhancing the lands and waters of the Turtle-Flambeau Scenic Waters Area." In subsequent years this fund has grown, thanks to additional contributions by friends of the flowage. The fund is administered by the Natural Resources Foundation, a statewide non-profit organization. The operational guidelines for the fund stress educational activities, especially those that involve students, as well as land improvements. Funds cannot be used for routine maintenance or maintenance equipment. The property manager of the flowage applies for support for projects that fall under the guidelines, and the Natural Resources Foundation then decides whether or not to fund the proposal and sets the funding level for approved projects. For several years, the endowment supported costs the WDNR incurred in connection with crib building.

Beginning in 2011, the endowment funds were directed toward erosion control projects. The presence of this fund has brought still others to the proverbial table where the future of the flowage is determined: namely, private individuals who believe the flowage to be of sufficient value to the state and its citizens to warrant its own ongoing revenue stream.

◦◦◉◦◦

From the very beginning of the Turtle-Flambeau Flowage, the state of Wisconsin, through its natural resource agencies, has made its presence felt on this resplendent body of water. Initially this presence was limited mainly to the fishery, and, with the exception of setting bag regulations, it had been somewhat episodic. The involvement of the WDNR in the Voigt case and its aftermath took the relationship another step, though, embedding the agency more deeply and on a continuing basis in the management of this fishery. The decision of Governor Thompson to purchase the flowage on behalf of the state, however, was a qualitatively different kind of step. For not only did the WDNR retain its preeminent role in the fishery and in wildlife management, but it also took on an added set of managerial responsibilities for the lands of the flowage and the human activities on them. Indeed, the purchase effectively entrusted to the state, through the WDNR, responsibility for the entirety of the Turtle-Flambeau Scenic Waters Area—leaving only the management of water flows to the CFIC, and these were to be governed by the memorandum of understanding between the company and the WDNR. By this reading, the master plan can be seen as the concrete expression of the state's goals for and obligations to the flowage.

The WDNR's acquisition of the flowage seems a fitting outcome, given that so much of the impetus in the direction of preserving it from private ownership and development had come from within the agency's ranks. And it was an outcome that certainly pleased those who had been so involved. But as a long-term arrangement, the purchase can only secure its stated goals if the new guardian of the property is strong enough to effectively carry out its fiduciary duties. In short, the future of the flowage will depend on a WDNR that is science-based, adequately staffed and funded, and as free as possible from petty political interference.

CHAPTER TEN

Continuity and Change: The Flowage Moves into the New Millennium

I n keeping with its character as a place at once timeless and ever-changing, the flowage during the latter years of the 20th century and the first decade and a half of the 21st century witnessed moments of business as usual as well as some developments of potentially far-reaching consequence. As noted in the previous chapter, the creation of the Turtle-Flambeau Scenic Waters Area (TFSWA) set a new and full agenda for those responsible for its growth and maintenance, and especially for the property manager; but it had little immediate impact on those who looked after the area's fauna. The role of the wildlife biologist pretty much remained what it had been—to focus on signature species in the area; and fisheries personnel sustained their intensive monitoring of the populations of major species. That said, the latter group undertook a bold initiative to identify angler preferences and to actively undertake measures to shape the fishery accordingly. The biggest changes, however, occurred with the entry on the scene of two new interest groups: the federal government and a flowage property owners' association. Though widely disparate in their powers and purviews, these two entities expanded the ranks of stakeholders and as a result rendered the politics of flowage management even more complex.

Wildlife Management

Over the 25 years spanning the turn of the century, the course of wildlife management on the flowage followed well-established lines. This was certainly the case when Bruce Bacon took up the position of wildlife biologist for Iron and Ashland counties in 1993. Bacon promptly immersed himself in a number of ongoing wildlife projects—in particular, those focused on ospreys, eagles, and loons. When John Olson, Jeff Wilson, and Mark Fort began this work in the 1970s, avian predators had started to rebound in numbers nationwide, thanks largely to the declining use of harmful pesticides. On the flowage, ospreys led the way, and by 1988 their numbers peaked at 22 nests, as compared with only three or four for eagles. From then on, however, osprey numbers began to decline, while those of eagles rose, until in 2012 and 2013 not a single osprey nestling fledged on the flowage.

This reversal of fortune for the flowage's ospreys set a research agenda that Bacon was to follow for some 18 years. With assistance from Jeff Wilson and four interns who he supervised, Bacon helped to capture and band over 500 osprey nestlings on the flowage and throughout Iron County. The research also involved placing cameras at nesting sites to capture behaviors that might adversely affect ospreys. In time this work led the researchers to surmise that the ospreys' problems might be attributed in large measure to harassment by the burgeoning eagle population. The issue was not the occasional fish that eagles steal from ospreys. Rather, the issue centered on the defensive activities of male ospreys to defend their nests from threatening eagles. The males, it seemed, spent so much time driving eagles away and pursuing them that they neglected their primary responsibility, which was to catch fish for their young. As a consequence, osprey fledglings set off on their first migrations underweight, which rendered them vulnerable to the many perils of long-distance flight and of survival in a new environment. It is not surprising that so few survived to return and nest in the area. Based on this assessment of the ospreys' plight, the researchers concluded that future efforts to increase osprey numbers on the flowage might benefit from strategic placement of nesting platforms at some distance from known eagle nests.

Eagles and ospreys were hardly the sole focus of Bacon's attention. He took part in loon surveys and assisted in some of the loon research projects on the flowage, and he participated in Northland College's Loon Watch program as a member of its advisory council. Picking up on another initiative from Olson's era, Bacon monitored the 90 remaining wood duck houses on the flowage. For the most part, these nest boxes produced mergansers rather than wood ducks, but one of them produced a clutch of common goldeneyes, a duck that rarely breeds in this area but one whose presence in the TFSWA he hoped to foster. This led to the placement of 10 new boxes with somewhat wider entry holes, which were designed with the goal of attracting more goldeneyes to the flowage.

Bacon also helped sustain the research initiatives of his predecessors by conducting, every five years, wildlife surveys for tracking loons, ospreys, eagles, and waterfowl on the flowage. Starting in 2000, the survey teams were joined by experts in identifying songbirds. Their participation led to the creation of a comprehensive list of bird species that inhabit or visit the TFSWA. With this addition, the survey has become, in effect, one means of measuring the biodiversity of the area. Bacon summarized the results of these surveys in an article entitled "Turtle-Flambeau Flowage Scenic Waters Area Wildlife Surveys, 1980-2006."

The rich avian life that the flowage supports drew not only the attention of WDNR biologists but of a number of scientists from academic institutions. Flowage loons were the focus of one doctoral dissertation and one master's thesis. Another master's thesis focused on resident merlins. Beyond these studies, at least 22 scientific articles, most of them on loons, have drawn on, wholly or in part, data from birds that are native to the flowage. This basic research not only speaks clearly to the value of the flowage to the scientific community, but it also confirms the reputation of the flowage as one of the state's premier sites for signature native birds.

Unlike birdlife, the four-legged animals present in the Turtle-Flambeau Scenic Waters Area have never received special attention from the Mercer wildlife biologists—primarily because the lives of most of these animals are not dependent on the waters of the flowage to the extent that the lives of loons, ospreys, eagles, and waterfowl are. The one exception to such benign neglect of mammals has been recommendations from biologists for selective timber sales within the scenic area (but away from the flowage viewshed) that would be beneficial to wildlife. Mammals in the flowage area have therefore been treated within the context of the two-county (Ashland and Iron) field of responsibility of the WDNR wildlife biologist in Mercer. These duties have traditionally included helping to set bag regulations for game species, as well as fostering, where possible, the well-being of species that have reintroduced themselves, such as American martens and fishers. But beyond these measures no major initiatives were taken to introduce or assist flowage-area mammals during these years.

This approach was consistent with Bacon's views, based on years in the field, on the limits of human intervention: namely, though we can take modest steps, consistent with our science-based understanding, ultimately "Mother Nature rules, whether she is dealing out mild or harsh winters, or contriving to bring about a more robust array of predators (bears, wolves, coyotes, bobcats, fisher) than the north has seen in a number of years." She remains the ultimate game manager.

Shaping the Fishery: Public Preferences and Planning

The state's purchase of the flowage and the establishment of the Turtle-Flambeau Scenic Waters Area, had, in effect, made the citizens of Wisconsin stakeholders in its waters and woods. And so it was fitting that when the WDNR set about to develop the statutorily required master plan for this property, it did so with considerable citizen input. The master plan had, of course, included sections on the flowage fishery, but these were brief and somewhat tentative in places. That is, the plan set the overall goal of maintaining "the current fish species assemblage and types of fisheries now available, with improvement in quality where feasible," and it suggested some possible ways in which four species—walleyes, sturgeon, smallmouth bass, and muskellunge—might be managed. This modest treatment of the subject left the door open for a more robust management plan to be developed in the future. It is not surprising, then, that the WDNR fisheries professionals in Mercer, as they became ever more knowledgeable of the character and composition of the flowage fishery and its trends, and as they were bolstered by some modest management successes, would undertake the creation of a more ambitious fishery management plan to guide their work into the future.

The first step toward the creation of such a plan took place in July of 2005 when Jeff Roth, the WDNR senior fisheries biologist in Mercer, and Dave Neuswanger, the WDNR fisheries team leader for the Upper Chippewa Basin in Hayward, "met with 54 stakeholders who were willing to volunteer their time to help develop a long-term vision for the fishery of the Turtle-Flambeau Flowage." The meeting was hosted by the Turtle-Flambeau Flowage and Trude Lake Property Owners' Association (TFF&TLPOA) under the leadership of its president, Arlen Wanta. Participants included 37 lakeside landowners, 15 area anglers, six fishing guides, two business owners, and one Conservation Congress board member. Most, though not all, were Wisconsinites. The session had two objectives: to rank order flowage fish on the basis of angler interest; and then to assess, for each of the major species, angler preferences for two sets of criteria: numbers versus size and catch versus harvest. The end purpose was to set overall goals for each species of interest, along with some precise operational objectives. The goals could be ambitious, but they were not to exceed the ability of the flowage to achieve them. No attempt was made at the meeting to prescribe the strategies that ought to be deployed to attain the goals and objectives. This task was reserved for professional fisheries managers.

It comes as no surprise that walleyes easily won the popularity contest. Fifty-one of the 54 participants rated their interest in them high, and the remaining three individuals rated their interest medium. The agreed-upon goal for walleyes called for "a population of moderate to high density with a moderate proportion of quality-size fish." In operational terms, this meant "four to eight adult walleye per acre in spring population estimates." Adults, as defined by the WDNR, are all fish over 15 inches and any smaller fish whose sex can be determined. Translated from technical language, the clear preference of the group was for a flowage with plenty of "eaters," a view with quite a history behind it.

Yellow perch and black crappie ranked second and third, respectively, in terms of interest, and bluegills occupied sixth place. For perch and bluegills, the population goal was set at a "low to moderate density with a moderate to high proportion of preferred size fish." For crappies, the bar was set a bit higher: "a population of moderate density with a moderate to high proportion of preferred-size fish and a low to moderate proportion of memorable fish." The goal for crappies likely represented a bow both to the historical role of this species in the flowage and to the need to have a sufficient population that exceeded the 10-inch minimum length limit. In aggregate, it seems that panfish anglers on the flowage wanted to put quality fish in the frying pan in preference to putting a lot of small fish back into the water.

Muskellunge came in fourth in the popularity poll. Those with strong opinions about this fishery expressed a preference for size over numbers and voiced overwhelming support for catch-and-release. The goals for musky management as specified in the plan precisely target these preferences. They call for a "population of low to moderate density with a moderate proportion of memorable-size fish." In operational terms, this goal means two things: a density of 0.1 to 0.2 adults per acre; and that 20 to 30 percent of all muskies 20 inches and over that are taken in spring netting should be 42 inches or longer.

Attitudes toward smallmouth bass, which ranked at number five, tended toward extremes: roughly as many participants expressed low or no interest in them as expressed a high interest in them. The plan, quite appropriately, drew on the interests of the latter group of anglers. It calls for "a population of moderate density with a moderate proportion of memorable-size fish." As was the case with the goals for the musky population, the goal for smallmouth coincided with broader trends in bass fishing: namely, trophy hunting and catch-and-release.

The final goal set by the group was, in effect, an endorsement of the kind of diverse fishery that had been in the making for some time, and which was to be confirmed in the survey of 2009 to 2010. Painting with a broad brush, goal number seven endorses "a diverse native fish community that fluctuates in species composition but generally experiences no net loss of native fish species and provides adequate forage for sport fish populations."

The report that contains these goals and objectives, and which elaborates in some detail on what has been and what might be done to attain them, was published under the title, *Fishery Management Plan, Turtle-Flambeau Flowage, Iron County, Wisconsin, March 2007.* The plan does not purport to be absolutely definitive and unchangeable. Rather, it recognizes that fisheries management involves both successes and failures, and that modifications of goals and objectives might well be necessary in light of new knowledge and changing circumstances. That said, the authors regard it as a "long-term strategic" plan that should be consulted on a regular basis as a part of the management of the flowage fishery. And in fact the benchmarks established in this plan have continued to inform the work of fisheries personnel since the time of its publication. Those who take to the flowage's waters with rod and reel in hand do so, whether consciously or not, under the shaping influence of this plan. And it is a plan that anglers themselves had a hand in creating.

The Unsettled Legacy
of the Voigt Decision

Once the court's final rulings had been handed down, and public protests and attempts to obstruct spearing activities had come to an end, the tribes could take some satisfaction from the outcome of the struggle. Their rights had been reaffirmed by law and the exercise of them had become a matter of routine. Moreover, the tribes had attained these goals through the courts and through activities that drew heavily on the principles of nonviolence that had been so prominent in the general struggle for civil rights in American society. But in spite of these positive outcomes, matters had not fully come to rest. Continued hostility to the process and its resolution on the part of non-Indians, and failure by the tribes to secure satisfactory agreements with the WDNR on harvest levels, were to rekindle, from time to time, the mindset of struggle that had been forged among the tribes during the years of tension and protests over walleye fishing. The result was a pattern of on-and-off conflict between the Chippewa bands and the state.

In April of 1996, for example, six Chippewa bands declared a 100 percent harvest on some lakes, including the flowage, where the declaration called for a harvest of 4,462 walleyes. Governor Thompson, concerned about the impact that reduced angler bag limits would have on business in the north, threatened to seek a court injunction to delay the harvest unless the numbers were reduced, which they eventually were. In retrospect, the episode seems to have been a first move in what became a prolonged chess match between the tribes and the state. The next move came in 1997, when the Lac du Flambeau tribe and the state concluded a memorandum of agreement (MOA) that permitted the tribe to sell state licenses, such as for fishing, hunting, all-terrain vehicles, and snowmobiles, and retain a certain portion of the fees. In addition, the state would make a cash payment to the tribe annually for carrying out these sales. This arrangement was expected to net the tribe approximately $100,000. In return, the Lac du Flambeau agreed to harvest walleyes at a level that would guarantee anglers three-fish bag limits on more than 200 lakes in the area around the reservation. This agreement went into effect in 1998.

So matters stood in 2008, the 25th anniversary of the ruling of the Seventh Circuit Court of Appeals that reaffirmed Chippewa treaty rights. Speaking to the overall impact of the implementation of these rights, Joseph Hennessy, the treaty fishing coordinator for the Wisconsin Department of Natural Resources, made the following, quite positive, assessment: "What we have seen over the last 20 years is that angler catch rates, the number of walleyes caught per hour, have been stable." In short, people have not seen their ability to catch walleyes diminish over that time span in spite of tribal harvests. Moreover, walleye populations remain strong in lakes with good natural reproduction. To put the tribal harvest in perspective, he noted that spearers had taken a total of 548,302 walleyes since 1985, whereas agency estimates put the hook-and-line harvest at 300,000 walleyes per year.

Hennessy's numbers were on target, but the overall tone of his remarks did not tell the whole story. It seems that members of the Lac du Flambeau Tribe had been growing increasingly discontented with the settlement of 1997, and some of them had begun to call for the revocation of the memorandum of agreement. In a communication on April 12, 2011, Quinn Williams, a staff attorney in the WDNR bureau of legal services, noted that "there is a perception amongst many of these tribal members that they are 'selling' their treaty rights, and there is pressure for LdF to provide 'more fish' for their members, guaranteed under the Voigt decision. Many of the most recent LdF votes on the issue of completely abandoning the MOA have been decided by single digits." Williams goes on to argue that the new WDNR Secretary, Cathy Stepp, faced with the possibility that the tribe might withdraw from the MOA, had little choice but to negotiate a modification of it to take effect in 2011. The terms of this modification permitted the tribe to "declare up to 10 lakes of their choice at a harvest level that would result in a two-bag limit. The remainder of the lakes speared by LdF should remain at a three-bag limit or higher.... LdF also agreed to 'rotate' these ten lakes each year, so no lake is declared to a two-bag limit in successive years."

This amendment of the MOA directly affected the TurtleFlambeau Flowage, as the tribes declared it to be one of their 10 lakes for more intensive harvest in 2011. This action, in turn, prompted the Turtle Flambeau Flowage Association, the organization that represented local business interests, to protest to the WDNR. In a letter to Secretary Stepp dated April 7, 2011, Scott Reinhard, the association president, objected to the recently negotiated two-bag limit, noting that this concession was not accompanied by any corresponding reduction in financial incentives to the tribe. Reinhard's case centered, as might be expected, on the potential economic consequences of a two-bag limit: "This new agreement will not only result in a negative economic impact to the resorts, restaurant and guides on the Turtle-Flambeau Flowage, but also have an adverse economic impact on all the businesses in the surrounding communities of Mercer, Park Falls, Butternut, Springstead and Agenda." He concluded by calling for a renegotiation of the arrangement so as to make a three-bag limit possible on the flowage. The WDNR response to this letter was Quinn's review of the context of the decision and his assertion that the settlement Stepp negotiated was, under the circumstances, "the best solution." The flowage association had no option but to live with this solution.

The agreement of 2011 between Secretary Stepp and the tribe did not, however, improve relations between those two parties. In a lengthy article in the December 1, 2012, issue of the *Wisconsin State Journal*, reporter Ron Seely explored the roots of a growing contentiousness between the tribes and the state. Walleye quotas remained at the heart of the dispute, but other issues had cropped up as well. The state had gone to court with the tribes to prevent them from introducing night deer hunting (Judge Crabb was to rule against the tribes in December of 2012). Discussions in the legislature about modifying environmental regulations for a proposed mine on the Penokee range and the passage by the legislature (later signed by Governor Scott Walker) of a bill establishing state wolf hunting seasons both contributed further to tensions between the tribe and the legislature. Finally, the tribe's decision to kill an elk in the vicinity of Clam Lake drew a rebuke from the state. Tom Maulson, speaking for the Lac du Flambeau, sought to downplay tensions between the tribe and the WDNR; but he did criticize the legislature for ignoring the tribes in its deliberations on mining legislation and for passing the wolf hunting bill, which tribal members found culturally insulting. Maulson was not alone in his concerns. In his article, Seely noted the following comments from George Meyer, now head of the Wisconsin Wildlife Federation: "I'm greatly concerned about the deterioration of the relations between the state and Wisconsin's tribes." Both Meyer and Maulson expressed the belief that negotiation, not litigation, was the only way to restore relations between the state and the tribe.

This notion received a severe test in early 2013, when the tribes put forth a declaration that called for a walleye harvest of 59,399—the second highest total ever. If this goal were to be met in reality, some 197 lakes would enter the open water fishing season with a one-bag limit. In response, Secretary Stepp called the declaration "significant, unprecedented, and a challenge to long-standing partnerships." And, after reminding the tribes how much they had benefited financially from the 1997 MOA, she raised the possibility of withholding future payments. Maulson took the position that the bad economy made additional fish essential to tribal freezers, but he did not discount frustration with the legislature over mining legislation and the wolf hunt. The resolution of the confrontation occurred on the water. The total walleye harvest was 28,382 fish, the lowest figure since 2009. Perhaps a shortened spearing season—the consequence of a late thaw—was responsible for these low numbers; or perhaps the tribes decided in the end to harvest at a more modest level for other reasons. Whatever the case, the events of 2013 did little to heal relations between the tribes and the state.

One casualty of this more than decade-long back and forth was certainty. From year to year, tribal declarations and harvests varied widely; and, in any given year, the disparity between declarations and harvests could be dramatic, as was the case in 2013. Anglers had to await news of declarations before knowing the likely bag limit on a given lake, and this number itself was subject to adjustment after the tribal harvest had been completed. What was an inconvenience for anglers, however, was a much more serious problem for businesses in the ceded area, as the complaint from the Turtle Flambeau Flowage Association made clear. It was against this background, then, that the state undertook a major initiative in 2014 when the Natural Resources Board declared that, beginning in 2015, the bag limit for walleyes would be set at three for all the lakes in the ceded territories.

To make such a regime work in a manner that would protect the resource, the WDNR needed a new way to allocate angler harvests across a wide range of lakes so that the total take—including tribal harvests—fell within a safe harvest number. WDNR and the Great Lakes Indian Fish & Wildlife Commission (GLIFWC) biologists assessed lakes based on three variables: abundance of walleyes, surface area of the lake, and time. The next step was to adjust the harvests by applying size limits appropriate to the differing types of lakes. The "baseline" size limits—ones that applied to the majority of lakes—called for a 15-inch minimum size limit, with a 20- to 24-inch protected slot (meaning no fish whose measurements fall within the slot may be harvested) This is a fairly conservative regulation, based on the premise that these lakes have limitations and vulnerabilities. But it is only one of a number of possible regulations designed to support a three-fish bag limit. For example, no size limits were to be imposed on the Turtle-Flambeau Flowage, as its regulatory regime presupposes that the flowage is not likely to have its walleye fishery degraded given the existing conditions of the fishery and the level of angler pressure.

More or less concurrently with the introduction of the new regulations for a three-fish bag limit, WDNR biologists also began to deploy a new model for determining what constitutes a safe harvest. Back in 1989, when biologists began to set safe harvest levels, they used a simple linear regression which relied primarily on lake surface area to predict adult walleye abundances. But over the years, the accumulated body of data from lake surveys made it possible to test a number of other models. Eventually, scientists concluded that so-called mixed-effect models were more accurate in predicting walleye abundances. These models included more variables, and did not assume, as the earlier models had done, that walleye populations were equal in lakes of equal sizes. Only time, and subsequent surveys, of course, will tell how the new regulations and the new methods of setting safe harvest numbers will fare in practice.

This is where matters stood as of 2016. Given how this whole tale unfolded, it must be considered a good sign that WDNR and

GLIFWC biologists meet, exchange data, and hash out, as scientists do, the meaning and implications of the data they have gathered. And so, also, one might take heart that the flowage and those who had relied on or simply enjoyed its bounty and beauty had survived yet another change. Chippewa bands spear, anglers fish, biologists sample and count, and the waters flow on. Yet behind this outwardly peaceful reality, and in spite of efforts at reconciliation by well-meaning people—Indian and non-Indian alike—there lies a legacy of bitterness and animosity. It simmers both among those who can neither forget the past nor reconcile themselves to the new reality, and among those who feel they have paid an inordinate price for the exercise of rights they considered so obviously theirs. And in the public arena, the affected parties seem to lack the trust, and perhaps the will, to work out long-term agreements that would benefit all interested parties. One chapter of this story has been written, but there will be more to come before the Voigt decision is woven seamlessly into the warp and woof of Wisconsin life.

The Ranks of Interested Parties Expand

The two big events of the late 1980s and early 1990s—the advent of Chippewa treaty-based spearfishing and the state's purchase of the Turtle-Flambeau Flowage—not only introduced a new party, the state's Chippewa tribes, to the scene, but they also significantly altered the balance of responsibilities among the existing ranks of flowage stakeholders. The WDNR, with its expanded portfolio, became the dominant party; and the Chippewa and Flambeau Improvement Company (CFIC), though it continued, critically, to manage the dam and to regulate water flows—had few, if any, obligations beyond that. In addition, the tribes and their newly established agency, the Great Lakes Indian Fish & Wildlife Commission, had gained a place at the table when it came to fisheries management. But changes to the ranks of stakeholders did not end at this point. In the 1990s, two radically different types of entities came forward to assert their interests in the flowage. At one pole, the Federal Energy Regulatory Commission (FERC) sought to bring the dam, and its owner, the CFIC, under the embrace of a federal agency. And at the other pole, a local citizens' organization, the Turtle-Flambeau Flowage and Trude Lake Property Owners' Association, Inc. (TFF&TLPOA), stepped forward as a "grassroots" advocate for the flowage. As great as the differences between these two entities were, both FERC and TFF&TLPOA laid claim to speak on behalf of the flowage, and their actions were of consequence.

Keepers of the Dam

From the time of its construction, the flowage dam fell under the jurisdiction of the state—in particular, the Railroad Commission and then its successor, the Public Service Commission (PSC). Dam inspections under their auspices took place regularly, starting in 1930. In 1935, inspectors found "some seepage around construction joints," though none was apparent the following year. In 1937, inspectors recommended some facing work in the near future, but this repair seems to have been postponed until after World War II. According to a 1978 report from the Army Corps of Engineers, the renovation of concrete surfaces finally took place, first from 1949 to 1951, and then again in 1956. These were the final actions taken under the supervision of the PSC; in 1967, following a major reorganization of the executive branch of the state government, the newly formed Wisconsin Department of Natural Resources took over from the PSC the regulation of dams, with the exception being those matters pertaining to electric rates, which remained under the jurisdiction of the commission. Since the Flambeau Reservoir generated no electricity, it came fully under the regulatory authority of the WDNR. The agency does not seem to have been in any rush to exercise its newly delegated authority. The available record shows that it inspected the dam in 1981 and did not recommend any maintenance at that time.

Design of the Flambeau Dam showing sluice gates, tainter gates, and log chute. From a marked-up U.S. Army Corps of Engineers Report of 1978. WDNR

Matters took a sharp turn, however, in the mid-1980s when a WDNR initiative led to a major overhaul of the dam and of some of its operating practices. In June of 1984, the WDNR sent Northern States Power—the actual operator of the dam—a memorandum requesting that the company prepare a written plan for regulating the spillways during major storms; develop a plan to notify civilian defense officials downstream in the event of an overtopping of the dam or dikes; obtain a stability analysis of the dam; clear brush from dikes; and create a maintenance and inspection program. Shortly thereafter, NSP brought Ayres Associates, an architectural and engineering services firm based in Eau Claire, into the matter, and by September of 1985 Ayres had prepared a "Project Manual" for the "repair and modification" of the Turtle-Flambeau Dam. The work took place during 1986. The most noticeable outcome of the project was the closing off of the essentially irrelevant log chute, but repairs to the basic structure of the dam were of decidedly greater significance. The following summer the WDNR inspected the dam and documented the site in a set of photographs. In a follow-up communication in June 1987 to NSP, the agency laid out three continuing concerns: the lack of an emergency action plan for "the area downstream;" the failure of the company to provide inspectors with keys that would give them access to the southern set of dikes; and the presence of wave erosion "on at least two of the saddle dams." In addition to noting these concerns, the agency set dates for rectifying them.

Enter the Federal Government

As noted earlier in this chapter, the WDNR learned during the course of the 1990s that another governmental entity had an interest in overseeing the flowage dam: the Federal Energy Regulatory Commission (FERC). FERC's decision to bring the dam, as well as the one at Rest Lake on the Manitowish River, under its jurisdiction emerged from the process of relicensing another NSP facility—the Big Falls Dam downstream on the Flambeau River in Rusk County. In the relicensing order for Big Falls, dated February 5, 1997, FERC signaled its intention to subject both the Turtle-Flambeau and Rest Lake dams to licensing proceedings. In a separate order issued the same day, the commission pointed out that the operation of these two reservoirs "increases downstream generation for all eight projects by about 9GW, which is worth about $270,000 annually to the downstream project owners." A power-generating contribution of that magnitude led FERC to conclude that "these facilities are part of the complete unit of improvement or development that includes the downstream licensed hydropower project and are thus required to be licensed." And so FERC ordered the CFIC to file for "licenses for continued operations" for both of these reservoirs.

Not surprisingly for a company on which E.P. Sherry left a stamp of firm opposition to regulation, the CFIC objected vigorously to this initiative by FERC, and it filed for a rehearing. FERC responded on November 16, 1998, with an order that exempted the Rest Lake Dam from the original licensing order. This dam, FERC argued, increased downstream generation by only 0.06 percent, and therefore was "neither used and useful nor necessary or appropriate to maintain or operate the downstream projects." This order left the Rest Lake Dam fully under the jurisdiction of the WDNR, where it has remained ever since. As for the Turtle-Flambeau Dam, however, FERC came to the opposite conclusion: its 5 to 6 percent contribution to downstream generation is significant to downstream operations and thus warrants licensing. This reiteration of its claim to jurisdiction over the dam set off a prolonged test of wills and lawyerly imagination between the two parties.

After receiving two FERC orders that rejected its arguments against licensing, the CFIC filed a petition on January 14, 1999, with the United States Court of Appeals, District of Columbia Circuit, for a review of FERC's orders. More than three years of jostling between the company and the commission passed before the court finally heard arguments in November of 2002 in the case of *Chippewa and Flambeau Improvement Company, Petitioner v. Federal Energy Regulatory Commission, Respondent.* When it handed down its decision in April of 2003, the court found the company's three main arguments unpersuasive and denied it a review of the commission's various orders.

FERC moved ahead to assert its jurisdiction by notifying the company that it would be conducting an inspection of the dam in late August of 2003, and FERC inspectors showed up again in 2004 and 2005. In advance of the latter inspection, an official with the commission promised the CFIC that he would he would be preparing a basic assessment prior to the inspection using the Dam Assessment Matrix for Security and Vulnerability Risk, familiarly known in "acronymese" as DAMSVIR. Although the company was still in the mode of denying FERC's jurisdiction over the flowage, it did permit the inspections to go ahead as a "courtesy" to the commission. Another apparent courtesy was the delivery to FERC in October 2004 of a nicely produced emergency action plan (a color photo of the dam adorns the cover). The document contains notification flow charts in the event of an overtopping, or the imminent threat of one; lays out the responsibilities of various personnel in the event of a problem; and calls for annual safety drills. It also contains maps of areas, as far downstream as Park Falls, that would be affected by a breach of the dam or of the dikes. Canoe travelers may or may not take comfort in knowing that, in the event of a breach-caused flood, it will take approximately 2.6 hours for flood waters to reach Holt's Landing on the Flambeau River, and a full 11 hours for the flood to reach its maximum elevation there.

The court battle was over, but not the war. Later in 2003, CFIC returned to FERC with a petition for a declaratory order under which FERC would give up its jurisdiction over the TFF reservoir if the company were to adopt a new operating regime. The company began its case by suggesting that it might alter the dam's head gates so as to allow water to flow freely, without regulation, in which case there would be no reason for FERC jurisdiction. Of course, the company noted, this course of action might make it hard for the Fraser Paper Mill in Park Falls to meet its point source pollution obligations and could result in the plant's closing and a substantial loss of jobs. To avoid such an unfortunate outcome, CFIC suggested an alternative course of action: namely, it would modify its operating regime so as to limit drawdown to 1.5 feet year-round (with the possibility of increasing the draw in drought conditions). Since such an operating regime would roughly halve the reservoir's contribution to downstream energy generation, the CFIC hoped that FERC would exercise its discretion and cease its claim to jurisdiction. FERC denied the petition in March of 2005, noting that even a halved contribution to downstream energy generation was, as a percentage, "well above the level at which the Commission asserted its jurisdiction in earlier cases." The company responded by seeking a rehearing. In its case, CFIC contended that the $750,000 it would have to spend to secure a license and comply with its stipulations was not worth the tiny amount of revenue the company would receive from the reservoir's contribution to downstream generation. It also threw into the hopper once again the possibility of ceasing all flow regulation. Apparently neither persuaded nor intimidated, FERC denied a rehearing on July 25, 2005.

The two sides finally came to an agreement after FERC suggested the possibility of adding the TFF to the licenses of several of the downstream power generators, thereby substantially reducing the licensing costs for the company. CFIC responded by suggesting that the flowage become a "project feature" under a license held by Northern States Power for its Big Falls facility. The company justified changing the responsible party from CFIC to NSP on the grounds that NSP "was a majority owner of the Improvement Company, and provides services... related to the operation and maintenance of the projects including Turtle-Flambeau." FERC agreed, and the licensing process began in earnest. In the consultation phase, NSP sought comments from various state and federal agencies, and FERC invited input via a public notice. Concerns over water flows and water levels dominated the latter submissions. Mrs. Carm Eheler, owner and operator of the Nine Mile Tavern and Canoe Rental Facility on the Flambeau River, complained about frequent low flows, as did the supervisor of the WDNR Flambeau River State Forest. Upstream users had their complaints as well. The Turtle-Flambeau Flowage and Trude Lake Property Owners' Association objected to the operation of the dam in drought years and noted that the MOU "is not only lacking in guidance but is flawed with contradictory principles and confusing language." This organization also called for a scientific study of the North Fork of the Flambeau River to determine what level of flow was needed to sustain its ecosystem. It was clear that no matter who controlled the spillways, the task of pleasing those above and below dams would never be an easy one. The WDNR weighed in neutrally with a recommendation that NSP install and maintain a permanent gauge at Springstead Landing, and, in addition, that it provide real-time internet access to information about water levels (a position also endorsed by the TFF&TLPOA).

The FERC licensing process also required NSP to secure a water quality certification (WQC) from the WDNR. This document, incorporated into the license itself, covers a wide range of issues, both operational and environmental, and, in effect, stakes out the contours of WDNR's continued role in management of the TFF. Regarding the critical issue of water levels and flows, the WQC requires NSP to "operate the Turtle-Flambeau Project in accordance with the August 23, 1990 Memorandum of

Understanding between the Wisconsin Department of Natural Resources and the Chippewa and Flambeau Improvement Company." In the event NSP were to foresee problems maintaining both minimum discharge *and* elevation requirements of the MOU, it is to "promptly" consult with the WDNR "to evaluate alternatives for modified reservoir operation." The certification also specified the "Property Manager of the Turtle-Flambeau Scenic Area" as the "Department's primary point of contact" in such a situation. In addition, the WQC requires NSP to develop a plan within a year to install water level gauges at select landings and to provide public access to data on levels and discharges. To improve navigation, the licensee is to consult with WDNR, the town of Mercer, and other cost-sharing partners to eliminate obstacles to navigation at two locations: the place where the Little Turtle River empties into the flowage, and the site where Trude Lake drains into the flowage. The WQC also laid out requirements for the licensee with regard to several environmental issues. In the absence of any plans to provide for fish passage around the dam, NSP agreed to make available annually $6,500 to the WDNR "for studies and efforts related to fish passage and/or lake sturgeon rehabilitation in the North Fork [of the Flambeau River] and Manitowish Rivers." The WQC made the company responsible as well for monitoring water quality in the event that citizen volunteers should no longer be able to do so, and it called on the company to cooperate with the WDNR on controlling exotic species. FERC reinforced the WDNR's position on exotics by requiring NSP to develop a full-fledged plan for monitoring invasive species. In addition, FERC specified that renovation or replacement of NSP's power transmission line that crosses the flowage would require regulatory approval, which would include notifying the property manager of the TFSWA. Finally, the company must, as best it can, pass downstream woody and other organic matter that accumulates near the dam spillways. It should be noted that FERC worked up its own 31-page environmental assessment of the flowage. One of its recommendations called for a "mandatory WQC" to be adopted as part of the amended license.

FERC issued an "order amending license" to NSP on October 14, 2008. At this point, the federal agency had formally asserted its jurisdiction over the Turtle-Flambeau Flowage. This order, quite expectedly, placed burdens on NSP to provide FERC with extensive documentation about the flowage dam facility and to report regularly on its flowage operations to yet another government agency. But the presence of this new stakeholder can hardly be said to have changed dramatically what are called today "the facts on the ground." The WDNR retained, in many ways, its front-line position. The memorandum of understanding that it had worked out with the CFIC continued to dictate operation of the flowage as a storage reservoir; and many longstanding environmental concerns of the WDNR found expression in the language of the order and in the obligations placed on NSP to work on those concerns in consultation with the WDNR. What changed was that the WDNR now appeared to have the backing, as it were, of a major federal agency, and one that had a strong environmental commitment of its own. How this relationship will play out over the long haul remains to be seen.

Flowage Folks Put an Oar in the Water

Unlike the arrival of FERC on the scene, the emergence of a grassroots organization speaking for the Turtle-Flambeau Flowage was neither prolonged nor contentious. Under the leadership of Paul Gottwald, a retired WDNR area director, and

Maryann and Rod Brown, flowage resort owners, 25 flowage residents gathered on June 8, 1996, to bring into being the Turtle-Flambeau Flowage and Trude Lake Property Owners' Association (TFF&TLPOA). Those present approved a set of bylaws for the organization; elected a slate of officers and board members; and set annual dues for members at $15 dollars per year. By July 23 of the same year, the association had a bank account (with a balance of $363.63) and a post office box (#631) in Mercer. The association was officially incorporated by the state in 1997 and received its federal tax exemption as a 501(c)(4) organization in 1998. In the fall of 2012, the association's membership had grown to the point where it represented the owners of approximately 180 parcels of property on or near the flowage.

No single, immediate threat to the flowage prompted the foundation of the association. The state of Wisconsin had only recently completed its purchase of the flowage bottom and shoreline from the Chippewa and Flambeau Improvement Company—thereby taking off the table the possibility that the flowage might someday be subject to extensive development. Nonetheless, the time seemed right to bring strong citizen involvement to bear on its long-term future. In the words of Paul Gottwald, the first president of the association, "we wanted to be prepared... to build some camaraderie with stakeholders [property owners] around the flowage... to make sure that nothing bad happened."

The association moved quickly to build that camaraderie, as well as a sense of shared aspirations, when it scheduled a cookout on Hot Dog Island for late September of 1996. It also sent out a survey to some 200 flowage property owners in an effort to gauge their hopes for and concerns about the future of the flowage. The returns were few, but their content was telling. Respondents described the flowage as "remote," "pristine," "peaceful," and "quiet," and they spoke as one about their jointly held belief that the flowage should be "preserved," "protected," and "kept as it is." In addition, they expressed concerns about declining fish populations, threats to the stability of the flowage, fluctuations in the water levels, and the need to control or limit high-powered boats, personal watercraft, and water skiing. A subsequent survey in 2001, this one with a 75 percent response rate, reiterated the concern about fish populations and added two new ones: water quality and the threat of exotic, or invasive, species. As befits a grassroots organization, the association leadership sought to reflect and to act on the expressed interests of its members from the very beginning.

Topping this agenda, as one might suspect, was the enhancement of fishing on the flowage. It seemed that almost everyone had memories of "the good old days" on the flowage when fish practically fought with one another for the privilege of ending up on someone's stringer. And these feelings had been passed on over the years to fisheries managers through informal comments, participation in creel censuses, or attending public gatherings, such as the listening sessions and open houses connected with the state purchase of the flowage and the preparation of the master plan. These communications, as varied as the views of the individual anglers who offered them, did not, for the most part, speak for any organized group (there were a few exceptions). Nonetheless, they provided data that were indispensable to the scientific analysis of the flowage fishery.

Sustained, organized citizen input into the flowage fishery can be traced to the formation of the TFF&TLPOA. From the outset, its members placed enhancement of the fishery high on their list of priorities, and over time they found a number of ways to actively contribute to this end. First and foremost, the association has worked to keep open lines of communication with the WDNR fisheries personnel at the Mercer Ranger Station and in Park Falls. The association leadership and members have regularly conveyed to the WDNR their aspirations for and concerns about the fishery, and they have worked closely with the fisheries biologists to disseminate scientific information about the flowage to all interested parties. In addition, fisheries biologists have at times made presentations at association meetings and exchanged views with members; and the association has published in its newsletter summaries of scientific studies about the flowage fishery and interviews with the fisheries biologists.

Members of the Turtle Flambeau Flowage and Trude Lake Property Owners' Association chat at the end of a long day of building cribs. TFF&TLPOA

The association's contribution to fish management has not, however, been limited to exchanging views and information; its volunteers have also engaged in some "hands-on" activities. In 2000, at the invitation of Warden Stuart Pfeiffer, association volunteers took part in their first "walleye watch," a springtime nocturnal vigil intended to protect vulnerable spawning walleyes at the falls on the Turtle River. An organized walleye watch became an annual event for the next half dozen years, and it continued informally thereafter. The association tackled an even more ambitious project in 2002 when it launched a major crib-building program. Association volunteers, joined by WDNR staff, assembled the cribs on the ice, stuffed them with brush, and weighted them with cement blocks. In the spring, WDNR personnel towed the cribs into place, and sank them. The association and the WDNR shared the costs of the materials; the association paid for the timber (starting in 2004), and the WDNR for additional materials and, of course, for the time of its staff. In 2007, the association donated to the WDNR a pontoon boat that was used to tow and place cribs. All told, the association built 425 cribs. Four hundred and seven were placed in the flowage, and 38 in Trude Lake.

What prompted the association to build cribs was a shared sense among its membership that the amount of woody cover in the flowage had noticeably declined over the years and that something should be done to replace it. The WDNR intention for the program, according to Jeff Roth, was to "provide 'hyper-cover' in the pelagic [open water] regions devoid of cover" (and fish) in the hope that these protective shelters might encourage fish to populate these areas. It was also the hope that, by maximizing the number of cribs, the potential for overharvest around crib sites might be diminished. As it turned out, no evidence was found, one way or the other, as to the effectiveness of the cribs in producing the results sought by the WDNR. There was, however, plenty of anecdotal evidence that fishing the cribs could pay off handsomely. Although the WDNR did not disclose the precise locations of the cribs, anglers and guides, aided by modern electronics, soon located them; and lists of GPS waypoints circulated among friends. Instead of protecting fish, it seemed to some that the cribs had concentrated them and made them more accessible to anglers. "They are fish cemeteries," one association member asserted. At that point, the association took stock of the program. Cribs had been placed throughout the flowage and in Trude Lake; but even so, the WDNR could point to no data showing that the cribs had established fish populations in previously unpopulated areas of the flowage. Moreover, many people had strong reservations about the tendency of cribs to concentrate fish. And so, after 28 cribs were sunk in Lake Bastine in the spring of 2012, the association decided to call a halt to the program. Thereafter, the association began to explore other means to add woody structure to the flowage.

Finally, association volunteers literally had a "hands-on" experience in fish management when they collaborated with the WDNR on two projects. The first instance came in 2012 when they assisted with biologist Lawrence Eslinger's study of the diets of walleyes and smallmouth bass, and the second occurred later in the same year when association volunteers helped WDNR personnel clip the fins of 2,908 musky fingerlings that were then released into the flowage. With this substantial track record behind it, the Turtle-Flambeau Flowage and Trude Lake Property Owners' Association remains committed to active involvement in fisheries management in cooperation with the WDNR.

In response to concerns expressed in the 2001 membership survey, the association soon turned its attention to some basic attributes of the flowage that shape not only the fishery but also the broader ecosystem of which it is a part. Protecting native flora and fauna against exotic invasives, monitoring water quality, and striving to assure adequate water levels soon became integral parts of the work of the TFF&TLPOA. With encouragement and assistance from Roger Jasinski and Bruce Bacon of the WDNR, the association launched what turned out to be a continuing battle with purple loosestrife. Since 1997, association volunteers have surveyed the flowage to locate infestations and have worked with WDNR personnel to eradicate plants or to prevent their reseeding by removing and destroying blooms. Diane O'Krongly, an association member and officer, led this effort, not only through organizing the association's activities but through her own efforts to raise and deploy beetles to fight loosestrife. In addition, association volunteers worked at boat landings for many years during the opening weekend of the fishing season, handing out information about invasives and counseling boat owners on the most effective ways to prevent the spread of these harmful exotics. In 2000, the association pressed the WDNR to post information on invasives at public landings on the flowage. After a bureaucratic hiccup, the recommendation was approved in 2001 and signs soon went up. In 2010, these signs were replaced on boat landing kiosks by a new generation of signs developed by the Iron County Land and Water Conservation Department (ICLWCD).

In the fall of 2009, the association brought together representatives from Xcel Energy (the parent company of Northern States Power), the WDNR, the US Geological Survey (USGS), and the ICLWCD to discuss water quality and invasives. Those present worked out a plan, which was funded in part by Xcel and in part by the WDNR, by which ICLWCD interns, working under the auspices of the Clean Boats, Clean Waters program, were to spread the word about invasives and how to combat them among boaters at the various put-ins on the flowage through the course of the summer. Finally, a 2009 grant from the WDNR enabled association volunteers to survey parts of the flowage to catalog beneficial plant species (some 34 different species were identified) and to search for invasives other than purple loosestrife (none were found). The results provided solid evidence of a healthy, diverse plant community in the flowage, which, in turn, reinforced the association's commitment to fighting exotic invaders.

Water quality—so critical to the long-term health of the flowage—found its way onto the association's active agenda in 1999 when Arlen Wanta (who was to become association president in 2000) became a certified water quality monitor. Wanta was soon joined in this work by Jim Leever, who in turn became the de facto dean and chief educator of numerous volunteers who gathered water quality information on an annual basis. The field data they recorded went to the WDNR for analysis. The next big step came in 2009 when the association under President Terry Daulton received a $10,000 grant from the WDNR to study flowage water quality in greater detail. The basic monitoring work was carried out by the USGS, which contributed $5,000 in staff time and expenses. The USGS concluded that there were no serious threats to water quality in the flowage, but they recommended that the association expand its monitoring program to more parts of the flowage and that it be especially attentive to possible problems upstream. Following their report, association volunteers began the systematic monitoring of all sites studied by the USGS. These efforts by the association and other interested parties have established solid baseline data on flowage water quality—data that could, in the future, facilitate prompt identification of adverse trends in water quality and lead to timely action to rectify them.

Fluctuating water levels, which had shown up as a concern in the initial survey of members in 1996, became a far more pressing problem as the flowage experienced the drought years of the first decade of the current century. The extreme low water level of 2007 prompted the board of directors to initiate a series of meetings with the WDNR and Xcel in an effort to encourage the company to adopt a more conservative program of water level management on the flowage. In 2008, when NSP was in the process of securing a license for the flowage from FERC, the association recommended (unsuccessfully, as it turned out) to the federal commission that changes be made to the memorandum of understanding that would diminish the likelihood of severe drops in the water level.

In addition to these actions, the TFF&TLPOA set up a water level committee, headed by James Bohmann, to closely monitor both the water levels and the discharge rates. Using these data, the committee developed its own set of guidelines for conservative water level management—which the committee dubbed the "reasonableness curve." In its direct talks with the association, Xcel rejected the group's recommended guidelines for a modified water management regime. The association board, however, persisted in its efforts to secure water levels that would be beneficial both to the ecology of the flowage and to the various recreational activities of members and the general public. In 2013, with advice from and initiatives by its legal counsel, the association once again entered joint discussions with WDNR and Xcel about water levels. The outcome this time was a verbal agreement by Xcel to a conservative discharge arrangement: namely, in low water conditions, drawdowns should follow rains, not anticipate them. This agreement was not put to the test in 2013, as generous rainfall enabled Xcel to comfortably maintain water levels at an elevation conducive to recreational activities throughout the open water period. The year 2014 began with good rainfall and high water levels, but in July, August, and September decreasing rainfall and high discharge rates drew the flowage down 3.5 feet from full pool—a number within the MOU but nonetheless problematic for recreational users. It remains to be seen whether Xcel will adhere to the agreed-upon conservative discharge regime in future years.

In addition to addressing perennial issues, the TFF&TLPOA tackled a number of one-time matters, either through lobbying efforts or through financial contributions. In 1999, for example, the association began to lobby the town of Sherman to adopt an ordinance on the use of personal watercraft that would be identical to that of the town of Mercer. This effort, led by Tom Mowbray, the association's treasurer, finally came to fruition in

2008 and made possible uniform enforcement of the rules across the entire flowage. In some instances, the association has taken public stands on issues that directly affect the flowage. It opposed both a proposed gravel pit near the flowage in Springstead and motor trolling on the flowage, and it supported a revised flow agreement for the Rest Lake Dam that would restore seasonal flows to the Manitowish River. When deemed appropriate, the association board has authorized financial assistance to such varied projects as building osprey nests on the flowage, fighting against legislation that would permit "dockominiums"(marinas where individuals own boat slips), and purchasing water quality monitoring equipment. Finally, the TFF & TLPOA has sought to disseminate a wide range of information about the flowage to its members via its newsletter, *Driftwood*, and to the public through its website, tfftl.org.

As the flowage entered the new millennium, its status as a State Scenic Waters Area under the aegis of the Wisconsin Department of Natural Resources seemed, on the surface at any rate, secure. The department's experience with and cumulative knowledge of the property and its wild inhabitants had led to numerous beneficial projects and to the development of a plan to reshape— however modestly—the fishery. Moreover, the department, wisely recognizing its obligations to the citizenry of the state and to local residents, directly involved the public in setting objectives for the plan, in research on walleyes and bass, and in other fishery-related activities.

The arrival on the scene of the Federal Energy Regulatory Commission, a heavyweight player to be sure, did little to threaten the dominance of the WDNR in the management of the flowage. In fact, by writing the WDNR's water quality certification into FERC's licensing agreement with Northern States Power, the commission endorsed the department's interests in and goals for the flowage. This endorsement, along with FERC's independently established environmental objectives, seemed to align almost perfectly the objectives of the federal government with those of the state. So far, however, its post-licensing interventions have centered primarily on dam safety and not on matters impacting the environment. It remains to be seen how much FERC will act on its environmental commitments by way of lending support to the WDNR.

The Turtle-Flambeau Flowage and Trude Lake Property Owners' Association is something of an anomaly among the various interest groups seeking to have a say in the management of the flowage. On the one hand, its connection with the flowage is more intimate that that of any other agency or institution. On the other hand, the association has no statutory powers. As an expression of civil society, it can advocate on behalf of its members' interests and aspirations, but it cannot, ultimately, secure its ends without cooperation from those parties who enjoy some measure of legal authority. As this chapter makes clear, the association's most important achievements have come through its ability to persuade empowered entities to act on its aspirations and recommendations. The inherent limitations of such an organization require that its members be persuasive, persistent, and, above all, patient.

And so the flowage added two new players: one powerful but distant, whose focus remains somewhat limited; the other without authority but close at hand. They joined an already established group, headed by the WDNR and Xcel Energy. What lies ahead cannot, of course, be foreseen. What is certain is that the contest for the future of the flowage will witness the largest number of players ever; and, who knows, perhaps there are more in the wings.

Epilogue

Viewed through the narrowest of lenses, one could say that the Turtle-Flambeau Flowage was the creation of a single person: E.P. Sherry. Keenly aware of the need of his paper company for water, both for manufacturing processes and for generating power, he devised a plan for bringing into being a storage reservoir a scant 15 miles as the crow flies upstream from the site of his Park Falls mill. The plan involved no small amount of financial risk, especially given the cyclical character of the industry, but it should also be noted that Sherry enjoyed some significant advantages. Setting aside the numerous landowners with whom he had to negotiate for the acquisition of land, there were only two significant parties whose concurrence was critical to the realization of his plan. He needed to persuade his colleagues in the Chippewa Valley of the merits of building yet another storage reservoir, and he had to obtain permission from the Railroad Commission for the project. Sherry, as it turned out, had the requisite business acumen and political skill to accomplish both these tasks. And so it was that the flowage came into being with relative simplicity—at least as compared to similar operations undertaken in the present century. It is, frankly, almost impossible to imagine the construction of a similar facility in northern Wisconsin today.

That said, historical actors function in specific contexts, and Sherry's success depended on the fit between his ambitions and broader forces at play in the state. First, he was the beneficiary of Wisconsin's rapidly transforming economy. A burgeoning demand for electrical power, both for industrial and residential purposes, turned the attention of the leaders of the power industry to the state's copious, and as yet only scarcely used, water powers. The power industry's efforts to harness water resources did not, however, go uncontested. Wisconsin's largest extractive industry, logging, had long used these waterways to move timber from forests to mills, and it continued to make use of them even as the industry was becoming increasingly dependent on railroads to move its product. The crux of the conflict between these two industries was management of the flow of the state's rivers: the power industry needed as even a flow as possible in the rivers, whereas logging relied on periodic large releases of water followed by lengthy periods of storage. To this contest between older and newer economic interests must be added yet another party with a stake in Wisconsin's water powers: namely, an emerging conservation movement, which had begun to make clear its intent to preserve and protect, both for intrinsic reasons and for public use, some of these very same rivers and streams that were so prized by industry. As this struggle came to a head, there can be little doubt that the power industry, with its potential to be transformative, represented the wave of the future.

In the end, it fell to the principles and politics of the Progressive Era to referee this three-sided conflict among power, logging, and conservation interests. The Progressives supported economic growth, but they wanted to temper its downside consequences by means of regulation. For them, a modern economy could be ushered in without abandoning fully or forever the notion of public trust—a doctrine deeply rooted in Wisconsin's constitution, statutes, and case law. In this instance, the pertinent regulatory agency, the Railroad Commission, gave the green light to the construction of the dam, even while protecting the public through its powers of oversight and through its assertion of the rights of the state to seize control of the facility should the Wisconsin Constitution ever be amended to permit such an action. But there can be no doubt that Sherry and his associates in the power industry came out best in this process. Not only did they secure authorization for the construction of the Turtle-Flambeau Dam, but they also carried the day in their subsequent legal tussle with the Flambeau River Lumber Company over the flow of the river. The state's regulatory regime had clearly thrown its weight behind Wisconsin's industrialization to the detriment of its once dominant logging industry. In the final analysis, Sherry's achievements surely owed as much to the broader historical moment as to his own hard work.

It is to the credit of the Turtle-Flambeau Flowage that it can trace its lineage back to this truly protean time in state history—the Progressive Era. But the flowage today might be nothing more than an artifact of that era, an aging storage facility tucked away in a sparsely populated county, had not an intricate series of events given it a life of its own. The waters of the flowage made their own contribution to this process by hosting a plentiful and varied fish population. This fishery, in turn, drew anglers, and the anglers brought forth the resorts and other services that supported their outdoor pursuits. The flowage emerged from all this activity as a recreation center that significantly boosted the economy of the immediate area, especially the towns of Mercer and Park Falls. But the flowage might never have prospered as it did had its development and use not coincided with a number of changing patterns of American life. The increasing ease of transportation—

thanks to convenient passenger rail service and a growing network of highways that fed the country's booming automobile culture—promoted travel in general and facilitated access to relatively remote locations. The one- and two-week vacation benefit that had become the norm for many workers was ideally suited to the rhythms of resort life. And patterns of family life—especially in those families with a single breadwinner and children who had yet to fall prey to the demands of organized activities—meant that everyone, Mom, Dad, and the youngsters, could carve out a vacation week together. All these trends combined to weave vacations at the lake in a much more integral way into the fabric of American life than ever before, and the flowage happily played its part in the process.

The flowage was but one of dozens of northwoods resort areas that drew sustenance from these major social and economic changes, but it nonetheless managed to differentiate itself from the others. Unlike those locations centered around some of the more glamorous—and populous—natural lakes of the north, the flowage could not boast of water ski shows, water slides or parks, or lumberjack contests. What it did have was remoteness and wildness, attributes that, along with good fishing, appealed to a special subset of outdoor-loving people. It is probably fair to say that the flowage was not as well known among the public as many other northwoods lakes, but people who knew the flowage could not praise it enough.

In time, the lure of the flowage reached beyond anglers and their families to a wide range of people with an interest in the natural world: canoeists, campers, bird watchers, wildlife photographers, and the like. And it also pulled in natural resource professionals who turned their scientific lenses on its lands and waters. The data they gathered confirmed the richness of its ecosystem, thereby building its reputation with the public as something more than just a good fishing hole. Even the years of controversy following the Voigt decision, for all their tensions and confrontations, failed to dim the flowage's image. In fact, the central role that its fishery played in Chippewa harvest plans only served to reinforce popular perceptions of this walleye-rich body of water. Subsequently, state and tribal fisheries personnel stepped up their efforts to monitor and manage this resource—actions that underscored the high value that they, and the public, placed on it. By the time the flowage reached its 64th anniversary in 1990, it had incrementally evolved from a little-known fishing spot to a statewide symbol of the natural and the wild. The time was right for the state's purchase of the land and its pledge to conserve it on behalf of present and future generations of Wisconsin citizens.

The character and magnitude of the flowage's trajectory can perhaps best be illustrated by two points of comparison. The first concerns the public's place in relation to the flowage. When E.P. Sherry built the dam for essentially private interests, the public was represented only secondarily by the Railroad Commission; and its task in this regard was to make sure that public interests were not significantly harmed by creating a more even flow to meet the needs of industry. In stark contrast, Governor Tommy Thompson's express objective in authorizing state acquisition of the flowage was to hold it in trust for the people. Beyond this, members of the public participated directly in the drafting of the master plan for the Turtle-Flambeau Scenic Waters Area, and later consulted with Wisconsin Department of Natural Resources (WDNR) fisheries personnel in setting goals for fisheries management.

This transformation of the public role is a reflection of the increased value of the flowage in the eyes of citizens and government alike—which leads to the second point of comparison. As noted above, only a few parties initially placed value on the resources affected by the construction of the dam and the flowage.

But as the flowage grew into something other than a big pool of water in private hands, more and more individuals, groups, and government agencies stepped forward to advance their interests in this resource. Today, the flowage finds itself at the center of a complex spider web woven by an ever-growing assemblage of institutions. At the anchor points of this web one finds the Chippewa and Flambeau Improvement Company, the state-chartered owner of the dam; Xcel Energy, the actual operator of the dam; the Wisconsin Department of Natural Resources; the Wisconsin Chippewa bands; the Federal Energy Regulatory Commission; the towns of Mercer and Sherman; the Iron County Land and Water Conservation Department; and the Turtle-Flambeau Flowage and Trude Lake Property Owners' Association. Also at play in this web are local promotional organizations, such as the Mercer and Park Falls chambers of commerce and the Turtle Flambeau Flowage Association. When some issue arises that affects the flowage, the interested parties scuttle to the center of the web to defend threatened interests or advance favorite agendas. Negotiating this web requires patience and great political skills—politics here understood in the broadest possible sense. Mother Nature, of course, has had a lot to say about the character of this flowage and will no doubt continue to do so. But it must be remembered that human decisions brought this body of water into being in the first place, and they have modified its character ever after. It would be foolish to think that the future will be otherwise.

--<@>--

The story of the Turtle-Flambeau Flowage lends itself to some broader kinds of observations about our world. First, acts destructive of natural systems do not necessarily impose a death sentence on these systems. They are surprisingly resilient and capable of reshaping themselves in response to disruption. Second, as much we may have tried to separate in our minds the "natural and the wild" from the "civilized" when thinking about or experiencing a location untouched by human development, we often overlook both overt and subtle connections between these two ideal realms. For no "natural" setting, once society encounters it, can remain pristine, or wholly apart from the humanly constructed world about it. This means, in turn, that our sense of the wild, if fully thought through, is necessarily touched by compromise. Third, over the course of time, as society itself grows in complexity, so too does the relationship between the natural and the civilized.

Slightly reconfigured, these observations lead directly back to the flowage and to a striking double dose of irony. In the first instance, human intervention, in an effort to tame the wild, inadvertently brought into existence this beautiful scenic area, one known and loved for its "natural" and "wild" character. And second, and perhaps even more telling, this natural and wild environment is not wholly self-sustaining, if by that one means keeping it pretty much as it is. As paradoxical as it may seem, continuing human intervention of a purposeful and knowledgeable kind will be needed if the flowage is to maintain its "wilderness" character into the future, even as it undergoes the kinds of changes that are inevitable for any naturally evolving ecosystem.

And what of the prospects for the future? One moment in the history of the flowage brings sharply into focus the element of precariousness that haunts our efforts to conserve the natural world. In October of 1940, August Frey, the state's research director, and James Formany, attorney for the agency Frey headed up, visited the Turtle-Flambeau Flowage. For Frey, this was a bittersweet return to hallowed ground. Well before the flowage had come into being, he and a handful of friends had built a camp along the banks of either the Turtle or Flambeau Rivers (the account of this moment does not specify which). When Sherry was securing lands for his proposed reservoir, these owners chose to sign away flowage rights up to the high-water mark in return for a cash payment and the retention of their unflooded land. As it turned out, though, this decision was followed by an unanticipated outcome: the waters of the flowage began their inexorable rise and lapped up within a few feet of the buildings. What now lay before Frey's eyes was a veritable nightmare: "Gaunt dead trees up to their necks or up to their waists in water. Their bark has rotted away, their trunks are bleached white, and their fallen branches are afloat on the waters. Mile after mile of desolate shore is covered by this driftwood."

As I have argued earlier, these conditions, while deplorable in the eyes of some, were a thrilling, even enticing, sight for others. Frey's misgivings, however, had a different referent, as this was the time when the state was considering buying land along the Flambeau River from below the Turtle-Flambeau Dam downstream to Hawkins. Frey's research department had opposed the purchase, in no small measure because of his experience with the Turtle-Flambeau Flowage. His worry, in short, was simple: what if the state acquired the land along the Flambeau River and then a power company put in a dam? A possible response to this concern had been put forward earlier by Judge Asa Owen of Phillips. Americans need, Phillips asserted, "Faith in their democratic institutions. They must trust that if a state forest is built on the Flambeau, the Conservation Department and the Public Service Commission will protect it." Frey remained a skeptic, and could imagine approving the project only if ironclad guarantees against its exploitation were written into any agreement.

Today, of course, we look out on a flowage of great beauty and natural richness—even if many an angler would find it even more alluring if some substantial portion of the lost driftwood were to reappear. But the same kind of concern that tormented Frey cannot help but creep into the back of one's mind. The state's purchase of the flowage rendered the Wisconsin Department of Natural Resources the long-term protector of the flowage. This situation is all well and good provided that the WDNR is a healthy institution with a proper measure of independence. Yet recent years have seen the department undergo severe budget cuts, reductions in scientific staff, and interference from hostile legislators; and an initiative to deprive the Natural Resources Board (the state agency that sets policy for the Department of Natural Resources) of its independence was only narrowly beaten back. More troubling still, plans to completely dismember the WDNR have circulated through the halls of Wisconsin government during the past two bienniums. One cannot help but question the capability of a diminished and denigrated WDNR—to say nothing of a disaggregated set of resource agencies were the WDNR to be broken up—to freely articulate a land ethic (to borrow a term central to Aldo Leopold's thinking) and to actively defend natural resources under challenge. That it be able to do both is absolutely critical if the Turtle-Flambeau Flowage is to retain its special character into the future.

Judge Owen would no doubt counsel us to have faith in our institutions, and Frey, one suspects, would mostly fret about the future. But neither sitting back and trusting nor being paralyzed in anticipation of the worst, it seems, is a suitable posture. We might, instead, look to history, which can indeed teach lessons. Here we have seen that the intricate interplay—sometimes in cooperation, sometimes in conflict—of industry, government, Chippewa tribes, natural resource professionals, and an interested citizenry has shaped the character of today's TFSWA. The lesson for all is both clear and admonitory: to expect the Turtle-Flambeau Scenic Waters Area, in all its richness, to persist well into the future without actively working on its behalf would be to ignore the very dynamic that brought it to its present state. Inactivity on the part of those who have responsibility for and a deep interest in the flowage would represent a dangerous indifference to history and could well imperil this storied and treasured resource.

Part II

Memorable—or at Least
Remembered—Moments

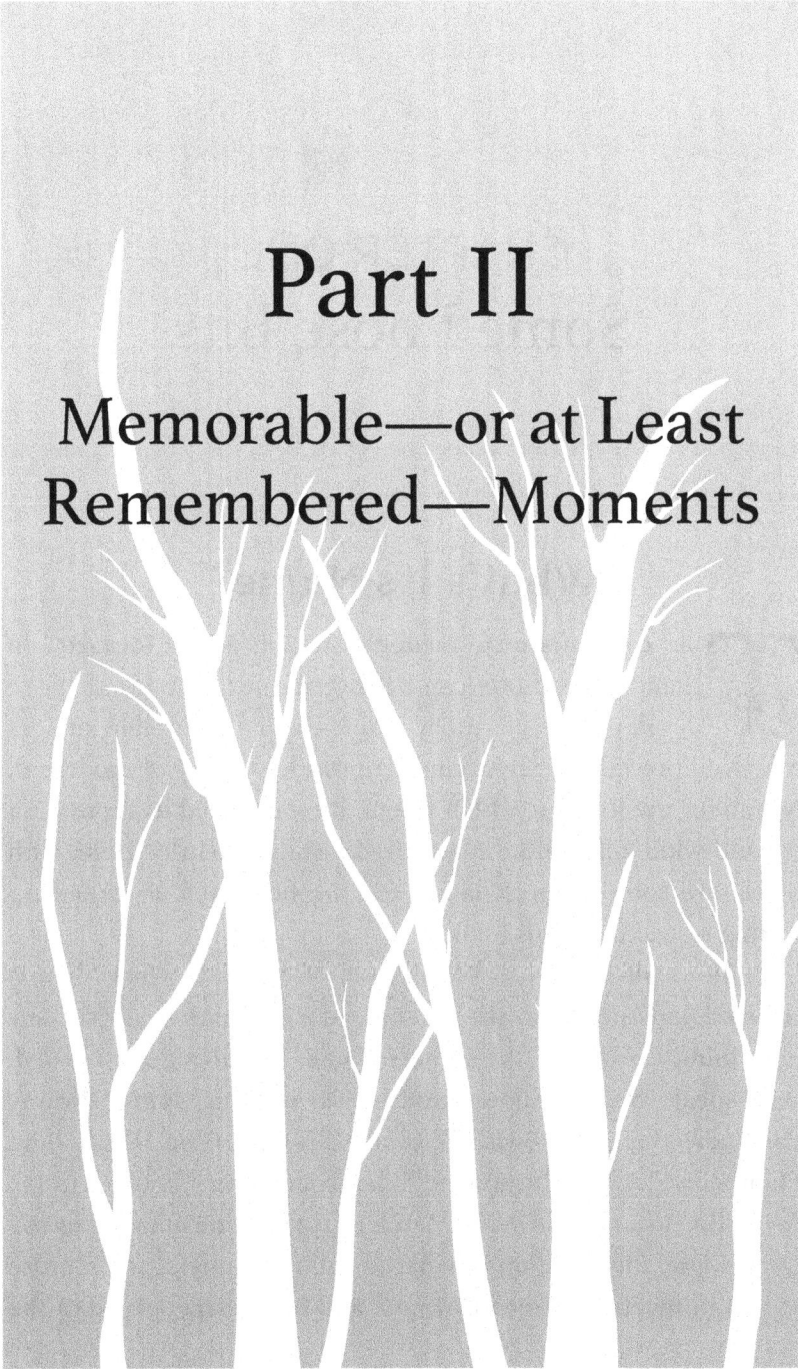

CHAPTER ONE
Some Loose Bits

What's Its Name?

The contemporary business world is so focused on branding that one can be forgiven for thinking that the development of catchy names and memorable images may well precede the creation of a product worthy of the brand. Not so for the flowage, which spread its waters and its reputation far and wide long before it acquired a stable identity. Here, with dates, are some various names for the flowage that turned up during research for this book.

Pride of place goes to the Byllesby Company, which in 1925 referred consistently to the "Flambeau Reservoir" in documents pertaining to costs of the project. Then, the floodgates opened, so to speak. We have "flowage of the Turtle Dam" (1927); "Norway Point on the Manitowish Flowage" (1933); "The Turtle and Flambeau Flowage" (1934); and "Flambeau River Flowage" (1935). According to an article in the March 12, 1937 edition of the *Ironwood Daily Globe*, the question of what to call this body of water arose at a joint meeting of resort owners and businesspeople from the towns of Mercer and Sherman. "A suggestion that the name of the Flambeau Flowage [another variant] be changed to the Turtle and Manitowish flowage was warmly debated, but no decision was reached." The confusion marched on: the "Flambeau and Turtle rivers flowage" (1941); "Sturgeon Bay on the Turtle Flowage" (1945); "the Flambeau or Turtle Flowage" (1946); and, from the Park Falls Chamber of Commerce in 1957, this reminder of which river flowed through its fair town: "the Flambeau Turtle Flowage." When the author and his wife purchased property on the flowage in 1972, we were told by one welcoming local, "Oh, you're on the Turtle part of the flowage."

Not so subtly folded into this saga of nomenclature was the matter of the size of the flowage. In 1946, George Klein of Butternut told *The Milwaukee Journal* that, at full pool, the flowage had a surface area of 33,000 acres, a number intended to compete well with the Chippewa Flowage, whose adherents put it at 38,000 acres. By 1942, however, the Turtle-Flambeau Flowage (TFF) seems to have shrunk by nearly half, to 18,000 acres, if the Wisconsin Conservation Department's supervisor of recreational publicity is to be believed. The press release at the time of the state purchase of the flowage in 1990 noted 11,395 acres of water and 3,700 acres of wetlands, for a grand total of 15,095 acres. The flowage master plan of 1995 adjusted that total downward to 14,300 acres. The Federal Energy Regulatory Commission, in fine Washington fashion, first enhanced the flowage to 17,800 acres in 2001 and then in its environmental assessment a few years later cut it back to "about 13,800."

Since the purchase of the flowage by the Wisconsin Department of Natural Resources, WDNR fisheries experts have brought an end to the shrinking lake phenomenon. The 2007 Fish Management Plan pegged the number at precisely 13,766 surface acres of water at full pool (1,572 feet MSL), and that number seems to be holding.

What the WDNR could not do in its efforts to set things right was to enable the TFF to lay sole claim to the title of the state's "crown jewel." For, as *The Milwaukee Journal* of July 28, 1988, informs us, the Chippewa Flowage "was acclaimed the crown jewel in Wisconsin's Vast Treasury of Public Land" by Governor Tommy Thompson at the dedication of its purchase by the state. But the same thing could be, and was, said about the Turtle-Flambeau Flowage a few years later. Thanks to Governor Thompson's want of a different metaphor, the flowage must, alas, share a place with the Chippewa Flowage in the glittering gubernatorial diadem. And so it is that today the proper nomenclature and descriptors for this fabulous body of water should (probably) read as follows: the Turtle-Flambeau Flowage, 13,766 acres, Crown Jewel, 2.0. As a final minor note, lovers of consistency can only thank the WDNR for settling on the flowage's properly hyphenated name.

The Woodland Bards

At a time when the idea of building a storage reservoir at the junction of the Flambeau and Turtle rivers was but a distant gleam in E. P. Sherry's eye, the Jerome Fishing and Hunting Club (JFHC) on Trude Lake had established a reputation as a place where important men went to do manly things... and also to be boys. In 1907, the three-year-old club was purchased by a group of about 20 men, led by Charles Comiskey, the fabled owner of the Chicago White Sox. Comiskey quickly turned Jerome into a primitive retreat for a veritable who's who of Major League Baseball owners, officials, managers, and players, as well as prominent politicians, businesspeople, and entertainers. All that was needed to take advantage of the club's many perquisites was an invitation from Comiskey, also known as the "Old Roman." For each year after the baseball season concluded, Comiskey gathered anywhere from

25 to 50 friends to hunt (deer, ducks, geese, and partridge), to fish (mostly muskies), feast (oysters on the half shell and huge mixed-game dinners), and drink (French champagne, among other choice offerings).

A cabin at the Jerome Fishing and Hunting Club. The visitor is a free range cow belonging to the club. Mercer Historical Society

Those guests not drawn to rod and gun could find other diversions while staying on the shores of Trude Lake. A woven wire fence, variously described as 12 or 16 feet in height, enclosed not only the camp itself but also a considerable amount of property beyond the camp. The enclosure (where loaded guns were prohibited), it turns out, was nothing less than a wildlife park or zoo, some of whose occupants were native to the area, while others had arrived from elsewhere as "gifts." The freely roaming animals had little difficulty in establishing a nourishing relationship with many of the assembled dignitaries who took great delight in providing handouts to the bold and begging fauna. Not surprisingly, given the close bonds that emerged between man and beast, the animals' human enablers could not resist the great anthropomorphic temptation to assign names: hence, Tom and Minnie Deer; Bill the Moose; Mr. and Mrs. Elk; and Monte the Antelope. The buffalo, however, remained anonymous, as did the ducks, geese, and partridge, perhaps because they were somewhat transient. Bill the Moose, who went in and out of cabins at will on foraging expeditions until his spreading rack checked him at the doors, eventually escaped the enclosure only to fall victim to a hunter many miles away.

Practical jokes, rendered all the more delicious when practiced on some of the substantial egos present each fall at Jerome, provided another entertaining diversion for those so inclined. One example should suffice to prove the point. Byron Bancroft "Ban" Johnson, president of baseball's American League, had proven himself over time to be one of the poorer shots at Jerome. In the hope of remedying this deficiency, Johnson had purchased a custom-made Parker shotgun, which he proudly showed to his colleagues on the long train ride from Chicago to Mercer. But when Johnson sat down to eat breakfast in the Mercer depot, some of his friends struck back against both his braggadocio and his newly bought solution to becoming a better shot. They invaded Johnson's gear, found his ammunition, poured out the lead pellets and then replaced them with innocuous stuffing of some sort. Next came the 12-mile wagon ride from town to the Jerome camp, during which the guests were permitted to shoot at any partridge that was flushed along the logging trail that served as a road. After an embarrassing number of misses, Johnson saw a tight-sitting partridge along the edge of the road, climbed down from the wagon, and—in violation of the rule that called for taking all birds on the wing—attempted to ground swat the bird. After it merrily flew away, a miffed Johnson is said to have attached a piece of paper to a tree and fired his gun at the target; when this close shot rendered no damage to paper or tree, Johnson figured it all out. His unhappiness with the stunt apparently lasted days.

For those of Comiskey's guests who neither wanted to pursue or pet nature's creatures or prey jokingly on their own kind, there was always lazing around and having "a few snorts," as Irving Vaughn, a sportswriter for the *Chicago Tribune*, put it in a retrospective article on the Jerome Fishing and Hunting Club. And so it happened that on one afternoon when libations and stories flowed freely among a group of visitors, Joe Farrell, a curious blend of songwriter and publicist for the Chicago Blackhawks hockey team, challenged his compatriots to write some verse. In Vaughn's words, "The poems were lousy, but Farrell thought them excellent, at least he said that, and in recognition of the alleged display of talent suggested that all become known as the Woodland Bards."

Little could Farrell have imagined the consequences of that casual hour of versifying. For as Charles Fountain, a historian of the White Sox, suggests, the practice of composing verse at the JFHC seems to have continued well beyond that initial session, and the term "Woodland Bard" rapidly gained currency as a designation of honor for anyone who survived a week or so of life at Jerome. Over time the number of people who could claim to be a Woodland Bard may have approached 250. The fraternity of Woodland Bards soon escaped the remote confines of Trude Lake and Mercer and extended its field of play to Chicago, where "Comiskey built a clubhouse for them in the ballpark and the revelry continued, not for one week each year, but every day and many times into the night."

The reader might wonder why this commentary on the Woodland Bards was not included in the following section on the flowage in the arts. The answer can be found in a precious fragment of bardic verse, recited at the commemoration of "Home Plate," a cabin built for Comiskey at the JFHC by his friends.

The Home Plate
Away up North there is a shack
   'Tis built of logs entirely
The owner has a million friends
   And prizes each one highly.
His front door never knew a key
   And you must all remember
The dear old shack is never locked
   From New Year's to December....

Camp Nokomis

It is highly unlikely that the patrons of the Jerome Fishing and Hunting Club could ever have believed that this male retreat par excellence would end its life as a girls' camp, but that is exactly what happened. In 1946 Samuel and Rose Lesher, the third owners of the Jerome parcel after the CFIC had initially gotten rid of it in 1931, sold the core property of the club to Edith Alderman and Charlotte Mendes, both of Chicago. The new owners quickly transformed the club's facilities into a summer camp, and that same year Camp Nokomis for girls opened for its first season. In 1957, the camp acquired additional parts of the Jerome Club through a land contract purchase from the Leshers, an acquisition that added more land as well as frontage on Sandy Lake. The camp, which had a capacity for 100 girls, ages nine to 16, flourished through 1984, when Mendes retired. In 1992, the property was sold and subdivided for private residences.

Camp Nokomis set high goals for its campers: to gain a love of the outdoors; to learn responsibility and cooperation; and to develop leadership skills so that they "may become useful citizens in the world of tomorrow." The girls pursued these objectives in a setting that included 186 acres of forest and three lakes—Trude, Little Bass (renamed Nokomis), and Sandy (formerly Bass Lake)—and through participation in a broad range of activities (58 are listed on a staff application form!), including the usual staples of camp life: swimming, sailing, canoeing, water skiing, camping, archery, riflery, horseback riding, fishing, and, for creativity, crafts, dramatics, and music. The camp was not inexpensive; an application form (undated, but likely from the 1970s) listed a price of $1,000 for a four-week session, plus an additional $75 dollars for horseback riding three days a week.

Nokomis campers enjoy the waters of Trude Lake where once the Woodland Bards flourished. Mercer Historical Society

Without a doubt, Charlotte ("Chuck," as she signed her letters) Mendes was the driving force behind the camp. An excellent athlete in her youth—a swimmer, a skier, and a horsewoman—she served in World War II in the Women's Auxiliary Ferrying Squadron (WAFS). These women "flew army aircraft from manufacturing plants to military bases, and from base to base." After that she taught physical education and served as a guidance counselor in the Chicago area school system. It was this background, along with the self-confidence it had given her, that Mendes brought to the tasks of founding and running a girls' camp. Charlotte Mendes died in 1991 at the age of 89. In Mendes' obituary in the *Chicago Tribune*, her niece summed her up as follows: "There was nothing that woman couldn't do. She could sew and crochet, and then get out her toolbox and fix the lawnmower." In short, she had the perfect qualifications for a successful camp director.

The Flowage in the Arts

Literature

No question about it, the Turtle-Flambeau Flowage has inspired a lot of stories, almost all of the kind that are told around campfires and wood stoves or at cozy northwoods watering holes; and they invariably center on ever-lengthening fish or likely world records that got off the hook. But there is one exception: *The Secret of the Flambeau*, written by H.M. Appel and published by the Goldsmith Publishing Company in Chicago in 1936 as a part of a series for young boys and girls. The book is certainly in good company, as the series includes such notable pieces of literature as *Little Women, Alice in Wonderland,* and *Robinson Crusoe.* Whether it deserves this company, however, is another matter. H.M. Appel, it turns out, was but one of three pseudonyms for Conrad Kimball, so prolific an author of "weird menace tales" that he needed the extra names so he could publish more than one piece in a single anthology. *The Secret of the Flambeau*, a straightforward mystery wholly free of the supernatural or the lewd, stands out like a "healthy thumb" among such titles as *The Bath of Blood* and *Hell Welcomes Lonely Wives!*

In a review written for the Winter 2000 issue of the newsletter of the Turtle-Flambeau Flowage and Trude Lake Property Owners' Association, Jim Leever summarized the plot succinctly: "The novel begins when a Hurley-based gang of smugglers threatens to kidnap Tom [the ultimate "All-American boy"] because his father, an Iron County District Attorney, is trying to prosecute them. Tom's father attempts to hide him with his friend, Al, who lives in a cabin deep in the Northwoods. He is introduced by his new protector to a group of colorful Northwoods characters and is quickly befriended by them. Sharing in a rough camaraderie with his Northwoods newfound friends, the story is an account of Tom's flight from the 'bad guys,' his capture, eventual rescue, and happy reunion with his father." Leever goes on to point out—ever so rightly—that the book "lacks the ethnic sensitivity that would be expected if it were written today." Would-be readers should keep this observation in mind if they have trouble reading literature from a different cultural era, as the bad guys fall right in line with a number of prevailing ethnic stereotypes of the 1930s. Billy Mob, for example, the obligatory half-breed Indian who works for the gang, is admonished by Tom to "be a white man." Subsequently, Billy helps in Tom's rescue and is later praised as a "good Indian."

Appel seems to know enough about the flowage and northwoods life to put in some evocative passages. Flowage boaters can appreciate the description of Tom and his helpers paddling "a circuitous course through drowned forests and across the open water of a vast overflow caused by the recent damming of the river." And readers can only wish for construction plans for the "log jumper," a motor boat that had the capability to take on stumps and other woody debris that make the flowage so hazardous to navigate. Then, too, anyone who has ever tried to contain a captured wild animal will read with gleeful anticipation as Tom and two of his friends put a bear, confined to a makeshift barrel trap, in a canoe and paddle off to a certain fate: canoe swamped; bear free. Some areas of the flowage are identifiable, but the "Red Banks" area where the criminals hid out just does not fit with the known topography. In the end, it is hard to see this book as anything other than the hasty work of a proficient storyteller who had plugged in just enough local color to be roughly believable, but not enough substance to move beyond the modest expectations of formulaic pulp fiction.

It should be noted that the flowage inspired one other work of fiction—this one by Bill Tutt, a noted guide, resort owner, and author of a great fishing story (see pp. 386-87). Unfortunately, it exists in typed manuscript only. The work could best be described as a roman à clef male fantasy, whose strongest suit lies in its detailed information about the flowage and the people associated with it.

Film

The Turtle-Flambeau Flowage celebrated its Hollywood film debut in July of 1962, when 20th Century Fox released *Hemingway's Adventures of a Young Man*. The plot line of the movie was based on Ernest Hemingway's semi-autobiographical stories about Nick Adams, a young man who came of age in upper Michigan and in Europe during World War I. Richard Beymer, who played Nick, was supported by a heavyweight cast that included Diane Baker, Arthur Kennedy, Ricardo Montalban, Paul Newman, Susan Strasberg, and Eli Wallach.

Mellen, Wisconsin, served as the base of operations for the crew and cast for about a month. The town had been selected by 20th Century Fox advance agents, allegedly because they were attracted to the picturesque charm of the local railway station. The role assigned to the flowage by Martin Ritt, the film's director, was to serve as an archetypal northwoods lake on the shores of which Nick's father, a local MD, and mother had their home—a structure woodsy and rustic on the outside but incongruously citified on the inside. Moviegoers can easily identify one specific location on the flowage fairly early in the film when Nick rows his girlfriend across the placid water toward a foreground shore. Easily visible in the background are the deteriorating remains of the old Mercer fish hatchery and the falls of the Turtle River. Once he beaches the boat near the site of the present-day west bank campground and boat launch, Nick proceeds to tell his lady friend that it's all over. This stormy moment in their relationship achieves added gravitas as the wind (wind machine?) cranks up and the shrubs, trees, and autumn leaves bend and flutter before its force. In addition to this moment, generic flowage scenes recur throughout the movie to reinforce the northwoods image, though it would be difficult to identify their precise locations.

A collage created by Doug Severt of scenes from the film Hemingway's Adventures of a Young Man. *Doug Severt.*

Two flowage area residents can boast of an association with the film. Norman Severt, brother of the guide Emil Severt, assisted in filming railroad sequences by driving a Soo Line hi-rail truck (he worked for the railroad) along the tracks with a crew of photographers operating out of the truck bed. During the days when the flowage scenes were being filmed, the Mercer guide Mitch Babic lent a boat to Beymer, Newman, and Hemingway for their personal use. Babic also had the pleasure of eating dinner with Newman for a week.

Hemingway's Adventures of a Young Man could hardly be called a critical success. Mellen Mayor Howard Peters, who attended the film's Midwest premiere at the Ironwood Theater in the Michigan city of the same name, described it as "long and boring." Bosley Crowther, the venerable critic of the *The New York Times*, translated the mayor's terse judgment into the arch language of a cultural arbiter. It was "a sappy, soggy movie" totally at odds with Hemingway's prose style and worldview. In Crowther's view, Beymer, as Nick Adams, turned out to be "just a big squashy figure, made from sodden Airfoam, that gropes its way through a succession of 'adventures' that develop no dramatic or emotional punch." And just to prove that he was not dazzled by stars, Crowther observed that "it is Paul Newman's very good fortune that he isn't recognizable in the role of an addle-brained vagrant prize-fighter, for he is simply terrible...." Curiously, Crowther was silent about the flowage. But in this author's humble critical judgment, the flowage performed gracefully, beautifully, and, one could even say, naturally.

Poetry

Lakes and waters have often stirred poetic instincts. One poem that can be linked with certainty to the flowage appeared annually in the advertising brochure for Camp Nokomis. The author is not known. Perhaps it was Charlotte Mendes; for certain it was not Wordsworth. That said, its verses touchingly summon campers to imagine a treasured northwoods setting bereft of their youthful presence.

When you leave Nokomis
"The friendly little path you know
Will miss your glad young feet.
The hillsides and the forests
The sound of laughter sweet;
The dancing waves upon the Lake
Will miss canoe and sail:
All Silent in the shadowed woods
Will be your well-worn trail.
The singing birds will miss your songs
The stars your wondering eyes:
The ever-changing sunsets
Your look of hushed surprise.
You leave behind the beauty
Of all the hills you trod.
But in your heart you take away
More lasting gifts of God."

CHAPTER TWO
Fishing the Turtle-Flambeau Flowage

Esox Masquinongy:
The Ultimate Quarry

Flowage muskies, like muskies everywhere, are cantankerous. Sometimes they bite readily and furiously; sometimes they don't bite at all. For sure, anglers must always work hard to catch them, except, of course, when the casual or ill-prepared person triumphs right off the bat. Muskies are excellent teachers, especially of vocabulary, but their most lasting lessons usually bring tears and gnashing of teeth. Musky fishing is a science, an art, and a pathology. Musky anglers are either outdoor enthusiasts on a noble quest or hyper-competitive narcissists with no end of excuses. All this, and more, is in the historical record of the Turtle-Flambeau Flowage.

Bert Claflin, the *Milwaukee Sentinel* outdoor writer who did so much to publicize the flowage, knew well the many faces of this unpredictable sport. His initial trips all followed the same route—

from the confluence of the Manitowish and the Bear rivers down into the flowage in the direction of the Turtle Dam. "Our first trip was on Decoration day [1933], we caught 11 muskies; on the Fourth of July we went down again, catching on that occasion six, and the third trip was made in October with nary a strike to reward us." Claflin returned to the Mercer area during the Labor Day weekend of 1934, but to less than ideal circumstances. The weather was utterly miserable. It rained "pitchforks and hoe handles," he wrote, "changing a country which at this time of year is usually one of gorgeous colors, 'wim and wigor,' to a dripping, dismal ensemble of mud and mad drivers." Claflin attributed his failure to catch a musky in the flowage's Lake Ten area to the never-ending need to bail his boat. But big fish were taken that weekend, several by doctors, which, in turn, prompted Claflin to speculate that doctors did so well at musky fishing that they must be anesthetizing their quarry. In these two accounts, Claflin does not capture all there is to be said about musky fishing, but he gets a lot of it: amazing luck, very good luck, no luck whatsoever, weather-borne misery, an explanation for failure, and (mock) hostility toward successful anglers.

It seems only fair that the flowage would reward this champion of its waters for his enthusiasm, and it did. In an article published in *The Post-Crescent* (Appleton) on April 27, 1937, Claflin recommends musky fishing in the Baraboo Lake part of the flowage, where, he notes, he had taken a 25-pound fish. A few years earlier he had advised anglers to be satisfied with a musky weighing 25 pounds, noting "for truly that is a regal fish." In recognizing how fortunate one is to catch a fish of this size, Claflin displays a maturity that often comes to musky anglers only when they reach the age when throwing giant baits against the wind and pumping them in is no longer age-appropriate behavior—if it ever comes to them.

Lest Claflin's account makes flowage musky fishing seem too like the pursuit of muskies elsewhere, one should take into account the following testimonial from another member of the sporting press. Writing in the June 21, 1970, edition of *The Appleton Post-Crescent*, the normally reliable Dave Duffey passed along, without qualification or comment, the following: "L.C. Rheaume, retired conservation warden supervisor, once, before witnesses, got 75 musky strikes on as many casts in the newly filled Turtle Flowage." If Claflin helped in tempered prose to build a legend for the flowage, then Duffey surely took it over the top.

Setting aside Rheaume's miraculous feat, anyone who has ever fished muskies knows that it would be a colossal mistake to assume that muskies were any easier to catch in "the good old days" than they are today. And the record bears out this judgment. One might cite in this regard Dr. E.A. Kingston of Lockport, Illinois. Kingston began his musky fishing in 1914 as a member of the Jerome Fishing and Hunting Club, caught at least one musky every year but one over a 35-year stretch, and in 1949 took a 35 ½-pounder out of Trude Lake with Leonard Scheels of Mercer as his guide. Nonetheless, as an article about him in the *Wisconsin Conservation Department Bulletin* of December of 1949 notes, "As to musky fishing in those days—Dr. Kingston will testify that they didn't jump into the canoe. You had to work for them, and with poorer equipment than is available today." But then again, take the case of Leonard Krueger of Pittsville, Wisconsin. In August of 1946, Krueger was fishing for crappies with a four-and-a-half-ounce fly rod, a 10-pound test leader, and a White Miller fly with a red tail when a lunker musky rose to his gently delivered offering. After a half-hour battle, during which it often "looked like this big 'un would be among the getaways," he landed a 50-inch fish that weighed in at 35 pounds. Witnesses to this feat include Krueger's wife, Martha Corbin (also of Pittsville), and Al Koshak, the resort owner.

But enough of the exception, and back to the rule. Even hard work was to no avail at those times when the fish just plain refused to cooperate. "Bad news for the 'feast or famine' crowd who fish for 'a muskie or nothing.' His lordship, Esox Masquinongy, is in one of those moods. It may be the cold weather. It may be the high water. Or it may just be the infernal contrariness of this fascinating fish." So wrote Gordon MacQuarrie in July of 1940 in the *The Milwaukee Journal*, in a column that went on to note that "this has been so far the poorest muskellunge season in many years." Flowage guides, he said, were trying to persuade customers to set aside their pursuit of muskies and to be content for catching some fish for the skillet. As Emil Severt, a knowledgeable flowage guide, put it: "You can't rush muskies. Give us some hot days and we'll show you some busters. Meanwhile I'm all for fishing for what's available and the other fish are as willing as ever." MacQuarrie himself, guided by Verner Gustafson, a Park Falls guide, had fished—with no action at all—in the Flambeau River below the Turtle Dam. "When I can't turn up a musky below the Turtle Dam with a live sucker, there's something wrong," a frustrated Gustafson noted. What was wrong, of course, lay somewhere deep in the genetic code of the musky.

Guides who focus on this fish are as one in regarding the musky as savage, lonely, and moody. Ed Robinson, the dean of the Flambeau River guides for whom the river landing below the dam has been named, put it this way: a musky that follows a bait to the boat without striking it looks at the angler and says, "What the hell are you doing here? You want to catch me?" For Robinson, musky fishing boiled down to a "personality contest" between fish and angler. And what kind of personality is it that pursues muskies? One answer would be individuals who rise to the challenge of a low-odds game with the potential for high rewards—including some major bragging rights. A somewhat more elevated answer would be those persons who seek a fair chase encounter with a legendary quarry in a majestic setting. Many of the old-time musky guides have an entirely different response: namely, that both they and their parties lack something upstairs—or in fishermen's lingo, musky anglers are "rowing with only one oar in the water." And then there is outdoor writer Gordon McQuarrie's assessment of "muskie fishing crews": "They are another breed of cats, given to expensive equipment, guides, exclusive accommodations and the right to holler after each day of total loss: 'We was robbed.' They are a clan apart, bellyachers as is the way with fanatics." (Obviously, not every outdoor writer is enamored of musky fishing.)

One suspects that most musky anglers combine, with varying emphases, a little of each of these personality types, garnished by an idiosyncrasy here and there. What is for sure is that musky hunters take their sport seriously, and that success in it is closely tied to the ever-fragile ego. Take, for example, an Ironwood man who in 1938 caught a musky in the flowage that was attractive enough to prompt a bystander at the landing to offer $10 for the fish. The proud angler turned down the money, saying that "it is worth more to bring it back and show it to people who think I can't fish." In the end, Robinson's notion of a personality contest between man and fish may be the most penetrating insight ever into the deeper dynamics of musky fishing.

But what of the notion of muskies as teachers? One fisherman turned pupil was Dave Van Wormer, a writer for *The Milwaukee Journal*. While on the flowage, this rookie musky angler succumbed to the monotonous, mind-numbing routine of casting and retrieving a surface lure, and so he failed to respond with a sharp hook set when the strike came. The fish got off about halfway to the boat, and Van Wormer quickly figured out his mistake. For the rest of his day, he remained on high alert during every retrieve; but the muskies, having taught him a lesson, had left the classroom. Novice journalists are not the only ones who find muskies to be harsh teachers, as the 75-year-old mother of Mercer guide Jerry Hartigan learned. While fishing with Jerry and another son for walleyes, she was calmly reeling in a nice 16-inch bit of table fare on an inexpensive rod with a push-button reel when a huge musky rose up and engulfed the walleye. As Mrs. Hartigan watched, practically frozen, the fish sounded slowly but powerfully. The rod hit the gunnel and broke apart, and the reel went flying off. The episode, brief and brutal, upset this experienced angler sufficiently that she announced her intent "to go home, have a Manhattan, and take a nap."

Wall-hangers and Wall-hangers... Almost

If catching *any* musky is fraught with difficulty, catching a really big one is, barring one of those freak moments of musky-bestowed grace, a task of yet another order of magnitude. But in spite of the poor odds, the possibility of encountering a monster fish— the meanest of the mean—is what drives almost every angler, experienced or novice, who sets out in pursuit of the musky. Indeed, the first order of business for oh-so-many musky hunters is to get some assurance that there are BIG fish in the waters they plan to fish. Tom Guyant of the *The Milwaukee Journal* sought that assurance, but only after a long and unsuccessful day on the flowage in 1970, when he asked his guide, Milt Zablocki, "Are there any big fish in here?" Zablocki's response, no doubt well-tested, was classic: "Must be, we haven't taken any out." People who know muskies and musky fishing, however, find the exceedingly high expectations of many of the anglers to be a potential source of frustration. Dan Vickers, the Park Falls postmaster and a leading figure in promoting fishing and tourism in the area, put his concern this way: "I feel sorry for the folks who pin their faith entirely on muskies. Sure, we've got the greatest musky fishing in the country, here in Wisconsin. But here is a fish whose temperament can never be depended upon.... But a fisherman comes up with his heart set on something around 30 pounds. Shucks, he isn't being fair with himself if he tries for muskies and muskies alone. That's not the way to have fun fishing. Muskies will break your heart if you let them." Dick Sleight, a man regarded by musky historian Eli Singer as "the king of the musky guides," believed that really big muskies would appear for only one week in a year, and after that, "Where they go, no one knows." If Sleight's conjecture is right, the prospects for landing a wall-hanger are exceedingly slim.

Even so, anglers have managed to find some big ones on the flowage. In his book, *A Compendium of Musky Angling History,* Larry Ramsell claims that, as of 1997, the Turtle-Flambeau Flowage (TFF) had given up five fish over 40 pounds, and two over 50 pounds. These data, compiled mostly from the records of the annual *Field & Stream* fishing contests, come from an era when, on the flowage as elsewhere, most legal muskies were killed and often weighed—especially the big ones. One can only wonder whether other fish in the 40-pound plus range came out of the flowage but were never registered anywhere. Surely this is possible, but, given the ego investment of some of the more fanatic musky hunters, it seems unlikely. Circumstances are somewhat different today. The prevailing practice in our "catch-and-release" era is to report the length of a fish, and any weighing as may be done is carried out with a hand-held scale—hardly a certified instrument. Again, one can only wonder whether, among released fish, there has been a 40-pounder or two.

In a classic exemplar of an old saw, *The Milwaukee Journal* of June 30, 1957, announced that musky fishing in the flowage "isn't what it was 10 years ago." Perhaps that was correct; but if so, matters were to take quite a turn for the better in the following decade. For what is for certain is that the 1960s were a good time for catching big muskies on the flowage... and an especially opportune time to be a female musky angler. In mid-August of 1966, Mavis Haines of Joliet, Illinois, and Mercer, pitched out a surface bait and soon found herself engaged in a 30-minute battle with a heavy-bodied musky. When the fish was finally gaffed and brought into the boat, Haines found herself in possession of a fish that measured 52 inches in length and weighed in at 46 pounds. As big as this fish was, it only earned her third place in what might be called the "TFF women's musky derby of the 1960s." Second place belonged to Mrs. E. Reinardy of Janesville, Wisconsin. In late October of 1962, Reinardy was fishing with a veteran flowage guide, Vern Sutherland, in the Baraboo Lake area. As lunchtime approached, Sutherland rowed up to a known picnic spot only to find another guide, Dick Sleight, and his party taking their break there. As a courtesy both to Sleight and the two parties of anglers, Sutherland rowed to a lunch site on the opposite shore. On the way into the bank, he had thrown out a couple of suckers... just in case. Before Sutherland could get a proper fire going, however, he heard Reinardy scream, "Fish on!" After a substantial fight, Sutherland whacked and then gaffed a fish that pulled the scale down to the 50 pounds and one ounce mark! The whole episode was viewed—no doubt with some complicated feelings—from across the water by Dick Sleight and his party. It seems they had spent a week heavily working the shoreline where Reinardy's fish hit.

Seven years later it was Sleight's turn, when he guided Rita Hillenbrand to an all-time flowage record fish, a monster that tipped the scale at 52 pounds, eight and three-quarters ounces. Once again, the fish hit while the angler was on the shore; only this time, it was not a lunch break that put her there. Rather, Rita had expressed a strong interest in working a sand point where she was confident a big fish resided. Sleight rowed her to shore, pitched out a sucker that sank to the bottom, and headed off with Rita's husband, Ray, to fish some different water. After some time, the fish picked up the sucker, Rita set the hook the best she could— being slight of frame—and the tussle began. Sleight returned quickly to help with the endgame, and the happy party headed off for the inevitable photographs and celebration. It should be noted here that Rita Hillenbrand's achievement was not a one-time piece of luck by a casual angler. She and Ray were avid musky hunters who put in serious time

Guide Dick Sleight, skilled angler Rita Hillenbrand, and the largest musky ever taken from the flowage in the "Redwing" cabin at Sleight's Resort. Russ Sleight

with Sleight year after year. Moreover, she seems to have had a special gift for the sport, to say nothing of the endurance needed to cast a sucker ("all day, never stopped"). As Sleight remarked, "She caught so many fish between 35 and 40 pounds that it was unbelievable."

These two 50-pounders were not the only TFF fish that Dick Sleight remembered. There was, of course, the one that got away; the one that might have been a world record. The story began, true to musky lore—if not always reality—with an approaching storm front. Hoping to get some action before being driven off the flowage by thunder and lightning, Sleight took his party to a favorite spot. "It's a big area, stumps and sand bars, some rocks and the whole works." At one moment when no one's lure was in the water, a huge fish surfaced about 20 feet from the boat, then slowly submerged and disappeared. Sleight compared both its size and its actions to a "submarine." The party failed to raise the fish before they had to flee the storm, but they returned to the same area for four days in a row and only raised a few small fish. The next day Sleight and his party launched an all-out assault on this fish, throwing every lure in the box, without success. Then Eddie Reddick put on a musky-sized Rapala, despite Sleight's warning that it would hang up in this stumpy water. Sleight was right, of course, and he had to stop several times to free the plug from snags as he worked his way through prime water. Then Reddick said something to the effect that he had hooked a really big snag this time. Sleight turned the boat toward the snag and began to row in its direction, and Reddick put his rod down in the boat to put some slack in the line. Then, suddenly, the head of this monster musky emerged from the water, Rapala in its mouth and gills flared, and headed toward the boat. As its head sank into the water—the fish seemed too heavy to jump—the slack line was sucked beneath the gill covers and instantly severed. The fish was gone, and the anglers were left with indelible memories and the inevitable what-ifs. What if the fish had reacted instantly and not mimicked a stump? What if Sleight had not pivoted the boat in preparation for retrieving the "snagged" lure? What if Reddick had kept a tight line, even though common sense told him not to? In Sleight's reminiscences, he states that he and his guests were all certain this had been a 70-pound fish. Sleight's clients, in recognition of the sight and sound of this musky as it emerged from the water heading toward the boat, named it Santa Fe. Fish as locomotive.

Sleight was far from being the only member of the "big-one-that-got-away club," a club whose sole perk was the painfully earned right to tell a tale that was never going to end well. Jerry Hartigan and one of his customers also qualified for the club. During one of his trips to the flowage, Hartigan took along two executives from the Caterpillar company. One of them was an avid musky fisherman, a man who owned "nearly every lure made" and who did his best to use as many as possible in a day's outing. The other executive, the boss of the musky enthusiast, had very little experience chasing muskies. In order to assess the boss's casting skills, Hartigan had the man begin casting no more than 20 yards from the put-in. And then—this story almost tells itself—up came a musky in the mid-50-inch range and it engulfed the whole bucktail. The novice could only say, "Look at that, look at that," as the fish slowly shook its head from side to side. His experienced companion, of course, was shouting, "Set the hook, set the hook," at the top of his lungs. But the hook was never set, the bucktail fell out, and the fish slowly disappeared. At that point, the junior executive screamed again and again at his boss, "Do you understand what that was [a fish of a lifetime, and then some]?" Hartigan finally had to do some yelling of his own to calm the man down—a task that took four or five minutes. As for the boss, he had no idea what was going on; even after things were explained to him more calmly, he had no basis in personal experience that enabled him to fully comprehend this lost opportunity.

Another member of the club was Bill Tutt. In 1966, Tutt and his wife, Marj, purchased Casey and Lu's Resort (formerly Popko's) and renamed it Flam-Bow Resort after Bill's previous occupation as a representative of a hunting bow manufacturer. A dedicated and skilled musky fisherman, Bill proceeded to catch almost 40 muskies during his first summer as a resort owner—including a 36-pounder. He went on to become a highly respected guide, advocate for muskies (later on he would serve as a president of the Flambeau Chapter of Muskies, Inc.), and author. Thanks to that latter talent, we have the most memorable single piece of writing about flowage musky fishing ever produced. The story, "Big George," appeared first in a newsletter of *Muskies, Inc.*, and then in the March 1980 issue of *Fishing Facts*. Tutt first encountered Big George (an anomalously named female!) in 1966 on a sandbar in one of the old natural lakes that are part of the flowage, but could not tease a repeat appearance from her that year. But during the following four summers, he raised the fish with mind-boggling regularity to the delight and awe of friends, guests, and guiding clients; it was as if the fish wanted to be seen and admired. Matters were to change, however, in August of 1970, when flowage muskies went on a tear. In one week, Tutt landed "nine fish in 10 short trips, ranging from 26-1/2 to 38 pounds." And then came the moment he had been waiting for. On a viciously windy evening, Big George finally struck, engulfing Bill's bucktail almost as soon as it hit the water. The fight played out at close range, with the fish displaying extraordinary power in the wind-blown waters, but eventually Big George wore down and was brought to the boat for the coup de grace. But then as a heavy wave made the boat pitch, the handle of the gaff, which was wielded by a companion, hit the side of the boat and delivered only a glancing blow to the fish—and the gaff hook itself severed the leader. Driven by the heavy wind, the boat quickly drifted away, leaving an exhausted Big George lying tantalizingly in water. But in the time it took to fire the motor and return to her, she managed to sound—never to reappear. Tutt continued to fish muskies, but never with quite the same verve as before this incident—even though he subsequently saw an even larger fish in the flowage. Whom the gods would destroy, they first take musky fishing.

Musky Tackle and Techniques: The Tried, the True, and the New

In the early years of the flowage, musky fishing was an altogether different undertaking from what it has become today. It was, in the first instance, much more leisurely, as getting around the flowage was accomplished either by oars or by wooden boats driven by motors of three to five horsepower. Mercer's Mitch Babic, who started guiding in 1938 and "put in 56 years in the boat," remembered those motors, staggeringly low-powered in relation to today's outboard motors and so heavy that they had to be transported in a wheelbarrow. Flowage boats, for the most part, were round-bottomed craft, a shape that was useful—but not foolproof—in avoiding getting hung up on stumps or other grabby wood. A few, including one owned by Babic, were pointed at both ends; these "double-enders," as they were sometimes called, rowed extremely easily and were ideally suited to trolling. By contrast, the Flambeau River guide Ed Robinson preferred flat-bottomed boats (some of which he built) as he negotiated the rapids-strewn stretch of water from the dam down to Park Falls. And all of the guides knew well how to work the oars—often leathered oars that could be feathered in the wind. Indeed, precise boat control was a critical part of musky fishing. For not only did it enable guests to cast to likely spots, but it also helped to position the boat during the fight, the goal here being to keep the line at a right angle to the boat.

Needless to say, wooden boats required a lot of maintenance. They had to be submerged or allowed to accumulate some rainwater in order to swell tight after a winter in storage, and their high moisture content had to be sustained throughout the season. From time to time they needed a bit of caulk, a new rib here or there, and, of course, occasional coats of paint. (Al Weseman, the second owner of Al's Place, put his engineering background to work by devising a machine that softened hardwood strips destined to be shaped into ribs.) Wooden boats also had other liabilities. They were vulnerable to damage from rocks or solidly rooted stumps and roots, and there were limits to the size of a motor that could be mounted on them—though the flowage itself had something to say about how big a motor made sense. And so, as beautiful as many of the wooden boats were, and as agile as they could be in the hands of a skilled rower, they began to be replaced in the 1960s and 1970s with aluminum boats—a triumph of low maintenance over beauty and maneuverability. In 1961, for example, Al's Place retired its Shell Lake wooden craft and replaced them with 12-foot Alumacraft boats. The motors still remained modest, however. Doug Severt, a chore boy at Al's Place at the time, recalls that most motors were 7.0 or 9.5 horsepower, and "only the daring would mount a 15 HP, and only a 'darned fool' would think of using something as powerful as 25 HP." That said, the gradual disappearance of wooden boats brought to a close a lengthy chapter in the history of freshwater fishing. The race was now on toward bigger and bigger boats and ever more powerful motors. The era of what might be called "row and reflect" was eventually to be replaced by the age of "run and gun."

The same evolution from few and simple to complex and many can be seen in tackle. There is remarkable uniformity in what guides, outdoor writers, and anglers have to say about the rods, reels, and lures deployed in musky fishing right into the 1960s. First came True Temper square steel rods, most notably the Trophy and Raider models. These rods, first patented in 1925, eventually went out of production in the early 1950s. Modeled after a fencing sword, they were made of forged and tempered steel, and the rod guides were wrapped with copper and then tinned. These square rods were eclipsed in the late 1940s and 1950s by the Heddon Pal tubular steel rod, a relatively short rod—the longest version was five-and-a-half feet—that had enough backbone to cast fairly heavy baits and to set hooks firmly into boney mouths. By the late 1950s, however, steel rods lost their dominant position, first to fiberglass ones, and then, in time, to rods made of carbon fiber, also known as graphite. The door had been opened to a broad range of rods, uniquely designed for different types of lures. One size no longer fit all.

There were a number of baitcasting reels on offer from such manufacturers as South Bend, Shakespeare, and Langley, for example, but by far the most popular among musky anglers were Pfleuger products—first the Summit and then the Supreme. The latter was simple of design, easy to maintain, and tough. But it could also be tough on the user. Early models of the Supreme had no drag, leaving the angler to control a sudden, violent run by a musky either by thumbing the spool or by trying to keep up with the rapidly spinning handle. Needless to say, line-burned thumbs and banged-up knuckles were an accepted part of the musky game. Later models of the Supreme included an optional second handle with a primitive drag feature that could be adjusted to let the spool slip when the handle was firmly held in place, but it was neither a smooth nor a reliable feature. The reign of the Supreme came to an end, starting in 1954, when the Swedish Abu Ambassadeur 5000 reel came on the American market. It featured a free spool for ease of casting, and a substantial star drag that could easily be adjusted while fighting a fish. The 5000, and successor models, quickly became reels of choice for musky anglers and inspired the manufacture of similar types of reels by a number of companies. But these new model reels masked, to some extent, the violence and power of a fighting musky. As Dick Sleight put it, "Everybody who wants to catch a musky and feel what a musky feels like, they should try a Pfleuger Supreme. When you put in this brake system [star drag], you don't really know what you're catching. It's just twisting the handle, that's all. But take a Pfleuger Supreme, where there's no drag, and you'll know what catching a musky feels like. Ha ha... Yeah, you can burn your thumb! Most of the time, everybody after they caught a big fish, they came up with a bleeding someplace."

As far as lures go, it did not take a very big tackle box to hold the ones that are mentioned time and again in reports about the early days of flowage musky fishing. A 1935 article by Claflin states that flowage muskies can be "caught by casting various types of wooden plugs, metal wobblers... also by trolling among the half submerged tree trunks with No. 7 spoons having heavy brown or white bucktails about 10" in length." The Pikie minnow, either solid or jointed, was an early favorite among solid wood baits, and starting in the early 1940s, Frank Suick's Musky Thriller, the classic wooden "jerk" bait, gained quite a reputation. Various iterations of Dardevle lures topped the category of wobblers. The No. 7 spoon mentioned by Claflin was, of course, the famous Skinner fluted spoon (often referred to as a "spoon hook"), whose blade rotated about a wire axis. The Flambeau River guide Ed Robinson favored this bait, especially one dressed with nine-inch long black feathers. Others liked their spoon hooks dressed with heavy brown or white bucktails. Dick Sleight found woodchuck tails to be an acceptable substitute for bucktails; in this instance, the whole tail was deployed, and the color was certainly "natural." There is perhaps no bucktail color that does not have its staunch defenders, but black and yellow seem, over the years, to have been the flowage favorites. Mitch Babic, who laid claim to having taken 2,550 legal muskies himself over his lifetime, was unambiguous about his color preference on the flowage: "If you didn't have a yellow bucktail, you might as well stay home."

Surface baits constituted yet another category of lures popular with flowage musky anglers. They had three advantages: they were much less likely to get snagged on the flowage's ubiquitous wood; they produced some heart-thumping moments as following muskies raised a menacing wake; and they gave anglers an opportunity, if only for a nanosecond, to witness the strike. Among the many surface lures on the market, a small handful dominated musky fishing: toppers with their twin propellers; mud puppies, the body of which detached from the hook upon the set; and globes, lures whose heads, outfitted with propellers, rotated while the bodies remained fixed. On the flowage, the overwhelming favorite seems to have been the globe—especially a version manufactured by Pfleuger that was known as the Yellowbird or Yellow Bird (possibly because it was a larger version of an 1897 lure of that name). Not surprisingly, this lure, yellow with gold spots, was Babic's favorite, but many other guides and musky chasers also remember the Yellowbird with fondness. William "Musky Bill" Siegert, one of the founders of the Driftwood Hunting and Fishing Club, was another passionate advocate of the Yellowbird. In the 1950s, crawlers and creepers joined the list of topwater favorites. Bud Wahl, for instance, who learned his craft from the legendary Joe Golumb, remembers the Heddon Crazy Crawler as one of his favorite musky baits.

Artificial lures have certainly proven their effectiveness, but live bait—particularly large suckers—have also been part and parcel of musky fishing. As noted earlier, the two largest muskies to come from the flowage were taken on suckers, and many more of trophy size have succumbed to the same bait. Although suckers can be fished throughout the season, autumn has traditionally been the prime time for sucker fishing on the flowage and elsewhere. Muskies are fattening up for winter, the argument goes, and there's nothing quite as toothsome as a two-pound sucker. The traditional technique was fairly simple. The terminal tackle consisted of a large, sturdy hook attached to a long, metal leader. The angler then tied the head of the sucker to the hook in such a way that the sucker could withstand repeated casts without coming off. Tying suckers was something of an art, and various guides had their proprietary techniques. The suckers could then be cast and retrieved in such a way as to imitate an injured fish; they could be placed below a bobber and allowed to swim freely; and they could simply be cast out and dragged behind the boat. When a musky takes a sucker, the angler must wait—sometimes for an agonizingly long time—for the fish to ingest the bait before setting the hook. The drawback to this approach to sucker fishing, of course, is that most fish become deeply hooked, a situation that makes releasing them highly problematic. As a consequence, the practice of fishing with suckers declined as the catch-and-release ethic gained in popularity; but the invention of quick-strike rigs— which are designed to hook fish in the mouth—has revived the use of suckers among some musky anglers.

Finally, there was the tackle used either to get a musky into the boat or to secure it sufficiently at boat side in order to remove the hooks and release it. For decades, the common practice was to boat and keep almost all muskies of legal size. The argument, to the extent that anyone bothered to articulate it, went something like this: catching a legal specimen of the "fish of ten thousand casts" surely warrants reducing that quarry to possession. But that task was easier said than done. Getting a powerful, live fish over the gunnel was a challenge of the first order, and dealing with its flopping antics—teeth bared and hooks flashing—in the bottom of the boat could be an exercise in chaos. A frequent solution in the early days was to shoot the fish, while it was in the water, with a small caliber handgun. A .22 or a .25 caliber slug, when placed in the head or neck, brought a quick end to the struggle. According to one of his clients, Earl Tomek used a .22 pistol, which lacked a front sight, to dispatch muskies. But, as one can easily imagine, this method had its shortcomings. Shots could fail to hit a vital spot or even go completely awry, sometimes dangerously so. Shots fired in excitement could—and sometimes did—go through the hull of the boat. Worst of all, a fish killed by a shot, if not securely hooked, could sink to the bottom. Dick Sleight put his pistol aside for good when a bullet to the head of a fine fish dislodged the hook, and the fish, fatally wounded, sank irretrievably to the bottom. Wisconsin finally banned the practice, but only in 1966. Vern Sutherland, by contrast, never shot a fish. Instead, he sought to break their necks by administering a sharp blow to the back of the neck with the handle of a gaff, followed quickly by hoisting the fish aboard with the gaff hook. As Bill Tutt's experience with Big George proved, however, gaffing was far from fail-safe. The net, the friend of anglers for centuries, had its limitations as well. At the urging of Ray Hillenbrand, Dick Sleight once attempted to net a large musky that Ray had hooked with a Saltwater Pikie. The outsized lure caught on the inside of the net before the fish's body was in the bag, and Sleight had no recourse but to drag the fish in by the gill cover, the danger to his hands be damned.

•-◄◉►-•

The practice of taking every legal fish, whatever the species, was soon to be challenged. A growing awareness of the finite number of game fish available, coupled with growing numbers of anglers, led to the increasing popularity of "catch-and-release." This practice, initially advocated by trout and bass anglers, quickly spread to other game fish species, including muskies. Under its influence, even some of the prominent musky guides who had escorted many a musky to the local scales and display coolers eased up some on taking fish. Both Sleight and Sutherland fell into this category; Bill Tutt had for some time been tagging and releasing fish in an effort to learn more about their behavior. Catch-and-release received an additional impetus from the appearance and spread of organizations dedicated to preserving muskies. With the practice of catch-and-release so widespread today, anglers can make use of new equipment, such as musky-sized landing nets and cradles, to contain fish destined for release. Those who still want to take their prizes home can dispatch them with wooden "priests," or even a rusty old ball-peen hammer.

Today's musky anglers on the flowage can, and often do, take to the water with the latest gear: specially outfitted boats, oversized motors, multiple rods, ever more advanced generations of reels, boxes of lures of all actions and materials, space-age lines, laser-sharpened hooks, and on and on, right down to "official" fishing clothing decorated with tackle manufacturers' logos. The pace of angling has certainly accelerated, the expectations of success have become more fervid, and the whole enterprise has been tainted by the language of hype and the jingle of the cash register. But there is no reason to believe that old Esox has bought into that vision of the game. Can one really say that she will be more cooperative with anglers who motor to her lair at warp speed than with those who row in cautiously? Will she be more attracted to a newfangled bait delivered by an expensive rod and reel combo than to a traditional lure cast out by a battered rod and squeaky reel? One simply does not know. What seems for sure is that she will show herself, taunt her would-be captor, and disappear, sometimes for days or weeks on end, all at her own pleasure and her own pace, and that she will eat when she damn well pleases—and not a second before. For her, the game is still a personality contest, one in which she absolutely controls the first move.

Michael Hittle

June Bug Spinners, Stump Dunking, and Crawlers Through the Driftwood: The Pursuit of Flowage Walleyes

The primary goal of the great majority of flowage anglers was, and remains today, to catch a good stringer of fish for the table. Candidates for such a meal include crappies, perch, bass, northerns, and, of course, that table fare par excellence, the walleye. In the magical, mythical early years of the flowage, before the great differentiation of tackle had taken place, to fish for one was to fish for all, and not much time was wasted on choosing tackle and technique.

Imagine, then, this scene: a guide rowing his party in a homemade boat through standing timber, stumps, and floating logs in pursuit of anything that bites. And what is on the end of their lines to lure the fish? "I always just put a minnow on a spinner and used that. Right through the two lips. Use a number four hook, I like a four hook.... That's plenty big for ah, you catch northern on them.... A lot of times we drift across, but I know the shallows or a good weed bed. There was a couple of places on the flowage where the water was thirty feet deep and the crappies would get down in there, and I used to drift across that. Then we'd pick up some nice big crappies in there. With that same spinner with a minnow, that's all I used on there." Fred Losby, an early Springstead guide, is referring here, of course, to the estimable June Bug Spinner, which, when tipped with a minnow, preferably a hardy mud minnow, was the presentation of choice among flowage anglers for several decades. Art Schmidt Jr., a licensed guide during his mid-teens and the son of a resort owner, was another advocate of the June Bug Spinner. "We would start out in the lake and drift toward the shore with the wind, casting and retrieving spinners with minnows. The minute you feel something, you let it go." Having given the fish time to swallow the minnow, the angler then set the hook. But just in case minnows were not on the day's diet for walleyes, Schmidt put a pole out behind the boat "with a big fat night crawler." Though this insurance policy sometimes paid off with a nice fish, he admitted that it "caught more snags than walleyes." In that simpler time, the only choice for the angler was color—a red and white blade seemed to work best for northerns, a gold or silver one for walleyes. Any color stood a chance at picking up the odd musky. Needless to say, pioneer flowage anglers did not need much by the way of a tackle box. The June Bug Spinner, though overshadowed in time by other lures, continued to put fish on the stringer. In 1982, for example, Jay Reed of *The Milwaukee Journal* got in some May walleye fishing on the flowage. Although cold weather had put the fish down, he tied on a June Bug Spinner and managed to pick up a couple of walleyes anyhow. Indeed, this revered lure can still be deployed to good effect on flowage waters.

Driftwood in Beaver Flats in 1994. The jam is smaller than it once was, but just as densely packed. George Rothenberger

The transformation of the flowage brought on by the decline of standing timber and the growing size and numbers of logjams along its shores was accompanied by a burgeoning walleye fishery. By the 1950s, a walleye-dominated flowage had attracted widespread notice among anglers and outdoor writers. And as the walleye fishery grew, so too did the range of tactics anglers deployed to pursue their quarry. Stump dunking, for example, focused on patches of standing timber in water of moderate depth. Anglers stopped at each tree, sometimes holding the boat in place with oars, sometimes attaching the boat to the tree with an ice hook or pick hammer and rope, and then dropping a minnow or night crawler into the roots. Getting the bait to the proper depth required a substantial weight. Joe Aski, a flowage resident who began fishing this body of water in 1937, recalls fishing standing trees and leaners with the following setup: a casting rod and reel, 20- to 30-pound test braided line, a spindle-shaped sinker, a short piece of 10-pound test gut for a leader, and a hook. He also remembers that this kind of fishing required a plentiful supply of hooks. Either the first or second time he fished the flowage, he went through 47 hooks in a week's stay, a costly—but memorable—adventure for a youth during the late Depression years. Joe and his father learned the tricks of the walleye trade from one of its greatest practitioners, Joe Popko, while staying at Popko's Resort and occasionally fishing with this legendary guide and northwoods character. Another client of Popko's, an Iowan named Tom, describes stump dunking as follows: "We only used night crawlers straight down the side of the boat at a log or stump. Three to four minutes was max time until either he [Popko] caught fish or he... said 'going up' and that meant to get your line in the boat immediately!!!!!" Once the lines were in, Popko was off to the next stump.

Casting jigs, tipped with minnows or crawlers, became—and

remains—one of the most popular approaches to flowage walleye fishing. This technique helps the angler to cover more water, and is especially suited to fishing gravel bars, humps, and broad flats where the fish may be widely scattered. Whether the color of the jig makes a difference seems to be a matter of personal opinion; but it should be noted that when color shows up in a story or reminiscence, it is often yellow. More important than color is the weight of the jig—the rule of thumb being to use the lightest possible jig that will get the bait in front of a wary walleye. Jig weights from 1/16 ounce to 3/8 ounce are appropriate for the flowage. Weed guards are advised both for reasons of economy and mental health.

Slip bobbers, which allow anglers to position bait with precision at any depth, also have their place in the arsenal of flowage walleye anglers. Whether fish are hugging the bottom or suspended higher in the water column, a slip bobber rig keeps the bait right at their level. Moreover, when fished deep, they are somewhat less likely to hang up on woody debris than are jigs; but nothing lowered into the flowage is proof against attack from wood. Joe Aski has been a longtime advocate of these rigs; and, when the south wind, his favorite, blows up a chop on the water, he has enjoyed many a successful outing with them. Don Pemble, a Mercer guide who has 50 years of experience on the flowage, finds slip bobbers particularly effective if one finds a pocket of fish in a fairly confined space.

That so many anglers used live bait to fish for walleyes does not mean that these fish could not be taken with artificials. As spinning tackle became ever more popular, walleye hunters found it possible to easily cast a wide range of lure types and weights. In particular, lightweight stick baits, such as the Rapala (first introduced into the United States in 1959) and its many look-alikes, turned out to be ideally suited to the flowage. Donald Bluhm of *The Milwaukee Journal* reported success in using a number seven black and silver Rapala (presumably a floater) to fish rocky shorelines and shallow stump fields. A black and silver Rap, with two split shot ahead of it for weight, was the only bait used by "Musky Bill" Siegert when he fished walleyes in the summer. Color options for stick baits have proliferated over the years; and, judging by the gaudy array of lures that the author has retrieved from the lakebed during low water, it seems clear that flowage anglers, woody structure, and possibly even some fish have been attracted to quite a range of colors. Spinner baits have also proven their ability to catch flowage walleyes in good numbers. Examples include the Mepps Spinner (originally a European import) and the Beetle Spin (designed by Virgil Ward, an American television fisherman). Both of these lures came on the market around 1960, and continue to have their advocates among flowage anglers.

The presence of walleyes at the edge of and beneath logjams was to give rise to a particularly exciting and highly productive mode of fishing. The *Milwaukee Sentinel* introduced logjam fishing to its readers on June 30, 1957: "One method of still fishing is to drop a line with minnow attached in openings among the snag and log choked bays." But carefully edging up to a jam and dunking minnows or crawlers through nearby driftwood was the most benign form of logjam fishing. A more aggressive version involved running a boat up onto a jam until it lodged there, at which point the fishing began. This approach had benefits beyond avoiding the hassle of dropping an anchor. According to Don Pemble, motoring into jams with enough force knocks various aquatic insects from the bottom of logs. As they drift toward the bottom, the fish move in and the anglers go to work. One of the most memorable days of guiding for Art Schmidt Jr. illustrates Pemble's point. While fishing in the Beaver Flats area of the flowage, Schmidt ran his boat up on top of the logs and his party began to catch perch, one after another, hauling the wriggling critters up through gaps in the floating timber. Then the walleyes showed up; the first 26 inches in length, the second only an inch shorter. It was no mean feat to get these prize walleyes into the boat, but Schmidt's party succeeded amid much "hooping and hollering." Of course, the arrival of the walleyes scared the perch off, and fishing was at an end. But this did not stop the happy party from hanging the two large walleyes and their stringer of perch from snubbed branches on a standing tree and taking photos of the moment. "I was king for that day," Schmidt said.

Fishing through the logs of a big jam. WDNR

The most aggressive way to fish jams, however, was to climb out of the boat and scramble across the logs in pursuit of a likely looking opening to fish. One flowage veteran found ways to reduce the risk to life and limb while on the jams. "I remember as a kid I would take a boat and row along the logjam from Popko's towards Norway Point. I'd have three 2x6s about 5 or 6 feet long with me. I'd fish the edge of the jam 'til it got slow and then put those boards out on the jam and walk around on it fishing in the holes. If I got a fish, usually a walleye or perch, I'd hang 'em on a branch sticking up and keep going. On the way back I'd put them on my stringer I had around my belt and head back to the boat. Ya couldn't do that if there was a strong wind blowing into the jam for safety reasons and also some evenings the mosquitos sounded like a squadron of B-17s!"

In all of its variants, logjam fishing was more about putting fish on the stringer than about sport. An expert flowage fisherman once showed the author his logjam rig—a Heddon steel musky rod, rigged with 20-pound test line (at the least), heavy sinker and hook. He explained that the instant the hook was set, the fish had to be muscled up to the surface and onto the logs, lest it find some underwater obstacle to wrap the line around and escape. As one old-timer noted: "I can remember the days of so many logs in the jams, and fishing between them for the 'eyes.' What a treat, and a pretty cool way to catch fish, if you can wrestle them out of there. 'If it is to be, it is up to me!'"

Sadly for the sake of tradition, logjam fishing on the flowage is pretty much a thing of the past. The seemingly inexhaustible supply of driftwood disappeared, for the most part "one piece at a time," as Don Pemble puts it, eventually to end up as lawn decorations, elements of taxidermy mounts, or craft items. And, perhaps worst of all, some of it was piled up on shore and burned in order to clear beaches for waterfront properties. By the time the state got around to prohibiting the harvest of driftwood in the 1990s, the bulk of it was gone. Fishing tightly to the edges of floating bog islands is about as close as today's anglers can come to replicating the logjam experience of yore.

As time passed and the standing timber turned to driftwood, most of it lodged against the banks, the flowage lost some of the eerie character that Losby had so vividly described. Yet it remained, and remains today, a formidable body of water to tackle. As noted, the flowage in its earliest days differed enough from most other northwoods lakes to force anglers to come up with some new strategies. And if it became somewhat easier to fish in the years when the logjams were at their greatest extent, the flowage changed yet again as the jams diminished in size and other woody structure deteriorated and disappeared. Emmet Skaggs, a flowage resident who has fished its waters for some 59 years, calls it a "tough body of water to fish" and "damned hard to fish" and adds, "You have to find just the right spots." Two Mercer guides, Don Pemble and Jerry Hartigan, who have between them over seven decades of experience, echo that sentiment. To begin with, the flowage is huge compared to most inland lakes. This fact alone makes it hard for novice anglers to figure out where to start. Then one must factor in the relative paucity of weeds, something that distinguishes the flowage from most northwoods lakes. Locating structures— some of them almost unimaginably small— that do hold fish is no easy task in a body of water so large. Jerry Hartigan's GPS has some 580 marks for the flowage. Moreover, the fish, especially walleyes, can relate to structures in unpredictable ways. They may lie deep in river channels one day and then move up onto adjacent flats the next. Or such movement can take place in an hour's time. In other locations, even a one-foot change in bottom contour can serve as a haven for fish. To some extent, this unpredictability can be attributed to the fact that the stained waters of the flowage allow walleyes to forage at almost any depth. During the dog days of August, with temperatures in the 90s, flowage walleyes are just as likely to be active in three feet of water as in 15 or 20. As in all fishing, there's no substitute for experience, but on the flowage a willingness to set aside conventional wisdom can sometimes turn a bad day into a very good one.

A Boater's Nightmare

Not only has the flowage proven to be a challenging body of water to fish, it has also gained a much-deserved reputation as a boater's nightmare. At full pool in the spring, the flowage can be deceptively forgiving of boaters who race hither and yon oblivious to what lies below. But as the waters drop over the course of the summer, as they so often do, unseen obstacles, whether wood or rock, begin to assert themselves with ever greater regularity; and they can wreak havoc on the experienced and the novice alike. The first casualty of these hazards was usually the outboard motor's shear pin. "Shear pins," writes George Rothenberger, a longtime flowage angler. "What a pain. Dad once fell out changing a pin. He said, 'Heck, it's easier standing in the damn water' and continued to replace the pin…. Don Hill once told us he replaced a shear pin with tripled up hook shanks he jammed into the slot—with a gale coming, damn near a tornado." Emmet Skaggs gave up purchasing factory-made pins and crafted his own from nails. Dealing with sheared pins at night was even worse, as another flowage veteran recalls. "We'd only go once a year, so we only knew the water well enough to be dangerous…. I learned a bunch of new swear words as my dad replaced shear pins in the dark as we drifted toward the dam on the way back from the big water."

The next to go were propellers. Gene Osterhaus, who spent two years as caretaker of the campsites for the DNR, recalled that his job was fun in the early part of the summer, but by August, as the water level declined, his boat began to take frequent hits from sand and rock bars and stumps—sometimes as many as six, seven, or eight hits a day—and his props suffered accordingly. A high-speed collision with an underwater hazard can damage the entire lower unit, or worse. Joe Aski, witness to a boat that hit a rock pile in the Big Water, said that "half the motor ended up in the boat." Finally, there was the danger that the hull of a boat could be damaged by coming down hard on standing wood or on rocks, particularly during the years when only wooden boats were in use on the flowage. In the early days of the flowage, Fred Losby claimed that stuffing a hole in the hull with pieces of clothing was the standard form of first aid at such moments. According to Tom Gargrave, this technique seems to have been alive and well right into the 1950s. He points out that Earl Barnhardt, an outdoorsman and owner of the Standard gas station in Mercer, punched a hole in his boat while transporting four deer hunters and one deer from down lake to Popko's Resort. Barnhardt stuffed some jackets in the damaged hull and got his party safely to the resort for a round (or two?) of celebratory beers.

The advent of aluminum boats substantially reduced the risk of a breached hull, but this new material did not eliminate what had been a longstanding problem: getting a boat stuck atop a submerged tree. Though not likely to be costly in financial terms, being stranded on a hidden forest remnant is surely the most frustrating type of encounter with a flowage navigation hazard. Sometimes a boater can work a hung-up craft free by shifting weight around the vessel; other times wet heroics are called for; but once in a while there is nothing to do but wait for assistance from a passing boat.

It is no wonder, then, that spotters were widely favored by many boaters on the flowage. As one experienced fisherman recalls: "In the early days every boat had a spotter in the front looking for logs at or just below the surface. I would guess that by the 1980s the spotter was no longer required." Maybe. Maybe not. What is for sure is that almost everyone who has extensively boated the flowage has made at least one memorable acquaintance with what lies below. For this author, it was a jarring, motor-raising encounter with the rock bar in Merkle Lake, a feat accomplished in the presence of his two sons who could not hide their delight in the explosive consequences of Dad's poor navigation skills. For sure, the potential for such moments is pretty evenly distributed across the entire flowage, but there is one stretch of troubled water that has earned itself a secure place in flowage lore: the route from Fisherman's Landing to Bonies Mound. This twisting, turning, tree-studded passage has been dubbed "stump alley" or "the minefield," and probably with a lot of unprintable phrases as well. That some people can run it at full throttle without a bump while others, carefully navigating it at no-wake speed, seem drawn to lumber like iron filings to a magnet only adds to the legend of this tricky passage.

"Treacherous," is what one old-timer called the flowage. But the caution of elders is not always the practice of youth, as the following story shows. Beginning in 1960, Don Hill frequently explored the flowage as a youth. One day, while fishing in Lake Ten and Rat Lake with his brother and a friend, the trio "killed them." When they returned to O'Meara's Resort with a groaning stringer, one guest inquired where the fish had been caught. When he found out where, he responded with alarm: "Past the dam? Are you kids nuts?" "That night my dad wanted to go where we had caught them," Hill recalls. "Once we got past the dam, he got nervous. Then we passed the two islands and got to Sandy Point and he saw what was ahead of us and he shut off the motor. I said, 'Dad, we've got another mile or two to go.' All he said was, 'I'm not going through that,' and we didn't. I think it was 5 or 10 years before I got him all the way down there." The young Hill was even brash enough to head out alone *and* at night, two circumstances that compounded the risks already inherent in plying the flowage's trouble-filled waters. On one evening he had reason to regret his boldness. "My lure landed in a tree on the west shore near the pink rock. It was around midnight. I beached the boat, climbed the tree, and got the lure. Climbed down and my boat was 40 feet away and drifting. Lucky as hell, I casted into the boat, the lure got tangled in the net, the net got caught under the seat, and I pulled the boat to shore. That ended my night fishing that trip. Scared the hell out of me." Hill thought it best not to recount the adventure—even with its fortuitous outcome—to his father, lest he be grounded from night fishing.

The Much-Prized "Eater"

What leads anglers to take on the flowage's navigational perils, as well as wind and waves and storms and bugs in order to fish its waters? The most likely answer is the chance to catch a limit of "eaters" in a classically rugged northwoods setting. Now the term eater has different meanings for different folks, but it should be understood as the preferred size walleye for the frying pan—not so small as to be embarrassing as it sizzles in grease, and not so large as to be tough of texture and strong of taste. These criteria would put an eater at somewhere between 14 and 19 inches, plus or minus an inch.

The flowage's bounty is on display in this photo of anglers and their families. A WDNR report labeled this photo "The good old days." WDNR

Joe Aski is someone who revels in the pursuit of eaters on the flowage. "I have enjoyed it fiercely; it can be as good or better than Canada." At one time or another, Joe has fished all over the flowage: Baraboo, Horseshoe, Bonies Mound, Merkle, and the logjams at the northeast end of the Big Water. And after he built a home near Four Mile Creek, he shifted his focus to that area. In the years when he and his father stayed at Popko's, Joe says the walleyes were super-abundant. "Ninety out of every one hundred fish were walleyes." It's not that they took a limit every day. During a typical week of fishing, they could expect three days when the bite was on and limits came quickly. Other days they had to work for two or three apiece. He does not recall ever taking a walleye over 26 inches, but this was a matter of no consequence, as the Askis had a different goal in mind: "For us, it was meat fishing, that's really what it was." Fish to eat in camp, and fish to take home. Perhaps that's why Joe's favorite memory harks back to a day when he took four walleyes, each 19 inches in length, from one spot in one hour. One suspects that moments similar to this one burn brightly in the minds of myriad of dedicated flowage anglers. The Askis took some northerns, of course, several in the 30- to 36-inch range, although they never targeted them. Perch occasionally came in the mix with walleyes; and as for crappies, Aski says, "You could fill the boat with them and not go more than a block from the cabin."

For such anglers, it was the stringer—not an individual fish here or there—that dominates flowage memories. Gene Osterhaus, who liked to drift with the wind either toward or away from the Pink Rock while gently working a jig over grabby bottom, remembers days when the walleyes were so aggressive that they picked up the jig and minnow combination well before it hit the bottom and could be worked. For him, fishing was best in the early 1980s, when walleyes seemed to run fairly consistently in the 16- to 20-inch range. Later on, he found that walleyes became smaller with each passing year. Emmet Skaggs has, amid his collection of flowage memorabilia, a photo of a truly impressive stringer of walleyes, though he is quick to point out that he had done even better the previous day; but, owing to a prolonged celebration at a local watering hole, he had neglected to get a photo of these fish. Photos from Bill Siegert's camp include one of a stringer of walleyes "too heavy to lift," or so the family memory has it.

That stringers full of "eaters" were the objective of the overwhelming number of flowage walleye anglers does not mean that really big fish did not attract attention. In June of 1943, two fishermen brought in a stringer of 10 fish that averaged seven pounds, with the top fish weighing in at 12 pounds. There could not have been an eater in the lot! The top fish in the 1957 contest sponsored by the Mercer Resort and Businessmen's Association measured 30 inches and weighed nine pounds and four ounces.

The winner two years later came in at 31 inches and 10 pounds and one ounce. Two accounts that rely somewhat on hearsay suggest that the flowage is capable of producing even bigger fish. Bill Tutt is said to have taken a 14-pound walleye while fishing suckers for muskies, and Don Pemble says the biggest flowage walleye he has ever heard of weighed in at 16 pounds. Unfortunately, it had been snagged while spawning. Impressive as these fish are, the flowage has never been regarded as a trophy walleye lake, a fact that WDNR sampling confirms; and it is the opinion of some that the number of really big fish has been in decline for several decades, in spite of the fact that many anglers routinely release the bigger spawners. The scarcity of wall-hangers, it should be noted, has never been a matter of concern for flowage anglers for whom eaters are the prize.

No one has ever claimed that walleyes are great fighters. They neither run off yards of line nor leap into the air shaking their heads. But there is something about the sight of a flowage walleye as it comes into view in the coppery waters it calls home that triggers a unique kind of excitement in the angler. Mostly, this excitement is a response to a flashing visual mix: the golden belly (or in some cases on the flowage, an orange cast to the belly), the characteristic white spot on the tail, the glowing marble eye, the dorsal fin in full display. But this excitement is also shaped, somewhere in the mind's eye, by the image of a platter of sizzling, golden brown fillets. There seems little doubt that fishing is connected to some deeply rooted primordial urges, and nothing satisfies these urges better than an eater walleye.

Shore Lunch

Many a stringer of eaters ended up as dinner in resort cabins, and others found their way into freezers and eventually into anglers' homes. Some, however, never got back to the landing, having supplied the makings for the king of all outdoor meals—the shore lunch. Anyone, of course, could prepare a shore lunch, but it was the guides who led the way and set the standards for this northwoods institution. In June of 1944, Gordon McQuarrie offered readers of *The Milwaukee Journal* a vivid description of what he called "heartburn season." It is "co-incident with the regular seasons, and is a special season, rigidly observed by those campfire boys, the fishing guides, who load up their city charges with bacon and beans at noontime." This description, alas, falls far short of the full program, as described by the *Milwaukee Sentinel*'s Don Johnson. In July of 1981, Johnson spent a day on the flowage with Joe Golumb, whose 44 years of experience and fishing savvy earned him the reputation as one of the most highly regarded guides in the history of the flowage. The walleyes weren't biting that day, so Golumb decided that northern pike should be the "catch of the day" for the shore lunch. When they had three northerns on the stringer, the two men headed for shore. Once Golumb, who had brought along his own firewood, got the fire going, he put two "huge" skillets on it, and divided a half pound of bacon between them to create fat. The beans, in their half-opened can, went on at the same time. When the fat was ready, the bacon was removed and made available for a snack while Golumb put potatoes and chopped green onions from his garden in one skillet, and northern fillets, dredged in flour, in the other. Shortly thereafter, he served up plates heaped with fish, potatoes, and beans. Bread and butter, radishes, onions, bananas, apples, and cookies rounded out the menu. Perhaps a bit much for lunch, but then again the anglers had spent the morning in the fresh air, an experience that is said to justify almost unlimited caloric intake.

At its heart, the shore lunch has an element of risk: what if the walleyes—the preferred table fare—do not cooperate? As

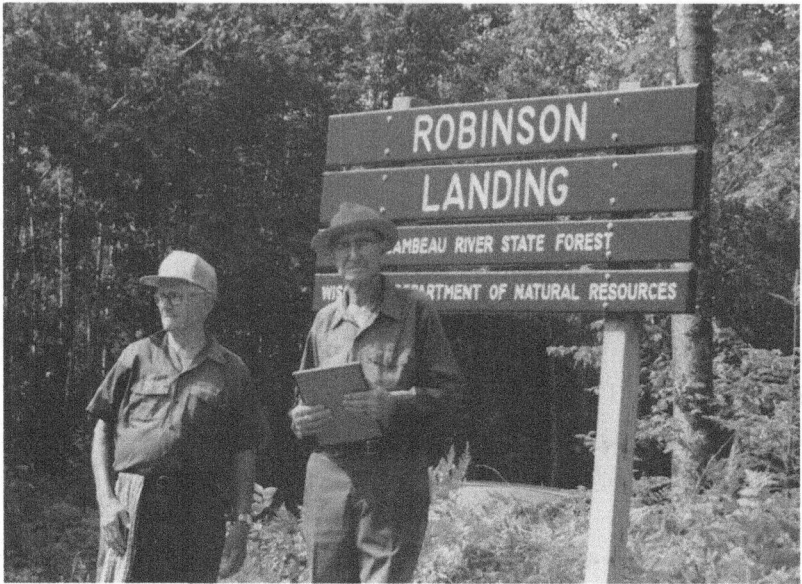

Flambeau River guide Ed Robinson (right) at the dedication of the landing named for him. Ed Beechler, another river guide, is on the left. Shane at the Midway

Johnson's story makes clear, turning to other species is the first line of defense. In this case, it was northerns, but even the rather pedestrian rock bass could be used in a pinch, as one knowledgeable party informed the author. In extreme situations, guides were forced to fall back on emergency rations from their packs. On one such occasion in 1968, Don Johnson and a photographer took a float trip on the North Fork of the Flambeau with guide Ed Robinson. The river was high and wild, and Robinson was not confident his party would catch fish. When they broke for lunch, the red-hatted guide apologetically told his party, "I wasn't too sure about you guys, so I brought along some fillets from the fish we caught yesterday." In Johnson's words, "We were not too insulted to eat at his table." Other backup menus featured meat from four-legged creatures. When Johnson had his aforementioned shore lunch feast with Joe Golumb, he noticed that one package of

An Accidental Jewel. Wisconsin's Turtle-Flambeau Flowage Flowage

food taken from Golumb's pack was not put in play. When he asked about it, Golumb replied, "Oh, that's ground beef. I stuck it in there. You never know." Sometimes steaks were on the menu from the get-go, something that made good sense when anglers were after muskies, or when they had had their fill of fish for the week. Many a T-bone sizzled away in Ed Robinson's huge, long-handled skillet on the banks of the Flambeau River. When the fish did not cooperate and there was no red meat backup, Emil Severt served his guests "cackleberries," known to most of the world as hen's eggs. With prodigious amounts of bacon and a dozen cackleberries, the starving anglers could eke by with a "shore breakfast." Indeed, one gets the sense that bacon, at least as much as fish, lay at the heart of the mystique of the shore lunch.

A shore lunch is more than just an opportunity to feed the body; it can feed the soul as well. Its elements, from preparation to cleanup, cannot be rushed; and while the guide/chef is working hard, his guests have an opportunity to explore the lunch site or to sit and observe the flowage and its natural inhabitants with a level of attention that they cannot always muster while fishing. It is also a moment to reflect on the day's happenings. In short, the very duration of the shore lunch can subtly adjust the participants to the rhythms of the natural world. But shore lunches are not without their downside. As Jerry Hartigan points out, properly done, a shore lunch takes a good two hours—not counting the lethargy or sleepiness that can follow in the wake of a bounteous midday meal. As such, the shore lunch has become, over the years, increasingly ill-matched both with the pace of life so many anglers are accustomed to and with their expectations for maximizing their time on the water during a guided day. Don Pemble notes another drawback of the shore lunch: the fish consumed during the meal count against an angler's bag limit. Those who want to take as many fish home as possible will likely find a shore lunch constraining. The upshot is that both of these guides, who have cooked many a shore lunch between them, have witnessed a steady decline in this much-beloved rite of flowage fishing. Today the shore lunch is a rarity; it has been replaced by cellophane-wrapped deli sandwiches, often wolfed down on board between casts.

Anglers as Campers:
The Ultimate Flowage Experience

Not everyone who spends a day or days fishing the flowage returns at night to the comfort of a resort cabin, a rental property, or even a home. Some head back to campfire and tent at one of the flowage's many campsites. A good argument can be made that combining fishing with camping—and especially when the camping is done on an island—is the ultimate flowage experience. And it can be habit-forming, as the saga of the Willing-Rothenberger clan so richly illustrates. In 1953, George G. Rothenberger joined his father-in-law, Ernest Willing, and two brothers-in-law, Don and George ("Cliff") Willing, on a fishing trip to the Turtle-Flambeau Flowage. They stayed at Al's Place—then under the ownership of Al and Millie Weseman—and fished with an Indian guide named Joe. Joe proved to be an ideal guide: he put them on fish, and he taught them a lot about his favorite area of the flowage—the southern end of the Big Water, including the south end of Beaver Creek. Indeed, this trip proved so successful that the four men decided to return the following year and camp on an island in the area they had fished.

In late May of 1954, the four of them pulled up on shore on an island close to Rat Lake, where campsite F-8 is located today. It is, in the words of George E. Rothenberger, son of George P., "a windy site, sheltered on the lee side by a small bay." Two considerations played into the decision to camp there. The site had to be near the area they had learned to fish the previous year, and it had to be close to a source of potable water. The latter consideration sprang from the challenge of getting all their camping gear from Al's Place (they continued to rent boats from him) to the southern end of the flowage in one trip. Their wooden boats with five-horse outboards could only carry a limited amount of equipment, and even then the trip through stumpfields and waves was slow and sometimes dicey. Carrying sufficient water for four to five days of camping would have taxed the capacity of the boats and made the trip even slower. The site they selected solved this problem. It was quite close to Pump Island, one of a number of nearby small islands where good water was readily available.

Apparently no one had camped at this spot before, and it needed some preparation. The men took down a handful of small birch and pine trees and cleared brush prior to setting up their camp. They also dug a pit some distance from the new campsite where they buried their garbage. The trip went so well that the four committed to returning the following year. Accordingly, to ease their logistical problems for the future, they stashed several items in the woods: "tables, chairs, live fish basket, toilet seat and frame, grill top for fire, etc." Little did they know what they had set in motion that year. Don and Cliff Willing and George G. Rothenberger returned annually to this campsite, sometimes bringing a guest, often a brother in law, through 1964. The following year, however, they decided to open the camp to any of their sons who had reached the age of 13. George E. Rothenberger met the criterion and joined them that year. His brothers Paul, John, and Reid were to follow as they came of age. This marked the beginning of an ever-expanding number of camper-fishermen from this family group who visited this island. It seems only natural that this campsite became, in the eyes of the Willing/Rothenberger clan, "our island," or "the island," or "unceremoniously, the Blow Hole."

Though prepared for wind and rain, the island campsite of the Willing-Rothenberger clan is here bathed in sunlight. George Rothenberger

All that is not to say that "their" island campsite remained a secret from the world. "Starting in the early 1970s we realized that someone else was using 'our' island as well," George E. writes. "Within a few years there were items added to the camping stash by others. I recall finding a full-size shovel one year and another time the fish basket was bad and needed new 2"x 4" timbers and a new screen. We brought the stuff the next year to do the repair, but the other group... had already repaired it." The two groups (assuming there were only two) never overlapped, and so these mutual benefactors remained forever anonymous to one another.

From their very first moment on the flowage, the participants in this family adventure began to weave an intricate fabric of memories, one that continues to expand, incident by incident and embellishment by embellishment, to the present day. At the center of this fabric looms, as recalled by George E., the figure of Joe, the guide who first introduced them to the flowage. "The spots we know best, all south of the dam, the names we have for spots, and fishing styles are a direct descendent of Joe's teachings. We used to fish in 'Joe's Hole,' which is a log-clogged quiet bay at the south end of Beaver Creek. We also seem to call Beaver Flats by another name, 'Northern Pines,' which all south TFF fishermen know was choked with logjams and leaners." As for fishing styles, George E. caught his first walleye on that tried-and-true flowage bait, a June Bug Spinner. And, of course, the family's founding fathers learned about Pump Island—so critical to their site selection—from Joe. This fabric also includes fond memories of Al Weseman, "a generous man." For it was from his resort that they rented boats and motors, and to his resort that they returned for much-needed showers before heading back to Illinois—but not before tipping Al amply for his assistance.

Not just people but things have earned their way into the collective memory of the Willing/Rothenberger clan as well. The 1950 Wards Sea King motor—a full five horsepower—is still operative, in spite of two seizures owing to improper oil/gas mixes. It was eventually joined by a "big motor," a 15-horse Evinrude that was purchased communally and used for runs up the flowage for boat gas and minnows. Or the automobile fuel pump that failed as the men were driving north one spring. "Popped the hood, removed air filter, emptied out coffee from coffee can, punched hole in bottom of can, poured gas in can, and GGR sat on top of the motor holding the coffee can aloft and dribbling gas in the carb as one of the others drove... a short distance, I assume." What people won't do to get to the flowage! Other memories, even succinctly recounted, are sure to trigger thoughts of "been there, done that, or almost done that" among people who have tackled the natural world head-on. "Stories would include some really tough weather, night-time crossings, a broken motor and the need to sleep on another island (slept on the rocks) until dawn, massive turtles, great and lousy fishing... and broken shear pins." As for the fishing, in the "old days" walleyes were "plentiful and largest was three lbs., huge was four lbs. Occasional small muskie. I (G.E.R) once caught a blue (aka Silver) Northern, approx. 21 inches." Smallmouth were a rarity.

Members of the Willing-Rothenberger camp head out from shore in the kind of wooden boats that once prevailed on the flowage. George Rothenberger

In the 1980s, the Willing/Rothenberger clan ran into trouble in their paradise. "None of us could catch a fish. An entire group of men could be skunked over five days and we knew the area and knew how to fish." So the group shifted their operations to various locations in the Upper Peninsula of Michigan. Then, in 1993, they decided to give the flowage another try. The fishing was good, and the men even returned in the summer, taking their wives with them to the island. In 2006, they resumed their annual trip and have not missed a year since. In recent years, they have found the fishing "better than ever," which they attribute to "better management," and they report occasionally limiting out on walleyes.

This renewed commitment to the flowage has been accompanied by a steady increase in the number of participants. By the summer of 2013, four generations of the family had camped and fished on the flowage, including the daughter of George E., who was the first female angler to join the group. Indeed, the party had grown so large that it had to occupy two different campsites—or even use a group campsite—in order to stay within current WDNR regulations for the number of campers per site. Over the years, such regulations, and others, chaffed at times on these veteran flowage campers who felt that their status as pioneers ought to have earned them an exemption here or there. One can easily understand George E.'s response when WDNR personnel stopped by at his Rat Lake campsite in 2009 and asked if this was his first year. "Whippersnappers," he called them.

The walleyes are fun to catch, and tales of quirky motors and misreads of the weather are worth the telling. But, as with most everyone who has come to know the flowage, the Willing/Rothenberger family, according to George E., has always found a deeper grounding for their attachment to this body of water: "It is the love of TFF and the ethics and generosity that the 'old men' instilled upon us that we carry to others, to enjoy this place, to respect the dangers, and experience the camaraderie and the fishing in the great outdoors.... TFF is dear to us."

Guides and Guiding

Without a doubt the Willing/Rothenberger clan demonstrated a great deal of initiative and independence as they took on the flowage over an extended period, but even they benefited at the beginning of their flowage saga from the tutelage of their guide Joe. And so it has been for many other anglers who have chosen, for various reasons, to have their contact with the flowage mediated by the talents of professional guides. In so doing, these anglers gave up the satisfactions of learning on their own (as well as avoiding the myriad mishaps lying in wait for those intent on self-instruction) in return for the opportunity to draw on the vast store of knowledge that experienced guides possessed. And that is to say nothing about the opportunity to meet some of the northwoods' most eminent characters. Happily, the flowage has had more than its share of successful guides, hard-working men whose collective legacy goes well beyond numbers of fish put in the boat, and who have, each in his own way, helped to shape the mystique of the Turtle-Flambeau Flowage.

What does it take to become a guide? The simplest answer is a license, which can be acquired from the state by anyone over the age of 18 who fills out a form and pays a fee—$40 today, only $5 back in 1957. Formalities aside, a passion for the sport, along with reliable knowledge of the water and the quarry, are two indispensable attributes of a successful guide. The passion is born into the person; the knowledge has to be acquired. Some guides, like Jerry Hartigan, learned as a youngster how to fish the flowage. He spent his summers at a family cabin on the Turtle River stretch of the flowage, fishing with family as much as humanly possible. His growing proficiency as an angler caught the attention of some nearby resort owners, who occasionally asked him, at the tender age of 10 to 12, to show resort guests some good places to fish—for which service he got some modest tips, though not guide fees. In his late teens, he began guiding in the summers, and he started full-time guiding in 1996. Later on, Hartigan built on the base of knowledge he had gained as a youth by doing creel surveys for the WDNR. This work expanded his knowledge of what was happening on the flowage, and where.

Other would-be guides benefited from informal mentors, who willingly passed on their hard-earned knowledge to novices. Earl Tomek would be a case in point. A Chicago firefighter, he came to the flowage area in 1950 with thoughts of resort ownership and guiding in mind. Tomek had the good fortune to be taken under the wing of Wilfred "Buck" Amo, the owner of Camp Buckhorn (a flowage resort). Amo taught him how to fish muskies on the flowage and on Butternut Lake, one of Amo's favorites. The lessons learned from Amo laid the foundation for Tomek's 50 years of guiding.

Bud Wahl, who took up guiding after retiring from the construction business in Chicago, owed his second career to the great Joe Golumb. Wahl had first fished the flowage in 1955, and, impressed by the walleye fishing, he bought a cabin in the Bastine area in 1960. He subsequently became close friends with Golumb, whose physical prowess, hunting and fishing skills, and rough-hewn personality Wahl had come to respect greatly. After Wahl closed up shop in Chicago in 1979, he moved full-time to the flowage. One day Golumb came by and asked Bud to help out guiding when Joe had parties too big to handle. It took some persuasion, and "about six beers," before Bud acquiesced. Bolstered by the endorsement of this renowned guide and armed with his trusty Pfleuger Supreme reel, Bud started taking out Joe's "overflow parties." Soon, however, he began to attract his own customers, and with that his career as a guide was launched.

Who taught some of the flowage's earliest guides is a matter shrouded in the mists of time, but some of these mentors certainly did their jobs well. Emil Severt, who had worked on the construction of the dam, began guiding shortly after the flowage was finished. Early on, he "commuted" to the flowage via logging railroads and found shelter "in the 'Hoodlum,' a homemade trailer house" built by his brother, Norman Severt. The Hoodlum was first parked near the dam and subsequently moved from place to place around the shores of the flowage. Emil later built his own cabin on Bastine Lake and went on to become one of the most respected and requested guides on the flowage. Another guide who looms large in legend is Gene Netzel. Described as "one of the most memorable and colorful guides," Netzel was a well-known if somewhat unpredictable presence in the Bastine Lake area. In his remembrances of Al's Place, Doug Severt, Emil's

A young Emil Severt with the uniform and tools of the trade for a day of guiding. Doug Severt

nephew, had the following to say about Netzel: "As I look back and remember Gene, he sort of reminds me of one of Blackbeard's pirates or one of those crusty old characters from the movie *Jaws*. He wasn't a bad looking man, face weathered before his time because of being out on the water so much, and he probably had a personality and vocabulary to match." Netzel enjoyed a reputation as a guide who could be counted on to come through with a full bag for his clients, time and again. "I never once fished with Gene but what we didn't come home with ten nice walleyes." Both Netzel and Severt, it should be noted, were also known for their talents as shore lunch chefs.

Passion and knowledge can make for a first-rate angler, but only when these traits are joined by people skills are the makings of a real guide fully in place. "Patience," Bud Wahl emphasizes, "a good guide has to have patience." This means, in the first instance, meeting people where they are in terms of their fishing experience and their level of commitment. Patience can take the form of putting a party of novices, with no fishing background or expectations, on to panfish for an action-filled outing. Or it can involve some narrowly focused instruction. Jerry Hartigan, for example, recalls introducing an English angler, a man who had never used anything but a fly rod, to the use of spinning tackle. Within no time, the Englishman had mastered the technique and proved to be the most successful angler in the boat that day. Patience can also mean forbearance in the face of some pretty annoying behavior by clients: this includes anglers who refuse to fish to markers that have been thrown out to indicate where the fish are lying, or anglers who fail to stick with a recommended lure and insist on switching lures practically every other cast, or anglers recently back from Canada who throw 18-inch flowage walleyes back into the water in expectation of still larger ones. The best response to such provocations, Hartigan says, is for a guide to go along agreeably, but at the same time to manage the situation so that a problem angler catches some fish. After that, tensions usually recede. Don Pemble also takes a tolerant view of another angler stereotype: the know-it-all. Sometimes, he observes, these individuals do know something (if not all of it), and one can learn from them.

Patience need not, however, be exercised to the point of indulgence. Earl Tomek had no use for "fishermen" whose main objective on the day was to drink. Though Earl himself, in his son Scott's words, was "a bartender's bartender," he did not allow any liquor in his boat. In the same vein, Don Pemble remembers one morning when he had to lay down some strict rules for a party of three. Two men were already in his boat at the dock, when the third man, clearly under the influence at this early hour, staggered from their cabin carrying a heavy cooler. He stumbled on the beach, the cooler fell and broke open, and full beer cans rolled every which way. At that point, Pemble announced that "this trip for three has become a trip for two," and he set a limit of two beers each for the two sober men in the boat. On one occasion, Pemble had to lay down the law in a way that crossed state lines. At the beginning of the morning while in the bait shop, he had warned two Indiana fishermen that the weather would be cold and rainy and asked if they had sufficient clothing. They answered affirmatively, pointing out that they had trash bags to use as parkas! Although Pemble repeatedly urged the men to outfit themselves with more appropriate gear, they insisted they were good to go. Several times during the day, he asked if the men were all right, and they assured him they were. By midafternoon, however, the two Hoosiers, soaked through and frozen, asked to be taken to their motel to get warm and to don dry clothing before resuming fishing. Pemble agreed to take them in and to cut the day—and the guide fee—by one hour; but he refused to return with them to the water. Once on shore, the men paid by check and headed for hot showers. Pemble deposited the check, only to learn several days later that the check writer had put a stop order on it. When he called to ask what was up, he was told that the two anglers were considering suing him because they had suffered hypothermia. Pemble reminded them that people in the bait shop had witnessed his efforts to encourage them to take more suitable clothing and that he had been solicitous of their welfare throughout the day. He also told them that he had "friends" where they lived—who would be happy to collect the money from them. Pemble got his money.

Guides themselves are not, of course, beyond error when it comes to getting along with their guests. Jerry Hartigan recalls, with a laugh, some "rookie mistakes" he made. "Never say to your party, 'You should have been here yesterday'—especially not early in the day." Nothing can deflate expectations like this phrase, which can imply that it is hardly worth continuing the day on the water. Nor should a guide ask his party, "Where do you want to go?" The question is genuine and legitimate, in that it seeks to find out what kind of water the party would like to fish, such as shorelines or deep water; but the takeaway for many clients is that the guide has no idea where to go and is asking them to do his job! Guides must also be careful not to put clients in situations that can be frustrating or discouraging. On the flowage, this means trying to keep folks from incessantly hanging up and losing lures. No matter how much a guide may reassure someone that snags and lost tackle come hand in hand with the flowage experience, some people feel guilty about going through a lot of terminal gear. Hartigan tries, through his choice of fishing methods, to keep his guests fishing as cleanly as they can in order to free them from bottom phobia and guilt trips. However hard they may try to keep their customers happy, even guides with lots of experience under their belts can still do something, quite by accident, that rubs someone the wrong way. Vadim, a Russian from Latvia, had the good luck to hook and land a trophy smallmouth—21 and 1/8 inches—while fishing with Hartigan. After measuring and admiring the fish, Hartigan released it without having explained to Vadim that he routinely encourages anglers to return to the water large spawners (especially walleyes, but this time a bass). Vadim was not a happy camper for the remainder of the day; yet he seems to have mellowed following the experience, as he fished with Hartigan again the next year.

All told, however, difficult clients and moments of tension and conflict were few and far between in the memories of guides. Those interviewed for this book, as well as ones who have gone on record elsewhere, speak emphatically about how much they enjoyed the people who fished with them and about what good and enduring friendships grew out of their hours on the water together. Though guiding was his second career, Bud Wahl has made friends with anglers from Iowa, Indiana, and Illinois, as well as Wisconsin; and he receives calls and notes from some of them throughout the year. For Don Pemble, meeting new people from all walks of life and chewing the fat with them about everything from aches and pains to the joys of fishing stands at the heart of the guiding experience. That, and the pleasure that comes from being in the boat year after year with return customers who have become friends. Ed Robinson had no complaints about his customers, who ranged from Dennis Morgan and New York models to anglers from England, Sweden, Germany, Russia, Japan, Africa, Australia, and Canada. One can only imagine the rich texture of the dialogue that took place daily in these guides' boats—some fish talk here, a bit of business chatter there, a level of banter that surely increased in proportion to familiarity of the participants, and, when no women were present, the inevitable guy talk. Only guides with genuine people skills could elicit such rich and varied conversations from their guests—all the while attending to the business of catching fish.

·-◦◉◦-·

One customer, rather more infamous than famous, perhaps warrants special mention: namely, Al Capone. Two area guides, Ray "Blacky" Schwartz and Mitch Babic, lay claim to having fished with the mobster, though Schwartz told an interviewer for *The Milwaukee Journal* in 1991 that "there's nobody guided Capone but me." Whether or not his claim to be Capone's only guide is correct, Schwartz seems to have satisfied his customer's expectations. For at a time (possibly the 1940s) when the standard fees for guides ranged between $3 and $5 a day, Capone paid him $20 dollars for each outing, plus a $20 dollar tip—"always in two brand-new $20 dollar bills." Schwartz's secret may well have been knowing enough not to jabber away at the gangster, whose taciturn manner was only occasionally interrupted by some pithy comment. In describing an outing with Al and his brother, Ralph, Schwartz said that "Ralph was the talker. We fished back and forth. I'd row and Al just trolled a minnow. He didn't cast at all. He had big hands and big eyebrows." Babic saw things in a different light. "The Capone brothers, they were all nice except Al. You know, I spent a week with him and every morning I'd go in and say 'good morning Al,' and he never once answered me." Taciturn or rude, Al Capone was clearly a personality to be reckoned with.

--◆--

While flowage guides had many traits in common, they also had their share of idiosyncrasies that distinguished them from one another and that earned some of them a lasting place in flowage lore. To illustrate this point, one might well begin with a look at some of the many faces of Joe Popko—guide, resort owner, and relentless fisherman—as remembered by a young Joe Aski: There is Popko getting a head start on the day by stopping by the Askis' cabin each morning to have a nip of a good whiskey that one member of the Aski party, a liquor distributor, had brought with him for the week; there is the jaunty and fearless Popko steering his outboard while standing up—presumably to watch for the stumps and debris that still littered the flowage in the 1950s; and there is Popko, the fishing addict, who at the conclusion of a long day of guiding could think of nothing better to do than to take his wife out fishing. Legend has it that when Popko once visited a dentist, the latter, to make conversation, asked Joe what he did for a living. Popko's response was short but true: "I fish walleyes."

Joe Miller, guide, resort owner, sometime hunter, and avid trapper, counted among his many talents the ability to spin some tall tales. As one person who knew him observed, "Joe wore a lot of different boots. And it's a good thing, too, because he was a master of BS." This author remembers his two sons listening wide-eyed as Miller told them that flowage muskies were so plentiful in the old days that almost no effort was needed to catch them in winter. "We drilled a few holes, and the muskies just popped up through them onto the ice." He also claimed that the WDNR was netting deer in deer-poor Iron County and transferring them to deer-rich Waupaca County. No matter that the

Resort owner and guide Joe Miller displays two 50-inch class muskies. Carol Zilinger and Carla Kloess

agency was paying Waupaca farmers huge sums to compensate them for crop damages from an outsized deer herd. Not only did Joe have the imagination to come up with these stories, but he also had the ability to rattle them off as if he were speaking the word of God. Neither the slightest twinkle of an eye nor the trace of a smile crossed his face at such moments.

Earl Tomek, like many other successful northwoods people, was a hard worker who did whatever it took to provide for his family in this remote setting. Sometimes this meant working at the St. Croix factory in Park Falls, other times working winters in the woods, and still other times caretaking for the Blue X Club. And, of course, he and his wife ran Tomek's Old Log Inn bar and restaurant (where Camp One now stands). Earl brought this same seriousness of purpose to his guiding. "When you paid him money, you were going to fish," his son Scott says. "He made you work. Some of them [customers] came back and weren't too happy with getting yelled at." Bud Sivertson, a veteran northwoods angler who had fished with Tomek, tells of an occasion when one of Earl's clients snubbed a musky, broke the line, and lost the fish. At an appropriate moment later in the day, Earl pulled out the man's shirttail and cut off a triangular piece of cloth with his knife. This was vintage Earl, who had long since practiced this little stunt on hunting companions who had missed deer. Indeed, many a shirttail remnant contributed to the décor of Earl's establishment. On balance, however, Tomek's customers "came back from a day on the water happy, with a fish, or with stories about catching fish." And some of his parties even saw quite another side to him. "Earl Tomek used to guide the river [North Fork of the Flambeau], too. He would always stop at a particular idyllic place and cast all around. After about 15 minutes he'd light his pipe, lean back and say, 'Never caught a fish here—but it sure is pretty, isn't it?'"

The beauty of the river that struck a chord with Earl Tomek was but part of a larger appreciation for nature that all generations of area guides have shared. Don Pemble speaks, almost reverently, of the quiet of the flowage, of the sight of resident ospreys and eagles—including a pet eagle that comes to his whistle for an occasional rock bass handout—and of migrants such as egrets, swans, and pelicans. And then there are the occasional encounters with swimming bears, mink, deer, or moose. Not surprisingly, protecting all the natural resources of the flowage environment, from fish to birds to mammals, is high on his agenda. He puts his trust in proper management of the waters and vigorous enforcement of fish and game laws to assure that the fishery and its setting remain a healthy, productive ecosystem. Jerry Hartigan, whose background includes an undergraduate degree in wildlife biology and field research on flowage loons and eagles, finds his clients quite receptive to his biological explanations for various wildlife behaviors they encounter on the water. Clearly, for these two currently active guides, showing clients the flowage entails a much broader agenda than just finding suitable places to wet a line.

No single anecdote can fully capture what the flowage, as a whole, meant to guides and their customers, but the following one comes close. According to Bud Wahl, his most memorable guiding experience occurred one October day when he took a man and his wife down to Beaver Flats to fish. While the man fished, the woman clutched her camera and indicated that what would make the day for her would be the opportunity to photograph some of the flowage's non-finny wildlife. Wahl was much too experienced on the water and in the field to think that nature's creatures can be summoned on command, but he also knew that sometimes those creatures can be inexplicably cooperative. And so it was on this day. A group of passing otters gave the woman her first opportunity to snap away. Then came a handsome buck, swinging his antlers as he stood on the shoreline not more than 20 feet away. Click, click. Next, a flowage eagle held its perch on a towering white pine until the customer took yet another "poster shot." This photographic grand slam concluded when a pair of loons persisted in popping up and down next to the boat, giving the now ecstatic shutterbug a chance to get some classic loon shots. Bud remembers the ride back up from the flats that afternoon as particularly rough, but no complaints came from his customers. Indeed, the wife conveyed her satisfaction with the day so enthusiastically to her husband that he left Bud with the biggest tip of his entire guiding career. Fish never entered the telling of this story. But, judging from the delight in Bud's eyes as he recounted the events that day, fish had little to do with it. What mattered was his wonder, and gratitude, that everything had fallen in place so that he could share with his guiding party some of the true riches of a world he knows and loves.

Don Pemble's words seem an apt conclusion to this discussion of guides and guiding. "It's such a beautiful body of water and I'm thankful I am part of it and that I can show other people what I can enjoy in a day's time. And what's enjoyable then are the rebookings, and making these people friends, and keeping these friends. It's a great way to make a living. It can be tough at times, but it can be very rewarding." Tough but rewarding is an equally apt characterization of the flowage itself.

The Driftwood Lodge Club

In the early 1920s, William Siegert of Milwaukee heard that an impoundment was to be built in Iron County and promptly purchased 40 acres for $40 in a location that promised waterfront access to its waters (roughly speaking, along the passageway from Merkle Lake into the Norway Point area of the flowage). In 1937, under Siegert's leadership, this property was incorporated as the Driftwood Lodge Club. Modeled along the lines of both the Jerome and Merkle Lake fishing and hunting clubs, the Driftwood Lodge Club served as a base camp for the activities of the 10 dedicated outdoorsmen who made up its membership. They hunted deer, bear, grouse, and ducks; and they fished for walleyes, crappies, and, of course, muskies. The hundreds of photographs now in the possession of Siegert's grandson, Robert Dralle, testify to the success of their activities: handsome bucks, groaning stringers of crappies and walleyes, and a tiger muskie that was at least 48 inches, caught by "Musky Bill" himself.

The guys from the Driftwood Lodge Club display a bountiful take from a day in the outdoors. Robert and Lisa Dralle

The camp flourished when regulations were fewer and enforcement less vigorous than is the case today. And so it was that in a low water year in the 1940s, Bill Siegert brought laborers, machinery, and material up from Milwaukee to bulldoze all the stumps and rocks out of the bay in front of the property (the rocks ended up in a pile that even today warrants a marker buoy) and then constructed a concrete block wall all along the waterfront. The coming winter's ice proved no respecter of expert masonry, however, and took out the entire wall. Then there was one fall when some of the members arrived apparently unnoticed in Mercer and headed promptly to the waters below the Lake of the Falls Dam. There they prepared a setline for sturgeon, part rope, part dog chain, and arrayed with hooks baited with chicken parts. They tied one end of the line to a stump, and secured the other end to a boulder. In a few weeks the men returned and retrieved through the ice two sturgeon whose total weight came to 180 pounds. The sturgeon, duly smoked and elegantly presented, next debuted at the Masonic Hall in Milwaukee at a holiday gala open only to guests who had been personally vetted by Siegert. This enterprising man also arranged one of the more colorful deer drives known to have occurred in the area, when he persuaded a camp of loggers working the Big Island to drive the entire island while beating pots and pans from their cookshack. Driftwood Lodge Club members, strategically posted on the ice off the island, had some fine shooting as the animals emerged from the woods onto the frozen flowage.

After 1945, the wives of the club members expressed an interest in coming up as well, especially if certain amenities could be provided. Thereupon the club divided the property into 10 four-acre sections, and each member put up a cabin on his parcel. The hunting and fishing did not abate with the arrival of the women, but some more genteel practices did emerge. Siegert built a large boat, named *The Queen Mary*, on which the members and their wives cruised the flowage, martinis in hand. And with a nudge from the distaff side, club members provided safe harbor and provisions for the many canoeing parties—mostly Boy Scouts and Girl Scouts—who were forced to take shelter from weather just across the bay from the club.

Summers spent at the club teemed with one fabulous experience after another for an outdoor-loving boy like Rob Dralle. There were the local characters: Checky, of the resort of the same name; Joe Popko, whose new resort was next door; Hugo, a resident of Yugoslavian background whose topless Elcho outboard could be heard from an amazing distance; Warden Holger, a frequent visitor to the camp; Selma Ingevold, a neighbor who made excellent snapper soup from critters "Musky Bill" did in with some heavy slug loads; and a celebrity or two, such as Tommy Gettelman of the brewing company and Governor Warren

Knowles. But Rob's most vivid memories came from visits to nearby Flam-Bow Resort, owned at that time by Bill and Marj Tutt. On one occasion, Rob and his mother walked over to the resort only to find a group of men, including Bill Tutt and the world-famous bowhunter, Fred Bear, sitting around a table fletching arrows and talking about nothing but game and fish. Life could not get more exciting than that for a young lad, unless it was when Tutt's musky bell rang out, calling the neighborhood to see the latest trophy. As Dralle puts it, the Driftwood Lodge Club was "ALL about huntin' and fishin.'" Today, the narrow, tree-lined road that leads to

William "Musky Bill" Siegert, the founder of the Driftwood Lodge Club and an ardent sportsman. Robert and Lisa Dralle

the property bears the name Siegert's Boulevard, honoring both the memory of the founder of the club and the insouciant spirit of its members. The boulevard also serves as a veritable memory lane, one that leads to the site of over 75 consecutive years of vintage flowage experiences.

CHAPTER THREE
Flowage Resorts Up Close

Art Schmidt and Al Koshak: Pioneers and Pals

Perhaps the best way to capture the essential character of flowage resorts is to examine the origins and development of a couple of the earliest ones—Art Schmidt's Muskie Camp and Al's Place. That neither place bore some generic name—like Whispering Pines or Sunset Shores—reflects the fact that their two founders were creators, not just owners, and that they were more than willing to be identified with their work. The story begins, then, with Art Schmidt and Al Koshak, two young men, who, with the aid and support of their wives, created vibrant resorts on the shores of the newly created flowage. They were, in effect, pioneers—literally in the sense of their self-reliant lives, and figuratively for their role in the nascent flowage resort industry.

Art Schmidt was born in 1908 in the town of Eisenstein, just to the east of Park Falls. After completing the sixth grade, Art worked in the area for a while, then sought his fortune in the West—in California and Washington state. In 1929 or 1930, he returned to the Park Falls area and in 1931 married Katherine Ernst. Shortly thereafter, he obtained, through a long-term lease from Wisconsin Realty, control over a parcel of land in the Bastine Lake area of the flowage and boldly began to put together Art Schmidt's Muskie Camp.

Initially the camp consisted of a number of tents, a couple of cabins, one of which had the bar, and a few rental boats. The owner and his wife—and from 1932 on, their son Art Jr.—occupied the other cabin. According to Art Jr., the lakeside cabin in which he was raised was far from airtight. When the wind blew, "the curtains stuck straight out." And he recalls his father's claim—perhaps a bit embellished—that there was once a snowdrift in his son's crib. The next step in the creation of the resort came with the building of a lodge—which housed a bar, dining room, and rooms for guests. Schmidt hired some carpenters from Eisenstein to do the work, but the wood—a lot of it hemlock—came from his property and had been run through his own sawmill. And then, incrementally, year by year, additional cabins were constructed.

The initial success of the enterprise prompted Schmidt to seek full title to his land. To do so, he borrowed $10,000 from a logger and timber broker by the name of Charlie Patterson. With that stake he purchased from the Wisconsin Realty Company on June 1, 1937, the property on which his fledgling resort was located and some adjacent property as well—for a total of 159.3 acres. Securing a loan of that magnitude while the country was in the teeth of the Depression was no small feat. There seems little doubt that Art's energy, vision, work ethic, and winning personality were already evident before he had reached 30 years of age. To ease the burden of the loan, he sold off some of the land, and then proceeded to further develop his resort.

Around 1940, the lodge was expanded to include a new kitchen and barroom. Beyond adding space, this renovation was the occasion for the crafting of an imposing stone bar and fireplace by Carl Nove, an area stonemason of considerable talent and repute. In this striking work, Nove created mosaics of various animals by setting small stones in cement panels three or four feet square. Inexplicably, however, these were African animals—lions, giraffes, and tigers to name a few—not the northwoods animals one might expect. (In the adjacent dining room, a mosaic panel featured a leopard, whose disproportionately small head reminded at least one observer of a frog.) The highlight of Nove's work was a stone mosaic depicting the head of an American Indian—carefully inset into the stones of the exterior of the chimney. The whole ensemble of mosaics became a signature landmark of Art Schmidt's Muskie Camp.

A stone mosaic giraffe overlooks the bar at Schmidt's resort. Doug Severt

Carl Nove's stone image of an American Indian became a signature feature of Art Schmidt's Muskie Camp. Neil Koshak

Al Koshak was born in the Town of Lake, west of Park Falls, in 1901. Leaving school after the seventh grade, he went to work with his father in the woods, cutting timber and skidding the logs out with oxen. In 1928, after a summer of working at Behr's Resort on the Chippewa Flowage (he guided by day and washed dishes at night), Al married Charlotte Van Camp of Draper, Wisconsin, who had grown up near Park Falls and had just completed her schooling as a beautician in Chicago. It was a classic elopement, with the couple tying the knot across the border in Minnesota.

After their marriage, Charlotte went to work at Bessie Goodin's beauty parlor (The Powder Puff) in Park Falls, and Al found work logging and as a temporary foreman for the Wisconsin Conservation Department. Soon, however, the idea of establishing a resort on the flowage came to dominate his thinking, and Al secured a 99-year lease in 1931 with either the Wisconsin Realty Company or the Chippewa and Flambeau Improvement Company (whichever entity had formal title to the land) for a parcel of land in the Bastine Lake area of the flowage that looked directly across to Big Island. The property, at one time in the possession of a homesteader, was mostly open, with few trees of any significance. At times of low water, the remnants of the homesteader's root cellar could be seen about 100 feet from shore. It was on this shore that Al Koshak set out to build a resort.

The initial steps were predictably modest. By 1933 an advertisement for Al's Landing (soon to become Al's Place) boasted of a boat landing, a bar, and hamburgers! The food and drinks were served in a 16-by-16-foot cabin that Al built and lived in during the summer months. But his commitment to the enterprise was unflagging, and so in that same year Charlotte set aside the career for which she had been schooled and joined him. Her reminiscences of that decision and its consequences tell it all. In spite of having done "a little fishing and played a little baseball" while growing up, she considered herself to have been "a perfect greenhorn" when it came to living in fairly primitive conditions and learning the ways of the woods. And as time went on and she found herself engaged in "everything" by way of work, she said she often wondered: "What ails me...to come up here [from Park Falls to the Flowage!] and scrub and make beds?" What ailed her, of course, was a firm resolve to work alongside her husband, Al, to make the place a success. And indeed they did. By 1935, Al had become sufficiently confident in the venture that he "pestered" Wisconsin Realty, which held the deed at that time, to sell the property for $1,500.

Each winter Al worked in the woods for the Hines Lumber Company, sometimes near Loretta, Wisconsin, sometimes in upper Michigan, visiting home for about 24 hours each week. Come spring, he returned to the flowage, built another cabin of spruce hewn with a veteran axe with a large letter K stamped on it, and made other improvements to the operation. Charlotte, for her part, tended bar, kept the books, drove on what amounted to a glorified fire lane to Mercer to pick up guests and bring them back to the resort, and managed the help in Al's absences. Apparently, Al was more than happy to see her assume the latter task, as he once remarked that "it is easier to handle 60

Al Koshak pulls a beer in the company of his wife, Charlotte, and son, Neil, in the bar at Al's Place. *Neil Koshak*

men in the woods than six girls in a resort." In the summer of 1937, Al built a lodge that could serve 100 meals a day; and he expanded the staff to 15. By 1947, Al's Place had a lodge, 13 cabins, a "girls' cabin" for the housekeepers and dining room workers, a laundry, an icehouse, a garage, 20 boats, and about a dozen motors and a sand beach—thanks to several loads of sand that Al dumped into the small bay that marked their waterfront. In addition, there was a small home for Al and Charlotte and their son, Neil, who was born in 1935 and lived full-time at the flowage from 1938 to 1947. Thanks to relentless hard work, Al's Place had become, in Charlotte's words, "a divin' roarin' place."

Art Schmidt and Al Koshak were certainly cut from different pieces of cloth—at least to hear the two of them described by their sons. Art was "ready to stick his neck out" and "ready to take chances;" he was the kind of guy who could have it all one day and nothing the next, according to Art Jr. He also could "do it all." After selling his camp in 1945, Art subsequently obtained a pilot's license and worked both as a licensed surveyor and a real estate broker. Neil Koshak remembers Art as a skilled promoter, citing his talent for whipping up enthusiasm for his camp and other ventures. And Art seemed to know just how to jolly people along, such as the client who inquired how the cabin Art was building for him was coming along. Though construction had yet to start, Art confidently sent the man the door key. But it was the big, affable personality, recalls Neil, that stands out most: "Everyone liked Art Schmidt."

Al, for his part, was "more the hard-nosed businessman." "He could smell a dollar over a hill," says his son, Neil. He would never, as Art was reputed to have done, have carried his money in a paper envelope rather than in a wallet. In addition to his business sense, Al had both the work ethic and skills needed to carry the burdens of resort building on his own shoulders. And he, too, enjoyed the kind of versatility so necessary to making a go of it in the northwoods. In 1937, Al took in his brother, George, as a partner in a logging business, and the Koshak Brothers operated until shortly after Al sold the resort in 1947. The brothers then incorporated as Koshak Construction Company, Inc., "Dirt Movers," which proved to be a successful earthmoving business. Though technically competitors, Al Koshak and Art Schmidt developed a deep personal friendship—in part out of their shared love for and knowledge of the outdoors, in part out of respect for each other's talents, hard work, and achievements.

What was true for these men was true for their families as well. Katy Schmidt and Charlotte Koshak both bore the heavy burdens of resort management and child-rearing. And their sons, Art Jr.—known then as Arty—and Neil, became playmates and schoolmates, and lived, in summers at least, a truly idyllic childhood. It would be highly misleading, however, to suggest that family life at these two resorts was a piece of cake. In the final analysis, the Schmidts and the Koshaks—and to some extent their guests, too—had to abandon the amenities of town and city and live like pioneers.

In the early years at Al's Place, the cabins lacked running water. All water came from the spigot of a single well. In summer, the cabin boy delivered water by the bucket to guest quarters, as well as a chunk of ice for the icebox. The absence of running water meant, of course, outside toilets for owners and guests alike. At Art Schmidt's Muskie Camp there was one large outhouse, which did have running water to sinks. But the facility could only accommodate so many people; and, as Art Jr. puts it, "There were times you had to stand in line." By 1947, Al Koshak had managed to "modernize" (a euphemism for indoor plumbing) three of his rental units, but wartime shortages of pipes and fixtures hindered further progress. At Schmidt's, the outside toilet was still in operation in 1945; and as late as 1960, Al's Place had a few remaining but functional outhouses—though all of the cabins had been retrofitted by then with indoor plumbing.

The other essentials, beside water and toilets, were heat and light. Both resorts employed wood stoves in the cabins, and wood stoves and fireplaces in their lodges. Firewood, of course, was readily available. Neil Koshak remembers his father and helpers corralling vast amounts of cedar in the flowage—trees that had been too small to harvest at the time the flowage was constructed—and dragging the boom to shore where the trees were cut up for firewood. To provide light, the resorts generated their own electricity. Windmills, about 80 feet in height, charged a bank of commercial storage batteries. These batteries, in turn, powered a 32-volt DC system that brought light to the cabins. This was a well-proven system that lighted as many as a million American farms prior to rural electrification. Gasoline or diesel generators produced 110-volt AC for the lodges. A six-cylinder Chevrolet gasoline engine generated 110 at Koshak's, while a four-cylinder diesel engine did the job at Schmidt's. Years later, this diesel engine was to cost the life of a subsequent owner of Schmidt's camp, a man by the name of George Greiner. He cranked away at the stubborn machine, which just wouldn't start, until exhaustion set in. Greiner went to bed and never woke up. The best machine, perhaps, was a Kohler unit at Shady Rest Resort, next door to Al's Place. A pull on a small cord set the generator in action.

Connections between these early resorts and the outside world left a lot to be desired. A promotional piece from Al's Place boasts, in big letters, "Good Road." Not so, says Neil Koshak. "That's a bald-faced lie!" The dirt and sand road surfaces, studded with rocks and boulders from the area's glacial till, readily deteriorated under heavy rains. Washouts and potholes were commonplace. Infrequent plowing added to the basic challenges of winter driving, but spring road conditions were by far the worst. As the frost left the ground from the surface, a soupy, greasy mixture of soil and rocks literally floated atop the deep frost. Art Schmidt Jr. remembers springtime potholes "a hundred feet long." In these conditions, his father would order all passengers out of the vehicle, then run wide open through the slop. Once back on solid ground, he would stop and wait for his passengers, who had circumvented the mess on foot. When they were back on board, off he would drive to town, or to another pothole, whichever came first. In Neil Koshak's remembrances, Netzel Hill on County Trunk F, between Midway Lodge and Deer Creek, "used to be about impossibly muddy in the spring." Travelers through this area often found themselves dependent on the assistance of a nearby resident, Martha Netzel, the mother of Eugene Netzel, guide and northwoods character. Martha was a sturdy, somewhat rough woman, given to wearing overalls and boots, but she was also a helpful soul. When an automobile bogged down at this particular location on F, she would connect the disabled vehicle to her team of horses and command the team to "Get up, you SOBs!"

Needless to say, the bad roads and the necessity of hauling everything from resort supplies to spare tires made pickup trucks the vehicle of choice—whether Ford, International, or Dodge. The pickup box also served, on occasion, to transport the boys to the nearest school—aptly, or wishfully, named the Smart School. Some of the pupils, including Art Schmidt Jr. and Louie Ledvina, rode to the school for a few years in the bed of Joe Ledvina's Model A pickup truck. No doubt that was a brisk ride in the winter, even at the relatively slow speeds dictated by poor road conditions. By the time Neil Koshak entered first grade, the students enjoyed the luxury of a proper 12-passenger school bus.

Like so many other features of everyday life, telephone service came slowly to the flowage. The first line, essentially a private one built to connect the dam keeper with the world, ran 18 miles from the dam keeper's house to the paper mill in Park Falls. In 1935, Al Koshak spent the winter at the flowage, while Charlotte, who was expecting, moved into Park Falls shortly before her due date to guard against being snowed in. It was only when Emil Severt, a local guide, skied to Al's Place from the dam that Al learned he was a father. Shortly thereafter, several branch lines were added, bringing service to the Koshak, Schmidt, Stangle, and Ledvina residences. The battery-powered phones had to be cranked into action, and even then the results left a lot to be desired. "If you had to holler any louder," Neil Koshak recalls, "you wouldn't have needed a phone." The ring at the Koshak residence was "three shorts."

"A little bit snowed in," is how Charlotte Koshak described winters at the flowage. Indeed, only a handful of people could be described as full-time residents in the 1940s. Besides the dam keeper, Neil Koshak recalls only his family, the Schmidts, the Millers (about whom more follows shortly), and the Popkos. Schmidt's lodge remained open through the winter with their ice toboggan slide serving as an attraction for those looking for a weekend outing. Initially, there was little ice fishing, though Art eventually got that going. Entertainment for the year-round residents involved visiting neighbors and, on Saturday nights, going dancing at Carl Newell's bar. It was a log cabin located on what is today Ashland County Highway F, on the north side of the road opposite the current Midway. This seems to have been the "happening" spot on cold winter evenings. For certain, these hard-working resort pioneers deserved some restorative socializing during the long northwoods winters.

Duff Downey and Joe Miller: Colorful Bastine Lake Resort Owners

The third resort to spring up in the Bastine area, Downey Brothers' Shady Rest, was owned and operated by Marvin "Duff" Downey and his wife, Mary. Legend has it that Downey, a Chicago area native, had, with the aid of a shotgun, supervised the comportment of guests at a dance hall known to be patronized by local wise guys. Put another way, he is supposed to have had ties with some of Chicago's Prohibition-era gangsters. Whatever the merits of this story, what is for sure is that Downey, who purchased property immediately adjacent to Al's Place, brought a bit of Chicago attitude to the flowage. Shortly after Downey's arrival, Al Koshak found a sawhorse with a "road closed" sign across the driveway that led to the two properties. Downey, it seems, considered the road to be on his property and decided to close it to his neighbor/competitor. It may well be that Downey thought the situation might be resolved in the Chicago fashion with a cash payment from his neighbor. But whether this was the case or not, Koshak responded with an end run. He headed to the town hall and laid out his predicament to the local authorities. There he was assured that if he were to improve the road—by adding enhancements such as gravel and culverts—the local authorities would declare it a town road. Al got the work done promptly, the town kept its bargain, and the problem was resolved for good.

Duff Downey, by all accounts, seems to have been a reclusive type who often lurked behind the curtains near the bar, as if to remain invisible. He interacted little with his guests and seemed to some who encountered him to be a bit on the menacing side. Whenever he got wind that his resort might be paid a visit by some folks from Chicago, he retreated to a small cabin on what was known as Duff's Island, presumably for safety. It was up to his wife, Mary, to carry the resort on her shoulders, which she did admirably thanks to an ever-mellowing personality that former guests remember fondly. As the Downeys departed the flowage at the end of each season, they did not participate in the winter rituals of the full-time residents and as a result were not a part of the small and close-knit community of resort owners.

Another resort owner in the Bastine Lake area who could lay claim to pioneer status was Joe Miller. Originally from the Chicago area, Joe found himself in the 1930s living on the family farm in the town of Agenda with his wife, Gertrude. An avid outdoorsman, Joe was equally at home fishing, hunting, or running a trap line. He did some guiding in the area, and he provided minnows on a wholesale basis to the Schmidt and Koshak camps. (His daughter Millie worked for a while for Art Schmidt.) Also an able craftsman, Joe helped in the construction of Downey's Shady Rest. Having been associated with these resorts and having watched them grow and prosper, Joe eventually decided to build one of his own. A piece of land on the north side of Lake Bastine caught his eye, and he took his daughter to see it. "Let's buy this, Butch," he told Millie, calling her by her pet name. And buy it he did. In 1939, Joe closed a deal with the Wisconsin Central Railroad for the 141-acre parcel and set about clearing the land and preparing to build.

From there on, the story is a familiar one: work and more hard work. The land was made suitable for construction with axes, shovels, and grub hoes. Wood for the cabins came mostly from Joe's land, along with some salvaged from the area. The icehouse—a resort essential—was the first building to be put up, followed shortly by the first cabin and a residence for the owner's family. The resort welcomed its first guests in 1942. All this work was done with planes, handsaws, and hand drills. Along the way, he accumulated a sizeable store of nuts and bolt, screws and nails, and parts for this and that. This stash saved numerous trips to town over the infamous local roads, and proved valuable not only for building but also for the never-ending maintenance that attended resort ownership. Joe also fashioned his own flat-bottomed boats, his preferred model for fishing the stumpy flowage. In short, as Joe's daughter Millie put it, "He done a lot of work." Though Joe never stopped working until his death in 1993, he did receive more than a little help along the way from family.

In the 1960s, the fifth and final cabin was built, bringing the total number of buildings at the resort to five cabins, a house for the owners, and assorted outbuildings. The cabins had two bedrooms and a living area equipped with all the facilities needed for housekeeping. Each cabin could accommodate four to five people, or more when guests arrived with cribs. Over time the older cabins were fully electrified—Rural Electric Administration lines got to this area in 1948—and retrofitted with indoor plumbing. For more than four decades, Joe Miller's cabins operated without a bar—though a large room adjacent to the owners' quarters served as a gathering spot for social events and a place to get ice cream and malted milks. Eventually the resort obtained a liquor license that had migrated from Shady Rest to Lakeview to Miller's. One other addition to the resort deserves particular note. In response to the rising popularity of camping, Joe Miller's added a campground in 1992. Initially it accommodated mostly tents and a few camper units, but in time the facility was modified to include 16 permanent places, each with water and electricity. Moreover, the introduction of the campground diversified the resort's offerings, enabling it to serve a significantly larger clientele.

In 2010, Joe Miller's Resort and Campground celebrated its 68th year of continuous operation, and it could lay claim to being the only resort still in existence to have been operated by one family. For this achievement, the resort received a Cornerstone of the Community Award from the town of Mercer. The obvious explanation for this achievement would be customer satisfaction, but it is what lies behind this satisfaction that tells the deeper story. Managing a resort "is 24/7, with no time for yourself," the family emphasized in an interview. Everyone has to do something. Moreover, no resort can succeed without someone on the premises who can do just about anything. Joe Miller was just such a man, and the operation he started greatly benefited from the presence of similar individuals in subsequent generations of the family.

❖

Success for the early flowage resorts depended on relentless hard work—with only the occasional respite—and an optimistic frame of mind on the part of the owners and their families. But something else was at play here that contributed to the success of the Koshaks, Schmidts, Downeys, Millers, and others: namely, the spirit of cooperation that was the hallmark of so many pioneer communities. The examples are many. When would-be guests showed up at a resort that had no vacancies, the owner would be on the phone immediately to try to find a vacancy at one of the nearby resorts. Helping hands were always available for a project beyond the resources of one person. Even financial support figured in the equation. Al Koshak, for example, made numerous loans to Harold Boyington (described by Charlotte Koshak as a "pompous Englishman") to the point where he ended up taking out a second mortgage on Boyington's resort. (This relationship did end, far from satisfactorily, when Boyington departed the area.) Perhaps the signature communal activity was the annual making of ice. When the flowage froze to a depth of around a foot or a bit more, the resort owners hauled out their ice machine—a

Chevy engine that drove a big circular saw blade. Once grooves had been cut in the ice, chisels were used to loosen it up. The ice blocks were transferred into trucks by means of another cobbled-together device and then delivered to the respective resorts. In the coming year, the ice would cool iceboxes in cabins, keep fish fresh, and chill whiskey sours at resort bars. Work-related cooperation spilled over into the social lives of these families as well—whether child sitting, spontaneous visits, or weekly get-togethers at a local watering hole. This strong sense of community—so highly emphasized by those who remember the early days—not only helped these resorts manage in sometimes trying conditions, but it led to numerous deep and lasting relationships. Today's resort owners who can recall stories of those times or who experienced them firsthand lament the absence of such a spirit today.

The Browns and the Boths: Latecomers to the Resort Business

There is a certain romance to the stories of early resort owners who built their establishments from the ground up by their own labors. But that certainly was not the experience of the vast majority of resort owners. Most of them bought going businesses whose owners had decided, for any number of reasons, that it was time to sell out. Without a doubt, the attraction of owning a business in the magical northwoods exerted a powerful allure on those who were eager to escape the urban grind; and there was no shortage of potential buyers when resorts went on the market. Two families who responded to the draw of the north, bought resorts, and managed them successfully were the Browns and the Boths.

Rodney Brown and his wife, Maryann, who purchased the Lakeview Resort on Bastine in 1976, fit in many ways the broad profile of those who took over established resorts. First of all, they were well-acquainted with the flowage and the particular location they were buying. During the 12 consecutive summer vacations they had spent at O'Meara's Resort, starting in 1964, they had fallen under the flowage's magical spell. "We loved it here," said Maryann. "It was a breath of fresh air." For sure, the flowage setting contrasted starkly with the character of their hometown, Calumet City, Illinois, which was located in the industrial belt that runs from East Chicago to Gary, Indiana. Second, Maryann brought an unwavering commitment to the undertaking—indeed, as she tells it, her insistence on purchasing the resort overrode all reservations her husband may have had about taking such a step. Third, she had the work ethic to match her high level of enthusiasm. Fourth, Rod, a pipefitter and plumber with Lever Brothers in Chicago, possessed a wide variety of trade skills so essential to maintaining and improving a resort. Finally, the Browns had two boys and a girl, ages 12, 11, and 10, respectively, who were to help with the

Maryann and Rod Brown behind the bar at the Lodge of Lakeview.
Maryann Brown.

operation, increasingly so as they grew older, until each one graduated from high school.

There was, however, one important way in which the Brown's story differs from so many others. Rod chose not to abandon his job in Chicago and the reliable source of income that it represented. This decision restricted his contributions to the operation of the resort to weekends, vacations, and the few other times when he could get away. As a result, full-time management of the Lodge of Lakeview fell to Maryann. There was, as Maryann readily admits, a fairly steep learning curve. She recalls, with amusement tinged with a sense of embarrassment, that the first year they "didn't know the need to have the resort up and running in time for the May opener." The Browns had always thought of flowage resorts in terms of the high summer months when they themselves had vacationed. As a young woman with three children and no resort management experience, it was clear that she needed help that first year. This help came in part from her father, and in part from a generous Mary Downey, who was the heart and soul of Shady Rest Resort. Even with this generous assistance, Maryann claims that she aged from 36 to 56 over the course of this grueling first year.

Fortunately for the Brown family, the resort they took over was "in fairly good condition." No major rebuilding was needed, though Rod recalled that "there were some things that I wanted to be a bit different." And so he swung into instant maintenance and modification gear—a gear that, owing to the nature of resorts, could not easily be reversed. Perhaps the most notable shortcoming of the Lodge of Lakeview was the absence of a liquor license, a valuable, if not absolutely necessary, commodity for a northwoods resort. It took about eight years to rectify that situation. When Shady Rest Resort was broken up into lots around 1980, the Browns purchased the license for $7,000. The bar, located in the basement of their home, quickly became the hub for storytelling and general socializing among the guests—with Maryann as a skilled and charming bartender-in-chief.

Bartending was but one addition to Maryann's full-time role as owner/manager. She also threw herself into public relations work. She became active in the Turtle Flambeau Flowage Association—a group that represented and still represents resort owners and businesses in the area—and the Mercer Chamber of Commerce. In off-seasons, she traveled on behalf of these two organizations to outdoor shows throughout the Midwest— including stops in Chicago, Milwaukee, Indianapolis, Rockford, and the Quad Cities. It was at shows in the early 1980s that she first began to receive inquiries about camping facilities—not for tents, but for towable camping units. Though the Browns did not, as the Miller resort did, establish a campground, they responded to changing recreational tastes by deciding to cater to a different but rapidly growing clientele: snowmobilers. With the last of their children having completed high school, Rod retired in 1987 after 31 years with Lever Brothers, and he and Maryann moved north permanently. Starting in 1987, the Lodge of Lakeview was open year-round.

Snowmobiling families brought enthusiasm and money to a northwoods area that had traditionally languished during the long winter months. The Browns enjoyed these new guests—who fitted so well into the resort's family oriented ethos—and the benefits they brought to the bottom line. But in a fast-changing world, it was not long before the winter clientele took on a decidedly different character. In the next decade or so, snowmobiling families were largely displaced by young male snowmobilers, whose love of speed and alcohol-driven behaviors were not compatible with a family resort. the Lodge of Lakeview ceased its wintertime operations in 2000.

That was not the only step taken by the Browns in response to changing times. Rising property values and taxes, the multiple demands on their time and energy, and the departure of their children from home persuaded them to scale back the size of their operation. In 1994, they decided to transform the original four cabins into condominium units. The actual sales took place four years later. They also divested themselves of their liquor license. As of 2017, the Lodge of Lakeview was comprised of the four condominiums, the owners' house, and two rental units. Though now decidedly nontraditional in configuration, the resort has successfully operated for 41 years and counting under the ownership of the Browns.

On Memorial Day weekend in 1971, Pine Trees Hideaway, a resort on the Turtle River area of the flowage, opened its doors under new management: Ernst (Ernie) and Aranka Both. The Hideaway had a storied past. Its founder, Joe Popko, was a true northwoods legend—a genial resort host, tireless fisherman, top-flight guide, and character of the first order. The resort, which Popko apparently built himself, comprised some 11 cabins along the Turtle River part of the flowage; and, according to the *Ironwood Daily Globe* of May 30, 1938, he had recently added a substantial new house for himself and his growing family. One story has it that Al Capone provided some financial assistance to this project by way of dispatching a personal obligation to Popko. Whatever the merits of this story may be, for sure Popko was rapidly sinking roots in the area. In 1938, he also built four cabins "near Norway Point on the Manitowish River side" of the flowage—clearly a harbinger of things to come. Having made a success of the Hideaway, Popko sold out to Christian Yeakle in 1953 and turned his energies to the Norway Point property. Popko's Resort, as this one was named, would flourish for years under his management and that of subsequent owners. In 1968, Marj and Bill Tutt purchased the resort from Casey and Lu Sliwicki and renamed it in keeping with Bill's bowhunting passion: Flam-Bow.

By the time the Boths took over Pine Trees Hideaway, it had fallen on hard times. One pair of owners apparently did nothing to keep it up and supposedly told prospective customers that if they wanted to rent the cabins that they could clean them up themselves! The Boths' immediate predecessors, Joe and Ethel Burda, had not been able to devote the necessary attention to the operation, in part because Joe continued to be employed full time in Chicago. So Ernie and Aranka found themselves in possession of a physically run-down resort with few customers. According to Ernie, the cabins were just as Joe Popko had built them—with no interior walls and gaps in the siding through which daylight could be seen. Two cabins had fallen into such disrepair that they had been closed down. In others, only curtains—not doors—separated the bedrooms from the main room. A herculean task lay before the Boths if the Hideaway were ever to rebound. "Nobody thought we were gonna make it," said Aranka, "but we never thought we weren't gonna make it."

Ernie and Aranka Both take time off from the chores of resort ownership to celebrate New Year's Eve. Marge Ervin

The family divided up the chores and went to work. Ernie tackled the cabins, starting with the worst one. He tore the roof off cabin number one, gutted the building down to the floor joists, changed rooms around, put in inside walls, and finished it off. If that was the most extensive of the renovations, there was still plenty to do on each of the remaining 10 cabins. Moreover, the Boths had decided to go after the snowmobile clientele, a decision that called for the winterization of all the cabins. Winterizing the cabins, in turn, required not only insulation but also the digging of a partial basement to provide heat and insulation for the water system. Fortunately, Ernie had worked in construction for most of his years in Milwaukee, so he was able to function as plumber, electrician, carpenter, insulator, and even concrete mason on this major rehabilitation project. During dining hours and on into the evening, he tended bar, graciously and efficiently.

Meanwhile, Aranka set about the task of applying her cooking skills to the benefit of the operation. First, she commandeered what had been the resort's bar, a basement room in the main house with a large rock fireplace, and turned it into the dining room. The remainder of the basement was divided into a kitchen and a large room fitted out with a bar and a few arcade games. Then she settled on a menu. To no one's surprise, it featured German food, though it did make some American concessions to the culinarily challenged. Finally, she introduced her children, ages 14, 11, and 9 in 1971, to the world of work. They set and cleared tables, and, as time went on, began to take orders and serve meals. Of course, in the daytime there were the inescapable housekeeping tasks to keep the children and their mother occupied.

The first year of business proved particularly tough, and cash flow problems forced the Boths to shut down the operation after Labor Day weekend. The following year went better, thanks to the presence of additional renovated cabins and to the restaurant's growing reputation. News about the meals that came from Aranka's kitchen quickly spread by word of mouth from the guests at the resort to the Mercer area in general, and then beyond. It was not unusual to encounter diners at Pine Trees Hideaway who had driven from as far away as Hayward for one of Aranka's German specialties. As the Boths readily and gratefully acknowledged, the Mercer Chamber of Commerce also played a strong supporting role by publicizing the resort and by directing people to it.

The Both family did indeed turn around the fortunes of Pine Trees Hideaway, and built quite a reputation—especially for the restaurant—as they did so. But the personal cost was high. In Aranka's words, "We had no life!" And to illustrate the point, Ernie recalled being awakened at midnight, or 2 a.m., or later, by snowmobilers looking to buy gasoline—even though they were not guests at Pine Trees. It was not the hard work that the Boths were ready to step away from; it was the relentless nature of the resort owner's obligations. And so, after an Easter vacation in warmer climes in 1979, they put the resort up for sale—not really expecting a buyer to show up anytime soon. One did, however, and by July 4 the Hideaway changed hands. The new owners took over a resort that was fully booked through the summer and into the fall.

The story does not end there, however. The resort lost momentum under its new management, and after three years ownership reverted to the Boths. Once again, they sold the property, and once again it fell back into their hands when yet another party failed to be up to the task. And so, in 1986 Ernie and Aranka began their second stint as owners of Pine Trees Hideaway. Luckily, their daughter, Margaret (Margie), and her husband, Colin (Erv) Ervin, were in the area and available to assist them. In 1990, the Boths sold the resort for the third and final time.

CHAPTER FOUR
Some Loose Bits from the Resort Era

Genealogy of a Resort: Art Schmidt's Muskie Camp

As noted earlier, most flowage resorts changed hands numerous times. By way of example, I have put together, with the assistance of the staff of the Iron County Register of Deeds, the following history of the ownership of Art Schmidt's Muskie Camp. It should be noted that some or all of the parcel Schmidt purchased for his resort had first been acquired from the government by Joseph Bastein in 1893. The property had changed hands several times before being acquired by the Chippewa and Flambeau Improvement Company (CFIC) prior to the construction of the flowage.

1930 or '31: Art Schmidt began operating the resort on land leased from the CFIC or from Wisconsin Realty.

June 1, 1937: Art Schmidt purchased government lots Three and Four and the West half of the SE quarter of Section Twenty Eight, T42N, R2E, from Wisconsin Realty Company.

1945: Schmidt sold the resort to Frank and Bea Kopecky. The resort opened in 1946 as Frank Kopecky's Musky Camp.

1946: The resort reverted to Art Schmidt.

1947: Art Schmidt sold the resort to Richard Gilbert and George Greiner and their wives. The resort name reverted to Art Schmidt's Muskie Camp.

1948: George and Bertha Greiner bought out the Gilberts. George died in 1948.

1950: Bertha Greiner sold to her sons, Gordon and Glenn Greiner, August 12. "Gordon E. and Glenn A. Greiner, co-partners, doing business under the firm name and style, of Art Schmidt's Muskie Camp...." Later, Glenn and Mavis Greiner became sole owners.

1955: Glenn and Mavis Greiner sold the resort to Thomas and Alyce Turnbull.

1966: Thomas and Alyce Turnbull sold the resort to Fred and Bertha Vick.

1966: Fred and Bertha Vick sold the property to Camp Kennedy. (Plans to open a special needs camp fell through because of dangers connected with a waterfront property.)

1966: Camp Kennedy sold the resort to Richard and Florence Amos. They renamed the resort Hiawatha Lodge.

1973: Richard and Florence Amos sold the resort to Gerald and Verena Campbell. In time they sold the resort to their sons John and Robert Campbell. John eventually became the sole owner.

July 13, 1998: John Campbell sold the resort to Hiawatha Investment. The resort's lodge was razed.

Partial Inventory of Personal Property of Schmidt's Resort

Should the reader be contemplating going into the resort business, the following *partial* list of needed items, taken from an inventory compiled in 1955 when the resort changed hands, may constitute a sort of cautionary tale.

Main Lodge -Kitchen -	Main Lodge - Kitchen	Main Lodge - Living Room:
1 lg. glass cake tray	30 water glasses	
1 4-pc. set porcelain mixing bowl	2 fruit and nut dishes	1 red table lamp 1 mounted beaver 1 mounted pheasant bookcase and books
3 lg. porcelain mixing bowls	1 Deluxe Cyclamatic Frigidaire	6 throw rugs oilcloth Flowage map small magazine stand
3 lg. porcelain dishes	3 Pre-way butane gas heater	1 arm chair 1 smoking stand
2 plastic juice containers	1 large Skelgas range	1 mounted hawk fireplace screen and fireplace tools
2 metal cannisters	1 table, 4 chairs	
12 asst'd. sizes square plastic freezer containers	1 telephone	Basement:
	6 aluminum kettles	1 new Speed Queen washing machine
1 lg. glass sugar cannister	2 small spiders	2 laundry tubs with stand 1 small butane heater
1 Universal meat grinder	8 dishup dishes	1 set ice tongs 1 wood meat carving table
1 Hanson Model 1509 postage scale	1 8-hole dep-freezer	extra used water system
16 asst'd. tin pie and cake tins	1 sm. toaster in lg. dishup table	Main Lodge - Upstairs:
		1 metal double bed, coil spring, innerspring mattress
2 round Pyrex cake pans	3 dixie cup pans	1 old dresser, 1 chair
2 Pyrex baking dishes	2 lg. roasting pans with tops	1 home-made dresser 1 smoking stand, 1 floor lamp
1 French fryer drip	2 med. roasting pans with tops	1 mattress pad 3 blankets, 2 cotton
1 aluminum teakettle	french fry cutter	2 pillows, 2 pillow cases 1 metal clothes rack
1 lg. aluminum coffeepot	1 lg. aluminum kettle	Main Lodge - Room 2 (Girl's room)
1 sm. aluminum coffeepot	2 sm. vegetable press	Main Lodge - Room 3
1 yellow upholstered stair chair	1 lg. earthenware mixing bowl	1 Double metal bed, coil spring, innerspring mattress
1 glass tray metal ash stand	2 med. size aluminum kettles	2 sheets, 2 blankets 2 pillows, 2 pillowcases 1 bedspread, 1 arm chair
25 porcelain lunchcups		1 home made dresser 1 pin up lamp 1 mirror

Main Lodge - Dining Rm:

1 lg. porcelain cooky
   cutter
1 sm. enamel roaster
1 card table
1 metal ironing board
1 N.W. deluxe tank
   vacuum cleaner
2 angel food tins
1 Electric waffle iron
1 pressure cooker
1 large iron roasting
   oven
1 Presto dixie fryer
1 Duo-therm oil
   heater
1 8-hole Frigidaire
   deep-freeze
   (office)
all cards, office sup-
   plies and stationery
   in office
1 desk & chair
1 4-drawer wood filing
   cabinet
1 electric fan

Main Lodge - Dining Rm:
   (office)

1 electric heater
1 Tower adding mach.
1 desk lamp
1 metal typewriter table
1 metal waste basket
1 movie screen and film
1 safe in office belongs
   to Town of Eisenstein

Main Lodge - Bar Room:

18 bar stools
1 old National cash reg-
   ister
2 mounted muskies
1 large scale to weigh
   fish
2 mounted bass
1 mounted walleye pike
1 malted milk mixer
1 Butane gas heater
   all bar glasses and
   equipment to run the
   bar
1 old relic shotgun
1 old relic rifle gas
   lantern
1 minnow tank
1 barrel wood heater
1 fish head with deer
   horns

Main Lodge - Living Room:

3 sets deer horns
3 mounted deer heads
1 piano, 10 chairs
   small writing table
   with lamp and matching
   chair
2 davenports
1 lg. coffee table
1 Butane gas heater
1 end table, wood
1 end table, steel
2 double reading lamps
   set of poker chips
   fireplace screen
1 set moose horns
1 mounted wild cat
1 magazine rack
1 deer horn clothesrack
1 ornamental small lamp

Main Lodge - Room 4:

1 double metal bed coil spring
   innerspring mattress
2 sheets, 2 blankets
2 pillows, 2 pillowcases
1 bedspread, 1 mirror
1 home-made dresser
1 pin-up lamp

Main Lodge - Room 5:

1 double bed (metal), coil
   spring, and innerspring
   mattress
2 sheets, 2 blankets
2 pillows, 2 pillowcases
1 bedspread, 1 mirror
1 home-made dresser
1 pin-up lamp
1 arm chair

Main Lodge - Room 6:

1 metal double bed
1 innerspring mattress
1 mattress pad
1 coil spring
16 blankets
6 bedspreads
2 pillows
1 home made dresser
1 arm chair
1 small wastepaper basket
1 bed lamp
1 sm. chest drawers
1 mirror

Hallway:

1 small butane heater

A Testimonial to Downey's Shady Rest, Cabin 7

This letter was written to the current owners of a cabin that had once been part of the resort. The tip of the tip of the iceberg of such letters written, usually to resort owners, by satisfied guests.

October 1, 2008

Dear Beth and Mike,

Here's a blow-up I had made for you of one of my old Shady Rest Cabin 7 postcards. I hope you enjoy it.

This was the 42nd summer that my family vacationed at the Flowage since our first visit in 1959. We stayed in Cabin 7 every year until Mary Downey passed away in the mid-1970s. The first several years the rate for the big cabins, 7 and 8, was a whopping $35 per week. At some point the rate for 7 and 8 went to $50 a week. The first few years my Dad rented the cabin for the first two weeks of August. We enjoyed it so much he got it for the entire month of August. It was like a second home. I could not begin to tell you how many great memories I have from our time at Shady Rest and Cabin 7. Mary Downey was like family. She insisted that we kids call her "Aunt Mary." Her husband, Duff, was still alive the first several years we visited. He was a real recluse and never left the living quarters or showed himself in public. My father spoke to him a couple of times. Duff's real name was Marvin. He and his two brothers, Woz and Bend, (I never knew their real names) were the original owners. In addition to Shady Rest they owned the island at the entrance to Lake Bastine, over across from Cry of the Loon. It had a cabin on it and was referred to as the Isle of Shady Rest.

A sun-dappled Cabin 7 that one family of happy guests came to think of as their own. Mike and Beth Myers

We had as good a time this past August as we've ever had, but it has really never been quite the same since we stopped staying in "our cabin," Cabin 7. As we did on the day we met you, we always like to ride over and take a good look at Cabin 7... and dream.

Very truly yours,
Dan Murray

CHAPTER FIVE
Highlights and Lowlights of Resort Life

F lowage resorts drew their guests with promises of good fishing, relaxation in nature, and family-oriented recreation—all made possible by the relentless hard work and attentiveness of owners and their staffs. And most resorts delivered on their promises. Yet there was more to a northwoods vacation than endless serenity brought on by whispering pines and gently lapping waters. Stuff happened that interrupted this idyllic world and brought a large dollop of spice, mostly flavorful and even exciting but occasionally bitter, to resort life. These moments and the characters involved in them often dominated the memories of guests, even years after they happened. Since these moments do not lend themselves to a coherent chronological narrative, I have grouped them under a few general headings.

"A Wee Dram"... or Two... or...

It might be a useful prelude to the following vignettes to note that the early history of flowage resorts coincided with the end of Prohibition in 1933. Whether there was a cause-and-effect relationship between the repeal of the 18th amendment and high life at flowage resorts cannot be determined with certainty. But what is for certain is that attitudes toward fermented beverages were a great deal more relaxed in the land of sky-blue waters and towering pines. Doug Severt, who was decidedly underage when he worked at Al's Place, remembers never being concerned about buying himself a beer or serving up a couple of brews to patrons at the bar. Enforcement was an alien concept in a world where families gathered around bars and serious imbibers kept owner Al Weseman, who also served as the bartender, on duty into the wee small hours. As Severt puts it: "Heck, if you were old enough to get on a bar stool, you were welcome, but you would have to be with your parents or other adults. That was then, but I believe that in the northwoods it's still pretty much like that today. It was then as now a different way of life and in many cases, better." But not always better. As Art Schmidt Jr. recalled of the guests at his father's musky camp, "There were some pretty good drinkers." "This drinking business," reflected Neil Koshak after relating a number of alcohol-fueled escapades, "some people just shouldn't start." And what was true for the guests was also true for some of the staff and guides. With good reason, then, alcohol played a starring role in some of the more memorable episodes of resort life and was best supporting actor in a number of others.

Alcohol just might be suspected as playing a role in the following story. A fellow pulled up to the Fort Flambeau Resort with a huge turtle in the trunk of his car. The man then headed straight to the bar where he spent an hour and a half celebrating his good fortune—and likely putting off the unpleasant task of rendering the turtle ready for the soup pot. Meanwhile, the snapper did what snappers do: used its ferocious beak to tear through into the interior of the auto, whereupon it ate up the upholstery and the better part of the dashboard. After discovering the damage to his vehicle's interior—the seat having been thoroughly destroyed—the poor man ended up sitting on a milk crate while driving home. On the way, he decided to let the turtle go free, allegedly because "he didn't need it." It is not without good cause that the flowage proudly bears the name "turtle."

Crappies were in such abundance in Bastine Lake in the early resort days that they were used to feed mink. Art Schmidt, however, found a better use for them. He smoked crappie fillets—"salted the hell out of them"—and then put them out as bar food. No wonder that thirsty anglers at his resort remained thirsty, beer after beer. Patrons at Schmidt's bar also enjoyed free entertainment from a couple of gregarious guides. Orvid Donner (later the founder of Donner's Bay Resort) "had a line that people really liked," and Herbie Himes, who played a harp guitar and sang, spun tales that kept folks on the edges of their barstools. Guests knew the drill: buy Herbie another beer, and he'll tell another story or sing another song.

That said, alcohol did not always inspire crowd-pleasing behavior. One autumn, a member of a well-known area clan, while a bit impaired, broke a window to gain access to the bar at Al's Place to appropriate a bottle of whiskey. Al Koshak was off logging, and Charlotte had forgotten (for the first and only time ever) to clean out the cash register and take the day's proceeds to the family cabin. With no one present and the cash register unlocked, this thirsty fellow helped himself to a till full of money as well as a bottle. It did not take long to identify the culprit, and restitution was made. Another guide, known for his atypical long woolen coat and a propensity to acquire and sell a wide variety of items, launched a different kind of assault on the till at the Lodge of Lakeview many years later. He persuaded the Browns' son Danny that he was in need of money for a meal; to which request the lad, somewhat intimidated by the guide's persona, complied. When the boy's mother learned what happened, she hopped in her car and headed to Idle Shores, where the suspect was found munching away on a hamburger. After receiving a tongue-lashing for picking on a child, he returned the money, except what had gone for the burger and a drink. Minor transgressions of this sort were soon forgiven, if not forgotten—especially when a good guide was involved. Moreover, many of these episodes occurred during the Depression, a situation that aggravated the already hardscrabble lives of many northwoods residents.

Another colorful local who knew how to mix it up with guests was Ed Robinson, the legendary Flambeau River guide (the landing below the Turtle Dam has been named in his honor). Robinson owned the Midway Bar, located halfway between Mercer and Butternut. A fun-loving fellow, Ed possessed a shot glass with a hole in it. When the occasion seemed right, Ed would serve an unsuspecting customer a shot in this trick glass. As the customer attempted to drink, the liquor dribbled down his front while Ed cheerily suggested that the man was so drunk he couldn't find his mouth. The embarrassed customer would then vigorously affirm his sobriety and demand another drink, and the game began again. The real test of sobriety lay in the speed with which the customer caught on to the game.

Guests were not the only ones to suffer the consequences of "over-serving." A bartender at Al's Place chose a night when his boss was fishing in Canada to raid the cash register, take Charlotte's new maroon Chevy, and head to Park Falls for some serious celebrating. Apparently he had a head start on the latter and failed to negotiate the 90-degree corner at Spring Creek. The Chevy came to a stop against a rock pile, damaged to the tune of $250 to $300 dollars—a lot of money in those days. By way of excuse, the guilty party claimed "to have ridden a polar bear on bareback from Kenora, Ontario." Of course, Charlotte fired the poor fellow—who was still inebriated—the next day. Restitution came many years later, after the Koshaks had moved to Park Falls. One day the errant bartender of long ago left Bush's bar, close to the Koshak house in Park Falls, and walked over to see his former boss. "Drunk as a skunk," he paid back the money he had stolen as well as the costs for repair of the car—and disappeared.

One of the more colorful characters at Al's Place was a cook whose formal name appears lost to history, but not, happily, his nickname. Before Charlotte Koshak would head off to purchase groceries for the kitchen, she would ask this persistently imprecise man how much of this or that ingredient he needed. How many potatoes? How much meat? How much flour? His response, after due reflection, was always the same: "a certain amount." Or: "There's a lot of people for dinner tonight, so we'll need... a... a certain amount of meat." It was, of course, not long before the kitchen girls began calling him "Certain Amount," and in no time the cook's new moniker was being heard throughout the resort. On one regrettable evening after finishing up his chef's duties, Certain Amount consumed a certain amount—not potatoes or meat or flour, needless to say. In his mellow state, he wandered over to Schmidt's to have a drink or two at the rock bar. On his way home, he failed to notice that Schmidt's outhouse had been removed from its location over the pit so that some repairs could be made. Certain Amount stepped into the open toilet and found himself up to his chest in a certain amount of another substance. His predictable outburst alerted people in the bar, and they quickly came to his aid—only to be rebuffed by the humiliated chef. They returned to the bar, leaving Certain Amount to think the situation through. Eventually he decided to accept help, whereupon he was extricated from the pit, thrown into the flowage, and escorted back to Al's Place, still smelling like... well... a certain amount.

Bars are equal opportunity facilities, even in the rugged northwoods. Charlotte Koshak, after noting that a lot of the women who accompanied their husbands or boyfriends to Al's Place went out fishing with the men, observed wryly: "Of course, some of the women fished in the bar, too." A particular case in point involved a bona fide local north country character whose "indoor fishing trips" featured a single, invariably successful angling technique. She would enter the bar, take in the scene, squeeze between a couple of guys sitting on barstools, and lean against the bar. She then reached into her purse, pulled out a quarter (even in those days not enough to buy a real drink), and slapped it on the bar, as if it was all she had. Almost always, the two gentlemen fell all over themselves to purchase her a drink. A truly skilled "mooch," one might say.

Pranks

Pine Trees Hideaway had its share of zany moments as well, going back to the days when Joe Popko was the owner. The basement floor of his house was at, or perhaps a little below, the high-water elevation of the flowage. On those occasions when the flowage came up to full pool, water seeped through the foundation into the basement— which, of course, was where the bar was located. One evening some fishermen returned from the flowage with a bucket of bluegills and other panfish only to find something like four inches of water in the barroom. They promptly dumped their catch into the water, and watched with glee as the barroom bluegills swam about in this novel variant of an aquarium. The high-water problem in the basement continued for years until Ernie Both installed drain tile and a sump pump. A less dramatic prank, but one that momentarily subverted a standard ritual of the bar-room, occurred when a customer at the Hideaway bar furtively removed his glass eye and placed it atop his money on the bar. At that point he arose, announced that he was heading for the bathroom, and then said loudly to any and all, "Look after my money, would you." Everyone looked at the money, and the detached eye stared back at them. Consternation soon yielded to relieved laughter.

Mishaps

Joe Miller's resort was once the site of a *National Lampoon* summer vacation moment. After a long drive to the resort, a family poured out of their car. The mother, who was having a smoke, headed to the outhouse amid some perfunctory cautions from the staff not to set it on fire, and her young daughter headed for the dock with appropriate admonitions not to fall in the water. For whatever reasons, these well-meaning words fell on deaf ears. For within five minutes of this family's arrival, the outhouse was afire and the daughter had fallen in. Fortunately, the fire was quickly put out and the daughter promptly fished out of the flowage and dried off. Once all was righted, the family vacation proceeded along more traditional—and sedate—lines. While this episode quickly took on a decidedly comic aspect, beneath its surface lurks a sobering reality: in the northwoods, a fine line separates humorously memorable moments from potentially tragic ones.

The flowage itself lies at the center of this balancing act. Large and complex, with stretches of open water that can become perilously rough when the winds are right, the flowage demands a high degree of attentiveness and caution from those who would ply its waters safely. Beyond this, the navigation hazards posed by the veritable forest of trees, stumps, and floating debris put boaters—especially the inexperienced and the overconfident—at continuing risk. No wonder resort owners have felt compelled to advise the utmost care when taking a boat out on the flowage. Whether their messages are listened to, however, is another matter. One guest at Miller's, for example, insisted, against the advice of those who knew better, on heading out in a pea soup fog, confident that he could navigate to his favorite fishing hole. But just as he was about to lose sight of land, he turned around and returned to camp—announcing like a town crier that the fog was too thick for any reasonable person to venture out in. On another day a guest, who was heading back to his cabin from fishing down lake, pursued a beeline toward two boats that were fishing near one another just out from the dock. Seeing the onrushing boat headed their way, the two fishing boats moved apart so as to create a passageway. The returning fisherman stayed the course and smacked dead-on into the stump that had drawn the two parties of fishermen so close together in the first place. That minor misfortune—the boat and the fisherman sustained no lasting damage—is reminiscent of a time at Al's Place when a guest, also motoring back to the dock, ran into one of a number of boats that Al kept slightly submerged so they would remain tightly swollen for the season. According to Neil Koshak, Al had some choicely crafted instructions for his errant patron who had paid no attention to the buoy that marked the sunken boats. Then there was the guest at the Lodge of Lakeview, whom Maryann Brown charitably described as "an excitable man," who motored toward the resort a bit on the fast side and docked his boat... on top of the dock.

At times concern for the safety of guests could even backfire. One hardy outdoorswoman, a Ms. Hummerson, had left Miller's to fish in the Lake Ten and Rat Lake areas. When she failed to return, a search party set out to find her. And find her, they did, happily sleeping under her boat, which she had propped up on the beach with a pair of oars. Far from relieved to have been found, she reproached her would-be rescuers: "You didn't have to come out, I knew where I was."

Being found when not lost was not the only peril for those who ventured out on the flowage alone. In October of 1971, Elmer Rehse of Horicon battled a balky outboard motor on the flowage. Whenever he could get it to start, it died immediately as he shifted it into gear. Rehse decided to eliminate one step in the process and to try to start the motor while it was in gear. The experiment worked, up to a point. The motor started all right, but with such a lurch that Rehse, a non-swimmer, went over the transom. The boat circled him as he thrashed around in the water, then came directly at him. Luckily, it was set at half throttle, and Rehse grabbed the gunnel and "sloshed aboard." He described himself as more than a little happy to return to "firm land."

No recitation of the downside of resort life would be complete without a fishhook-in-fisherman story. A guest at Al's Place came off the flowage with a hook firmly embedded in his ear. Al, ever the handyman, began sterilizing his jackknife with a flame in preparation for extracting the hook. Before the procedure began, however, a noted doctor from Marshfield, who was enjoying himself in the bar, asked Al what he was up to. Upon hearing about the impending jackknife surgery, the good doctor intervened and put the poor fisherman under his personal care. Experienced hands removed the hook, to the relief of the fisherman, and probably Al as well.

Al's Place was the venue for another tale of intervention by a physician—but this time in far more grave circumstances. Here is the story as Neil Koshak recalled it.

"Probably the worst thing that ever happened at the place [aside from the drowned deer hunters] was the time a guest got drunk and was making a play for the dining room girl, or someone. Pa had told him to lay off and had things generally under control. We'd had a general pool of fishing guides, and Art Schmidt had his pool, however sometimes we borrowed back and forth. On this particular evening, a young guide—not one of our regulars—took it upon himself to confront this guest, and an argument erupted, which escalated into a fight outside. The guy was drunk, and not a fighter, and the guide hit him over the head with a beer bottle and then jumped on top of him, slashing his face with the jagged end of the broken glass. By the time they pulled him off his victim, he had cut the guy up pretty bad. At that time we had another guest who was a doctor/surgeon from Pekin, Illinois. Ma said he was about three-quarters drunk himself, but when he saw all that blood he snapped into "cold sober" immediately. They sent me to get his doctor's bag out of cabin No. 5. I couldn't find it, so an adult got it. They cleared off the kitchen table, which was about ten feet long, laid the guy on it, and Doc proceeded to sew him up. Later, the guy had plastic surgery, and they [the surgeons] marveled at the excellent work of the doctor at the resort."

A Tragic Tale

Not every tale had a happy ending, however. For the flowage has taken a number of lives over the years, some attributable to weather, others to carelessness. By far the most tragic single accident was a combination of both. It occurred on Monday, November 21, 1938, when three deer hunters—Steven Mangold, Clyde Bleil, and Kaare Dreyer—and their guide, Eddie Polacheck of Park Falls, perished on the flowage while on their way back from Big Island. The men had been guests at Al's Place, where they were told by James Van Camp, Al's father-in-law, to take two boats so as not to go out overloaded. One of the hunters, who had served in the Coast Guard, announced that he was not "afraid of that little puddle," and the four men departed in a single boat. The party came back to the resort at noon with two bucks, and then returned to the island in the afternoon to get a wounded buck. Although the day had started out calm, an early winter storm came up in the afternoon, and waves on the flowage reached three to four feet in height. When the party failed to show up at camp that evening, it was presumed that they had chosen to spend the night on the island. With the men still missing on Tuesday morning, a rescue party set out to search for them on the island, but in vain. That night the flowage channel froze, and the next morning would-be rescuers spotted an overturned boat embedded in the ice about 200 feet from Big Island. It seemed likely that the four men and their buck had not been under way for long before their boat swamped. Thin ice precluded any recovery effort that day. But by Friday the flowage had opened up once again, and the bodies of Bleil and Mangold were retrieved from the water; the other two men were not recovered until the following spring. Unfortunately, this incident is but one of a long list of fatal accidents that have befallen flowage boaters and fishermen. As noted in Part I, this list also includes Mark Fort, an employee of Northern States Power, whose love for the flowage and concern for its future contributed much to the process by which the state came to purchase it. He died in 2002 in an ice fishing accident.

Bad Apples

Things could go awry on shore as well as on the flowage. However much resort owners liked and befriended their guests, there were always a few bad apples. Pine Trees Hideaway once had a guest who departed early one morning without having paid the entirety of his bill. Thinking that he could get on Highway 51 and out of the area before anyone knew better, he took the cutoff road from County FF to Mercer. To the man's consternation, the sheriff, who had been notified when the rascal had departed Pine Trees, was more than familiar with the cutoff road. The two met; and with the sheriff's encouragement, the bill was promptly paid in full. That was a one-of-a-kind moment for the Boths, and pretty rare overall at the resorts. Not so rare were those occasions when guests behaved boorishly or offensively. The owner of Idle Shores once entered a cabin for housekeeping purposes and encountered a gutted deer hanging from the ceiling—not only a poor housekeeping decision by the guests, but also an incredibly inept way to treat a fresh kill in need of cooling. And then there was the guest who washed muddy and greasy snowmobile parts in the shower, an activity that left housekeepers with an industrial strength mess to clean up. Resort owners took these occasional lapses in stride—it was not worth the time or the possibility of bad publicity to seek legal redress—but they did not have to welcome such guests back another year, and they did not.

Guests who got out of control in the barroom and those who made unwelcome advances to female staff members also found reservations hard to come by in subsequent years. "I just crossed them off," Charlotte Koshak said, by which she meant that future requests for reservations would be met with the stock phrase: "nothing available." Sometimes, however, resorts had to put up with some unpleasant behavior from regulars whose business helped to pay the bills. Spirited bear hunters, for example, made life for the Boths more than a little taxing. One successful hunter claimed ignorance of the procedures for dressing a bear and asked Ernie to do the job for him. Ernie, a certificate-holding butcher, complied with the request, and a subsequent one, before retiring permanently from bear gutting. The reason was simple: "They [bears] stink." These same bear hunters, who rented out every cabin, also partied over-aggressively, leaving in their wake cabins that needed far more than routine cleaning. Even so, Aranka found it in her heart to say that they were basically good guys.

Boys Having Fun

It would, of course, be narratively inappropriate to end this chapter with stories of death or mayhem on the flowage and its shores. A better place to turn would be to the bright years of childhood, as lived by the sons of two of the flowage's earliest resort owners: Arty Schmidt and Neil Koshak. As their parents labored to establish businesses, there was fun enough, and trouble enough to get into, to satisfy a dozen boys. Charlotte Koshak remembered that Neil simply "ran wild," a view that Neil's reminiscences confirm. Arty's childhood apparently followed suit.

The intrigue of meeting guests—whose lives were so different from theirs—was but a youthful version of their parents' more mature interest in those who visited their resorts. The kindness and occasional benevolence of many guests impressed Art Jr. He was well-thanked and occasionally tipped generously as a teenager for carrying motors to and from the dock, or repairing a broken eye on a fishing rod, or similar tasks. Guests could also expand young horizons dramatically. Neil Koshak, who had never seen a black person in his life, observed one next door at Downey's resort and promptly went home to describe to his family a man with the most amazing suntan.

Then there were the little things that loom so large in memories of childhood. For Arty, a rough ride to Park Falls over terrible roads to buy groceries was the price to be paid in order to watch a Tarzan movie. For Neil, there was an overly ambitious building project on a logjam in the flowage that depended on his wielding an axe that was much too heavy for a boy of his age and size, an undertaking that almost resulted in disaster. For the two of them, there was a game of catch with a hammer, which came to an abrupt halt when the hammer went through the rear window of Al Koshak's new pickup truck. Neil recalls hiding in a grove of mosquito-infested balsams and paying such a price in bites that his family, relieved to eventually find him, spared him a "licking."

Finally, no list of childhood memories would be complete without at least one act of calculated mischief. The setting was the icehouse, that all-important resort outbuilding, where anglers stored their catch. At Al's Place, and other resorts as well, the occupants of each cabin were given a wooden stake with the number of the cabin on it. This stake was implanted in the sawdust that covered the ice to indicate the location of that cabin's fish. Whether acting under the harmful influence of "city kids," as claimed by Neil, or responding wholly to a self-generated idea, Neil switched the stakes around in an entirely random fashion. This simple act of misdirection sparked a frantic effort by the resort's guests to return the right stakes to the right fish. Anglers being what they are, setting this matter right demanded the highest form of justice—namely, the restoration of each and every fish to its rightful owner. Parental retribution for this bit of fun has never been disclosed.

A young Neil Koshak displays his casting form from the dock at Al's Place. Neil Koshak

A young Art Schmidt Jr. gingerly holds the tail of a boy-sized musky at his father's resort. Art Schmidt Jr.

Afterword

I n the loft of an Iron County cabin sits a scarred mahogany
library table, crafted by my father as a school project about
100 years ago. On the table, in piles and semi-sorted arrays,
lie books, copies of documents, note cards, memos to the self,
and other miscellany of the writer's trade. There's a computer, of
course, whose lurid glow seems so at odds with the color palate of
the building and its surroundings, a machine that has, because of
the ease with which it can be made to overcome slips of mind and
fingers, driven the clackety Remington typewriter of my youth to
the museum shelf or the landfill. And on one corner of the table,
in isolated splendor, resides a stack of folders, each containing a
completed chapter of a project that has taken so much longer than
I could ever have anticipated, but which has, at the same time,
brought the rewards of discovery and understanding along with
new and valued friendships. The end of the task is near at hand,
and it is time to shake the cobwebs spun by threads of thought and
syntax—cobwebs that have entrapped fragments of sentences,
whispers of ideas, and ineffable emotions, as well as superfluous
facts, stray punctuation marks, and formalities of format. It is time
to leave the glow of the lamplight and computer and head outside

to renew my ties with that which I have been seeking to chronicle for these many years.

Daybreak comes ever so gently upon the Turtle-Flambeau Flowage on this still summer's morn as I paddle across its dark, stained waters. The haze, the mounting bird calls, the cries of loons, the beat of unseen duck wings, and the almost cinematic transformation of threatening shoreline shadows into towering pines—all conspire to cast a calming spell. All around me nature seems to be putting on a show, choreographed eons ago and performed to perfection yet again this morning in response to cues we cannot entirely fathom. I feel certain, at this instant, that what is going on around me is how it has always been in the north country, where lakes and forests give off a powerful, yet comforting, aura of the eternal and unchanging.

Eager to capture the moment, I gently set my paddle across the gunwales, take in the scene, and reflect upon it. But a discordant thought soon works its way into my reverie. It takes the form of a memory of last fall's musky fishing, when autumnal winds rocked the boat and pitched lures about in mid-cast, and when slate-gray skies gave promise of approaching winter. The flowage, memory reminds me, has all manner of moods, many of them replete with turbulence and change. This sense of the flowage's changeableness crowds its way into my reverie, and jostles uneasily with my previous sense of the timeless and the immutable. After all, the very word, flowage, representing as it does the gathering, storage, and release of water, betokens continual change and renewal. Is there some paradox here, I wonder? How can it be that our experience of a world of change can bring about a sense of stability, of security? These thoughts, prompted by a struggle between moment and memory, gradually lead to memory writ large—that is, to history, or, better yet, to two intertwined histories. Nature itself has a readable past—one of great forces clashing over periods of time as well as subtle transformations too finely wrought for the eye to see. Natural history, then, stands as the gateway to understanding the rivers, lakes, marshes, swamps, and forests that became the flowage, as well as the creatures that inhabit them. And human history, the record of a late-arriving actor on this vast stage, carries the stories of all whose lives shaped and were shaped by the flowage. Perhaps, I conclude reverentially, to see one's self within these two great flows is to recognize that the transience of human life is deeply rooted in the mysteries of still greater transience. With this reassuring notion of belonging to something far beyond this emerging day or evocative location, or the limits of the self, I pick up my paddle, dig into the flowage's coppery waters, and glide off appreciatively into the rising mist.

M.H. Mercer,
Wisconsin
August 15, 2017

Some Acronyms that Appear in the Text

CFIC: Chippewa and Flambeau Improvement Company

FERC: Federal Energy Regulatory Commission

FPC: Flambeau Paper Company

FRC: Flambeau Reservoir Company

FRIC: Flambeau River Improvement Company

FRLC: Flambeau River Lumber Company

GLIFWC: Great Lakes Indian Fish and Wildlife Commission

MOA: Memorandum of Agreement

MOU: Memorandum of Understanding

NSP: Northern States Power

PARR: Protect Americans Rights and Resources

STA: Stop Treaty Abuse

TFF: Turtle-Flambeau Flowage

TFF&TLPOA: Turtle-Flambeau Flowage and Trude Lake Property Owners' Association

TFSWA: Turtle-Flambeau Scenic Waters Area

WCRR: Wisconsin Central Railroad

WDEG: Wisconsin Division of Emergency Government

WDNR: Wisconsin Department of Natural Resources

WGRA: Wisconsin Greater Recreational Association

WVIC: Wisconsin Valley Improvement Company

WWPA: Wisconsin Water Power Association

Sources for Part I

Note to reader:

Rather than prepare an alphabetically organized bibliography, I have chosen to list the sources on which the book's narrative has been based in chronological order on a chapter-by-chapter and section-by-section basis. When a single archive is the dominant source throughout a chapter, I have listed it only once, corresponding to the point in the text where I first begin to draw on it.

CHAPTER ONE
The Long, Slow Stretch

A Rocky Start

Dott Jr., Robert H. and John W. Attig. *Roadside Geology of Wisconsin*. Missoula, Montana, 2004.

Martin, Lawrence. *The Physical Geography of Wisconsin*. Third Edition. Madison: University of Wisconsin Press, 1965.

Paull, Rachel Krebs and Richard A. Paull. *Geology of Wisconsin and Upper Michigan*. Dubuque, Iowa: Kendall/Hunt, 1977.

Black, Frederick Michael. *The Geology of the Turtle-Flambeau Area: Iron and Ashland Counties, Wisconsin*. Master of Science dissertation. University of Wisconsin, 1977.

Cannon, William F. and Doug Ottke. "Preliminary Digital Geologic Map of the Penokean (Early Proterozoic) Continental Margin in Northern Michigan and Wisconsin." USGS Geological Survey Open-File Report 99-547. 1999.

Sternberg, Ben K. and C.S. Clay. "Flambeau Anomaly: A High-Conductivity Anomaly in the Southern Extension of the Canadian Shield." *The Earth's Crust*. 501-530. Published online, March 19, 2013.

Buchanan, Rex. "The Flambeau Anomaly." *Geology of Wisconsin*, part 3 (1978): 10-12.

The Ice Age Cometh

Andersen, Bjorn G. and Harold W. Borns Jr. *The Ice Age World*. Oslo, 1994.

Clayton, Lee. "Pleistocene Geology of the Superior Region, Wisconsin." *Wisconsin Geological and Natural History Survey*. Madison: 46, 1984. Large scale map included.

Beatty, Marvin T., Ingvold O. Hembre, Francis D. Hole, Leonard R. Massie and Arthur E. Peterson. "The Soils of Wisconsin." *Wisconsin Blue Book*, 149-170. Madison, 1964.

The Flambeau River

Doty, James Duane. "Northern Wisconsin in 1820." *Report and Collections of the State Historical Society of Wisconsin for the years 1873, 1874, 1875 and 1876*. Vol. 7, 195-206. Madison, 1876.

King, F.H. "Geology of the Upper Flambeau Valley." *Geology of Wisconsin. Survey of 1873-1879*. Vol. 4, Part 6, 585-621. Madison, 1882.

Norwood, J.G. "Geological Report of a Survey of Portions of Wisconsin and Minnesota, Made during the Years 1847, '48, '49 and '50." In Owen, David Dale. *Report of a Geological Survey of Wisconsin, Iowa, and Minnesota; and Coincidentally of a Portion of the Nebraska Territory*. Philadelphia: Lippincott, Grambo, & Co., 1852.

Vogel, Virgil J. *Indian Names on Wisconsin's Map*. Madison: University of Wisconsin Press, 1991.

Smith, Leonard S. "The Water Powers of Wisconsin." *Wisconsin Geological and Natural History Survey. Bulletin XX. Economics Series No. 13*, 206-228. Madison, 1908.

Sprucing Up

Davis, Margaret Bryan. "Vegetational History of the Eastern United States." *Late-Quaternary Environments of the United States. The Holocene*. Edited by H.E. Wright, Jr., vol. 2, 166-181. Minneapolis, 1983.

Webb III, T., E.J. Cushing and H.E. Wright Jr. "Holocene Changes in the Vegetation of the Midwest." *Late-Quaternary Environments of the United States. The Holocene*. Edited by H.E. Wright Jr., vol. 2, 142-165. Minneapolis, 1983.

Tallis, J.H. *Plant Community History. Long-term changes in plant distribution and diversity*. London: Chapman Hall, 1991.

Griffin, Duane. "Wisconsin's Vegetation History and the Balancing of Nature." *Wisconsin Land and Life.* Edited by Robert C. Ostergren and Thomas R. Vale, 95-112. Madison: University of Wisconsin Press, 1997.

Curtis, John T. *The Vegetation of Wisconsin: An Ordination of Plant Communities.* Madison: University of Wisconsin Press, 1959.

Wisconsin Public Land Survey Records: original field notes and plat maps. digicoll.library.wisc.edu/SurveyNotes/SurveyInfo.html

Whose Woods Are These?

Cleland, Charles Edward. *The Prehistoric Animal Ecology and Ethnozoology of the Upper Great Lakes Region.* Ann Arbor, Michigan: University of Michigan Press, 1966.

Strong, Moses. "List of the Mammals of Wisconsin." In *Geology of Wisconsin: Survey of 1873-1879,* vol. I, ch. 10, 436-440. Madison, 1883.

Schorger, A.W. "Changing Wildlife Conditions in Wisconsin." *Wisconsin Conservation Bulletin* (June 1948): 53-60.

Mason, Ronald J. "The Paleo-Indian Tradition." *Wisconsin Archaeology* 67 (September-December 1986): 181-206.

Mason, Carol I. *Introduction to Wisconsin Indians. Prehistory to Statehood.* Salem, Wisconsin: Sheffield, 1988.

Mason, Ronald J. *Great Lakes Archaeology.* Caldwell, N.J.: Blackburn, 2002.

Mason, Carol I. "The Historic Period in Wisconsin Archaeology." *Wisconsin Archaeology* 67, (September-December 1986): 370-392.

Stiles, Cynthia M. "Archaeological Sites and Historical Structures in the Turtle-Flambeau Flowage." June 1992. Report prepared for the group drafting the master plan for the flowage. On file at Mercer Ranger Station.

Hickerson, Harold. *The Chippewa and Their Neighbors. A Study in Ethnohistory.* New York, 1970.

Claude, Charles Le Roy and Bacqueville de la Potherie. "History of the Savage Peoples who are Allies of New France." In *The Indian Tribes of the Upper Mississippi Valley and Region of the Great Lakes,* vol. I, 275-277. Translated and edited by Emma Helen Blair. Cleveland: The Arthur H. Clark Company, 1911.

Cleland, Charles E. "The Inland Shores Fishery of the Northern Great Lakes: Its Development and Importance in Prehistory." *American Antiquity,* 47, (1982): 761-784.

Bieder, Robert E. *Native American Communities in Wisconsin, 1600-1960*. Madison: University of Wisconsin Press, 1995.

Adams, Arthur T., Ed. *The Explorations of Pierre Esprit Radisson*. Minneapolis, 1961.

Bersing, Otis. "Trade and Travel in Montreal Country." *Wisconsin Academy Review* 21, (Spring 1975): 11-14.

Norwood, J.G. "Geological Report of a Survey of Portions of Wisconsin and Minnesota, Made during the Years 1847, '48, '49 and '50." In Owen, David Dale. *Report of a Geological Survey of Wisconsin, Iowa, and Minnesota; and Coincidentally of a Portion of the Nebraska Territory*, 277-280. Philadelphia: Lippincott, Grambo & Co., 1852.

Chamberlain, T.C., Chief Geologist; R.D. Irving and Moses Strong, Assistant Geologists. *Atlas of the Geological Survey of Wisconsin*. No date or place of publication. [Presumably 1883]. Plates XXI and XXII show upper portion of Flambeau Trail.

Smith, Alice E. *The History of Wisconsin. Vol. 1. From Exploration to Statehood*. Chapter 4. Madison: State Historical Society of Wisconsin, 1973.

Malhiot, Francois Victor. "A Wisconsin Fur-Trader's Journal, 1804-05." *Collections of the State Historical Society of Wisconsin*, vol. 19, 163-233. Edited by Reuben Gold Thwaites. Madison, 1910.

Turner, Frederick Jackson. *The Character and Influence of the Indian Trade in Wisconsin*. New York: Burt Franklin, 1891.

Gilman, Rhoda R. "The Fur Trade in the Upper Mississippi Valley 1630-1850." *Wisconsin Magazine of History* 55 (Autumn 1974): 3-18.

Enter the United States

Smith, Alice E. *The History of Wisconsin. Vol. 1. From Exploration to Statehood*. Chapter 5. Madison: State Historical Society of Wisconsin, 1973.

The Northwest Ordinance. "An ordinance for the government of the Territory of the United States northwest of the River Ohio." July 13, 1787. In *Documents of American History*, edited by Henry Steele Commager, 5th ed., 128-132. New York: Appleton, Century, Crofts, 1949.

Satz, Ronald N. *Chippewa Treaty Rights. The Reserved Rights of Wisconsin's Chippewa Indians in Historical Perspective*. In *Transactions of The Wisconsin Academy of Sciences, Arts and Letters*, 79, no.1, 1994.

From Pinelands to Papermaking

Smith, Alice E. *The History of Wisconsin*. Vol. 1. *From Exploration to Statehood*, Chapter 15. Madison: State Historical Society of Wisconsin, 1973.

Current, Robert N. *The History of Wisconsin*. Vol. 2. *The Civil War Era, 1848-1873*. Chapter 13. Madison: The State Historical Society of Wisconsin, 1976.

Nesbit, Robert C. *A History of Wisconsin*. Vol. 3. *Urbanization and Industrialization, 1873-1893*. Chapters 2 and 3. Madison: State Historical Society of Wisconsin, 1985.

Buenker, John D. *A History of Wisconsin*. Vol. 4. *The Progressive Era, 1893-1914*. Chapter 3. Madison: State Historical Society of Wisconsin, 1998.

Area Facts and History. Dunn County, Wisconsin. Accessed April 28, 2015. Menomonie.com/facts_frame.html.

Millard, Lee C., Editor. "Chippewa Falls History," 1950. Accessed April 28, 2015. chippewafallsrotary.org/Chippewa_falls_history

Bailey, Judge William F., Editor-in-Chief. *History of Eau Claire County Wisconsin, Past and Present, 1914*. Chicago: Cooper & Company, 1914. Accessed April 28, 2015. Eauclaire.wigenweb.org/histories/1914ecco/index.html

Fries, Robert F. *Empire in Pine. The Story of Lumbering in Wisconsin 1830-1900*. Madison: State Historical Society of Wisconsin, 1951.

Smith, Ernest F. "The Chippewa-Flambeau Rivers." *Transactions of the Wisconsin Academy of Arts, Sciences and Letters*, 53, part A (1964): 27-33.

"Weyerhaeuser, Frederick 1834-1914." *Dictionary of Wisconsin History*. wisconsinhistory.org/dictionary/index

Martin, Roy L. *History of the Wisconsin Central*. Boston: The Railroad and Locomotive Historical Society, 1941.

Goc, Michael J. *100 Years on the Flambeau. Park Falls, Lake Eisenstein*. Park Falls, Wisconsin: Park Falls Centennial Committee, 1989.

Burns, Mary. "History of the Area." *Mercer Remembers... Pictures and Stories of its Past*. Mercer, Wisconsin: Mercer Area Historical Society, 1998.

CHAPTER TWO
The Origins of the Turtle Dam

Conflicts Over Water Powers

The Northwest Ordinance. "An ordinance for the government of the Territory of the United States northwest of the River Ohio." July 13, 1787. In *Documents of American History,* edited by Henry Steele Commager, 5th ed., 128-132. New York: Appleton, Century, Crofts, 1949.

Wisconsin Constitution of 1848. Article IX, Section 1.

Schmid, A. Alan. "Water and the Law in Wisconsin." *Wisconsin Magazine of History* 45 (1962): 203-15.

"AN ACT to authorize Henry Sherry and A.L. Maxwell to build and maintain a dam across the Turtle River in Iron County." *Laws of Wisconsin* (1895), Chapter 60. March 23, 1895.

Jones v. Pettilone (1853) 2 Wisconsin. 308, 320.

Title of fish and game in state. *Laws of Wisconsin* (1899). Chapter 312, section 26.

Opinion of the State Attorney General (Walter C. Owen) on the failure of a 1907 amendment to the Wisconsin Constitution with respect to water powers and forestry. *Opinions of the Attorney General of the State of Wisconsin.* Vol. 1. Bancroft-Owen. July 1, 1912, to April 1, 1913, 105-109. Opinion of February 18, 1913.

Brown, Ray A. "The Making of the Wisconsin Constitution." Part II. *Wisconsin Law Review* (January 1952): 23-63.

McGovern, Francis E., Governor of Wisconsin. "Message to the State Assembly, January 11, 1911." *Assembly Journal* (1911): 34-37.

Water Power Law of 1911. *Laws of Wisconsin* (1911). Chapter 652. July 13, 1911.

Goc, Michael J. *Stewards of the Wisconsin. The Wisconsin Valley Improvement Company.* Friendship, Wisconsin: New Past Press, 1993.

Gettle, Louis E. "The Railroad Commission." *Wisconsin Blue Book,* 197-203, Madison, 1929.

McDonald, Forrest. *Let There Be Light. The Electric Utility Industry in Wisconsin 1881-1955.* Madison: American History Research Center, 1957.

Scott, Walter E. "Water Policy Evolution in Wisconsin: Protection of the Public Trust." *Transactions of the Wisconsin Academy of Sciences, Arts and Letters* 54 part A (1965): 143-197.

The Sherry Family Enterprises and the Chippewa and Flambeau Improvement Company

"Henry Sherry." Biographical entry in *History of Northern Wisconsin*. Chicago: The Western Historical Company, 1881.

"Death of Aged Pioneer Resident." Obituary of Henry Sherry. *Neenah Daily News*, November 7, 1919.

"Sherry, Laura [Case]." *Dictionary of Wisconsin Biography*. Madison: State Historical Society of Wisconsin, 1960.

Archival Materials: Unless otherwise noted, all references to activities of E.P. Sherry and the Chippewa and Flambeau Improvement Company in this and subsequent chapters are based on materials in the following collection:

Edward Paddock Sherry: Sherry Family Business Papers, 1853-1961. Wisconsin Historical Society Archives/Milwaukee Area Research Center. Materials consulted for this project include:

> Organizational Records. Box 1. Flambeau Paper Company, Flambeau River Improvement Company Articles of Incorporation.
>
> Wisconsin Realty Company, Incoming 1895-1947. Boxes 13 and 14. Chippewa and Flambeau Improvement Company.
>
> Wisconsin Realty Company. Boxes 144-149. Flambeau Reservoir.
>
> Wisconsin Water Power Association. Box 152.
>
> Legal Records 1884-1941. Box 178. Hearing Transcript, Wisconsin Supreme Court. *Flambeau River Lumber Company v. [Chippewa and] Flambeau Improvement Company, and Railroad Commission of Wisconsin*. August 1930.

Sherry, Edward Paddock. Untitled manuscript history of the Flambeau Paper Company from the surveying of the area in the 1840s and 1850s through 1914. 54 pages, single-spaced. From Box 1 of the Sherry Family Business Papers.

"AN ACT to authorize the improvement of Bear Creek for log driving purposes." *Laws of Wisconsin* (1887). Chapter 329. April 22, 1887.

Connor, Sara Witter. "Bear Creek Dam and Reservoir." From a manuscript on the history of the Turtle-Flambeau Flowage.

Vogel, John N. "Round Lake Logging Dam." Historic American Engineering Record. HAER WI-7. 1980.

"Articles of Organization." Chippewa and Flambeau Improvement Company. February 4, 1909. Wisconsin Department of Financial Institutions.

"AN ACT to authorize the Chippewa and Flambeau Improvement Company to...." *Wisconsin Session Laws, 1911.* Chapter 640. July 12, 1911.

Overturn of Water Power Law of 1911. *State v. Bancroft. 34 N.W. Rep. 880.* January, 1912.

Kannenberg, Adolph. "The Water Power Situation in Wisconsin." *Wisconsin Blue Book,* 75-96. Madison, 1939.

Seeking Authorization for a Storage Reservoir

"Articles of Incorporation of Flambeau Reservoir Company." November 19, 1919. Wisconsin Department of Financial Institutions.

"AN ACT to amend...." *Wisconsin Session Laws, 1921.* Chapter 399. June 24, 1921.

"Articles of Association of Flambeau River Improvement Company." June 26, 1923. Wisconsin Department of Financial Institutions.

"Power Owners' Agreement" Signatories: Chippewa and Flambeau Improvement Company; Eau Claire Dells Improvement Company; Wisconsin Minnesota Light and Power Company; Lake Superior District Power Company; Chippewa Power Company; Cornell Wood Products Company; Great Western Paper Company; Flambeau Paper Company; and Flambeau Power Company. March 1, 1924. Railroad Commission Copy.

Draft of a Lease Agreement Between the Flambeau River Improvement Company and the Chippewa and Flambeau Improvement Company. No date.

"Resolution For Dissolution of Flambeau River Improvement Company and Certificate." May 15, 1924. Wisconsin Department of Financial Institutions.

"In the matter of the Application of the Chippewa and Flambeau Improvement Company, pursuant to Chapter 640 of the Laws of 1911 of the State of Wisconsin and Acts Amendatory Thereto." Ruling of January 20, 1925. Railroad Commission of Wisconsin, File WP-215.

"In the Matter of the Application of the Chippewa and Flambeau Improvement Company for Approval of Plans and Specifications for the Construction of a Reservoir on the Flambeau River in the State of Wisconsin...." Ruling of May 27, 1925. Railroad Commission of Wisconsin, File WP-221.

Confirmation of Dissolution of Flambeau Reservoir Company. Office of Register of Deeds, Chippewa County. June 4, 1926.

CHAPTER THREE
Of Cutovers and Virgin Stands:
Sherry Acquires a Future Lakebed

The Sherry Strategy and The Big Acquisitions

Edward Paddock Sherry: Sherry Family Business Papers, 1853-1961. Wisconsin Historical Society Archives/Milwaukee Area Research Center. Except as noted below, materials consulted for this chapter come almost entirely from the following part of this archive: Wisconsin Realty Company. Boxes 144-149. Flambeau Reservoir. Each folder contains correspondence related to purchases of land or to the acquisition of flowage rights on land from specific individuals or companies.

The Tough Acquisitions

Homestead Certificate 2927 to Matias Ledvina. General Land Office, Wausau, Wisconsin. March 23, 1892. Online search at www.glorecords.blm.gov

Map of Sec. 6, T42N R3E for Flambeau River Improvement Company. February 23, 1925. Surveyed and drawn by J.W. Harris. Wisconsin Historical Society.

"In the matter of the application of the Chippewa and Flambeau Improvement Company for approval of plans and specifications for the construction of a reservoir on the Flambeau River in the State of Wisconsin; the valuation of lands proposed to be flooded under said construction; the damage to state-owner land involved; and the approval of certain stock and bond issues in connection with the construction of such reservoir." Supplementary Order. Railroad Commission of Wisconsin. File WP-221. May 10, 1930.

Three Costly Acquisitions

Certificate No. 20973 to John Merkel. General Land Office, Wausau, Wisconsin. February 21, 1890. Online search at www.glorecords.blm.gov

Small Acquisitions of Varied Historical Interest

Certificate No. 21802 to Martin Drott. General Land Office, Wausau, Wisconsin. April 27, 1894. Online search at www.glorecords.blm.gov

Certificate No. 21838 to Martin Drott. General Land Office, Wausau, Wisconsin. May 19, 1894. Online search at www.glorecords.blm.gov

Patent Number 163872 to Leo Shienbeck [Schienebeck]. General Land Office, Wausau, Wisconsin. December 1, 1910. Online search at www.glorecords.blm.gov

Homestead Certificate 3112 to Joseph Bastein. General Land Office, Wausau, Wisconsin. March 27, 1893. Online search at www.glorecords.blm.gov

Script No. 2387 to Ezra Cornell. General Land Office, [Washington, D.C.]. August 5, 1869. Online search at www.glorecords.blm.gov

Warranty Deed. Flambeau Paper Company to Chippewa and Flambeau Improvement Company. February 17, 1925.

Warranty Deed. Wisconsin Realty Company to Chippewa and Flambeau Improvement Company. February 17, 1925.

"In the matter of the application of the Chippewa and Flambeau Improvement Company for approval of plans and specifications for the construction of a reservoir on the Flambeau River in the State of Wisconsin; the valuation of lands proposed to be flooded under said construction; the damage to state-owner land involved; and the approval of certain stock and bond issues in connection with the construction of such reservoir." Supplementary Order. Railroad Commission of Wisconsin. File WP-221. June 11, 1929.

"In the matter of the application of the Chippewa and Flambeau Improvement Company for approval of plans and specifications for the construction of a reservoir on the Flambeau River in the State of Wisconsin; the valuation of lands proposed to be flooded under said construction; the damage to state-owner land involved; and the approval of certain stock and bond issues in connection with the construction of such reservoir." Supplementary Order. Public Service Commission of Wisconsin. File WP-221. December 26, 1934.

"In the matter...." "In Re Application of Chippewa and Flambeau Improvement Company for Authority to Include an Additional $400.00 in the Capital Account of the Flambeau River Reservoir, to Acquire Flowage Over the SW 1/4 of the S/W 1/4, of Section 31, township 42 North, Range 3E, Iron County Wisconsin." Supplemental Finding. Public Service Commission of Wisconsin. File WP-221, 2-WR-576. July 22, 1942.

CHAPTER FOUR
A More Even Flow at Last

The Roddis Connection
Huston, Harvey. *The Roddis Line; the Roddis Lumber and Veneer Co. Railroad and the Dells and Northeastern Railway.* Winnetka, Illinois. 1972.

Edward Paddock Sherry; Sherry Family Business Papers, 1853-1961. Wisconsin Historical Society Archives/Milwaukee Area Research Center. Wisconsin Realty Company materials on Flambeau Reservoir. Roddis Company File.

Annual Report of Park Falls Spur of Roddis Lumber and Veneer Company to Railroad Commission. 1924.

Construction Plans and Financing

Railroad Commission of Wisconsin. Files WP-215, WP-221, WP-268, and WP-287. These contain information on the construction and maintenance of the dam, as well as late property acquisitions, operational practices, and one miscellaneous item. Pursuant to the creation of the Wisconsin Department of Natural Resources in 1965, responsibility for oversight of the Turtle-Flambeau Flowage dam was transferred from the Public Service Commission to the newly created WDNR. PSC files pertaining to the dam, as well as files of the Railroad Commission, the predecessor of the PSC, were turned over to the WDNR. These materials are on file in microform at the Wisconsin Department of Natural Resources, Madison. Materials generated by the WDNR subsequent to 1965, along with some early documents from the Railroad Commission era, can be found in Field File FF 26.5.

Flambeau River Basin. Flambeau Reservoir Dam. North Fork of the Flambeau River, Iron County, Wisconsin. Inventory No. 00041. St. Paul: St. Paul District, Corps of Engineers, 1978. Field File FF 26.5. WDNR, Madison.

Flambeau River Lumber Company, Respondent v. Railroad Commission of Wisconsin, Appellant. Supreme Court of Wisconsin. 204 Wis. 524; 236 N.W. 671; 1931 Wisc. LEXIS 371.

Flambeau Reservoir. Estimate of Cost of Construction by Byllesby Engineering & Management Corporation. February 24, 1925. WP-215. WDNR, Madison.

Flambeau Reservoir. Estimate of Cost of Construction by Byllesby Engineering & Management Corporation. March 25, 1925. WP-221. WDNR, Madison.

Contract between The L.E. Myers Co. and the Chippewa and Flambeau Improvement Company for the Construction of a Dam, Headworks and Dikes to form or create the Flambeau Reservoir. Chicago, March 28, 1925. WP-221. WDNR, Madison.

Letter of October 24, 1924, from Donald Boyd, Secretary, Chippewa and Flambeau Improvement Company to Paul Reiss, c/o Cummins, Roemer & Flynn [the law firm of the CFIC], with trial balance of CFIC on October 21, 1924. Sherry Archive.

"In the Matter of the Application of the Chippewa and Flambeau Improvement Company for authority to issue Stocks and Bonds." Memorandum of Opinion. Certificate of Authority to Issue Stocks and Bonds. The Railroad Commission of Wisconsin. File WP-221. May 13, 1926. Sherry Archive.

Report on Disposition of Stocks and Bonds. To the Railroad Commission of Wisconsin from the Chippewa and Flambeau Improvement Company. May 23, 1925. Sherry Archive.

The Flow Stopped: The Flambeau Reservoir Dam

"In the Matter of the Application of the Chippewa & Flambeau Improvement Company for Authority to Issue Stocks and Bonds. Supplemental Certificate of Authority." Railroad Commission of Wisconsin. February 15, 1926. Sherry Archive.

Letter of May 13, 1925, from Guy Waldo on behalf of Flambeau Paper Company to C.A. Halbert of the Railroad Commission of Wisconsin. WP-215. WDNR, Madison.

Letter of July 20, 1925, from John W. Harris to H.W. Fuller, Vice President in Charge of Engineering, Byllesby Engineering & Management Corporation. Sherry Archive.

Annual Reports of Park Falls Spur of Roddis Lumber and Veneer Company to Railroad Commission. 1924, 1925.

"IN RE Application of the Chippewa and Flambeau Improvement Company.... Memorandum of Decision." Railroad Commission of Wisconsin. May 27, 1925. Railroad Commission Proceedings.

The Flow Resumes

Telegram from Railroad Commission of Wisconsin to Paul Reiss. April 2, 1926. WP-221. WDNR, Madison.

REPORT OF OPERATION OF FLAMBEAU RESERVOIR From March 16 to May 21, 1926. [Water level elevations and conditions (open or closed) of sluice gates 1, 2 and 3, as measured at 8:00 a.m. and 5:00 p.m. daily.] WDNR Files, Mercer Ranger Station.

FLAMBEAU RESERVOIR ELEVATION AND DISCHARGE 1926. WDNR Files, Mercer Ranger Station, Mercer.

Tresnak, George. "Placid Turtle-Flambeau Flowage gives no clue of past troubled waters." *The Park Falls Herald*, June 8, 1989.

PROGRESS REPORT Monthly Statement for Chippewa and Flambeau Improvement Company. Byllesby Engineering and Management Corporation. April 30, 1926. WP-221. WDNR, Madison.

Boyd, Donald, Secretary of Chippewa and Flambeau Improvement Company. Letter to First Wisconsin Company. March 18, 1931. Income account and balance sheets for period 1927 through 1930. Sherry Archive.

Boyd, Donald. Letter to Flambeau Paper Company. November 15, 1926. Sherry Archive.

Materials on the escapades of the Jerome Fishing and Hunting Club animals come from the Sherry Archive.

Regulating the Flow

Minutes of the Special Meeting of the Directors of Chippewa and Flambeau Improvement Company. Chicago, June 29, 1926. Sherry Archive.

Flambeau River Lumber Company, Respondent v. Railroad Commission of Wisconsin, Appellant. Supreme Court of Wisconsin. 204 Wis. 524; 236 N.W. 671; 1931 Wis. LEXIS 371. This document contains information about the companies and the facts of the dispute.

"In the matter of the investigation on motion of the Commission of reasonable and proper rules and regulations to be promulgated for the operation of the reservoir of the Chippewa and Flambeau Improvement Company on the North Fork of the Flambeau River in Iron County, Wisconsin." Railroad Commission of Wisconsin. March 4, 1927. WP-268. WDNR, Madison.

"IN RE Investigation, on motion...." Railroad Commission of Wisconsin. March 3, 1928. WP-268. WDNR, Madison.

Flambeau River Lumber Company, Plaintiff v. Chippewa and Flambeau Improvement Company and another, Defendants. Supreme Court of Wisconsin. 204 Wis. 602; N.W. 679; 1931 Wis. LEXIS 372.

"In the matter of the Decision of the Supreme Court of Wisconsin in Flambeau River Lumber Company, Respondent v. Lewis E. Gettle, et al., Constituting the Railroad Commission, Appellant." Public Service Commission of Wisconsin. August 22, 1933. WP-268. WDNR, Madison.

The Flambeau-Turtle Flowage [motion picture]. [Wisconsin Conservation Dept.] No place of creation or publication. Date: circa 1930. Wisconsin Historical Society Archives.

CHAPTER FIVE

Lands and Waters of the Turtle-Flambeau Flowage: The Early Years

The CFIC and the Lands of the Flowage

Information on fires comes from the following newspaper sources: *The Milwaukee Journal,* July 31, 1933, and August 1, 1933; *Rhinelander Daily News,* October 16, 1948; *The Milwaukee Sentinel,* May 22, 1958, and May 27, 1958 (Dave Duffey article).

The CFIC response to the fire of 1958 comes from the following: *Milwaukee Sentinel,* March 20, 1959, and March 21, 1959; *The Milwaukee Journal,* April 4, 1959; and the *Ironwood Daily Globe,* April 6, 1959.

A New Fishery in a New Body of Water

Losby, Fred and Arvella. "Bringing Up the Old Times of Springstead." Accompanied by Charles V. James and George Daggett. Typed manuscript, transcribed from tapes recorded August 1996.

Eslinger, Lawrence. WDNR Fisheries Biologist. Personal communication to author via e-mail.

Turtle-Flambeau Scenic Waters Area: Master Plan & Environmental Assessment. Appendix I, Table 2: Fish Species Found in the Turtle-Flambeau Flowage and Trude Lake. No place of publication. March 23, 1995.

Claflin, Bert. *Milwaukee Sentinel* outdoor writer.

Schmidt Jr., Art. Interviews.

Vickers, Dan. Quoted in the outdoors column of Gordon MacQuarrie. *The Milwaukee Journal,* July 5, 1940.

Johnson, Don L. Golumb's comments are in "Fisherman Finds Shore Lunch Worth the Wait." *Milwaukee Sentinel,* July 4, 1981.

Guyant, Tom. *The Milwaukee Journal* outdoor writer.

The First Interventions

Fish rescue of 1929 and the possibility of remedies for lack of fish movement around dams in 1929. Sherry Archive: CFIC General Correspondence file.

Elevation and Discharge Records for the Flambeau Reservoir (and starting in 1996, the Turtle-Flambeau Reservoir). Prepared by the Chippewa and Flambeau Improvement Company from 1926 to 1942, and by Northern States Power from 1943 on. WDNR, Mercer Ranger Station.

Babic, Mitch. Guide. Interview.

Mercer Remembers... Pictures and Stories of its Past. Information on Fish Hatchery, Mercer Area Historical Society, 1998.

Sanctuaries proposal of 1931. Sherry Archive: CFIC General Correspondence file.

Re: Fishway of 1936. See Wisconsin Public Service Commission file 2-WP-287. WDNR, Madison.

Enter the State of Wisconsin

Early regulations. Information from WDNR files in Minocqua, courtesy of Lawrence Eslinger, WDNR fisheries biologist.

Gjestson, David L. *The Gamekeepers. Wisconsin Wildlife Conservation from WCD to CWD.* Madison: WDNR, 2013.

The County Game Commissions and Conservation Congress were created by the Conservation Department. In 1972, legislation gave them statutory authority. Wisconsin Statute 15.348.

Leopold, Aldo. *Game Management.* New York: Charles Scribner's Sons, 1933.

Fox, Stephen. *The American Conservation Movement. John Muir and His Legacy.* Madison: University of Wisconsin Press, 1981.

Fish Under Surveillance:
The First Comprehensive Study of the Flowage

Morrison, W.J. and C.W. Threinen. "Summary of a Voluntary Cooperative Creel Census for the Flambeau Flowage, Iron County." WDNR, 1950.

Klingbiel, John and William Morrison. "Summary of a Voluntary Cooperative Creel Census for Flambeau Flowage, Iron County-1951." WDNR, 1951.

Lealos, James M. and Gerry G. Bever, Park Falls. *Fish Management Report 110. The Flambeau Flowage Fishery.* Madison: Bureau of Fish Management, WDNR, March 1982.

Interviews with and personal communications from Jeff Roth, WDNR inland fish manager for Iron and Ashland counties, and with Lawrence Eslinger, WDNR fisheries biologist for Iron and Ashland counties.

CHAPTER SIX
A Place to Rest Along the Way:
The Resort Era

Resorts on the Rise

Advertising map for Al Seifert's Glennwood Resort. Photocopy received from a member of the Turtle-Flambeau Flowage and Trude Lake Property Owners' Association.

Losby, Fred and Arvella. "Bringing Up the Old Times of Springstead." Accompanied by Charles V. James and George Daggett. Transcribed from tapes recorded August 1966.

"Map of the Famous Flambeau Flowage." D-1018. Northern States Power Company, Distribution & Engineering Department. Eau Claire, Wis., March 4, 1938. Wisconsin Historical Society Archives.

An incomplete set of promotional brochures can be found at the Mercer Historical Society. A similar set resides at the Mercer Chamber of Commerce.

Scribbins, Jim. *The Hiawatha Story.* Milwaukee: Kalmbach Publishing Company, 1970.

Scribbins, Jim. *The 400 Story: Chicago & Northwestern's Premier Passenger Trains.* Minneapolis: University of Minnesota Press, 2008.

General information about the resort industry in Wisconsin in this section and the next comes largely from the following articles:

Shapiro, Aaron. "Up North on Vacation." *Wisconsin Magazine of History,* 89 no. 4 (Summer 2006): 2-13.

Monthey, Lawrence G. "The Resort Industry of Wisconsin." *Transactions of the Wisconsin Academy of Sciences, Arts and Letters.* 53, part A (1964): 71-94.

Monthey, Lawrence G. "Trends in Wisconsin's Tourist-Lodging Industry." *Transactions of the Wisconsin Academy of Sciences, Arts and Letters.* 58 (1970): 71-99.

Monthey, L.G. and Daniel Zielinski. "Vacation Resorts in Oneida County (Wisconsin); A Study of 1950-1968 Trends and Owner-Operator Characteristics." *Transactions of the Wisconsin Academy of Sciences, Arts and Letters.* 61 (1973): 207-227.

Pioneering Resorts

The principal sources for this and the following section of the chapter are interviews, conversations, and correspondence with current resort owners and with descendants of resort owners.

Millie and Walter Kloess, and Carol and Joe Zilinger: Joe Miller's Resort.

Charlotte and Neil Koshak: Al's Place.

Art Schmidt Jr.: Art Schmidt's Muskie Camp.

Ernst and Aranka Both: Pine Trees Hideaway.

Maryann and Rodney Brown: Lodge of Lakeview.

"Cabin Builders of Mercer are Active." *Ironwood Daily Globe*, May 30, 1938 (information on Joe Popko).

Latecomers

MacQuarrie, Gordon. "Right Off the Reel: Real Estate Man Comments on Resort Buying." *Milwaukee Sentinel*, June 2, 1946.

Reaching Out for Customers

Advertisement for Schmidt's Camp. *Milwaukee Sentinel,* June 16, 1944.

Brochure from Art Schmidt's Muskie Camp courtesy of Art Schmidt Jr.

Iron County booths at Chicago and Milwaukee shows. *Ironwood Daily Globe.* March 13, 1958.

Information on regional and statewide promotion of northern Wisconsin comes from the following articles in the *Wisconsin Conservation Bulletin (WCB)*:

"Movie Advertising." *WCB* 4 (January 1939): 49-50.

"Second Annual All-Wisconsin Show at Chicago." *WCB* 5 (June 1940): 64-66.

"Wisconsin's Famous Recreational Regions." WCB 6 (February 1941): 39-40.

Coon, C.L. "Advertising All Year Around Vacation Lands." *WCB* 6 (May 1941): 42-46.

Coon, C.L. "This Business of Vacationing." *WCB* 6 (August 1941): 37-38.

Coon, C.L. "1942 Participation in Outdoor Shows." *WCB* 7 (March 1942): 16-17.

Coon, C.L. "Vacation News and Views." *WCB* 7 (June 1942): 18-19.

Coon, C.L. "Wisconsin at Two Outdoor Shows." *WCB* 8 (June 1943): 13-15.

Coon, C.L. "Victory Vacation Year in Wisconsin." *WCB* 11 (June 1946): 12-13.

Resorts in Decline

See general articles on tourist industry and interviews, as cited above.

Data on prices come from the Art Schmidt brochure, cited above.

CHAPTER SEVEN

The Voigt Decision and Its Aftermath: The Past as Present and Future

The Voigt Decision: The Courts Speak

"Chippewa Off-Reservation Treaty Rights: Origins and Issues." State of Wisconsin Legislative Reference Bureau. Research Bulletin 91-1, December 1991. Includes a bibliography of the subject.

Satz, Ronald N. *Chippewa Treaty Rights. The Reserved Rights of Wisconsin's Chippewa Indians in Historical Perspective.* Madison: The Wisconsin Academy of Sciences, Arts and Letters, 1994. This book contains a full text of Judge Crabb's final judgment of March 19, 1991.

"A Brief Chronology of the Chippewa Treaty Rights Issue." WDNR. No date or place of publication.

"Ojibwe Treaty Rights." Online document prepared by the Milwaukee Public Museum, 2014.

"A Guide to Understanding Chippewa Treaty Rights." Odanah, Wisconsin: Great Lakes Indian Fish and Wildlife Commission, 1991.

"Ojibwe Treaty Rights." Odanah, Wisconsin: Great Lakes Indian Fish & Wildlife Commission, January 2014.

The State of Wisconsin Responds

The narrative of events that begins after the summary of the judicial process is based primarily on news stories from *The Milwaukee Journal* and the *Milwaukee Sentinel* (and after the merger of April 2, 1995, the *Milwaukee Journal Sentinel*).

Meyer, George. Speech at Great Lakes Indian Fish and Wildlife Commission Treaty Symposium. July 28-30, 2009. Online at www.glifwc.org/minwaajimo/Speech/GeorgeMeyer.pdf

Hanaway, Donald. Attorney General of Wisconsin. "History of the Chippewa Treaty Rights Controversy." Updated, March 1990. Madison.

Lines in the Sand of the Landings; Confrontation Comes to the Turtle-Flambeau Flowage; The Flowage Sits Out a Critical Year; and The Flowage Returns to a Gradually Dimming Spotlight.

"Protect Americans Rights and Resources." Pamphlet. Bloomer, Wisconsin, no date.

National Parr Issue. Winter Edition. Volume I, Issue 8. 1988.

Wisconsin Division of Emergency Government. "Emergency Police Services treaty rights files," 1986-1992. 6 cartons. Wisconsin Historical Society.

"Files created and/or kept by the Division, largely by the deputy director of Emergency Police Service, concerning the controversy over Indian rights to spearfish on off-reservation lakes. Subjects include manpower costs, communications, crowd control training, operational plans/basic plan, Protect Americans Rights and Resources, pre-planning meetings, meetings at the Governor's mansion, public information, reimbursement costs, and Mutual Aid Bill. Forms include tribal harvest quotas, daily situation reports, annual reports, landing reports, and reports from Great Lakes Indian Fish and Wildlife Commission wardens. Mutual aid files include correspondence from local and county law enforcement personnel." The narrative on the flowage during the early years of spearing is based on these files.

Short-Term Reactions and Long-Term Impacts

Brown, Maryann. Resort owner. Interviews and informal conversations.

Ledvina, Louis. Flowage area resident. Interview and informal conversations.

Maulson, Tom. Lac du Flambeau tribal leader. Interview and informal conversation.

Tomek, Scott. Flowage area resident. Interview.

Loew, Patty and James Thannum. "After the Storm: Ojibwe Treaty Rights Twenty-Five Years after the Voigt Decision." *The American Indian Quarterly.* 35 (Spring 2011): 161-191.

Whaley, Rick with Walter Bresette. *Walleye Warriors: An Effective Alliance Against Racism and for the Earth.* Philadelphia: New Society Publishers, 1994.

Fisheries Management Under the New Court Rulings

Interviews and personal communications with Jeff Roth, WDNR inland fish manager for Iron and Ashland counties, and with Lawrence Eslinger, WDNR fisheries biologist for Iron and Ashland counties.

Roth, Jeff and Dave Neuswanger. *Fishery Management Plan. Turtle-Flambeau Flowage, Iron County, Wisconsin.* March 2007.

AveLallemant, Steve. Fisheries Management, Department of Natural Resources, Woodruff. "Walleye: Safe Harvest and Reduced Angler Bag Limits." March 1990.

Chart on angler bag limits. WDNR, Mercer Ranger Station.

Roth, Jeff. *Turtle-Flambeau Flowage. Summary of Fisheries Management Surveys 1975-1997.* WDNR. No place or date of publication.

CHAPTER EIGHT
The Shaping of a Long-Term Vision for the Flowage

The Flambeau Flowage Recreation Plan of 1970

Flambeau Flowage Recreation Plan. First Draft. No authors identified. February 25, 1970. WDNR, Madison.

Doll, Arthur. Letter to Jerry Kripps. April 16, 1970. WDNR, Mercer Ranger Station.

Kripps, F.J. Letter to Arthur Doll. May 22, 1970. WDNR, Mercer Ranger Station.

Doll, Arthur. WDNR Intra-Departmental Memorandum to Lester Voigt. May 26, 1970. WDNR, Mercer Ranger Station.

Mark Fort: Caretaker and Catalyst

This and the following section draw primarily on the following three sources:

Fort, Mark. Untitled report on the Turtle-Flambeau Flowage, 1983. (Copy of typescript provided by Jeff Wilson.)

Olson, John. Telephone interview.

Wilson, Jeff. Several conversations as well as written comments on a draft of this chapter.

Management and Science

Koper, Terry. "He Keeps Tuned in on Loons." *Milwaukee Sentinel,* August 1, 1987.

Bibliography of scientific papers based on studies of flowage loons. Personal communication from Dr. Jerry Belant. February 20, 2014.

Taking the Long View

Olson, John (WDNR). Letter to Anthony Schuster (NSP). January 16, 1986. WDNR, Mercer Ranger Station.

Schuster, Anthony (NSP). Letter to John Olson (WDNR). March 24, 1986. WDNR, Mercer Ranger Station.

Fort, Mark (CFIC). Letter to John Olson (WDNR). April 14, 1988. WDNR, Mercer Ranger Station.

Olson, John. "DNR Involvement in Turtle-Flambeau Flowage Management Plan." Memorandum to files. October 14, 1988. WDNR, Mercer Ranger Station.

Fort, Mark (CFIC). Letter to John Olson (WDNR). December 19, 1988. WDNR files, Mercer Ranger Station.

"Chippewa and Flambeau Improvement Company. Turtle-Flambeau Flowage Management Plan." Prepared by Chippewa [and] Flambeau Improvement Company, Wisconsin Department of Natural Resources. Management Team: John Olson, Leader; Mark Fort, Marko Hanson, Dennis Scholl, and Don Peterson, Members. No date and place of origin. WDNR, Madison.

CHAPTER NINE
From Storage Reservoir to "Crown Jewel"

The Big Buy

Probst, Erin. "Warren Knowles-Gaylord Nelson Stewardship Program." Wisconsin Legislative Fiscal Bureau. Madison, January 2011.

Gottwald, Paul. Retired WDNR Area Wildlife Supervisor. Interview and follow-up conversations.

Information on negotiations for purchase, initial reactions, and editorial comment come from the following editions of *The Milwaukee Journal:* January 5, 1990; January 8, 1990; and January 9, 1990.

"Memorandum of Understanding Between the State of Wisconsin Department of Natural Resources and Chippewa and Flambeau Improvement Company." August 23, 1990. WDNR, Mercer Ranger Station.

Approval of the purchase by the Natural Resources Board and details of the transaction come from the following editions of the *Milwaukee Sentinel:* August 24, 1990; and August 14, 1990.

Olin, Rick. "Taxation and Regulation of Public Utilities." Informal Paper 8. Madison: Wisconsin Legislative and Fiscal Bureau, January 2013.

"Remarks by Governor Tommy Thompson: State Purchase of Turtle-Flambeau Flowage." August 25, 1990. Marquette University Libraries, Tommy G. Thompson Collection, Series 2: Gubernatorial Speeches. Online at www. marquetter.edu/library/archves/DC/CDM/062.pdf

Making a Master Plan

Information on the process of developing the master plan comes in large part from interviews and follow-up conversations with Roger Jasinski and Christine Paulik, the successive property managers of the Turtle-Flambeau Scenic Waters Area.

For early attitudes toward the master plan, see *The Milwaukee Journal*, June 9, 1991.

Scholl, Dennis. Recommendations for Turtle-Flambeau Citizens' Advisory Committee. WDNR Memorandum. February 13, 1991. Mercer Ranger Station.

Scholl, Dennis. Letter to citizens who attended an open house forum on August 9, 1991, and expressed opinions about the future of the flowage. September 3, 1991. WDNR, Mercer Ranger Station.

"T-F Flowage plan nearly final." *Daily Globe* (Ironwood, Michigan). March 17, 1995.

Letter from Doris Cihak, Citizen Advisory Committee, to the *Daily Globe* (Ironwood). June 21, 1995.

"Turtle-Flambeau Scenic Waters Area. Master Plan & Environmental Assessment." Wisconsin Department of Natural Resources. No place of publication. March 23, 1995.

Daily Globe (Ironwood). September 9, 1995.

The Flowage Under the Master Plan

This section depends heavily on interviews and follow-up conversations with Roger Jasinski and Christine Paulik, the successive property managers of the Turtle-Flambeau Scenic Waters Area.

Wisconsin Administrative Code. NR 45.04 (3) (v). Viewed online.

"Turtle-Flambeau Master Plan Variance—Group Campsite." Memorandum from Roger Jasinski [WDNR] to Laurie Ostendorf [WDNR]. July 14, 2005. WDNR, Mercer Ranger Station.

"The Turtle-Flambeau Scenic Waters Area Fund." Brochure. Natural Resources Foundation of Wisconsin. No date.

Information on procedures for implementing grants from the NRF courtesy of Christine Paulik.

The Big Blow

Information on the tornado came from interviews with Christine Paulik, Thomas Mowbray (flowage resident), Stacy Ofstad (Iron County Emergency Management Coordinator), and the following online sources: National Weather Service, Duluth, Minnesota, September 16, 2010; JS Online, July 28, 2010; BusinessNorth.com, July 28, 2010; Lakeland Times.com, July 28, 2010; Wisconsin Radio Network.com, July 29, 2010; Lakeland Times.com, July 29, 2010; WDNR News Release, August 6, 2010; Northlandoutdoors.com, August 11, 2010; *Wisconsin State Journal*, September 4, 2010.

CHAPTER TEN
Continuity and Change: The Flowage Moves into the New Millennium

Wildlife Management

Bacon, Bruce. Retired WDNR wildlife biologist. Interview.

Bibliography and copies of publications courtesy of Terry Daulton and Jeff Wilson.

Shaping the Fishery: Public Preferences and Planning

Roth, Jeff and Dave Neuswanger. *Fishery Management Plan. Turtle-Flambeau Flowage, Iron County, Wisconsin.* March 2007.

The Unsettled Legacy of the Voigt Decision

The narrative of events from 1996 through 2013 is based primarily on news stories printed in the *Wisconsin State Journal*.

Brown, Maryann. Resort owner. Interview.

Whaley, Rick with Walter Bresette. *Walleye Warriors: An Effective Alliance Against Racism and for the Earth*. Philadelphia: New Society Publishers, 1994.

Imrie, Robert. "Spearfishing Anniversary. A Federal Court Ruling 25 Years Ago Led to the Resumption of Off-Reservation Spearfishing by Chippewa Indians in Northern Wisconsin." Associated Press: April 26, 2008.

Reinhard, Scott. Letter to WDNR Secretary Cathy Stepp, April 7, 2011.

Williams, Quinn. Letter to Scott Reinhard, April 12, 2011.

Three-fish bag limit and new model for determining safe harvests. Interview and follow-up communications with Zach Lawson, WDNR fisheries biologist, Iron and Ashland Counties.

Keepers of the Dam

Water Power Inspection Report. Railroad Commission of Wisconsin. October 12, 1930; and subsequent reports in 1935, 1936, and 1937. Field File FF 26.5 (Flambeau Reservoir Dam). WDNR, Madison.

Flambeau River Basin. Flambeau Reservoir Dam. North Fork of the Flambeau River, Iron County, Wisconsin. Inventory No. 00041. St. Paul: St. Paul District, Corps of Engineers, 1978. Field File FF 26.5. WDNR, Madison.

WDNR Memo to NSP. June 22, 1984. Field File FF 26.5 (Flambeau Reservoir Dam). WDNR, Madison.

"Project Manual for Northern States Power Company. Turtle-Flambeau Reservoir Dam Repair." Prepared by Ayres Associates, Eau Claire, Wisconsin. September 1985. Field File FF 26.5 (Flambeau Reservoir Dam). WDNR, Madison.

Coke, John, P.E., Water Regulation Section, WDNR. Letter to Mike Popko, CFIC. June 22, 1984.

Popko, Mike. Letter to John Coke. September 17, 1984.

Parent, John (WDNR). Communication to Chippewa Valley Improvement Company [sic]. June 30, 1987. Field File FF 26.5 (Flambeau Reservoir Dam). WDNR, Madison.

Enter the Federal Government

"Order Finding Reservoirs Required to be Licensed." Federal Energy Regulatory Commission. FERC 62, 088. February 5, 1997. This and subsequent FERC files were accessed online at: www.ferc.gov/

"Order on Rehearing." Federal Energy Regulatory Commission. 85 FERC 61, 234. November 16, 1998.

"Order Denying Rehearing." Federal Energy Regulatory Commission. 95 FERC 61,327. June 1, 2001. This order reviews the case to date.

Chippewa and Flambeau Improvement Company, Petitioner v. Federal Energy Regulatory Commission, Respondent. United States Court of Appeals, District of Columbia Circuit. No. 01-1329. April 18, 2003.

Inspections of 2003, 2004, and 2005. Field File FF 26.5 (Flambeau Reservoir Dam). WDNR, Madison.

CFIC Emergency Action Plan. Field File FF 26.5 (Flambeau Reservoir Dam). WDNR, Madison. Public access to this document is no longer permitted.

"Order Denying Rehearing." Federal Energy Regulatory Commission. 112 FERC 61,115. July 25, 2005.

"Order Amending License." Federal Energy Regulatory Commission. 125 FERC 62,048. October 14, 2008.

"Water Quality Certification." Application for Amendment of License for the Big Falls Hydroelectric Project. FERC Project No. 2390-056. Wisconsin Department of Natural Resources. March 28, 2008."

"Environmental Assessment. Application for Amendment of License. Northern States Power Company of Wisconsin d/b/a Xcel Energy, Inc." Big Falls Hydroelectric Project. FERC Project No. 2390-056. Washington, D.C., October 2008.

Flowage Folks Put an Oar in the Water

The section on the Turtle-Flambeau Flowage and Trude Lake Property Owners' Association, Inc., is based on interviews and conversations with Paul Gottwald and Maryann Brown; on the minutes and files of the organization; on newsletters of the organization; and on personal experience as a director and officer.

Walleye/Smallmouth Feeding Study. Report by Lawrence Eslinger to Turtle-Flambeau Flowage and Trude Lake Property Owners' Association, Inc., Annual Membership Meeting, June 22, 2013.

Epilogue

Luening, F.W. "Waters Bring Timber Waste." *The Milwaukee Journal*, October 23, 1940.

Sources for Part II

CHAPTER ONE
Some Loose Bits

Fountain, Charles. *The Betrayal: The 1919 World Series and the Birth of Modern Baseball.* New York: Oxford University Press, 2015.

Maclean, Malcolm. "When Baseball Magnates Unmask." *Baseball Magazine*, 1913.

Vaughan, Irving. "Woodland Bards Wrote Bum Poetry and Colorful History in Wisconsin Camp." *Chicago Tribune*, February 4, 1951.

Camp Nokomis. Brochures, maps, application form, employee application form, calendars, yearbook for 1974, and land purchase documents courtesy of Chris Ederer, a Trude Lake property owner.

Worthington, Rogers. "Charlotte Mendes, Teacher and Counselor." *Chicago Tribune*, March 1, 1999. From chicagotribune.com

Appel, H.M. *The Secret of the Flambeau.* Chicago: The Goldsmith Publishing Company, 1936.

Bill Tutt's manuscript courtesy of Steve Tutt.

Hemingway's Adventures of a Young Man. Martin Ritt, Director. 20th Century Fox, 1962. Film.

Moe, Doug. "Newman Remembered in Wisconsin." *Wisconsin State Journal*, October 2, 2008. Accessed via internet.

Crowther, Bosley. "Screen: Adapted from Hemingway: 'Adventures of a Young Man' has premiere." *The New York Times*, July 26, 1962.

CHAPTER TWO
Fishing the Turtle-Flambeau Flowage

Since the majority of the materials used in this chapter contain information relevant to several of the subheadings, I have chosen to list them by category, rather than try to match them to the various sections of the chapter. Here and there, a bit of personal experience may also have crept into the chapter. I should also note that my treatment of musky fishing draws heavily (with permission) on the texts of interviews, as well as other information, contained in the works of Larry Ramsell and Eli Singer, and in the sound track of the video, "The Old Masters of Musky Hunting."

Books:

Ramsell, Larry. *A Compendium of Musky Angling History*. 2nd ed. St. Germain, Wisconsin: Musky Hunter Publications, 1997.

Ramsell, Larry. *A Compendium of Muskie Angling History*. 3rd ed. 2 vols. Infinity Publishing.com, 2012.

Singer, Eli. *That Big Fat Musky Book*. Park Falls, Wisconsin, 2005.

Singer, Eli. *The Musky Chronicles*. Park Falls, Wisconsin, 2001.

Articles:

Huizinga, A.T. "Fishing Around Horn: Where You Get Thrills as Well as Big Fish." *Outdoor Recreation,* September, 1926.

"Musky Fisherman For 35 Years." *Wisconsin Conservation Bulletin,* December 1949.

Tutt, Bill. "Big George." *Musky Hunter*, March 1980.

Video:

The Old Masters of Musky Hunting. Video Art Productions LLC, 1998.

Typed Manuscripts:

Losby, Fred and Arvella. "Bringing Up the Old Times of Springstead." Accompanied by Charles V. James and George Daggett. Transcribed from tapes recorded August 1996.

Severt, Doug. "Al's Place." Memoir with photos. 2014.

Newspapers:

Newspaper accounts, mostly columns by outdoor writers but sometimes articles on noteworthy happenings, have been drawn from the following papers: *Appleton Post-Crescent; Ironwood Daily Globe; The Milwaukee Journal; Milwaukee Sentinel; Racine Journal Times;* and *Miami Daily News Record* [Miami, Oklahoma].

Personal Communications via e-mail:

Eslinger, Lawrence. WDNR fisheries biologist.

Rothenberger, George. Fisherman/camper.

Rothenberger, Paul. Fisherman/camper.

Internet Threads:

Mercer & Turtle Flambeau Flowage Reports. Topic ID: 1245. Begun July 26, 2006.

Mercer & Turtle Flambeau Flowage Reports. Topic ID: 1529. Begun March 9, 2007.

Popko's question. Begun March 30, 2102.

Website:

"WCD/DNR History." The South Central Wisconsin Association of Retired Conservationists. www.wisarc.org

Interviews and Informal Communications:

Joe Aski. Flowage resident.

Mitch Babic. Guide.

Robert Dralle. Flowage property owner.

Tom Gargrave Sr. Fisherman.

Jerry Hartigan. Guide.

Gene Osterhaus. Flowage resident.

Don Pemble. Guide.

Bud Sievertson. Area resident.

Emmet Skaggs. Area resident.

Scott Tomek. Area resident.

Bud Wahl. Guide, Flowage resident.

CHAPTER THREE
Flowage Resorts Up Close

Interviews, Conversations and Shared Documents:

Ernst and Aranka Both: Pine Trees Hideaway.

Maryann and Rodney Brown: Lodge of Lakeview.

Millie and Walter Kloess, and Carol and Joe Zilinger: Joe Miller's Resort.

Charlotte Koshak and Neil Koshak: Al's Place.

Art Schmidt Jr.: Art Schmidt's Muskie Camp.

Scott Tomek: Area resident.

"Cabin Builders of Mercer are Active." *Ironwood Daily Globe*, May 30, 1938. (Information on Joe Popko).

Severt, Doug. "Al's Place." Memoir with photos. 2014.

CHAPTER FOUR
Some Loose Bits From the Resort Era

Partial Inventory of Personal Property of Schmidt Resort. Register of Deeds, Iron County, Wisconsin.

Testimonial letter on Downey's Resort courtesy Mike and Beth Myers.

CHAPTER FIVE
Highlights and Lowlights of Resort Life

See interviewees as listed in sources for Chapter Three above.

Severt, Doug. See above.

Turtle story courtesy of Sandy Gitzlaff, flowage resident.

Guyant, Tom. "Accent on the News." [Rehse's mishap] *The Milwaukee Journal*, October 7, 1971.

"Relate Story of Drownings." *Ironwood Daily Globe*, November 24, 1938.

"Bleil's Body is Recovered." *Ironwood Daily Globe*, November 26, 1938.

Index

Printed in the United States
by Baker & Taylor Publisher Services